THE
COOKING OF
SOUTHWEST FRANCE

ALSO BY PAULA WOLFERT

Couscous and Other Good Food From Morocco

Mediterranean Cooking

Paula Wolfert's World of Food

Mediterranean Cooking, Revised Edition

The Cooking of the Eastern Mediterranean

Mediterranean Grains and Greens

The Slow Mediterranean Kitchen

THE COOKING OF SOUTHWEST FRANCE

RECIPES FROM FRANCE'S MAGNIFICENT RUSTIC CUISINE

Paula Wolfert

WILEY

John Wiley & Sons, Inc.

Library of Congress Cataloging-in-Publication Data

Wolfert, Paula.
    The cooking of southwest France : recipes from France's magnificent rustic cuisine / by Paula Wolfert.—2nd ed.
        p. cm.
    Includes bibliographical references and index.
    ISBN 0-7645-7602-X (alk. paper)
    1. Cookery, French. I. Title.
    TX719.W64 2005
    641.59447—dc22   2005009747

Printed in the United States of America

10 9 8 7 6 5 4 3 2 1

For My Mother and Father and for Bill

Contents

A Note on Attribution

A WOMAN CHEF I KNOW, WHO TAKES HERSELF VERY SERIOUSLY AS A FEMINIST, made the point to me that since the cooking of Southwest France is really women's cooking, it was odd that I was collecting and publishing so many recipes obtained from men. My response was that I wanted to write a living cookbook, a book that encompassed the traditional recipes of the region as well as the new ones adapted from the old. Any recipe that appealed to me was worth considering for inclusion. And then I said that as far as I was concerned, one could no longer draw the line of gender in the kitchen; it must be the result, the food, that is the point, and not the man or woman who produced it.

Still, of course, recipes generally have a source, and we food writers must be scrupulous about assigning credit. I've developed my own way of acknowledging sources, a system that is used throughout this book. If a recipe bears no attribution at all, then it is my version of a new or traditional dish belonging to no one, a dish in the common domain. I don't invent recipes, at least not for a regional book like this. When I develop a recipe, I base it on my various tastings of the dish, the literature and oral lore that surrounds it, and my own amalgam of methods and techniques, most taught to me by various cooks through the years. If a recipe bears this line at the end: "Inspired by a recipe from …," then, in fact, that is just what happened—I've taken a recipe taught or imparted by a specific individual and made *definite* changes to it. These changes include not just substituting ingredients more available in the United States but also making simplifications or improvements that would better serve my readers. Finally, if a recipe bears the name of a specific individual in its name or is fully attributed in its introduction, then that is the recipe as it was given to me, and I am imparting it with some changes, having tested it in this country and adjusted it for a good result.

Introduction to the New Edition

THERE ARE NUMEROUS WAYS TO ENTER SOUTHWEST FRANCE. You can fly into Bordeaux or Toulouse, train in from Paris, drive in from Provence to the east or through the Pyrenees from the west. I've done all the above. But recently, after deciding to revise this book, I entered in a completely different way—by sea, via a British ship that turned into the Gironde to reach the outskirts of Bordeaux.

It was a remarkable journey, moving slowly, effortlessly up the river, past the beautiful King's Lighthouse, then into the estuary, which may be the least polluted in Europe. Here sturgeon, eel, shad, shrimp, oysters, and numerous types of river fish flourish. The banks are lined with some of the finest wine producing vineyards in the world.

Commentators disagree about just which areas are encompassed by the term "Southwest France." I've seen texts that ignore the Ariège portion of the Pyrenees, that omit every part of the Languedoc, and that delineate Gascony as a special and separate culinary zone. Certainly each province has its own specialties, but there is a land the French call "Sud-Ouest," which can be gastronomically defined. As shown on the map on page xxii, it is the land of preserved meats, or *confit*, a preparation that unifies such diverse regions as the Basque country, the Béarn, the Quercy, the Gers, and the western portions of the Languedoc.

You will be reading often of these regions in this book, and also of the Landes, the Rouergue, the Tarn, and the Périgord, so I suggest we take a brief tour of the whole area to catch a glimpse of each subdivision, to meet the people, and to gain a notion of what they eat.

As often as I heard that "one eats well in the Southwest," I was also told about how kind the people were, how warm and generous-spirited. Indeed, both assertions turned out to be true; the people are as wonderful as their food. From the proud Basques and the zany Catalans to the earthy Périgourdines and Quercynois, from the gentle Landais and Tarnais to the sophisticates of Bordeaux, the gallants of Gascony, and the sunny-tempered people of Toulouse, I never failed to find help and encouragement, a special kindness, or a smile. These are not the sort of provincial French who eye you with suspicion, nor do they behave falsely, only pretending to be your friend. Their friendship, when given, is serious; their hospitality, despite their relative poverty, generous to a fault. They have not been corrupted by *le grand tourisme*, nor are they xenophobic, as many provincial Europeans tend to be. There is more than a touch of Spanish honor in them, tempered by French intelligence, decency, forbearance, sympathy, and an ability to share humor. There is also the spirit of the Mediterranean, an attitude of live and let others live as they desire.

For the Bordelais, Bordeaux wine is blood; without it they would be poor and, worse, have not much to talk or argue about. Their city is elegant, their lifestyle serious, their tempers sturdy but never mean. They grill their steaks over vine cuttings, honor the shallot, the crayfish, and the caviar of the Gironde. They cook lamprey in red wine and then thicken the sauce with its blood; they eat their beloved silver-tinged oysters with spicy sausages and wash them down with chilled white Graves.

The Périgord, also called the Dordogne, is the land of old castles perched on hills, lazy rivers, forests, rocky precipices with towns clinging to them, caves hiding the artwork of prehistoric man, and the earth filled with the black diamond of gastronomy, the black truffle of Périgord. The men here are spiritual descendants of Cyrano de Bergerac, at least concerning romance. Their women stuff goose necks and make the best hare à la royale in France. They press the oil out of walnuts and use it to dress their salads.

The Corrèze reminds me of Great Britain: rolling hills and soft green valleys, touched sometimes by mystery and mists. The houses are topped with the same black tiles as those in the Périgord.

In the town of Brive-la-Gaillarde, at the marketplace on place de la Guierle, I stood among boxes of chanterelles, cèpes, tarragon, live rabbits, red plums, and fresh white beans, listening to the quacking of the poultry and the cackling of the women. I thought I was in some paradise of produce—with a bounty such as this, I knew, the food could never fail. Back in 1980 I visited the walnut liqueur factory of a certain Monsieur Denoël who reminisced about serving with the Americans during the First World War, and then sang "Yankee Doodle Dandy" for me while he spontaneously danced a jig.

In Cahors, in the Lot, also called the Quercy, they drink vin de Cahors, their namesake inky black wine, and eat chicken and salsify tarts, stuffed cabbage, and sausages, both black and white. Here I met a chef whose dog wore a plaid golf cap identical to his own, while another day I dined with three generations of truffle growers on an omelet that contained more truffles than eggs. Each farm has its pigeon house and its personalized weather vane. In a cave in Pech-Merle I saw a child's hand stenciled on the wall, a personal mark made tens of thousands of years ago, which I've never been able to put out of my mind.

Moving down to the Languedoc, we enter the country of troubadours. The red town of Albi, birthplace of Toulouse-Lautrec, called the Florence of France, marks the place where garlic meets shallot, the link between the Mediterranean and the Southwest. The people of the Tarn are rightly known for their stability as well as for their peaches, sausages, and *confits*. This is the land of cassoulet, the three famous versions of Toulouse, Carcassonne, and Castelnaudary, and also of a certain pastel blue tint, locally called *coca*, employed in the church frescoes, which gives this area the name pays de cocagne.

To the west is Gascony, a land of rolling hills studded with farms and bastides, red-roofed, fortified towns. This is the country of D'Artagnan, and it's no coincidence that the local chefs have banded together and now call themselves *la ronde des mousquetaires*. Their monthly dinners at one another's restaurants reflect the sharing quality of Gascons: laughter and fellowship and exchange of information, including the trying out of new dishes—there are no secrets here. They eat their grilled duck breasts bloody rare, use foie gras and truffles as if they were mere condiments, adapt their menus to the availability of wild game, and turn thick cabbage soups, called *garbures*, into glorious cuisine.

Things are calmer in the Landes, a sandy land of swamps and brooks and pine forests so thick they darken the midday sun. The people here are truly sweet; their idea of a burning issue is whether one should put white wine or red in a wild mushroom ragout. The local summer pastime is the *course landaise*, a modified, less cruel version of the corrida of Spain: The bull is never killed. The people of the Landes are specialists in *gavage*, the force-feeding of ducks and geese to produce the delicacy foie gras.

The Basques are known for their code of silence, their stoic acceptance of life, their pride, and their dishes enriched with a pipérade of tomatoes and peppers. On the Atlantic coast, one finds the famous ham of Bayonne. Back in the hills, in villages of timbered white stucco houses, one is apt to be served garlicky sausages called *louquenkas*, followed by hake, asparagus, and peas, then a sweet cake stuffed with black cherries or pastry cream.

When I think over my memories of the Southwest, I am struck by how varied the country is. I recall the smell of cheese that permeates the town of Roquefort-sur-Soulzon; the pilgrims lighting candles before the grotto at Lourdes; the oil-rich people of Pau, France's answer to Dallas; a market day in late October in Mirande in the Gers, where a car drove up with a fattened turkey nestled in straw strewn over the backseat. The turkey was to be sold for Christmas dinner.

One day my friend André Daguin sent me to the half-abandoned town of Poudenas in Lot-et-Garonne so that I could interview a well-known Gascon restaurateur. She received me graciously, talked food with me for hours, then telephoned the château on the hill above the village to see if I could spend the night there, since there was no local hotel. "Yes," said the count, "of course she may stay, and she should come up right away since she is interested in food. I am serving a very typical dinner."

I hurried up the hill. The hunting party guests were assembling for dinner. People from all over the Southwest were arriving, from Casteljaloux, Gimont, Mont-de-Marsan, Sarlat, and Bordeaux. The *chasse* was to be for stag, hunted from horses in the forests at dawn, and there was an aura of excitement, a sense of a purposeful adventure about to be undertaken. Local wines were served, and then a feast consisting of fresh foie gras, duck breasts grilled rare, an intensely flavored daube of onions cooked in red wine, fresh goat cheese whipped with young Armagnac and sugar, and a *croustade*, a closed flaky pastry filled with apples and pears. The guests began to sing hunting songs, which they all seemed to know, sipped from their glasses of Armagnac, and occasionally rapped the table with their fists. This delirium went on for hours. I felt myself entranced. At one point a young man turned to me. "You want to know about the Southwest?" he asked. I looked up at him and nodded. "Welcome," he said, gesturing with his hand. "You are here. This is it."

Revising this book, I decided to expand the borders of my own culinary Southwest, expanding north into the Charente, so I could include more Atlantic fish, toward the center into the Auvergne, so I could include Michel Bras and his inimitable Southwestern approach, and a bit further south into the Languedoc-Roussillon, to catch sight of the Mediterranean, my region of speciality.

Though many aspects of the Southwest culinary scene remain as they did when I wrote the first edition of this book, there have been changes. And I have altered my own outlook, too. The good news: The phrase so often used by the French to describe the Southwest—"They really eat well down there!"—remains true to this day. Certainly, the food of the Southwest is still wonderful, and the home cooks are still as good as I remember them. Artisanal foods are still produced on a small scale, and the foundations of the cuisine remain the same: cheese, cèpes, foie gras, truffles, confits, cassoulets, game birds, pork, lamb, beef, seafood, fish, and wine.

When I wrote this book more than twenty years ago, nouvelle cuisine was all the rage. Some of the dishes I included then are no longer served. Fascinating as they were, they didn't "wear" well, so I've dropped them from this edition. The excitement I remember, creative reactions to the old ways of cooking, has settled down, and, not surprisingly, the mainstays, the great traditional farmhouse and local town dishes, remain beloved. This isn't to say that inventiveness is dead. Southwest French chefs continue to explore fresh approaches.

The Cooks

When I first visited the French Southwest, the most important culinary figures were the highly talented, enormously generous and ebullient chefs of *la ronde des mousquetaires*, an association with a nod to the panache of Alexandre Dumas's heroes. They were the best chefs in Gascony. You will read much about them in these pages.

Jean-Louis Palladin has sadly passed away after a distinguished career as a chef first in Gascony, then in Washington, D.C., Las Vegas, Nevada, and New York. André Daguin no longer cooks in Auch; he is now president of a hotel-restaurant industry association, based in Paris. The great Toulouse chef Lucien Vanel, whose kitchen sensibility was the closest to my own, has retired. (I was flattered to find myself mentioned in his cookbook-memoir, *Saveurs et Humeurs*.) Roger "Zizou" Duffour and Maurice Coscuella have also retired from their stoves, but their disciples still speak of them with affection and awe. Dominique Toulousy, at his restaurant Les Jardins de l'Opéra in Toulouse, and Gérard Garriques, at his restaurant Le Pastel in a suburb of Toulouse, continue to elevate the rustic food of the Southwest. Christian Parra, formerly of the Michelin two-star La Galoupe now teaches cooking to small groups in the Basque region. Now there are "new voices" in the Southwest, chefs such as Michel Trama of Aubergade in the Agen, Thierry Marx at the Château Cordellan-Bages in the Medoc, Raymond Casau at Chez Pierre in the town of Pau, and, of course, the brilliant, iconoclastic, self-taught genius Michel Bras in the Auvergne, several of whose recipes you will find in this new edition.

In Bordeaux, I hastened to meet pastry chef Daniel Antoine, who confirmed my work on *canelés de Bordeaux,* a recipe that was published in *The Slow Mediterranean Kitchen.* Francis Garcia and Jean Ramet are still cooking great food there, as is the luminous and portly Jean-Pierre Xiradakis, whose La Tupina is my destination of choice in that city. He continues to prepare the best regional dishes before an open hearth.

André Daguin's daughter, Ariane, a teenager when I first met her, has made a huge impression here in the United States, having cofounded, with George Faison, the firm D'Artagnan, the number one domestic purveyor of foie gras, prepared confit, and other Southwest French products to chefs and consumers alike. It's safe to state that D'Artagnan has changed the face of restaurant cooking in this country.

Newly Available Ingredients

There has never been a better time in America to make the great dishes of the Southwest. The availability of new culinary products over the past twenty years has made the inclusion of numerous new recipes possible. Farmers' markets are now commonplace, and their arrays of fresh vegetables and wild mushrooms, formerly considered "exotic," are a blessing.

Hudson Valley and Sonoma County Artisan duck foie gras is now as good as foie gras found in France. Various types of delicious fattened ducks are available here with which to make proper confits and *magrets.* We now have domestically rendered duck fat and domestic *verjus* and artisan breads and cheeses, as well as fresh black truffles imported from France and China, Gironde River caviar, melt-in-your-mouth Tarbais beans from the Pyrenees, piment d'Espelette (moderately hot paprika) from the Basque Country, *moutarde violette* (purple mustard flavored with grape must) from the Corrèze, ventrèche (the French version of pancetta) and jambon de Bayonne (salt-cured ham), chestnut liqueur from the Limousin, and frozen demi-glace with which to make delicious and memorable sauces.

Our stores and markets have been transformed over the last twenty years from utilitarian sources of food into a food-lovers' cornucopia, providing us with free-range chickens, organic vegetables, organically fed lamb, beef, and pork.

When this book was first published, confit was barely known. Today duck confit is ubiquitous on restaurant menus. I believe our approach to eating has begun to change as well. When I was writing this book and traveled the country teaching the recipes at cooking schools, I found that the most difficult concept to convey to my students was not how to cook the food, but how to consume it—take pleasure in it and enjoy it slowly and in moderation. I believe that in the past twenty years we've moved closer to the Southwest French approach to the culinary pleasures of the table.

The Recipes

It was enormous fun revising this book, revisiting dishes I hadn't cooked or eaten in years. In preparing this revised edition, I've tested and rewritten nearly every recipe—refining, clarifying, even in some cases modifying them entirely. Some outdated recipes have been dropped, but more important, I've added over sixty recipes, including over thirty completely new ones and about two dozen from another one of my books that is now out of print, which have been completely updated and which properly belong in this collection.

After some debate, I've taken out the timings. Each of us prepares food at a different pace, and I wanted to remove any feeling of pressure from the home cook. In the rewritten recipes, I've sometimes simplified the steps, though never at the expense of flavor. Southwest French farmhouse cooking has always been intricate. The complexity of such peasant classics as *poule au pot*, *garbure*, and cassoulet is integral to their glory. I've also changed many ingredients to include more authentic products now readily available that were not imported when the first edition was published.

In preparing this revised edition, I approached three French chefs in the San Francisco Bay Area, where I now live, who practice Southwest French–style cooking. Gerald Hirigoyen re-creates his native Basque food at his fine San Francisco restaurant, Piperade. Though Gerald works mostly in a combination of old and new cooking styles, he shared with me his simple, delicious, flawlessly balanced potato, leek, and white bean soup garnished with olive puree (pages 57–58). Laurent Manrique, a Gascon chef, uses mostly American ingredients at Aqua, where he specializes in fish. He gave me two new recipes: a traditional recipe for braised short ribs in porcini-prune sauce (pages 261–263), inspired by his grandmother, and a bright new creation that employs fresh yellowfin tuna with avocado, and the mildly spicy Basque pepper, piment d'Espelette (pages 81–82).

Finally, Jean-Pierre Moullé, the downstairs chef at the famous Berkeley restaurant Chez Panisse for twenty-five years and who also runs a summer cooking school in Bordeaux, taught me a wonderful complex brine for pork belly, which makes it unbelievably succulent and flavorful (see Salt-Cured Pork Belly With Fresh Fava Bean Ragout, pages 301–303).

Sonoma, 2005

Introduction to the 1983 Edition

TO PARAPHRASE CHARLES DE GAULLE, I once had a "certain conception" of the cooking of Southwest France—ducks, goose fat, and cassoulet, with Michel Guérard working alone in the wilderness, practicing *cuisine minceur*. I knew the food was good down there; nearly every French person told me so. But the impression persisted of an overly rich, hearty peasant cooking, a rustic change, perhaps, from the elegance and excitement of the culinary scene in Paris, but nothing that could possibly tempt me to spend half a decade writing a book.

Indeed there are ducks, foie gras, mushrooms, goose fat, and cassoulet; the purpose of my first serious trip, in fact, was to seek out the perfect cassoulet. But on that journey I caught sight of something else: magnificent peasant cookery in the process of being updated. The food was modern, honest, yet still close to the earth—a true *cuisine de terroir* (of the soil) barely touched upon by other commentators. Here was the cuisine I'd been searching for; it struck a resonance with certain beliefs that had been quietly growing within me for years.

These ideas seemed contrary to the spirit prevailing at the time, and so I kept them to myself. They had to do with a love of logic in recipes in which a dish is built, step by step, inexorably toward a finish that is the inevitable best result of all the ingredients employed. They had to do with simplicity and healthiness and the pleasures of dining upon foods that bear natural affinities, as opposed to wild experimentation, gratuitous gestures, complexity for its own sake, and striking dramatic contrasts and effects. I found that my favorite restaurants in Paris were not the citadels of haute cuisine or the laboratories of nouvelle, but rather Alain Dutournier's Trou Gascon in a working-class area on rue Taine, and (the late) Antoine Magnin's Chez l'Ami Louis in the third arrondissement. Dutournier updates and lightens great regional specialties, most of them from Southwest France. Magnin takes traditional country dishes and elevates them to exquisite bliss.

As I explored the Southwest, I found many chefs doing the same sort of thing: first trying to reproduce the regional dishes they remembered from childhood, then working to refine them. If good country "mother's cooking" can rival the finest bourgeois cuisine (and I think a strong case can be made for this), then sophisticated versions of "mother's cooking" might just be the very best cooking around.

When I returned from my first expedition and began to teach Southwest cooking to my classes, I found my students reacting just as I had. They were seduced by its succulence, its deep taste as opposed to its dazzle, and like me, they could not get enough. And so, to satisfy our mutual desire for more, I launched a series of trips. What had started out as a simple venture to supply material for a few articles and classes turned into a passionate long-term enterprise.

Now let me tell you what is in this book and also what is not. Here is a personal collection of favorite Southwest regional specialties, most of them updated by chefs, home cooks, or myself. There is country food here and bourgeois food, but no haute cuisine. Some of these dishes are very modern, while some are purely traditional. You'll find "mother's cooking" and adaptations of "mother's cooking."

There is a sampling of the cooking of regional chefs. It is not an attempt at a definitive work or at encompassing everything. The criteria for inclusion were that first of all, the dish had to be very good to eat; second, it had to be practical to prepare here in the United States; and third, it had to interest me on account of something special in the recipe, a unique touch— a *truc*, or secret, as the French like to say—or, as I prefer, an element of finesse. From time to time there are comments on these *trucs* at the end of the recipe, called "Notes to the Cook."

This book does not cover the geography or history of the Southwest, or the customs and folklore. It is a cookbook first and foremost, a book of recipes, and the recipes are detailed, sometimes even long. This lengthiness does not necessarily connote difficulty. Rather, it stems from needs I've felt since I've begun to teach: to be as precise as I possibly can; to answer as many questions as I can anticipate; and to impart those elements of finesse that can turn the preparation of food into a joyful art. Truly lengthy recipes are presented with advance warning.

One could write a rich and anecdotal book about the region, the people, and the land, the sights and smells and moods. I've tried to put some of that sensibility into this book, but my primary intention has been to describe the making of food. I want to show you ways to actually bring the Southwest into your home in the form, for instance, of a rich Oxtail Daube (pages 264–266) or a satiny and delicate wild mushroom tart (Cèpe and Walnut Cream Tarts, pages 88–90), a deeply aromatic dish of chicken and garlic with Sauternes (see Chicken With Garlic Pearls in Sauternes, pages 138–140), or a haunting *croustade* containing apples, orange-flower water, and Armagnac (see pages 370–372). The idea is that you, too, can possess the Southwest not merely in words, but in that most tangible and sensuous necessity of people's lives: the wonderful food they eat.

Most cooks were generous with me. I never found a professional cook who was not willing to demonstrate a dish. The days when chefs gave out recipes but forbade observation of their cooking because the recipes left out something essential now seem to be a thing of the past. The tendency toward secretiveness is still prevalent, however, among some of the older, bony-faced "mothers" in the tight black hats who when surveying a marketplace can tell the difference in taste between two squawking chickens. I thought at first it was me, the American, with whom they didn't want to share. But one day, on a train between Cahors and Brive-la-Gaillarde, I happened to witness an encounter between two such women, and I have never heard such recipe-dangling in my life. Each would begin to tell the other how she made a certain dish. Her voice would start off clear, then she would begin to mumble, and then the description of the recipe would peter out. They took turns torturing each other this way, smiling as they did it. I was fascinated. Was this some kind of ritual? Perhaps, but not in the way it seemed. Those old women of the Southwest hold a certain matriarchal power over the region by virtue of controlling the preparation of its food. I felt a flood of sympathy for them: Their secrets were their usefulness. To give them up would be to diminish themselves, their glory, and their honor. So sometimes it was their daughters or their sons who showed me those famous *trucs*, those special touches. These touches always have a purpose, and they can elevate a dish to excellence: to cut mushrooms into matchsticks so that they will expose more surface and thus absorb more liquid from a sauce; to wipe the moisture off the bottom of a cover when cooking a potato cake so that it will not drip back and make the cake soggy instead of crisp. It is these little details that I call the "finesse of cooking," which to me is its joy.

The great cliché about the dishes of the Southwest is that they are good but heavy and therefore not healthful. I disagree emphatically, and I have made a special effort in this book to include recipes that have been lightened. Please read what I have to say about the fats of the Southwest (page 18) and about double degreasing principles (page 266). I have applied these techniques to nearly every traditional dish, with a few obvious exceptions such as cassoulet, whose very essence is its richness and which, if lightened, would simply not be the same. As for the stock and sauce recipes, they represent a long-term effort to develop ways of making first-class dishes in the home without a band of cooks to achieve consistent and professional results.

New York, 1982

Map of the Greater French Southwest

La Rochelle

Île de Ré

Île d'Oleron

Arachon

FRANCE

Paris

Limoges

LIMOUSIN

Clermont-Ferrand

AUVERGNE

Brantôme

Tulle

Périguex

PERIGORD

Brive

Laguiole

Gironde

Bay of Biscay

Bordeaux

BORDELAIS

Dordogne

AGENAIS

QUERCY

Cahors

Lot

ROUERGUE

GUYENNE

Garonne

Agen

Montauban

St-Affrique

Mont-de-Marsan

GASCOGNE

Albi

Dax

Auch

Toulouse

Bayonne

BÉARN

Masseube

Montpellier

Espelette

PAYS BASQUE

Pau

Oleron

Garonne

Carcassonne

LANGUEDOC

St-Jean-Pied-de-Port

Tarbes

St-Girons

Gulf of Lion

Bagnères-de-Luchon

Foix

Gavarnie

Perpignan

SPAIN

Port-Bou

N

0   50 miles

0   50 kilometers

THERE IS A QUADRUPLE overlapping of place names in Southwest France that may require some explanation. The entire area encompassed by this book is sometimes thought of as two distinct regions: the Aquitaine, whose most important city is Bordeaux, and the Midi-Pyrenees, whose "capital" is Toulouse. Additionally, cutting across these two regions are the two old duchies of Gascony (Gascogne) and Guyenne—and Gascony consisting of the Landes, Gers, and some other parts—Guyenne consisting of the Bordelais, the Dordogne, parts of the Quercy, and the Rouergue.

The region that constitutes Southwest France has expanded since I wrote the first edition of this book. It now includes the Limousin, the Charente, the Languedoc, and the Auvergne. But now the real confusion begins: There are names for the old provinces and names for the new *départements*; and the borders of the provinces and *départements* do not always precisely coincide. Still, one can make up a table of place names that are more or less equivalent. Thus traditionally one can speak of the Périgord, Quercy, and Rouergue while contemporaneously speaking of the Dordogne, the Lot, and the Aveyron.

What to do with all this confusion? One approach would be simply to go with the old provincial names and leave out words for regions such as Gascony. What I have done instead is to speak of these places as the people of the Southwest speak of them. So if Lucien Vanel tells me a certain dish is "quercynoise," that is how I identify it. And if André Daguin speaks of an "old Gascon recipe," I have so recorded it. But if I am limiting my discussion to that area of Gascony called Gers, that is the place name I use. A little complicated, perhaps, but I feel serious readers will soon come to appreciate the intent behind these usages and will find a visual guide on the map.

THE TASTES OF THE
FRENCH SOUTHWEST

Armagnac

On a market day in Eauze, one of the great centers of commerce in Gascony, you can see men buying and selling Armagnac the old way: opening the bottle of brandy, rubbing a few drops into their palms, cupping their hands, sniffing, looking for extraordinary depth and aroma, which are the signs of a great Armagnac. Some say you can find the scent of violets when Armagnac is young, and of peaches and vanilla when it matures.

Others use vivid words like "ripe plums," "crushed hazelnuts," "prunes," "violets," "sun-ripened peaches"—the comparisons spin out. But the words I like best come in phrases more simply grasped: "taste of the earth," "dancing fire," and "velvet flame." For you do not merely drink Armagnac; you sip it, sniff it, and literally breathe it in. The initial excitement comes at the first inhalation. It is here that the *gout de terroir*, or taste of the earth, is experienced. The glass, warmed in the hand, causes fumes to rise from the liquid. And at their first contact with the tongue, you are touched by the "dancing fire."

The Gascons are more than happy to instruct you: Inhale the Armagnac as you chew it, and you will experience the "dancing fire," followed shortly by the "velvet flame." Do not wash the glass afterward, they say, and it will keep its bouquet for another day, a phenomenon called *fond de verre*.

My friend the retired chef Roger Duffour, proprietor of the Relais de l'Armagnac in the Gascon town of Luppé-Violles, competed in a double-blind tasting of Armagnacs and was the only connoisseur to get all the bottles right—twice! Considering how many different vintage bottles circulate in the Gascon countryside, this was considered an amazing feat. He is my authority on the subject. I find his collection astounding, with many bottles more than a hundred years old. He offered me a drink from one, and I experienced the classic sensations from the red-black brandy: the dance of fire on my tongue followed by the velvet flame, a definable perfume of violets, and a slight pepperiness as well.

When I visited Duffour, I found him not only a great connoisseur of Armagnac but also a master at catching small flocks of ortolans in aerial nets. These much-coveted, lark-sized birds of the French Southwest are now a protected species, but when I visited him back in the seventies, I tasted birds he had caught, fattened, and fed Armagnac in bowls until they fell over and drowned. This final "drink" gave them an extraordinary flavor and aroma when roasted on a spit.

With Armagnac, vintage is not as important as blend, but the blend may well include some of these very old vintage brandies. (Bottles from the 1920s and 1930s may cost hundreds of dollars.) Actually, quality in Armagnac is based on four things: the origin, or *terroir*, of the grapes; the distillation process; the length of time the liquid is aged in oak casks; and the brilliance of the cellar-master's blend.

Recently, *Los Angeles Times* food columnist Leslie Brenner published an excellent and up-to-date column with tasting notes of Armagnacs available in the United States. With her permission, I quote her here:

Château de Laubade VSOP Bas-Armagnac. Vanilla and hazelnut nose; earthy and pleasant, if a little rough.

Château de Pellehaut Réserve Armagnac Ténarèze. Beautiful plum tart aromas with hints of fig, vanilla and ginger.

Francis Darroze Bas-Armagnac Réserve Spéciale. Pretty pear and almond aromas. Bright honeyed fruit on the palate—mirabelle? Santa Rosa plum?

1979 Château de Ravignan Bas-Armagnac. Lots of ripe late-summer fruit and serious caramel. Velvety and complex, with tremendous length.

In the old days, Armagnac was distilled from local grapes on practically every Gascon farm, in traveling stills hauled about by oxen. These were strange contraptions consisting of a potbellied stove and copper pipes, operated by an expert who would listen to the puffs and gurgles and make adjustments as he saw fit. Copper is still used in alembic stills, which today are mostly owned by farmers' cooperatives. The special hand-hewn and increasingly rare local dark oak barrels in which the raw fermented firewater is aged and smoothed are beautiful objects in themselves and often last a hundred years in service.

The question most often asked about Armagnac is how it differs from Cognac, which is better known and is produced in ten times the quantity 150 or so miles to the north. The Gascons are quick to give you answers ranging from the technical to the poetic. Intellectually, some argue, the distillation process is different. The thinner base wine of Cognac must be double-distilled, while Armagnac is distilled only once, which preserves its earthy bouquet and drier taste. Here are three reflections on Armagnac:

From Alain Dutournier, chef-proprietor of Carré des Feuillants in Paris: "Cognac is dependable, but Armagnac, like the Gascons who make it, is more forceful, more complicated—even excessive at times—and more exciting."

From Georges Samalens, Armagnac producer and author of an authoritative book on the subject: "Cognac gains its distinction by finesse, while Armagnac gains its distinction by its power. We are a bit rougher, but we are closer to the soil, and as a result we need more age."

From a Gascon friend who prefers to remain anonymous: "Cognac is a pretty girl in a freshly laundered smock carrying a basket of wildflowers; she pleases you by the sight of her. Armagnac is a tempestuous woman of a certain age, someone you don't bring home to Mother, someone who excites your blood."

Armagnac is wonderful to cook with—great in daubes, poultry dishes, and desserts. It can be used in sherbets, to preserve fruits, to cut the richness of a sauce of wild mushrooms, to perfume and flavor apples and pears. It will add depth and mellowness, a rich soft quality obtainable by no other means. Only the strongest condiments, such as mustard, capers, and vinegar, do not blend well with it. A touch of Armagnac added to a cassoulet will give that famous dish extra finesse.

RASPBERRIES IN ARMAGNAC

➤➤ *Framboises à l'Armagnac*   MAKES ABOUT 2 CUPS

THESE RASPBERRIES CAN BE served within two weeks of being soaked in Armagnac and should be eaten within a month. Otherwise, leave them for four to six months, strain through a coffee filter (the raspberries are no longer edible), then add the liqueur to Champagne for an evening aperitif, a "kir royale, Southwest style." For each drink, put 1 ounce liquid in a glass; then fill with chilled dry Champagne.

1 dry pint perfect, but not too ripe, red raspberries

¾ cup superfine sugar

1½ cups Armagnac, or more to cover

1 Wipe each raspberry very gently with a damp paper towel, then drop one by one into a very clean bottle. Add the sugar, then enough Armagnac to cover.

2 Let stand in a cool dark place for 2 to 4 weeks. Shake gently from time to time to help the sugar dissolve. Serve chilled in small glass cups.

Cèpes

Cèpes, to use the French word for the wild mushroom *Boletus edulis*—the same mushroom that is called porcini in Italy or king boletes in the United States, are the least expensive and simplest way to put the flavor of the Southwest into your cooking. While dried cèpes have always been plentiful, these days in the autumn, more and more fresh cèpes appear in markets in all parts of the United States.

In the region of the Landes, I was served very fresh, very small oval-shaped raw cèpes, thinly sliced and dressed simply with lemon and oil. They were extraordinary. But Southwesterners insist that cèpes require long, slow cooking both to bring out their deep woodsy flavor and to become digestible. They claim that many types of boletus mushroom are naturally filled with water and need to go through three stages of cooking: first, drying in a slow oven to rid them of excess moisture; next, a slow stewing in their own juices; and, finally, sautéing to caramelize and develop flavor.

Ads for real estate in France often include the phrase *"terrain à cèpes"* indicating that cèpes sprout on the land in autumn, which makes the property more valuable. People who love wild mushrooms and forage for them often have secret places called *nids*, or nests, they find them year after year. Wild mushrooms should not be gathered unless you're certain you know how to identify them or are with an experienced group that specializes in mushroom gathering. If you do pick cèpes, never pull them out by the stalk (unless you're are going to use them for identification), but cut them off at ground level with a knife, so that they can sprout again next year.

If you do find a nest of cèpes or other choice boletes and an expert in mushrooms has approved their edibility, or if you find a cache of fresh cèpes in your market, here is what to do: Choose only young, firm mushrooms and carry them home in a paper—not plastic—bag. If the stems are firm but tender, peel them and cut lengthwise to check for insects; set aside.

Hard and fibrous stalks should be discarded. Wet, spongy, soft undersides of the caps should also be removed and discarded. Brush the caps clean or quickly run under cool water. Wipe dry and gently press out moisture, or dry out in a slow oven. Then prepare the very traditional dish, *cèpes à la bordelaise*—cèpes sautéed in oil with garlic—a dish that retains their sweet, delicious nutty flavor best (see Cèpes Sautéed in Oil in the Style of Bordeaux, page 338).

There are many kinds of boletes in France, many shapes and sizes and colors; but the best and most coveted is the cèpe de Bordeaux, with its firm, blackish head. This mushroom, which grows as far north as the Périgord and as far south as Spain, has a superb earthy flavor and an aroma of woodlands. I first gathered the cèpe de Bordeaux in the woods of Saint-Jean-de-Marenne in the Landes. We were a group of American cooking teachers; our guide and mushroom expert was the local pharmacist; and our host, the owner of the woods, was an impoverished baron. From his château, on the high ground, we descended into the woods, where strange animals called *pottoks* wandered about at will. These are the descendants of prehistoric horses, harmless creatures often depicted by ancient man on the walls of caves.

There were many kinds of mushrooms in the woods, including three varieties of cèpes and an orange look-alike called by its scientific name *Lactarius deliciosus*, which, to the Catalans, is the best wild mushroom to be found. Its cup is chalice-shaped, and its taste slightly resinous. A Catalan will make sure it's the right mushroom by squeezing the stalk. If carrot-colored juices come out, he takes it home, since even one specimen of *Lactarius deliciosus* will make a fabulous omelet. On this same outing, we found the sought-after coulemelles and the somewhat less exciting russulas, as well as a vast number of various other mushrooms that were either unpleasant or dangerous to eat.

Fresh cèpes are available in season in many markets. If unavailable in your part of the country, you can mail order quality and flavorful cèpes from any number of sources. A typical and easy way to cook them is to trim, wipe dry, and quarter the fresh cèpe caps. Cut the stems into rounds. Heat oil or duck fat in a skillet until very hot. Add the cèpes, stir once, cover, and reduce the heat at once to very low. Cook, covered, for 5 to 10 minutes. Add a traditional *hachis* of chopped garlic and parsley, stir once more, and cook, covered, for 5 minutes longer. Season with salt and serve at once. You will find many more variations throughout this book.

Canned French cèpes are expensive but are available in many grocery stores. The German *Steinpilze* are an especially good variety. A ten-ounce can will serve four people. Drain canned cèpes, give them a quick rinse in a colander, dry them on a towel to press out excess water, then cook as if they were fresh. Cook the caps in oil to render their water; they are ready when the oil is clear, in about 15 minutes.

Dried cèpes (similar to porcini in Italian markets) are available in almost every city and are very reasonably priced in ethnic markets. The best are from France. I've included many recipes that use dried cèpes in this book. Even one ounce of dried cèpes of this type mixed with a pound of fresh cultivated mushrooms will give an extraordinary quality to a dish.

They always require soaking for 30 minutes, and it will not harm them to soak longer than that. You can enhance their flavor by adding a pinch of salt or sugar (or both) to the soaking water and also a dash of Armagnac. Be sure to reserve the soaking water after straining it through a coffee filter or several layers of damp cheesecloth to remove any grit. This tasty liquid can be added to the reconstituted cèpes as they sauté. The cèpes should be rinsed after soaking, then blotted dry and sautéed.

Cèpe-Scented Oil

➻➤ *Huile de Cèpes* MAKES 1½ CUPS

THIS IS A DELICIOUS woodland flavoring to use as an enhancement with cultivated mushrooms and with duck salads and as a basting liquid for lamb and pork.

⅓ cup dried cèpes, in large pieces	2 imported bay leaves
12 sprigs of thyme	1½ cups green-hued French olive oil

1 Wash the cèpes under running water, rubbing them with your fingers to rid them of grit and dirt. Pat dry on paper towels.

2 When they are absolutely dry, place them in a jar. Tuck in the thyme and bay leaves and pour the olive oil over all. Let stand in a cool, dark place for at least 1 month.

Cheeses of the Southwest

I was twenty years old when I ate a great Roquefort cheese for the first time, and I shall never forget the experience. It was my first meal at Brasserie Lipp in Paris. When the cheese was brought out, it was a revelation: not dry and crumbly, as it had always been in the United States, but creamy-soft and spreadable, with the *persillage*—the blue-green mold—distributed evenly throughout. Roquefort is, of course, one of the great cheeses of France, certainly the most important cheese made in the Southwest. The name Roquefort is now controlled to the extent that lawsuits have been filed against producers of other blue cheese who have tried to sell their products as Roquefort.

For me, one of the best desserts imaginable is a luscious wedge of Roquefort, some plump fresh black mission figs, and a glass of chilled Sauternes. The combination of the rich, nectarlike wine, the sweet ripe fruit, and the pungent, salty cheese is as perfect a trio of taste affinities as one is likely to encounter on this earth. An excellent walnut bread will enhance the experience.

Roquefort is made from raw sheep's milk and matured in the famous limestone caves of Combalou, north of Gascony, upon whose cliffs the town was built. These caves are notable in that they maintain a constant temperature and humidity year-round, perfect for the maturation of the *Penicillium roqueforti* mold, the source of the blue veins that give Roquefort its unique taste. (The apocryphal tale of the simple shepherd, who accidentally left behind some ewe's milk on a slice of rye bread in a cave, and upon returning to fetch it, discovered Roquefort has been told all too many times.)

Roquefort, known in France as "the king of cheeses and the cheese of kings," is always salty, but some of the brands seem too salty to me. (Salt is added for flavor, of course, and also to inhibit the spread of molds other than the desirable *Penicillium roqueforti*.) I suggest tasting for saltiness as well as condition before buying and be sure to look for the red, round seal indicating true Roquefort. The cheese should be evenly marbled throughout, moist at the center. Before serving, be sure to let it come to room temperature.

Recently, I tasted Le Vieux Berger. The explosion of tastes and textures was as good as any Roquefort I've ever eaten. This cheese is produced by a small firm and is extremely rich and creamy, a little less salty than others, and its flavor is more complex.

There are other great blues in Southwest France. Look for Roussel's cow's milk Bleu d'Auvergne, which is wonderfully moist and pungent and slightly sweeter than Roquefort; the full-bodied Bleu des Causses, made from cow's milk in the Languedoc; and Onetik's generous veined Bleu de Basques. Many wines pair well with blue cheese: Sauternes, tawny Port, sweet Banyuls, and late harvest Semillon. Try a ripe pear with a sweet red wine from Banyuls-sur-Mer.

Other sheep cheeses of the western Pyrenees are nutty and rich. One name to look for, Ossau-Iraty, is perfect with black cherry jam or quince marmalade, luscious melted on a potato gratin or tomato tart, or a portion tucked inside a croque monsieur with a thin slice of jambon de Bayonne.

Of course, the Southwest also produces goat's milk cheese, the tangy Cabécou of Quercy being the most famous. Since goat cheese passes through several different stages as it ages, each with its own special qualities, different styles of preparing the cheese has evolved. When first made, fresh goat cheese is very soft—fresh like milk, silky, and sometimes a little cottony, too. There are two problems with fresh young goat cheeses: They don't travel well, and they are at their best in season (i.e., summer). At this stage, they are best served simply with a coating of crème fraîche and a light sprinkling of chopped chives. If a young Cabécou is not available, a good substitute might be a creamy fresh goat cheese from California or Vermont.

As the cheese begins to firm up, it enters the second stage, at which point it is called *affiné*. It becomes more intense, piquant, and almost fruity. A yellowish rind begins to form outside, but the cheese is still silky at the core. At this point, the round can be cooked to great advantage, first brushed with a little walnut or olive oil, then set under the broiler to crust. Or it can be brushed with oil and folded in aromatic grape or fig leaves or flavored with herbs. Broiled goat cheese served on toasted rounds of French bread with a crisp green salad dressed with a smattering of walnut oil is one of the great simple delights of the Southwest French kitchen. Simply drizzled with chestnut honey it becomes a simple but lovely dessert.

Goat cheese at its third and final stage, when it has hardened into dried-out disks that resemble shriveled silver dollars, require some tampering. In the French Southwest, it is soaked in eau-de-vie de prune and white wine spiked with pepper, then wrapped in chestnut leaves for several days before being served with thin slices of walnut bread. My friend Georgie Géry, a great Southwest gastronome, instructed me never to throw out a "dying" goat cheese unless it smelled of ammonia—in which case it would be truly "dead." It can be enjoyed with some of the Muscats from California or the Languedoc, or you can slice it, grate it, or crumble it over oven-ready gratins.

There is a fresh goat cheese called chèvre frais from Poitou, which is available all year round in many cheese stores in the United States. It's sold in a crock, tastes light and fresh, and is so mild that in Gascony it is whipped with white rum or Armagnac, then flavored with sugar until it becomes *fromageon*—ready to be spread on dried bread and served as a snack to children after school.

Not all parts of Southwest France are blessed with great cheese. The land around Bordeaux is marshy, excellent for fisheries and the famous Pauillac lamb, but not appropriate for rearing cows and goats. On the other hand, the Rouergue and the Auvergne, where the food is oriented toward the cuisine of the Languedoc, produce numerous extraordinary mountain cheeses, such as the blues mentioned above. Also, some of the best cheeses for cooking come from this area: Saint Nectaire, Cantal, and its farmhouse brothers, Laguiole and Salers. There are some French gastronomes who place the cheese from Laguiole in the Aveyron so high that they compare it to their beloved Roquefort.

Cantal, a nutty cow's-milk cheese from the Aveyron, is often compared to Cheddar; but while similarly sharp in taste, its texture isn't as dense, and it melts lighter and more evenly. Cantal, Saint-Nectaire, and another farmhouse cheese called Salers are often matched with potatoes, green apples, raspberries, hazelnuts, and lightly grilled country bread.

All of these cheeses have a curious, mellow nuttiness and an unusual ability to melt smoothly. I recently read about a dish in the Auvergne, a regional version of a Swiss fondue, made in the same sort of caquelon, a one-handled, shallow clay pot. The dish is called *la fondue du Mont-Dore*, made with a combination of these smooth mountain cheeses, garlic, wine, seasoning, and nutmeg, all heated slowly while stirring constantly until the cheeses simmer. At this point some ground walnuts and an eau-de-vie are added. When ready, the diner dips slices of baguette into the fluid warm cheese. It sounds a bit ersatz . . . and also quite delicious.

Jean d'Alos, the most famous *affineur* in France (4 rue Montesquieu, Bordeaux), ripens cheeses to perfection in a series of rooms in his shop in Bordeaux. It was there that I tasted another moist and tasty Auvergne cheese, Saint-Nectaire fermier, made from Salers cows that feed on rich pastures. It was a beautifully textured, aged cheese of incredible butteriness and nutty, sweet flavor. Jean d'Alos exports a whole series of cheeses to Artisan Cheese in San Francisco and Philadelphia.

CHEESE TERRINES

→← *Terrines aux Fromages*

ROQUEFORT AND LAGUIOLE are two of the great cheeses of the French Southwest. Put them together, as in this recipe, and you will have something truly sublime. For a slightly less ethereal experience, other excellent blue cheeses can be used in place of Roquefort, and a really good French Cantal or California Monterey Jack can be substituted for the Laguiole. This terrine is not unlike a soufflé, except that its lightness and unusual creaminess derives from the addition of whipped cream. Serve hot or lukewarm with a semisweet white wine, such as a Riesling.

3 to 3½ ounces Roquefort cheese	Freshly ground white pepper
2 ounces walnut pieces	¼ cup heavy cream, chilled
2 egg yolks	3 egg whites, at room temperature
2 tablespoons walnut liqueur, or substitute any nut liqueur, such as Nocciole or Frangelico	1 ounce Laguiole cheese, Cantal, or Monterey Jack, shredded

1 Preheat the oven to 450°F. Butter four 6-ounce or six 4-ounce ramekins. Combine the Roquefort, walnuts, egg yolks, walnut liqueur, and pepper in a food processor. Process until very smooth. Transfer to a mixing bowl.

2 In a cold metal bowl, using chilled beaters, whip the heavy cream until stiff. Gradually fold the whipped cream into the cheese-walnut mixture.

3 In a clean bowl with clean beaters, whip the egg whites until stiff but not dry. Stir one-fourth into the cheese-walnut mixture. Carefully fold in the remaining whites. Spoon a enough of the mixture into each buttered ramekin to fill about one-third full; then divide the shredded cheese among the ramekins and cover with the remaining mixture. Fill each ramekin three-quarters full. Sprinkle any remaining shredded cheese on top and place the ramekins in a water bath of hot but not boiling water.

4 Bake for 8 to 10 minutes, or until the terrines are puffed and golden. Remove them from the water bath as soon as they are cooked. Serve warm.

(continued)

→→ If the Roquefort is quite salty, use the smaller amount.

→→ To keep the walnuts from turning into an oily paste, grate them in a nut grinder, or put them through the shredding disc of your food processor.

Chestnuts

It was in a country house in the Dordogne that I first experienced the pleasures of grilling and cleaning fresh chestnuts. Keep in mind that in this region nearly everyone has a chestnut tree in the garden, and this was during chestnut gathering weather, one of the first cold days of autumn. Here's what we did: A small knife with a short curved head was used to slit each chestnut on its rounded side. The nuts were then thrown into a special long-handled skillet with about a dozen holes in its bottom. The skillet was set over hot coals in the fireplace and shaken every so often to stir the nuts about. We knew they were cooked when we smelled their sweet aroma.

As soon as the nuts were roasted, they were placed in a basket lined with a heavy cloth soaked in wine to keep them moist and warm. (Cold chestnuts are impossible to peel.) A cooked chestnut is firm but mealy throughout. I was taught to squeeze each nut with my fingers so that the shell cracked open and the moist, tender nut slithered out. This method is easier than peeling off the bitter inner skin with a small knife. The French have a vulgar nickname for this squeezing procedure—*técot*—local slang for the nipple of a breast when it is full of milk and ready to be pressed.

Much as I enjoyed my lesson in slitting, roasting, and peeling chestnuts, I also learned that chestnuts once played a crucial role in the lives of the very poor peasants who inhabited the rocky, poverty-stricken region of the Cévennes. Before they learned to cultivate potatoes in their poor soil, chestnuts were their staple. One spoke of a chestnut tree as *l'arbre à pain* (the bread tree), since everyday bread was made of chestnut flour. Just as we sometimes speak of a subsistence diet as being one of "bread and water," so the people of the Cévennes are often referred to as those who "live on chestnuts and water."

Roasted whole chestnuts, vacuum-packed in jars or packed *sous vide*, are available in fine food stores and by mail from Frenchselections.com. Fresh chestnuts are available in early winter. They taste best when "shown the flames." A chestnut-cooking pan—a long-handled pan with large perforations—is available in many cookware stores and specialty equipment catalogs. The Basques' solution to the problem of having to double-peel chestnuts is to drop them into boiling oil—in and out just once.

PEELED FRESH CHESTNUTS

THE FOLLOWING TWO-STEP METHOD I learned for preparing chestnuts ensures that they won't break apart. It is typical of the shrewd approach to cooking developed in Southwest France.

1 Soak the chestnuts in cold water for about 1 hour to soften the shells. Preheat the oven to 450°F.

2 Drain the chestnuts. Use a small sharp knife, or a chestnut knife if you have one, to slit the rounded side of each chestnut. Bake in the oven for 8 to 10 minutes, until the cut shell begins to separate from the meat. While they are still hot, peel off their shells and inner skins. They are then ready for further cooking.

NOTES TO THE COOK

→► Wrap the peeled chestnuts in a thick layer of blanched cabbage leaves, then set in a deep pot with a small quantity of water flavored with stalks of celery or fresh fennel—vegetables that go well with chestnuts and tend to enhance their flavor. Cover the pot tightly and cook slowly for 45 minutes, until the chestnuts are very tender. Discard the cabbage leaves and use the chestnuts in salads, in stuffings or in an autumnal mixed vegetable garnish; or briefly sauté the chestnuts in butter and serve in a side dish.

→► When you want to puree chestnuts, simmer them in flavored water until tender.

→► Fresh chestnuts may be cooked up to one day in advance. Keep them in the refrigerator, covered, until 15 minutes before use.

The Pelou of Languedoc

→►──◄←

Mix 2 tablespoons sweet chestnut liqueur and ½ cup Sauvignon Blanc; chill and drink with Croustade With Apples and Prunes in Armagnac (pages 370–372).

Chocolate

Jews exiled from Spain brought the art of making chocolate to Bayonne, where chocolate has been famous ever since. The Bayonne chocolate of the seventeenth century, heavily spiced with cinnamon and cloves, had an almost diabolical reputation. Madame de Sévigné wrote about it in one of her letters: "Chocolate eventually seduces you, then you are inflicted with a fever leading to death."

In Bayonne's famous chocolate shop Cazenave, under the Arceaux du Port-Neuf, I drank a cup of extraordinarily rich-tasting hot chocolate called *chocolat mousseux* (frothy chocolate), which rose like a soufflé an inch above the top of my porcelain cup. The proprietress served it, not with a glass of cold water to clear the palate, but with two huge slabs of buttered toast!

In traditional Southwest cooking, chocolate rarely appears in desserts. (The only important chocolate dessert I know of is the gâteau de Saint-Émilion, which, to my amazement, is barely known in Saint-Émilion.) But in the Landes, chocolate is used in assorted cakes and other desserts, as in the Marie-Claude's Chocolate Cake With Fleur de Sel (pages 378–379). It is also added to sauces reminiscent of Mexican moles, for rabbit and also for fish dishes of eel, lamprey, or trout. The fish are cooked, then covered in a red-wine sauce with glazed onions, leeks, or prunes. A small amount of bitter chocolate or cocoa is then substituted for the old traditional thickener, blood, to enrich the sauce, as in Fish Fillets in Red Wine and Cocoa Sauce (pages 127–128).

Confits (Preserved Meats and Poultry)

"A Gascon will fall to his knees for a good confit," goes the saying. The citizens of Gascony may be the most extreme devotees of this splendid food, but they are not alone in their passion. Go into any traditional home from Périgord to the Pyrenees—farmhouse, town house, or château. Descend to the cellar and inspect the wines, then ask to see the storeroom. There you'll find shelves lined with stoneware or glass jars embellished with handwritten labels and containing preserved fruits, jams, and, above all, confits, virtually the signature of Southwest cooking.

Confit—from the French *confire*, "to preserve"—is simply preserved meat (duck, goose, pork, hen, wild birds, turkey, rabbit, or whatever) that has been salted to draw out the moisture, then cooked in and put up in fat. When you preserve a meat, you change it, creating an entirely new taste and texture. Confit is a phenomenon that has no close counterpart in the rest of French cuisine.

The method is applied most often to the splendid duck, goose, and pork of the Southwest. So clearly has it left its stamp on great reaches of the Southwest that you can construct an accurate map of culinary boundaries simply by the presence or absence of confit. Where there is confit, you'll find a constellation of other ingredients and approaches adding up to the uniquely rich and vigorous culinary style of the Southwest.

Confit-making was devised so that the local poultry and pork butchered in the late autumn could be preserved and enjoyed throughout the year. In past generations, it was an intrinsic part of the farm kitchen routine, a way of making use of every part of the animal, from good pork shoulder and meaty duck legs to such humble odds and ends as duck and goose gizzards, wings, and necks, or the tongues and ears of pigs. The process enables you to transform such bits of meat and poultry into the stuff of innumerable dishes, some of which, incidentally, can be produced in minutes—once you have confit on hand. When large quantities are involved, confit-making also provides by-products, such as crackling and rillettes, as well as generous amounts of good cooking fats.

Confit will add another dimension to any dish in which it is used. Those who have tasted some of the great Southwest classics know how telling its presence is. To many Southwesterners, cassoulets are not worthy of the name unless they contain a piece of confit. Confit also often appears in that magnificent regional dish called *garbure*, a soup that is based on cured pork (ventrèche or pancetta), cabbage, and beans and has innumerable local variations enriched with other meats and vegetables.

The secret of a great confit lies in a fortuitous combination of factors: the choice of meat, the choice of seasoning; the length of time spent in marination; the temperature at which the fat and meat are cooked; the length of time the meat is left to ripen; and the method of reheating. Freshly cooked confit can be superb; one-month-old confit is even better. As time passes, the flavor deepens. You can keep confit up to six months in the refrigerator.

Despite the large amounts of rendered fat used in the preparation and storage of confit, there is nothing fatty about properly made confit. Rather, the texture is nutty, silky, delicate, and almost fat-free. One secret is gentle heat and patient cooking. Traditionally, confit was cooked in an earthenware crock or iron pot set in the dying embers of the hearth. Slow methods are still the best. A good principle to follow—one taught to me by chef Alain Dutournier—is to gradually raise the temperature of the fat along with the pieces of meat, allow the confit to cook evenly, and then cool it in the fat as slowly as it was heated.

The slow initial heating allows much of the fat under the skin to melt out, the slow cooking inhibits stringiness, and the slow cooling prevents the meat from falling apart or losing its shape. (Incidentally, it is the meat of mature, rather than young and tender, animals that makes the best confits, since such meat is firmer and less likely to break down during cooking.)

When handled with this kind of care, the rendered fat can be reused for several batches. It stores well in the refrigerator or freezer and is excellent for sautéing and braising. But like all animal fats, confit fat is fragile and burns much faster than oil. Once the fat gets hot enough to smoke, it is "spent" and not usable again in cooking. To duplicate the best qualities of the ember method and keep the fat at a gentle simmer, I suggest that you use an electric slow cooker or poach the confit in a very low oven.

Though the versions of confit presented in this book are intended to be kept in the refrigerator, the method long predates refrigeration. In the Southwest, confits were traditionally kept in heavy stoneware jars in cool, dry cellars or storage rooms. If you have a storage area that will remain at a constant low temperature without fluctuation, you may let your confits ripen naturally, embedded in fat in tall stoneware containers, for several months. But be sure you have not overlooked anything; I know of one batch of confit that was ruined because the cook had forgotten about the heat of the basement furnace!

To remove confit from a jar of fat, gently heat the opened jar in a pan of warm water and carefully pull out the pieces with a pair of tongs or two forks. To remove confit from a boilable pouch, run the pouch under warm water until the cold fat breaks away from the duck flesh. Immediately open the package and separate the meat and fat.

You might think that the tastes and aromas of different types of confit would be enhanced if each kind of meat were cooked in its own fat. Surprisingly, this is not the case. If goose, duck, and pork are cooked together in a mixture of duck and pork fat, they will be all the better, and the fat will be tastier.

See pages 201–203 for the Confit of Duck recipe, page 213 for the Confit of Goose recipe, and pages 292–295 for the Confit of Pork recipe.

CONFIT OF PORK RINDS

→ *Confit de Couennes de Porc* MAKES 6 ROLLS

IF YOU ARE LOOKING for the balance, luminous taste, and satiny texture of Southwest French cooking, you should have some confit of pork rind on hand. You can make it up in batches, then freeze small rolls of it. This will provide you with a rich, addictive, and smooth addition for lentil and bean dishes; meat, poultry, and fish stews; soups and salads with a strong vinegar dressing and bitter greens; or whenever a recipe calls for pork rind or salt pork. Pork rind confit is also one of the secrets to a great cassoulet.

You can purchase a whole pork belly with the rind on, remove it, and cut it into 4-inch by 8-inch strips. Use the pork belly to make the Salt-Cured Pork Belly, pages 301–303—one of my favorite new recipes.

You will need a scale to prepare this dish properly.

3 pounds pork belly rind with fat

2 cups rendered pork or duck fat

4 to 5 tablespoons coarse kosher salt

1 Lay the rind out on a work surface. Use a long, thin-bladed knife to cut away most of the fat. Cube the fat; place it in a heavy saucepan. Add ½ cup water and up to 2 cups rendered pork or duck fat to cover the cubes. Slowly cook over very low heat until the pork fat cubes are rendered and the liquid fat has turned a golden color; remove from the heat. Strain the fat, let cool, and reserve for cooking the rinds two days later.

2 Meanwhile, divide the pork rind into 4-inch-wide strips and lay cut side up on a flat pan lined with paper towels. Sprinkle coarse salt over the rinds. Cover the strips with paper towels, refrigerate, and let cure for 3 to 4 days.

3 Wipe the salt from the pork rind strips. Roll each strip, as if you were rolling a carpet, and fasten tightly with string. Heat the reserved pork fat in a wide, heavy saucepan. Add the rolls and cook slowly, covered, until the rinds are tender enough for a toothpick to penetrate easily, about 3 hours. Cool the packets of pork rind in the fat. Remove and discard the string. Pack each roll individually in a small self-seal plastic bag with a little of the strained fat. Vacuum-pack and refrigerate or freeze. The confit of pork rinds will keep for up to 6 months.

Adapted from a recipe in La Mazille's La Bonne Cuisine du Périgord.

Fats of the Southwest

Classically, the food of France breaks down into three culinary zones, each with its corresponding cooking medium: olive oil (Provence), butter (Normandy and the North), and goose, duck, and pork fat (the Southwest). It's important to understand how to cook with these animal fats to obtain good-tasting results without fears of contributing to high cholesterol levels.

"Sans beurre et sans reproche," said Curnonsky of Périgord cooking—"without butter and above reproach." He meant it as a compliment. There is a cliché, and a false one, that Southwest food is greasy and heavy. In careless hands, it can be; but at its best, good Southwest food is actually enhanced by the fats it is cooked in.

I often use these animal fats for taste, the way I use a cinnamon stick in a red-wine compote of fruits: I add it for flavor in the cooking but take it out before the fruits are served. Goose, duck, or pork fat is employed to give flavor to a sauce, but almost all of it is removed before serving, so that the food is actually extremely lean.

This is possible because many of the elements that give the flavor to fats are, in fact, water-soluble; that is, they can be separated from the fat itself. My friend Dr. Adam Drewnowski, prominent in the field of public health and nutrition, puts it this way: "Animal fats contain volatile flavor molecules that may be soluble in both lipid and water. When fat is removed after cooking, the water-soluble flavors remain. When most of the fat is gone, the remaining fat emulsifies (think skim milk), but there is still enough to hold the flavor molecules in lipid-water phase."

I discovered an interesting fact in the U.S. Department of Agriculture Nutrient Database: Rendered poultry fat (goose, duck, and chicken) contains only 0.1 percent cholesterol, and lard contains a bit less than that. Butter contains twice as much cholesterol. When it comes to saturated fats, another dietary bête noire, duck and goose fat win webbed feet down, too: Butter is one-half saturated fat and duck fat is only one-third. Since you'll need less poultry fat, oil, or lard than butter to sauce meat or vegetables, you'll ingest far less saturated fat if these cooking media are used.

Many cooks recommend browning in a mixture of oil and butter to avoid burning. My suggestion is either to use poultry fat alone or to mix it with oil, and forget the butter for the true taste of the French Southwest.

I use grapeseed oil for high-heat searing for lamb or beef sauces or for pan roasting (as in the Fillet of Beef With Roquefort Sauce and Mixed Nuts, pages 258–260). Since this oil has a slightly odd taste, I dilute it with poultry fat in a ratio of two to one (oil to fat).

Garlic

Robert Landry, a French writer on herbs and spices, offers a *truc de trucs* for neutralizing the effect of raw garlic upon the breath: Chew three cardamom seeds for four minutes. Of course, if you cook any *Allium*, its strong odor and taste will disappear. However, if you want to eat garlic—or any *Allium*—raw, it's better to chop than to crush. Food and wine writer Matt Kramer offers the following explanation:

> The pungent aroma of garlic is contained in an odorless compound called alliin. When the garlic clove is intact, this compound is stable. But when the clove is chopped or crushed, it comes in contact with an enzyme that hangs around in another part of the clove. This enzyme converts alliin into three parts: ammonia, another sulfur compound, and pyruvic acid (which resembles acetic acid or, in the vernacular of the street, vinegar). It is the sulfur compound that is ultimately responsible for the characteristic odor of garlic. In short, chopping brings less of the alliin into contact with the enzyme, which sets all this into motion; crushing creates a more intimate mingling, the result being an unpleasantly strong garlic flavor and aroma.

Try this test: Slam a garlic clove with the flat side of a knife or cleaver to peel it and slice another clove in half. Smell and taste the difference. The smashed garlic is much more pungent. Since so many dishes in the Southwest French kitchen call for strewing hand-chopped raw garlic over food, it requires more delicate handling so as not to overwhelm the food.

In winter, you'll often find a green shoot protruding from each clove. This shoot, or "germ" as it is called in France, is thought by many garlic eaters to cause indigestion. If you ask a Mediterranean cook if she takes it out, nine times out of ten she'll tell you she does.

→≻ ≺←

One does not live by how one eats, but by how one digests.

Southwest French saying

ROASTED GARLIC

→ *Ail au Four*

THE CONCEPT OF an entire head of garlic roasted in embers will appeal to all garlic lovers. In France, the round white garlic of the Limousin and the flatter, white variety from Lomague in Armagnac are roasted when the heads weigh about four ounces. They are served as a sweet and creamy "vegetable" accompaniment to grilled meats and stews. Restaurateur Huguette Melier roasts them in embers to accompany meat and hearth-roasted potatoes. I've eaten them with fresh whipped goat cheese and have found them delicious with any kind of peppered cheese and toasted bread.

The best time to make this dish is late spring when plump young tender white garlic bulbs become available. Avoid using elephant garlic, which does not taste very good when cooked; also avoid garlic heads that are dried out.

ROASTED GARLIC I   SERVES 1

1 whole head of garlic

Coarse kosher salt and freshly ground pepper

1 tablespoon butter, cut into small pieces

1 Preheat the oven to 350°F. To prepare the garlic for roasting, carefully cut away the outside paper skins of each head with a small knife, starting from the top and stopping halfway down, leaving just a thin skin around the upper portion of each clove so that it will not dry out during roasting.

2 Place the garlic heads in a buttered shallow baking dish just large enough to hold them snugly in a single layer. Sprinkle with salt, pepper, and chips of butter; place in the oven to roast. When the heads are lightly colored, after about 20 minutes, add ½ cup hot water. Continue to roast the garlic for a total of 1 to 1½ hours, depending upon the size of the heads, basting with the cooking juices in the pan every 10 minutes and adding more hot water whenever necessary.

ROASTED GARLIC II

1 whole head of garlic

1½ ounces fatty prosciutto ham, finely chopped

1 teaspoon butter, cut into bits

Coarse salt

Freshly ground pepper

Dried thyme

Sugar

2 teaspoons chopped fresh flat-leaf parsley

1 Preheat the oven to 350°F. Place the heads of garlic in a saucepan filled with enough cold water to cover. Bring to a boil; drain and rinse under cold running water. Return to the saucepan with fresh cold water to cover and repeat; drain. Using a sharp paring knife, peel the skins back from top to bottom, leaving a single layer of papery skin on each clove as protection against the oven heat.

2 Scatter the ham on the bottom of a lightly buttered shallow baking pan just large enough to hold the garlic heads snugly. Arrange the garlic heads, root side down, in a single layer on top of the ham. Dot with the butter and season lightly with a pinch each of coarse salt, pepper, thyme, and sugar. Sprinkle the parsley on top.

3 Set in the oven and roast for 15 minutes. Add ½ cup hot water and continue to roast the garlic for a total of 1 to 1¼ hours, depending upon the size of the heads, basting with the cooking juices in the pan every 10 minutes and adding more hot water whenever necessary. Serve with the bits of ham and the pan juices.

Inspired by an unsigned article in the Quercy *magazine entitled "Les Produits de Nos Terroirs."*

Bayonne Ham

Jambon de Bayonne

There is a famous anecdote about a wet nurse from the Béarn who went to the Louvre to visit her former charge, the grown-up King Henry IV. Noticing that there were no hams hanging from the ceiling, a sign of wealth in a Béarn home, the nurse exclaimed, "Henri, my Henri, you must be so hungry! I'll send you a ham as soon as I get back home!"

Ah, the Basques and the Béarnaise and their fine-textured jambon de Bayonne! It has been famous since the Middle Ages; on the portal of the Église Sainte-Marie in Oloron I saw sculptures of a man slaughtering a pig and then preparing ham from its legs. Contrary to what has been written about Bayonne ham in many source books, it is not smoked; it is a salt-cured country ham dried over a period of at least a year.

We eat Bayonne ham raw like prosciutto or Serrano ham, but the Basques like it best cut into thick slices and sautéed (see Cured Ham With Vinegar and Caramelized Shallots, at right). Another favorite Basque dish consists of eggs fried in goose fat, served with sautéed ham sprinkled lightly with vinegar.

The taste of the peppery ham permeates many dishes in the Landes, the Béarn, and the Pays Basque. Often dishes are accented by the addition of a regional version of *hachis*, a mixture of hand-chopped raw garlic, chopped fresh parsley, and chopped-up fatty bits of Bayonne ham, which is simply strewn over food. The bone of a Bayonne ham is so highly regarded that it will be used again and again to flavor soups and stews.

The justified fame of Bayonne hams depends upon the use of two different salts, each with its own special properties. The first is the famous salt from Salies-de-Béarn, reputed to have been discovered by accident by a boar hunter in the eleventh century. This salt is rubbed into the pork legs for three days, preserving the meat, imbuing it with an extraordinary flavor, and giving it color.

The second salt is a gray crystal variety called sel de Bayonne, which is used in the giant salt boxes where the hams are kept while being cured. After curing, the legs are lightly rubbed with piment d'Espelette, a local moderately hot red pepper, and air-dried.

You will not find true Bayonne ham in America, as it is illegal to import it. The real stuff is always labeled with a red seal, *Marque Déposée Véritable Jambon de Bayonne*. This means it has been treated with the specific salts and then air-dried. However, you will find some delicious approximations, one prepared in the New Jersey city of Bayonne, excellent though lacking some of the velvety smoothness I remember. This ham can be purchased from several sources in this country. The best substitute hams I've come up with for my recipes are the mild Serrano ham from Spain or quality brands of prosciutto.

CURED HAM WITH VINEGAR AND CARAMELIZED SHALLOTS

→→ *Jambon Poêlé aux Échalotes*   SERVES 2

2 slices (2 ounces each) jambon de Bayonne or Serrano ham

1½ tablespoons milk, if using Bayonne ham

12 small whole shallots (5 ounces) plus 3 tablespoons coarsely chopped shallots

2½ tablespoons rendered duck fat or butter

1 sprig of thyme

1 imported bay leaf

1 whole garlic clove, peeled and halved

3 teaspoons sugar

1 tablespoon very fine red wine vinegar or quality sherry vinegar

1 To remove excess salt from the Bayonne ham, soak the slices in a mix of milk and 2 tablespoons water for 2 hours. Drain and pat dry.

2 Meanwhile, preheat the oven to 200°F. Place the whole shallots in a 10-inch gratin or other flameproof baking dish greased with about ½ tablespoon of the fat. Add the thyme, bay leaf, and garlic. Cover with foil and bake for 1 hour.

3 Remove the foil. Sprinkle 1 teaspoon of the sugar over the shallots and continue to bake, uncovered, until they are soft and golden brown, about 30 minutes longer. Remove the shallots from the baking dish and cover with foil to keep moist.

4 Put the ham slices in the gratin. Set over low heat to slowly fry the slices, turning once, for 10 minutes.

(continued)

5 In a heavy medium skillet, heat the remaining fat over moderate heat. When it sizzles, add the chopped shallots and sauté until golden, about 2 minutes. Sprinkle on the remaining 2 teaspoons sugar and stir once. Add the vinegar, 2 tablespoons water, and the cooked whole shallots. Bring to a boil, stirring to heat the shallots and coat them with the glaze, pour the contents of the skillet over the ham.

Wine Mustard With Grapes

Moutarde Violette

In the region called the Corrèze, I tasted a wonderful whole-grain black mustard, which looked like caviar. This particular mustard was an old recipe from the fourteenth century that somehow got lost in time, but in the past thirty years the Denoix family, who produce great walnut products, brought it back into the marketplace. The condiment is made from black grapes cooked, strained, and left to form a must that is then mixed with mustard powder.

A dollop of this heady mustard is splendid on grilled duck breast, veal chops, or black sausage. Another great use of *moutarde violette* is as an accompaniment to pot-au-feu and charcuterie. It also makes an extraordinary vinaigrette. Keep an opened jar in the refrigerator, and don't heat this mustard for too long because it loses its taste.

MÂCHE SALAD WITH MOUTARDE VIOLETTE

SERVES 4

1 tablespoon *moutarde violette*

1 tablespoon fresh lemon juice or *verjus*

3 tablespoons walnut oil

Salt and freshly ground pepper

4 large handfuls of mâche, rinsed and dried

1 cup walnut pieces, lightly toasted

Whisk together the moutarde violette, lemon juice, and walnut oil. Season with pinches of salt and pepper to taste. Toss with the mâche and sprinkle the walnut pieces on top.

Salt

My old friend the Gascon chef Maurice Coscuella once remarked to me: "Have you noticed there are some salts that don't actually salt?" He went on to explain that some salts are much saltier than others, some are merely salty, and others have a real flavor.

The taste, aroma, and texture of salt differ from place to place around the world and also within regions. Since some commercial salts contain additives that leave a strange aftertaste, I suggest you use pure salt, such as Diamond Crystal coarse kosher salt for cooking all the recipes in this book unless the ingredient list states otherwise. If you use the same salt, my salt measurements will be exact.

In the French Southwest, large quantities of rock or large crystal salt are also used to encase whole ducks, duck breasts, lamb shoulders, and chickens in a crusty shell in order to seal in the flavors during cooking. The hot salt also forces seasoning and aromatics deep into the meat's flesh. After cooking, the meat will stay warm in its crust for up to 30 minutes. Often it is brought to the table in its shell, then cracked opened before the diners (see Duck Breasts Baked in Salt, pages 183–184).

SEA SALTS

When cooking fish, I prefer to use sea salt, which is available in most supermarkets. Since it dissolves well in vinegar and creates a fresh briny flavor, I also use sea salt in vinaigrettes. When finishing a dish as opposed to seasoning it before cooking, you will want to use one of the recently available coarse salts from France for added crunch and zip. The finest salt in the French Southwest is farmed on the flats of the Ile de Ré in the neighboring Charente-Maritime. The first skimming of this famous salt is referred to as the fleur de sel, an immaculate rosy-white salt, treasured on account of its wonderful flavor, crisp texture, and delicate aroma. I often sprinkle it on at the last moment to bring a dish into harmony and to add a little crunch. Gourmets come to the Ile de Ré from all over the world to taste this salt with the local fresh fish.

POTATOES BAKED IN SEA SALT

Pommes de Terre en Sel   SERVES 4

OF ALL THE POTATO DISHES I know, this is the easiest. Small new potatoes, or *primes* as they are called on the Ile de Ré, are washed, dried carefully, and then placed in a closed pot on a small bed of sea salt. As cooking proceeds, a reaction takes place. The hot salt releases an aromatic steam that penetrates the flesh of the potatoes, augmenting their flavor with that of the sea and keeping them moist.

Traditionally this dish is cooked in a *diable charentais*, an unglazed earthenware potbellied utensil with a fitted cover. If you happen to own one, let it heat up slowly over a flame tamer for about 10 minutes; then raise the heat and cook, shaking the pot often, until the potatoes are done. (By the way, the *diable* is never washed; before using, its insides are rubbed with garlic, which the Charentais believe inhibits rancidity and strengthens the pot.) Lacking a true *diable*, please don't substitute the sort of unglazed pot that needs to be soaked. Instead, use an enameled cast-iron casserole. Considering the price of French sea salt, I combine a little bit of grey salt with ordinary coarse kosher salt, layering them so the grey salt is in contact with the potatoes.

On the Ile de Ré, a home cook will accompany these potatoes with a spread made from a whole head of garlic cooked in hot coals, peeled, then kneaded with a little fresh butter and white cheese. These potatoes are also served locally with fresh sardines that have been rolled in grey sea salt, then grilled over thick grapevine cuttings—a combination I can only describe as divine.

1½ pounds small creamer potatoes

1 cup coarse kosher, pickling, or rock salt

½ cup coarse sea salt, preferably grey sea salt from the Ile de Ré

Butter

1 Preheat the oven to 450°F. Wash and dry the potatoes. Spread the coarse salt in an even layer on the bottom of a wide casserole. Top with the sea salt, and arrange the potatoes on top side by side. Cover and bake 45 minutes to 1 hour.

2 Remove the pot from the oven. Set the cover askew and let the pot stand 5 minutes. Remove the potatoes and brush off the salt. Serve hot with butter.

→ If using an unglazed *diable,* cook on a flame tamer over low heat for 45 to 60 minutes.

→ The salt can be reused. Reheat it in the hot oven, covered, for 15 minutes, let cool, and store separately until the next time you wish to cook potatoes this way. Always add some fresh sea salt to each batch.

Salt for Confit

→ ◦ ◦ ←

In the Southwest French kitchen, salt must be precisely weighed and measured when preserving meat and poultry for confit. If you have made confit and found it too salty, the fault may have been the salt rather than the amount. The same is true when brining pork belly, duck breasts, and other meats, starting the aging process with cheese, and flavoring and storing ham.

Note the differences in weight between common salts in the marketplace.

→ 1 tablespoon fine table salt equals 21 grams

→ 1 tablespoon Morton kosher salt equals 17 grams

→ 1 tablespoon Maldon sea salt equals 14 grams

→ 1 tablespoon Diamond Crystal coarse kosher salt or grey sea salt from the Ile de Ré equals 12 grams

Truffles

Here is Colette on truffles; it is the most eloquent passage I've read on this wondrous subject.

> If you love her, pay her ransom regally, or leave her alone. But, having bought her, eat her on her own, fragrant, coarse-grained, eat her like the vegetable that she is, warm, served in sumptuous portions. She will not give you much trouble; her supreme flavour scorns complexity and complicity. Soaked in a good very dry white wine, not oversalted, peppered discreetly, she will cook in the covered black pot. For twenty-five minutes, she will dance in the constant bubbling, trailing behind her in the eddies and foam—like Tritons playing around a black Amphitrite—some twenty pieces of larding bacon, half-fat, half-lean, that fill out the stock. No other spices! Your truffles will come to the table in their court bouillon; take a generous helping, the truffle stimulates appetite, aids digestion. As you crunch this jewel of impoverished lands, imagine those of you who have never been there, the desolation of its realm. For it kills the wild rose, saps the strength of the oak, and ripens beneath barren rocks. Imagine harsh Périgordian winters, the grass whitened by the hard frost, the pink pig trained to its delicate prospecting. . . .

> *Passages et Portraits*

There is a famous saying about truffles: "Those who wish to lead virtuous lives had better abstain." The gist being that something so magnificent will, inevitably, corrupt. Well—truffles will certainly ruin your bank account, but if you're lucky your virtue will emerge unscathed!

What's all the fuss about? What tastes so good that it sells for upward of $700 a pound? After all, it's only some strange kind of underground fungus that must be sniffed out by pigs and dogs. All true—and if you've just tasted a little bit in a pâté or a sauce you may have good cause to wonder. But if, at least once in your life, you take Colette's advice and eat a Périgordian truffle as a vegetable, then you, too, may begin to rhapsodize.

I ate my first whole Périgordian truffle *(Tuber melanosporum)* at the Château de Castel Novel in the Corrèze, the very place where Colette spent some of her latter days. It was baked in a salt crust and served on a doily. The waiter cracked the salt crust open with a small mallet, releasing the powerful, penetrating bouquet. I sliced the truffle myself and ate it on toast, with a light sprinkling of walnut oil and a pinch of salt. As I ate I sipped a glass of Médoc.

That truffle seemed to me like earth and sea. I felt at one with nature, my mouth was filled with the taste of the earth. There was ripeness, naughtiness, something beyond description. A gastronomic black diamond, it was total luxury and simple earthiness combined.

Another time I ate a whole truffle raw, the way one eats radishes and butter. I sliced it thin, spread salted country butter on the slices, and gobbled it up. Of course, such a feast on the most expensive lump of dirt in the world cost me a small fortune, but it was wonderful— an experience I shall never regret.

Truffles range in size from as small as a pea to as large as a small melon. They range in color from black to white; they can be as fleshy as a mushroom or as firm as a nut. Their taste will vary greatly: Some are bland, others taste almost like garlic, and the best taste faintly nutlike, yet not like any ordinary kind of nut.

I went to Cahors to visit Jacques Pebeyre, one of the leading truffle harvesters in France. A tall, trim, balding man with large blue eyes, he comes from a family of famous *trufficulteurs.* His land, studded with craggy oaks, is perhaps the richest truffle ground in the area.

It was too early in the year to observe a truffle hunt, but just a look at that land was a revelation. The area surrounding each gnarled oak was absolutely bare to a radius of twenty feet—a bit like a baseball mound. "You always know where the truffles are," Pébeyre explained. "They eat up all the vegetation around the roots, so that if there are truffles, you won't ever see a single weed near the tree."

Some twenty-five varieties of truffle grow in his fields, but the only good ones, the ones he harvests, are *Tuber melanosporum,* the famous black truffles of Périgord. "It's humble work," he told me. "I plant a tree and wait ten years and often the truffles will not come." And then, when they do come, he still needs trained dogs or pigs to find them. The animals smell them out, and then are distracted while the hunter scoops them from the earth. Another way to find truffles is to look closely at the ground to see if any golden flies are hovering about, since they, too, are attracted by the truffle smell. If a man just digs around looking for truffles by himself, he'll likely disturb and break up those too young for harvest and thus waste a precious commodity.

Truffles are hunted every day during the season, collected at just the moment they are ripe. If they're too ripe, they turn soggy and cannot be sold. A good truffle must be firm and untouched by insects.

An expert truffle buyer will choose by aroma. The best market is in Périgueux in January, though in December there's an important market in Sarlat. If you buy canned Périgord truffles (a generic term; Quercy actually produces more truffles than Périgord), look for ones marked *surchoix* or *1er choix* (the latter tend to be irregular in shape).

Monsieur Pébeyre is quite annoyed by so-called summer truffle breakings *(Tuber aestivum)*, which have barely any taste or aroma and yet are frequently palmed off as the real thing. These second-rate truffles are exported in large quantities to America, where, unfortunately, many restaurants use them and people purchase them because they seem to be a "buy." They're black on the exterior, but white and yellow inside. At the great truffle markets in France, truffles are notched so the purchaser can see they are black through and through.

How can you buy a quality truffle? It's best to purchase from a trusted source, such as Plantin America (see Mail Order Sources, page 417), during the winter months when they can be bought fresh. Other times of the year they're sold packed in tins.

The "poor man's truffle" is the imported Chinese variety *(Tuber indicum)* that appears almost identical to the untrained eye, smells milder than the true *Melanosporum*, and even has some feeble flavor when consumed raw but tends to become tasteless when cooked. Chinese truffles are one-twelfth the price of the top French and can be used in some recipes for a colorful and flashy-looking garnish. (For example, I use them in my adapted version of the brothers Pourcel's Carpaccio of Pig's Feet, Celery, and Black Truffles, pages 86–88.) You can purchase them from Frenchselections.com.

BAKED WHOLE TRUFFLES IN SALT

→> *Truffes au Gros Sel* SERVES 4

FOR DREAMERS AND TRUFFLE "rustlers," here's a dish you'll remember all your life. Serve along with a cruet of imported walnut oil and a good bottle of Médoc.

4 small whole raw truffles of similar size, or substitute 4 canned truffles, preferably *première cuisson* (first cooking)

4 paper-thin slices pork fatback, blanched if salted

¾ pound coarse kosher salt

2 large egg whites

1 About 35 minutes before serving, preheat oven to 425°F.

2 Wrap each truffle in a slice of fatback.

3 Line four brioche molds with aluminum foil.

4 Mix the salt and egg whites in a bowl. Make a layer of the salt mixture about ½-inch deep in the bottom of each mold. Place a truffle in each and spoon the salt mixture around the sides of each truffle, pressing the mixture with your fingertips to pack. Spoon at least a ½-inch layer of the salt mixture over the tops of the truffles. Press firmly with your palm to completely seal truffles in salt. Flatten the salt so that when it's turned out, the casing won't wobble. *(The recipe can be prepared to this point 1 to 2 hours ahead.)*

5 Bake 25 minutes for medium-sized raw truffles, 15 minutes for canned (cooked). Remove from the oven; turn out and remove the foil.

6 Place each truffle on a serving dish. Crack each casing lightly and remove the truffle. The truffles will not be salty. In fact, you will probably need to season them with a pinch of salt.

NOTES TO THE COOK

→> To preserve truffles raw, or once you've opened the can, place the unused quantity in an airtight bottle with a light olive oil to cover. The truffles will keep for a month. Truffles pass on their aroma to fats and oils better than to alcohol. (Often people store truffles in Madeira or port or Cognac, but Monsieur Pébeyre advises against this, calling it wasteful.) You can get good use from the olive oil afterward in salads, on cold cooked leeks flavored with fresh mint, or simply on some blanched thin slices of celery root.

The Tastes of the French Southwest 🌸 31

→ To preserve whole fresh truffles, keep them packed in raw rice for 1 to 2 weeks in the freezer or refrigerator. (The rice can later be used in a wonderful risotto.) Freezing for long periods is not a good idea, since truffles tend to dry out. If you do freeze them, do not defrost. Use them straight from the freezer just as you do herbs.

TRUFFLED SCRAMBLED EGGS
→ *Œufs Brouillés aux Truffes* SERVES 6 TO 8

IN THIS DISH, the truffle is not merely decorative, nor is its purpose to convey a sense of luxury and ostentation. Gently heated with the eggs, it endows them with an earthy taste and aroma. Since these scrambled eggs are cooked in a double boiler or in a heatproof bowl set over simmering water, they have a creamy, almost curdless consistency. Close to a tablespoon of butter per egg makes for a rich dish, but served in small quantities in little porcelain ramekins, these eggs make a mouthwatering light supper dish or first course.

Be sure to cut the truffles into very small cubes so that you can eat a little bit with each spoonful of scrambled egg. And remember the Quercy tradition: "The truffle is a delicate lady"—apart from salt, no other seasoning except a hint of pepper is needed.

2 black truffles, fresh or canned, peeled if necessary

10 jumbo eggs

6 to 8 tablespoons unsalted butter

½ teaspoon fine sea salt

Pinch of freshly ground white pepper

2 tablespoons heavy cream

1 About 1 hour before serving, finely dice 1 truffle. Cut the other into 8 or 10 thin slices; reserve for garnish.

2 Break the eggs into a fine wire sieve set over a bowl. Gently crush the yolks with the back of a wooden spoon. Let them drip through; this takes about 1 hour.

3 Lightly butter the insides and bottom of the top of a double boiler or a 2-quart ovenproof glass or porcelain bowl, and set over a saucepan half-filled with barely simmering water. Add the eggs and 2 tablespoons of the butter. Cook over low heat, stirring constantly with a silicone or wooden spatula, for 1 to 2 minutes.

4 Add the salt and white pepper and continue to cook, stirring, for 7 to 8 minutes longer, until barely thickened. Be sure to move the spatula along the sides and bottom of the pan where the eggs tend to settle. Rather than stirring in circles all the time, make a figure "8" through the eggs. Gradually add the remaining butter, 1 tablespoon at a time.

5 When the eggs begin to hold together with as few curds as possible but are still very creamy, stir a little faster. Whisk in the cream and the diced truffles. Cook for 1 minute longer.

6 Spoon equal amounts of egg into 6 to 8 small warmed ramekins. Garnish each serving with 1 truffle slice.

Vinegars and Verjus

VINEGARS

The vinegars of the French Southwest include apple cider vinegar, red and white wine vinegars, and raspberry vinegar. Cider vinegar is used in poaching liquids for fish and shellfish, for cooking the famous apple dishes of the Limousin, and in vinaigrettes for vegetable salads in the region of the Périgord and the Quercy.

Red wine vinegar is used for salads and for deglazing duck dishes. White wine vinegar is employed for game marinades, fish dishes, and the famous sauce béarnaise. And raspberry vinegar, which for a time became something of a cliché among chefs, is still used in Southwest France, especially for deglazing sautéed duck breasts. In the 1929 edition of *La Bonne Cuisine du Périgord*, author La Mazille suggests adding a teaspoon of it to cold water to make a refreshing summer drink.

Vinaigre de Banyuls is another Southwest product now imported into the United States. One of my favorite condiments, it's comparable to sherry wine vinegar but has a sweeter component, which provides a very smooth flavor. It is wonderful for deglazing after sautéing duck and in walnut oil-dressed salads, too.

VERJUS

Summer is the season to make *verjus*, the juice of sour grapes. But there is no closed season for using this wonderful condiment to enhance the flavor of chicken, salads, foie gras, beans, game birds, river fish, and stewed wild mushrooms, or just to deglaze a sauté pan to make a sauce.

Unlike vinegar, *verjus* is wine friendly. With its subtly sharp, refreshing taste, it has always played a prominent role in regional Southwest French cooking, especially in the Périgord, and it is now making a comeback, despite the fact that the proper grapes—bourdelois, gressois, and farineau—are no longer grown. I recently purchased two extraordinary bottles of *verjus* from the Périgord and another from California (see Mail Order Sources, pages 415–417). All three served me well in updating and retesting the recipes for this book. You can also make your own, if you can obtain sour green grapes.

To make *verjus*: Choose the sourest green grapes available, still in the midst of ripening. (If the fruit is too ripe, its liquor will be too watery; if it is too "green" and not ripe enough, the fruit flavors will not have developed enough in the grapes, and your *verjus* won't taste good.) Holding a bunch of grapes by the thick stem, dip into boiling water for three seconds to kill the yeasts. Remove at once and drain on a clean kitchen towel. Repeat with all the grape bunches. One by one, roll each bunch of grapes in the towel while removing the grapes from the stems. Discard any blemished grapes. When dry, place the grapes in a food processor and puree for 10 seconds. Strain, pressing down on the grapes to extract all the juice. Let stand for 10 minutes, then ladle the juice into a sieve lined with damp cheesecloth and strain again. Use at once, or freeze in plastic ice cube trays. When hard, store the cubes in a sealed plastic bag in the freezer for up to 3 months. For maximum flavor, use frozen or immediately upon defrosting.

Walnuts From the Périgord

The Southwest concept that no part of any ingredient should go to waste is summed up beautifully in a peasant's aphorism from the Périgord: "Nothing is lost of the walnut except the noise when it is cracked!"

Since walnuts are foraged, they must be carefully used, or else the labor of their gathering cannot be justified. The shells are ground up and used for fuel. A digestif is made from the tender walnut leaves by infusing them with old red wine, sugar, and some marc. Another drink is made by macerating fresh walnuts in 90-proof eau-de-vie. (This is an excellent aperitif, by the way, served over ice; it is also makes an interesting ice cream.) The walnuts themselves are employed in salads, cakes, and candies, with green beans and fish, and joined with Roquefort or endives. In the Corrèze, neighboring the Périgord, I once ate an extraordinary dish of sautéed duck in which the pan juices had been deglazed with the black juices of unripened walnuts.

In the Périgord, there's a class of elderly women who specialize in shelling walnuts. Called *les énoiseuses* (the nutcrackers) they travel from house to house, village to village, during the walnut harvest season, bringing their special wooden mallets and round wooden boards upon which they rhythmically crack open the nuts, five to the minute, without ever smashing one to powder.

Some people prefer their walnuts peeled, believing the skins are indigestible. This is easily done by pouring some boiling water directly over the nuts, after which the skins may be slipped off easily.

Freshly shelled walnuts are available in the fall. Store walnuts in the freezer. Out of season, I always purchase them vacuum-packed. In the old days in the Southwest, housewives resuscitated walnuts by burying them overnight under about a foot of soil, then using them right away. Another *truc* of the Southwest is to soak them in milk. Still another way to resuscitate them is by sprinkling them lightly with sugar, then warming them in the oven.

A smooth-tasting, slightly bitter cooking ingredient from the Périgord is walnut wine (*vin de noix*). Since it isn't fermented, it isn't really a wine. Rather it's a beverage made by soaking chopped green walnuts and their shells in eau-de vie along with red wine, vanilla, cinnamon, nutmeg, and sugar. After ninety days this mixture is filtered and bottled. It tastes similar to a good port and is often served as an aperitif. Nostalgie, a walnut liqueur made by a California winery, Domaine Chambray, is similar, but sweeter and stronger. In the English version of *The Walnut Cookbook* by Jean-Luc Toussaint, steeping warm walnuts in sweet vermouth is suggested as a substitute.

You can make your own very simple vin de noix during the month of June when green walnuts are available. You'll need about half a dozen. Crack them open; place the husks and nuts in an earthenware crock; pour over a bottle of red wine; cover with cheesecloth, and let stand for 6 weeks. Strain and discard the walnuts. Add about ¾ cup eau-de-vie or vodka to the wine along with ½ cup sugar and a few spices, such as cinnamon and nutmeg, to taste. Stir to dissolve the sugar, bottle, cork tightly, and leave for at least 3 months. Southwest cooks use this wine to flavor sauces for fish, game birds, and poultry. One of the nicest uses is to use it for poaching pears.

One of the great by-products of walnuts is their extraordinary oil—"all of the Périgord in a bottle," in the words of Zette Guinaudeau-Franc, author of *Les Secrets des Fermes en Périgord Noir*. Soft, fragrant, green, and golden-hued, this oil is delicious on salads. But please remember, some French walnut oil is very strong tasting, and you might want to dilute it. Two parts olive oil or French peanut oil to one part walnut oil is an excellent formula. And once opened, always store in the refrigerator. Try a few drops on white beans or add some to a cassoulet.

And if you get to the Southwest, consider making a visit to a walnut oil mill. I especially recommend the hundred-year-old mill in Sainte-Nathalène outside Sarlat. There, they make stunningly delicious walnut oil. This stream-driven mill cracks open the walnuts by gentle crushing. The crushed nuts are then placed in a wooden cauldron and heated to about 120°F before being pressed. The resulting oil is then directly bottled.

LANGUEDOC WALNUT, GARLIC, AND OIL LIAISON

➤➤ *L'Aillade Toulousaine*   SERVES 4 TO 6

THIS SAUCE IS CALLED *Alhada Tolosenca* in the Languedoc dialect. It is made with a good handful of freshly shelled walnuts pounded in a mortar with sweet and aromatic soft-white or pink-hued garlic, then made into a smooth paste by the addition of cold water. After the paste is seasoned with salt and pepper and a tablespoon of fresh chopped parsley, walnut oil is slowly beaten in. Often the flavor is enhanced by the addition of a splash of *verjus* or mild cider vinegar.

If you suspect that your walnuts are not fresh enough, heighten their flavor by toasting them in a 325°F oven for 10 minutes. Let cool before using. The sauce is usually served with fish, duck breast *(magret)*, or veal chops grilled over charcoal or grapevine cuttings.

Though it is not authentic, if you make this sauce in a food processor, you might want to an add an egg yolk as a binder; the sauce will come out a good deal fluffier.

3 ounces broken walnut meats

4 to 6 garlic cloves, peeled

¼ teaspoon coarse kosher salt

Pinch of freshly ground pepper

½ cup French walnut oil and ¼ cup French peanut oil

1 tablespoon chopped fresh flat-leaf parsley

A few drops of *verjus* or cider vinegar

1 Grind the walnuts in an electric blender or food processor for 30 seconds, stopping and scraping down the bowl twice. Add the garlic and 2 tablespoons ice water and process for 5 seconds longer. Season with the salt and pepper. With machine on, add the oil in a slow, steady stream.

2 Transfer to a bowl and fold in the chopped parsley. Taste and, if desired, add the verjus or vinegar. Let stand at room temperature for 1 hour before serving.

The Périgord Paradox

→>‑<←

The statistics are stunning: The people of the Southwest lead the rest of France in general good health and length of life. You've heard of the "French paradox," but what about the "the Périgord paradox"?

Jean-Luc Toussaint, the author of a book devoted to cooking with walnuts, coined the phrase because he believes the protective properties of walnuts are a major contributor to the good health of Périgourdines. The Périgord diet, which consists largely of confit, pork, wild mushrooms, and river fish, features numerous appetizers, salads, sauces, and desserts that employ walnuts.

A Few Words About the Local Wines

The wines of the Southwest include some of the greatest and most illustrious ever produced, as well as hundreds of brands never seen beyond the bounds of their domains. Bordeaux wines are readily available in the United States and are the classic accompaniments to many dishes in this book. For an excellent treatment of the great whites and reds of Bordeaux, I refer readers to *The Wines of Bordeaux: Vintages and Tasting Notes 1952–2003* by Clive Coates.

Madiran, an intense, solid, inky, and very tannic wine, is often the choice on the Gascon table. Made from Tannat grapes, often blended with Cabernet Sauvignon, Madiran keeps well and improves markedly with age. It has recently become more widely available in the American market and pairs wonderfully with the rich, hearty food described in this book. When a Madiran is unavailable, try a hearty Syrah from the Rhône Valley, such as Cornas or Hermitage, or an earthy old-vines Zinfandel from Amador County in California.

I have a special affection for the intensely aromatic local white wine, Pacherenc du Vic-Bilh (the old name for Madiran is Vic-Bilh), which I drank every night during my annual research sojourns at the Hôtel de France in Auch, to accompany my evening bowl of *garbure*. Unfortunately for Americans, almost all Pacherenc du Vic-Bilh is consumed locally. Try a white wine from Rueda, Spain, a Riesling from Australia's Clare Valley, or an Alsace Gewürztraminer with your *garbure*.

Cahors, the famous "black wine" of the Quercy made mostly from the Malbec grape (known locally as *Auxerrois*) blended with Merlot, is wonderful for picnics. It is very tannic and creates a compelling, intense contrast with goat cheeses, rillettes, and other charcuterie. As they age, Cahors wines become acceptable mates for rich meat dishes, mushroom dishes, game, and fowl. If you can't find a Cahors, ask your wine merchant to order one, but while you're waiting, try an oak-aged Malbec from Argentina.

The region of the Béarn produces a soft, velvety, sweet wine called Jurançon, famous for its yellow color. Made from grapes so overripe that they are almost raisins, Jurançon is a good match for rillettes and cheeses. The legend, which everyone who lives around the area will be quick to tell you, is that when Henri IV was christened, his lips were rubbed with garlic and moistened with a few drops of this wine. If you can't find Jurançon, try a Coteaux du Layon from the Loire Valley, a semidry Riesling from the Finger Lakes in New York State, or a Moscatel de Setúbal from Portugal.

In the Landes, there is a special appreciation of the aromatic, very dry white Tursan, made from the local grape, known as "baroque," which has the reputation of being able to "knock you to your knees." And there is a curious and barely known Landais light red, smelling of violets and tasting "meaty," that is grown in sandy soil, such as the vin de table from the Domaine de Mallecare. If you are looking for a dry white with a knockout punch, try a white Condrieu from the Rhône Valley, made from the Viognier grape.

Sweet red wines are rare in the Southwest. A good one from the Languedoc-Roussillon region is the Banyuls produced at Domaine de la Rectorie, which enhances anything made with dark chocolate. It is also excellent with blue cheese. It is hard to replace Banyuls, but try a Recioto della Valpolicella from Veneto, Italy, a Mavrodaphne of Patras from Greece, or Quady "Elysium" from California.

If you travel in the region, you'll find numerous good local wines served with the local cuisine. The vineyards of the Périgord are at least as old as those of Bordeaux, though far less known. The best among the reds are the Bergeracs, many of which are light in body. Look for the Domaine du Haut Pécharmant, which ages beautifully. The white sweet Monbazillac from the Dordogne is called the "Sauternes of the poor;" look for the

The Human Touch

→>–←

I've often heard the assertion that in the best wines grapes must be crushed by human feet. It was only when I read *The Generous Earth* by Philip Oyler that I found this fascinating explanation:

"No machine can equal human feet, which are scrupulously washed of course before operations. These do not squeeze out too much acidity from the skins nor break the grape pits, which give a disagreeable flavor to the wine. Moreover, the mush is aerated better and the ferments mix more thoroughly with the juice."

Château Ladesvignes and try it with foie gras or Home-Cured Duck Ham (pages 82–84). On the left bank of the Garonne, on the hillsides west of Agen, you'll find some of the new "star" red wines of the Southwest, notably the Bordeaux-style Buzet (formerly Côtes de Buzet).

The Basques in Southwest France produce reds and rosés called Irouléguy, which are full-bodied and acceptable with the local food. Irouléguy is rarely available in export markets, but try a Spanish rosé from the Basque province of Navarra, or the most famous rosé in the world, Tavel, from the southern Rhône Valley, as a stand-in.

When a recipe calls for a red table wine, I usually cook with a food-friendly wine such as a Syrah or a California Pinot Noir. The wine you cook with does not have to be as expensive as the wine you drink, but a good basic rule is never to cook with a wine you wouldn't happily drink. Any inferior wine won't get better as it reduces, concentrating its flavor, during cooking; it will only get worse. Another guideline: "Wine in the sauce, wine in the glass." For example, if you braise with Syrah, serve Syrah with the dish, "bridging" or "echoing" the food and the wine.

Garbure, Pot-au-Feu, and Other Soups

"*Faire bien la soupe!*" ("Make a good soup!") That's what mothers teach their daughters in Southwest France. If France is a country of soup-eaters, the Southwest is the land of soup-lovers. Here soup is often eaten more than once a day, and an entire evening meal might well consist of only a fine, rich soup.

The soups of the Southwest range from very simple, to extremely hearty, to ravishingly elegant. I believe there are more varieties of soups eaten here than in all the other regions of France. The Périgord cooks are the most famous soup-makers in the region. Theirs are rich in nutrients, medicinal qualities, and the fortifying powers attributed to the classic chicken soup of Jewish mothers.

Most of these soups, of course, are never made the same way twice. The ingredients change from season to season, there is much room for improvisation, and each cook makes her own adjustments, "feeling" her soup as she goes along.

All great makers of soup have their special secrets. One cook uses her mother's old earthenware *toupin* (a high, round-bellied pot that sits in the fireplace) for soup and nothing else. She cleans it once a year on Ash Wednesday, she told me. She'll cook everything else on her modern stove, but "never a soup," she says.

One Southwestern cook always adds a few ribs of Swiss chard to give her soups a certain indefinable smoothness. Another swears by an old iron kettle, and still another contends that a fricassée (the Périgord habit of browning a portion of the cooked vegetables* in fat and then returning them to the kettle) is her secret.

Seventy-five years ago, a wedding night in the Southwest of France was unthinkable without a heavily peppered soup on hand for the bride and groom. (In the Landes, it was often served in a chamber pot!) And then there was a soup made to warm both the stomach and the bed. It was made in the evening, left in the dying embers to cook during the night, reheated to boiling in the morning, then placed under the covers of the bed to keep the bedding warm during the day. At noon, a piece of bread was left to soak in it, so that by nightfall the soup had turned into one big *panade*. It was then devoured for the evening meal, and a new soup was put into the embers to provide the next night's nourishment and to keep the bed warm during the cold winter day.

*A mixture of chopped turnips, carrots, cabbage cores, onions, leeks, and wild greens. In the Quercy it is called a *fleuri*; in Gascony, a *sabous*.

Thick Mixed Meat and Bean Stew

➤➤ *Garbure*   SERVES 12

THERE ALWAYS COMES a point while people are talking seriously about French gastronomy when someone quotes Curnonsky, the so-called Prince of Gastronomes, who was active in French culinary circles early in the twentieth century. And usually when he is quoted, people nod their heads, believing that if Curnonsky said something, it must be true. Among his most famous statements is the one in which he lists the four great regional dishes of France: *choucroute garnie*, bouillabaisse, cassoulet, and *garbure*. Almost everyone has heard of the first three; yet very few know anything of the last.

I am not too sure about some of the pronouncements of Curnonsky, but I have to admit that *garbure* in the right hands is most assuredly a great dish. Basically, it is a soup—a relatively simple one at that—made up of salt pork, cabbage, and beans. But, of course, like many "simple" peasant dishes, *garbures* are not as easy as they seem. It is in the embellishments, the variations, that the really great *garbures* come about.

Garbure is the very symbol of Béarnais cookery, but it is eaten widely in Gascony, the Landes, and the Pays Basque, too. It's usually served as the evening meal—one of those soups that is a meal in itself. Preferably cooked in an earthenware *toupin*, *garbure* has all kinds of variations, depending on local ingredients. The best *garbures* are made in spring with the second shoots of young cabbages *(broutos)*. In the late fall, grilled chestnuts are added; and in the Landes during the summer, cooks add roasted red pepper strips. In winter, the bean of choice is the Tarbais bean, which doesn't fall apart when reheated but also manages to maintain a melt-in-your-mouth texture. Some cooks will add a fricassee of onions and vegetables fried in goose fat during the last hour or so of cooking; others will add Swiss chard to make the soup more succulent, and still others will serve it as a gratin with layers of bread and cheese. On the average weekday night, a cook will often add a *hachis* or a *sahit* (a mixture of aged pork fatback minced with garlic and herbs) and perhaps a spoonful of goose fat. But a truly luxurious Sunday *garbure* requires a *trébuc*, a final embellishment of confit.

Here is a little story about confit and *garbure* that sums up, in an amusing way, the mystique of the "secret" in Southwest French cookery. A gastronomic reporter asked a famous local cook just precisely when she added the leg of goose confit to her deservedly famous *garbure*. The cook replied that first she took the preserved goose leg in her hand and

(continued)

stirred it around in the soup. She kept stirring and stirring until all the surface fat melted off and flavored the soup. Then she stirred some more until she could actually feel the confit imparting its wonderful flavor to the liquid. "I keep stirring," she said, "and stirring . . . and stirring . . . and then finally I let it drop in."

"Yes, yes," said the impatient gastronomic reporter, "but explain to me precisely when."

There was a long silence, and then the cook whispered her "secret": "When my hand gets too hot to keep holding it," she said.

For optimum flavor, make the soup 3 to 4 days in advance.

½ pound dried white beans, such as Tarbais or cannellini

PORK AND POULTRY STOCK

1 fresh meaty ham hock or pig's knuckle, or 1 small bone from a country ham

1 duck carcass, cut up, or duck back bone and neck bone, or ⅓ pound chicken feet, nails trimmed

¼ pound pancetta or ventrèche, in one piece

1 small head of garlic

Salt and freshly ground pepper

FRICASSEE OF LEEKS, CELERY, AND ONIONS

3 tablespoons rendered duck fat, preferably from confit

¼ pound pancetta or ventrèche, diced

3 medium onions, sliced

2 leeks (white plus 2 inches of green leaves), split lengthwise in half, and carefully rinsed

2 ribs celery, sliced

Herb bouquet: 3 sprigs parsley, 1 sprig thyme, 1 imported bay leaf, and 3 sprigs marjoram (if available), tied together with string

HACHIS OR SAHIT

3 sprigs parsley

A good pinch of piment d'Espelette, or moderately hot red pepper to taste

2 medium turnips, peeled and quartered

3 thick carrots, peeled and cut into 2-inch chunks

3 medium boiling potatoes (about 1 pound), peeled and cut into 1-inch chunks

1 medium head of savoy cabbage, quartered

2 Duck Legs Confit (pages 198–200), at room temperature

2 large slices of French bread or country-style bread, dried in low oven

Pickled wild leeks or pickled hot peppers, as accompaniment

1 Pick over the beans to remove any grit. Soak them in water to cover by at least 2 inches for 12 hours.

2 Make the stock: Place the ham hock, duck carcass, or ham bone, and the pancetta in a medium-sized saucepan. Add 6 cups water and bring to a boil, skimming. Add the garlic head and 1 teaspoon salt and a pinch of pepper. Reduce the heat to low and simmer, partially covered, for 1 hour.

3 Make the fricassee: Melt the duck fat and the diced pancetta in a heavy 3-quart casserole set over moderately low heat. Add the sliced onions, leek, celery, and herb bouquet. Cover tightly and cook until the vegetables are soft but not browned, about 45 minutes.

4 Strain the bone stock and set aside the pancetta and garlic. Pick meat off bones and set aside. Discard all the bones. Cool, cover, and refrigerate the stock and bits of meat.

5 At the same time you are soaking the beans, make the hachis: Crush the cooked garlic to express the pulp, add to a food processor along with the reserved pancetta, the parsley, and piment d'Espelette. Puree until smooth. Scrape into a small bowl, cover, and refrigerate overnight.

6 The following day, drain the beans and place in a deep, heavy saucepan, preferably copper. Degrease the bone stock and add to the saucepan along with 1 quart water; bring to a boil, skimming. Cover and cook the beans for 20 minutes over medium low heat.

7 Add the leek and onion fricassee, the turnips, carrots, and potatoes, and simmer, uncovered, until beans and vegetables are tender, about 1 hour.

8 In a large pot of boiling salted water, blanch quartered cabbage, uncovered, for 10 minutes. Drain and coarsely chop.

9 Remove the pieces of confit from its softened fat; scrape off excess. Add to the saucepan along with the cabbage, the bits of meat, and the pureed hachis and bring to a boil over moderately high heat. Reduce the heat to moderately low and simmer slowly, uncovered, for 30 minutes. Cool, cover, and refrigerate for several days, up to 2 to 3 days. The garbure improves in flavor as it sits and mellows with time.

10 Just before serving, check the consistency of the garbure; it should be so thick that a wooden spoon stands up straight in the center. If it is too thin, boil down. Stir in the remaining 1 tablespoon reserved confit fat, if desired. Season with additional salt, pepper, and piment d'Espelette to taste.

(continued)

To make a gratinéed variation, which is called a *panade*, layer slices of country-style bread, the boned duck, and the vegetables in a deep ovenproof or earthenware bowl. Moisten everything with the soup, sprinkle with grated cheese, such as Cantal or mild Cheddar, and set in a preheated 350°F, oven to bake until the top is crusty and brown, about 45 minutes.

CREAMY BEAN SOUP WITH CROUTONS AND CRISPY VENTRÈCHE

→→ *Crème de Haricots de Maïs*   SERVES 4 TO 6

I ASKED CHEF Martin Etchemaite, from the Basque country town of Larrau, to tell me the secret of his very famous bean soup. He confirmed that the thin-skinned, sweet-tasting, buttery textured Tarbais bean is the key. (As its French name—*haricot de maïs*—indicates, it is a climbing variety that grows up stalks of corn.) But that wasn't all: "Duck fat is essential, too, because it adds depth," he told me, and then he went on to extol the Basque paprika, called piment d'Espelette, without which, he said, the cooking would not be properly made. So here it is: a Basque version of a bean and chile soup—a stunning and wonderful soup for winter.

1 pound dried Tarbais beans or large white beans, such as cannellini

1 carrot, cut into ¼-inch dice

1 large onion, cut into ¼-inch dice

4 tablespoons duck fat

Salt and freshly ground pepper

1 cup diced crustless dense country bread

3 ounces lean ventrèche, pancetta, jambon de Bayonne, or Serrano ham, slivered (about ½ cup)

2 tablespoons minced fresh chives

1 cup heavy cream

Pinches of piment d'Espelette or moderately hot red pepper

1 Pick over the beans and soak them in water to cover by at least 2 inches for 12 hours.

2 The following day, rinse and drain the beans and set aside. Meanwhile, in a heavy, 4- to 5-quart flameproof pot, preferably earthenware, such as a Yankee bean pot or a Chinese sand pot, gently

cook the carrots and onions in 2 tablespoons of the duck fat, stirring, until tender, 5 to 10 minutes. Scoop out and reserve about ¼ cup of the onions and carrots. Add the drained beans and 2 quarts fresh water to the pot. Bring to a boil, reduce the heat to moderately low, add a pinch of salt and pepper, and simmer for 2 hours, or until the beans are tender and the liquid is reduced.

3 In a medium skillet, heat the remaining duck fat. Add the diced bread, slivered ventrèche, and the reserved carrots and onions. Fry, stirring, until crisp. Remove to a side dish, add the chives, and set aside.

4 Let the beans cool slightly, scoop out about ⅓ cup for garnish and set aside. Press batches of the remaining beans and liquid through the fine blade of a food mill or puree in a food processor or blender. Add the bean puree to the soup. Stir in the cream; bring to a boil and simmer for 5 minutes. Correct the seasoning with salt, pepper, and red pepper to taste.

5 To serve, divide the reserved beans among soup bowls, ladle the hot soup over the beans, and garnish each portion with a spoonful mixture of the fried onion and ventrèche mixture. Serve at once.

POT-AU-FEU WITH STUFFED BREAST OF VEAL

→→ *Pot-au-Feu à la Faouda*   SERVES 4 TO 6

THIS IS A DELICIOUS family pot-au-feu from the Languedoc. It is a little different from most in that a small stuffed breast of veal *(faouda)* is cooked in a rich broth along with the various soup meats and vegetables. To make the dish even more substantial, you can serve it with green beans and new potatoes dressed with a light vinaigrette. The Fresh Tomato and Caper Sauce (page 49) is a lovely accompaniment.

For relaxed preparation, make the stuffing a day in advance.

(continued)

1¼ to 1½ pounds veal knuckle

1 beef shin (1¾ pounds) with marrow "soup bone"

1¾ to 2 pounds thick-cut, lean beef brisket, trimmed of excess fat

1 tomato, halved

2 medium onions, halved, plus 1 onion stuck with 2 cloves

1 small head of garlic plus 2 garlic cloves, finely chopped

Coarse kosher salt

Herb bouquet: 4 sprigs parsley, 1 imported bay leaf, 2 sprigs thyme, 2 to 3 celery leaves, and 4 leek greens tied together in cheesecloth

8 ounces pork sausage meat

2 slices of country-style bread, crumbled, soaked in milk, and squeezed dry

1½ ounces jambon de Bayonne, Serrano ham, or prosciutto, chopped

2 shallots, finely chopped

1 egg

1 tablespoon chopped fresh flat-leaf parsley

¼ teaspoon quatre épices

Freshly ground pepper to taste

½ veal breast (1¾ to 2 pounds), with pocket for stuffing

4 large carrots, peeled

2 turnips, peeled, and halved if large

2 large leeks, well washed, trimmed, and tied in a bundle

Grainy mustard, cornichons, and fleur de sel, as accompaniments

Fresh Tomato and Caper Sauce (at right)

1 Place the veal knuckle and beef shin bone in a large pot. Add 4 quarts cold water and slowly bring to a boil. Simmer for 15 minutes, skimming. Add the brisket; return to a boil and simmer for 45 minutes longer, skimming often.

2 Meanwhile, place the tomato and onion halves under the broiler. Remove the tomato when just slightly blackened and soft. Remove the onion when the cut side is totally black.

3 When meats have simmered for 1 hour, add the tomato and onion halves, the onion stuck with cloves, the whole head of garlic, 1 tablespoon salt, and the herb bouquet. Simmer for 1 hour longer.

4 Make the stuffing for the veal breast, la fouada: Combine the sausage meat, bread, chopped fresh garlic, ham, shallots, egg, parsley, quatre épices, and ¼ teaspoon each salt and pepper; blend well. *(The dish can be prepared to this point up to a day in advance.)*

5 About 2½ hours before serving, stuff the pocket of the veal breast and sew up to secure. Add the stuffed veal breast, carrots, turnips, and leeks to broth in the pot. Partially cover, return to a simmer, and cook over moderately low heat 1½ hours.

6 Remove the vegetables, beef, and stuffed veal breast. Carefully strain the cooking liquid and skim off as much fat as possible. Discard the onion stuck with cloves and any debris. Remove and reserve about one fourth of the cooking liquid. Store the remainder for soups and sauces. Pour the reserved cooking liquid back into the pot; return the vegetables, beef, and veal breast to the pot.

7 About 20 minutes before serving, reheat the dish over moderately low heat for about 10 minutes. Remove the veal breast and cut into thick slices; divide the beef into chunks. Arrange the meats and vegetables attractively on a warm serving platter and cover loosely to keep warm.

8 Quickly boil down the cooking liquid in the pot to further intensify its flavor. Season with pepper and additional salt to taste. Sprinkle over the meats and vegetables to moisten. Serve hot. Pass grainy mustard, cornichons, fleur de sel, and Fresh Tomato and Caper Sauce on the side.

FRESH TOMATO AND CAPER SAUCE

Sauce Tomate aux Câpres   MAKES 1 CUP

This is a light and tasty sauce. It cannot be made successfully in a food processor, but it can be made many hours in advance and refrigerated.

1 hard-boiled egg, shelled

1 tablespoon finely chopped shallots

1 tablespoon finely chopped fresh flat-leaf parsley

3 tablespoons aged red wine vinegar

½ cup peeled, seeded, and finely chopped plum red-ripe tomatoes

⅓ cup extra virgin olive oil

1 tablespoon nonpareil capers, drained but not rinsed

Salt and freshly ground pepper

1 In a small bowl, coarsely mash the egg with a fork. Add the shallots, parsley, vinegar, and tomatoes and toss to mix.

2 Whisk in the olive oil in a slow steady stream.

3 Fold in the capers. Season with salt and pepper to taste. Serve at room temperature.

Stuffed Cabbage Soup

→ *Poule Verte* SERVES 6

WHENEVER A POACHED CHICKEN is stuffed—and in the Southwest of France it is always stuffed when poached whole—enough extra filling is made to form a basketball-shaped construction of overlapping cabbage leaves. Such a fabrication, called a *poule verte* (green chicken) is extremely popular in Southwest France, where it may often be seen in the family kitchen, bobbing like a big dumpling in a pot of simmering soup.

The *poule verte* is just further proof of this region's love of stuffings, the best of which are made from stale bread that is half wheat, half rye. Cream is added for moisture and eggs for body so that the stuffing can be sliced. And for firmness and extra flavor, pork or ham and veal along with a medley of herbs and spices are included.

Be sure to begin this recipe a day in advance so that the stuffing has time to mellow.

½ pound dried bread with crust (about 3 cups torn pieces)

¾ cup milk or cold stock

½ pound lean veal, finely chopped

5 ounces lean pork, finely chopped

4 ounces fatback, pureed in food processor

1 large shallot, finely chopped

3 garlic cloves, finely chopped

1¼ teaspoons salt

½ teaspoon freshly ground pepper

8 allspice berries, crushed

¼ teaspoon freshly grated nutmeg

3 tablespoons finely chopped fresh flat-leaf parsley

2½ tablespoons finely chopped fresh chives

3 tablespoons heavy cream

2 eggs

1 tablespoon Armagnac

1 head savoy or green cabbage

5 quarts unsalted chicken stock (storebought or homemade—page 405) or 2 bouillon cubes dissolved in 5 quarts of water

24 creamer potatoes or very small Yukon golds, scrubbed

4 carrots, peeled and cut into 1-inch pieces

6 tablespoons unsalted butter, at room temperature

1 Up to 24 hours in advance, make the filling: In a large bowl, combine the bread, milk, chopped veal and pork, pureed fatback, shallot, garlic, salt, pepper, allspice, nutmeg, 2 tablespoons of the parsley, 1½ tablespoons of the chives, and the cream and eggs. Mix with your hands to blend well. Drizzle the Armagnac over the top of the filling; cover and refrigerate for at least 12 hours or overnight to allow the flavors to develop.

2 The following day, remove and discard the outer leaves from the cabbage, then cut out the core. Drop the whole cabbage into a pot of simmering salted water and cook for 15 minutes, or until the leaves separate easily; drain. Let the cabbage cool, then pull back the leaves and separate them. Trim away all hard ribs.

3 Line a deep mixing bowl with damp cheesecloth or a washed string shopping bag. Line with half the cabbage leaves, overlapping them to fill all spaces. Place the filling in the center and cover with the remaining leaves to enclose completely. The poule verte should be round like a basketball. Tie up the cheesecloth firmly so that it retains its shape. *(The recipe can be prepared to this point up to 3 hours in advance; cover and refrigerate. If made ahead, remove from the refrigerator about 1½ hours before cooking to return to room temperature.)*

4 In a large deep kettle, bring the stock to a boil. Gently lower the poule verte into the liquid. If the ball is not completely covered with liquid, add more boiling water. Cover the pot, reduce the heat to low, and simmer for 1½ hours.

5 Uncover the pot and ladle 4 cups of the cooking liquid into a 3-quart saucepan. (Continue simmering the poule in the remaining liquid in the kettle for 30 minutes longer.) Quickly skim the fat off the stock in the saucepan. Add the potatoes and carrots and cook until tender, 12 to 15 minutes. Season the stock with additional salt and pepper to taste.

6 After the poule has simmered for 2 hours, check for doneness: Stick a larding needle or thin metal skewer into the center and leave it there for 1 minute. Remove and place the point of the needle on your palm. If it is burning hot, the poule verte is fully cooked. If it is merely warm, cook a little longer. Remove the poule and set in a colander to drain.

7 Cut the poule into 6 wedges and place one in each soup plate. Garnish with the carrots and potatoes. Ladle the cooking liquid in which the carrots and potatoes were cooked over all and add 1 tablespoon soft butter to each bowl. Sprinkle with the remaining parsley and chives and serve at once.

POT-AU-FEU IN THE STYLE OF ALBI

↠ *Pot-au-Feu à l'Albigeoise*

SERVES 10 TO 12

THIS VERSION OF POT-AU FEU, the famous boiled dinner of meats and vegetables served with assorted condiments and beef marrow, is a specialty of Albi, the beautiful red-brick city, sometimes called the "Florence of France," on the Tarn River. In this variation, the addition of confit gives this nationally popular dish a distinctly Southwest character. During the winter months, the cooks of the city add beans as well—at times, one suspects that the Albi pot-au-feu might almost be called *garbure*! Sometimes the Albi cooks will also add Preserved Stuffed Duck Neck (pages 207–208).

Making a pot-au-feu can be a no-win situation. If you start cooking the meat in cold water, you end up with slightly bland meat and a great broth; if you add the meat to boiling water, it will be delicious (because of the quick sealing in of the juices), but the broth will be so-so. In this recipe, however, you can win both ways: The broth is made in advance with chicken and beef bones, and the meat is cooked the next day in the hot broth.

Eight 3-inch pieces of beef marrowbones, with the marrow intact

1 pound (3 or 4 links) fresh pork and garlic or Toulouse sausage

Tomato Fondue (pages 54–55)

4 quarts unsalted chicken stock (storebought or homemade—page 405)

2½ pounds beef shin or brisket, in 1 piece

3 pounds beef top round, in 1 piece

1 small head of garlic

Herb bouquet: 3 sprigs parsley, large sprig thyme, and 1 imported bay leaf, tied together in cheesecloth

2½ teaspoons coarse kosher salt

½ teaspoon freshly cracked peppercorns

2 pounds meaty veal shank, sawed crosswise into 2-inch pieces (ask your butcher to do this)

4 medium carrots, peeled and cut into large chunks

3 small turnips, peeled and cut into large chunks

8 small leeks, split lengthwise in half, carefully rinsed, and tied in a bunch

½ small head green cabbage, cored

4 to 6 Duck Legs Confit (pages 198–200), at room temperature

10 to 12 small boiling potatoes, peeled

10 to 12 thin rounds French bread, lightly toasted

2 tablespoons salted butter, softened

Freshly ground pepper

1½ tablespoons chopped fresh flat-leaf parsley

Cornichons, fleur de sel, and grainy mustard, preferably *moutarde violette*, as accompaniments

1 A day in advance, extract the marrow from the bones by soaking them in lukewarm water until the marrow can be pried out easily with a thin skewer. Soak the marrow in salted ice water in the refrigerator until it is time to cook it the next day.

2 Cook the sausages in a large saucepan of simmering water for 15 minutes. Let cool, then wrap and refrigerate.

3 The following day, about 4 hours before serving, bring the chicken stock to a boil. Slip all the beef into the pot and return to a boil. Skim off the scum as it rises to the surface. Lower the heat and simmer slowly (the liquid should quiver rather than boil), uncovered. Continue to skim until the liquid is clear, about 15 minutes.

4 Add the garlic, herb bouquet, salt, and cracked peppercorns. Partially cover and continue to simmer very gently for 1½ hours, skimming if necessary.

5 Add the veal shank to the soup and continue to simmer, partially covered, for 1 hour, skimming often. Meanwhile, make the Tomato Fondue.

6 When the soup has simmered a total of 2½ hours, add the carrots, turnips, leeks, and enough cold water to cover. Return to a boil, then reduce to low and simmer, partially covered, for 30 minutes.

7 Meanwhile, in a separate pot of salted water, boil the cabbage over moderately high heat for 15 minutes.

8 Remove the confit pieces from the softened fat; scrape off most of the fat clinging to it. Divide the legs into thighs and drumsticks. Add the confit and potatoes to the cabbage. Return to a boil, reduce the heat to low, and simmer for 15 minutes. Check to see whether vegetables are tender; remove to a warm bowl when they are done. Moisten with a few tablespoons of hot cooking liquid and cover with foil to keep warm.

9 Meanwhile, cut the 4 chilled sausage links into bite-size pieces and reheat. Remove the confit and sausage to the large warmed serving dish; tent with aluminum foil to keep warm.

(continued)

10 Prepare the marrow toasts to serve as part of the first course. Have ready the lightly toasted rounds of French bread, buttered with the salted butter. Place the marrow pieces in a small saucepan of simmering salted water. Poach gently for a few minutes, removing pieces with a slotted spoon as soon as they turn pinkish gray. Divide the marrow among the buttered toast rounds, mashing lightly to spread over each slice. Preheat the broiler.

11 To serve the first course, remove and discard the marrow bones, herb bouquet, and garlic head from the soup. Ladle 3 quarts through a fine-mesh sieve into a soup tureen or other serving container. Run the toast rounds under the broiler for just a few seconds, or until the marrow is heated and glistening. Lightly sprinkle with pepper and serve at once, very hot, on a separate platter with the soup.

12 To serve the second course, slice or chunk the meats and arrange them on a warmed large platter; surround with the vegetables. Sprinkle lightly with parsley and season to taste with salt and pepper. Serve accompanied by Tomato Fondue, cornichons, fleur de sel, and grainy mustard.

TOMATO FONDUE

Fondue de Tomates   MAKES ABOUT 1½ CUPS

Pot-au-feu is a spectacular winter dish, and a highly seasoned thick tomato sauce like this one is a very popular accompaniment; it rounds out the flavor of boiled meats and blends well with the usual sharp accompaniments to the dish. Organic canned tomatoes can be substituted for fresh with excellent results.

½ cup chopped onion

2 tablespoons extra virgin olive oil

2 cups seeded, cubed plum tomatoes (there is no need to peel tomatoes; the sauce will be strained after cooking)

Pinch of sugar

Herb bouquet: 4 sprigs parsley, 2 sprigs thyme, and 1 small imported bay leaf, tied together with string

1 garlic clove, halved

Salt and freshly ground pepper

1½ cups stock or liquid from the pot-au-feu

Cayenne

1 In a small, heavy enameled casserole, cook the onion in the olive oil over moderate heat until soft but not brown, about 3 minutes. Add tomatoes, sugar, herb bouquet, and garlic. Season with salt and pepper to taste.

2 Bring to a boil. Cover tightly, reduce the heat to very low, and cook for 30 minutes, or until well reduced.

3 Add the stock and boil until the sauce is reduced to 2 cups. Strain through a sieve to remove any skin and seeds, then return to the pot and reduce, if necessary, to 1½ cups. If too thick, thin with a little water or stock. Season with salt, pepper, and cayenne to taste.

NOTE TO THE COOK

If you wish, this tomato sauce can be made up to a day ahead.

CHESTNUT AND CÈPE SOUP WITH WALNUTS

➤➤ *Crémeux de Cèpes et Châtaignes*   MAKES 3 QUARTS; SERVES 4 TO 6

MANY OF THE CHESTNUT SOUPS I've tasted have been filling and nutritious but also somewhat bland—even in the Auvergne, where they are an autumn evening staple. Not so this version, which I've loosely adapted from a recipe given to me by the late, great Gascon chef Jean-Louis Palladin.

Jean-Louis used a rich poultry stock as a base, to which he added a consommé made with a great assortment of vegetables. He also garnished the soup with quenelles of venison, crispy cubes of wild mushrooms, bits of cured ham, fragments of chestnuts, and cubes of sweetbreads. Needless to say, it was heavenly!

However, lacking a full kitchen staff to do all that work, I've opted to simplify the soup. It is still deliciously toothsome, a warm, creamy, beige soup, studded with crunchy walnuts and chestnuts, and I think the addition of walnut oil gives it a bright finish.

(continued)

2 chicken wings and 1 back

4 medium new potatoes, peeled and halved

1 onion, thinly sliced

3 tablespoons butter

2 celery ribs, sliced

1 imported bay leaf

10 juniper berries, bruised

Pinch of ground cinnamon

Salt and freshly ground pepper

½ ounce dried French cèpes or Italian porcini (½ to ⅔ cup)

1 pound steamed or roasted chestnuts, shelled and peeled

1 cup heavy cream

1½ ounces jambon de Bayonne, Serrano ham, or prosciutto, slivered

¼ cup shelled walnut pieces

1 tablespoon chopped fresh flat-leaf parsley

1 tablespoon chopped fresh tarragon leaves

Lemon quarters and a cruet of walnut oil

1 Make the soup base: Crack the wings and back of the chicken into small pieces. Place in a heavy saucepan with the potatoes, onion, and half the butter and slowly allow the contents to brown and lightly stick to the bottom of the pot. Deglaze with 1 cup of water. Add the celery ribs, bay leaf, juniper berries, cinnamon, and 2½ quarts of water. Bring to a boil, skimming. Season with salt and pepper. Simmer the soup base, uncovered, for 45 minutes.

2 Meanwhile, soak the cèpes in 1 cup water until soft. Strain, reserving the soaking liquid. Finely dice the mushrooms; set aside for Step 6.

3 In a blender or food processor, grind 2 cups chestnuts with 1 cup cream and the reserved cèpe soaking water until smooth. Chop the remaining chestnuts and reserve for garnish.

4 Remove the soup base from the heat. Use a slotted spoon to remove the chicken bones, bay leaf, and juniper berries. Add the chestnut puree to the soup base and simmer for 30 minutes longer. Press the soup through a tamis or fine-mesh sieve. *(The recipe can be prepared to this point up to a day in advance.)*

5 Return the soup to a saucepan and slowly heat to boiling. If necessary, add more water or reduce to reach the desired consistency. Season with salt and pepper to taste.

6 In a large nonstick skillet, quickly sauté the slivered ham, diced cèpes, chopped walnuts, and chestnuts in the remaining butter over moderate heat until golden brown, about 5 minutes. Ladle the hot soup into bowls and garnish with the chopped parsley and tarragon. Serve at once with some lemon quarters and a cruet of walnut oil.

Potato, Leek, and White Bean Soup With Olive Puree in the Manner of Ciboure

→→ *Soupe de Haricots Comme en Ciboure* SERVES 4

THIS VERY SIMPLE, utterly delicious soup shows off the talent of Biarritz-born Gerald Hirigoyen, chef-owner of the restaurant Piperade in San Francisco. Gerald's gift is to take a country-style dish, such as this simple bean soup, and make it sing. In his restaurant, he coaxes flavor out of tomatoes, peppers, cheese, and beans, re-creating the magnificent flavors of his region.

1 cup dried white beans, preferably Greek gigantes or French Tarbais

5 tablespoons extra virgin olive oil

1 sprig of rosemary

3 large garlic cloves, peeled and halved

1 large leek (¼ pound), trimmed and thinly sliced

Salt

½ pound baking potatoes, peeled and thickly sliced

6 cups light chicken or vegetable stock, lightly salted

2 ounces Picholine or other green olives, pitted

Freshly ground black pepper

8 thinly sliced rounds of French bread, toasted lightly and rubbed with garlic

1 Pick over the beans to remove any grit. Soak them overnight in enough water to cover by 2 inches. Drain and rinse.

2 In a heavy 3- or 4-quart saucepan, heat half the olive oil. Add the rosemary, garlic, and leek and cook over moderately high heat until golden but not brown, about 5 minutes. Add the beans, a pinch of salt, potato slices, and stock to the saucepan and bring to a boil. Cover, reduce the heat to a simmer, and cook for 1½ hours, or until the beans are tender. Remove and discard the rosemary sprig. Allow the soup to cool slightly.

3 Meanwhile, soak the olives in several changes of water for 20 minutes to remove excess salt and brine. Drain the olives and place in a blender or food processor. Add the remaining olive oil and 1 to 2 tablespoons water and puree until smooth. Scrape the olive puree to a small bowl. Add the bean and potato soup to the blender or processor in batches and puree until smooth. *(The recipe can be prepared to this point up to a day in advance; cool and refrigerate.)*

4 About 10 minutes before serving, gently reheat the soup. If necessary, add a little water to thin to desired consistency. Bring the soup back to a boil, then remove from the heat. Swirl in the olive puree and adjust the seasoning with salt and pepper. Serve at once and pass the garlic toasts on the side.

THE ARCHBISHOP'S TOURAIN WITH CONFIT OF DUCK

→→ *Tourin d'Archevêque*

A TOURAIN IS A SOUP made with onions, garlic, or tomatoes, or a mixture of two or three of these ingredients. (These soups are sometimes called a *tourin*, a *tourri* in the Pyrenees area, or an *ouliat* in the Béarn.) Most *tourains* are thickened at the last minute with a mixture of egg yolks and vinegar, and sometimes too beaten egg whites are stirred in. There are quick *tourains*, which can be made in half an hour, hardly longer than it takes to open up a can and heat its contents, and then there are *tourains* that must be "mothered" for two or three days. This one, particularly wonderful, will cook in about 1 hour.

 Tourains are the mainstay of most evening meals in the French Southwest except for the Béarn and Bigorre areas, where heartier *garbures* are served nearly every night. Evening soups—*tourains*, *garbures*; their Périgord cousins, *sobronades*; and their Basque variations, *saldas*—are often so thick that a spoon will remain upright if placed in them. After all the bread on the soup plate is eaten, and there is only a spoonful or two of soup left, diners will sometimes pour some red wine into their plates, mix the wine and the soup, raise the plate to the mouth, and drink off the mixture. This act, called *faire chabrot* (or, in the Béarn, *faire la goudale*) is considered restorative or quaint, depending on one's point of view.

½ pound of mixed pieces of duck confit (wings, thighs, and drumsticks), store-bought or homemade (see Traditional Confit of Duck, pages 201–203)

3 to 4 tablespoons fat from confit

3 medium onions, chopped (about 2 cups)

1 large fresh ripe tomato, peeled, seeded, and coarsely diced, or ⅔ cup drained imported canned peeled tomatoes

1 teaspoon chopped fresh garlic

Salt and freshly ground pepper

2 jumbo egg yolks

1 tablespoon red wine vinegar, preferably a strong-flavored variety

4 to 6 thin slices of country-style bread or good-quality seedless rye

1 About 4 hours before beginning main preparation, set out the crock of confit in a warm room or in a deep pan of warm water to soften the fat.

2 Carefully remove the confit pieces and scrape off the fat. Place 2 tablespoons fat into a flameproof 4-quart casserole; reserve remainder in a bowl. Heat the fat in the casserole over moderate heat to rippling. Set thigh and drumstick pieces aside; add the onions and neck and wing confit to the hot fat. Cook for 5 minutes, stirring often.

3 Add the tomatoes and garlic; cook for 2 to 3 minutes. Add 5 cups warm water and heat to boiling. Skim any foam from surface. Season with pepper and a little salt. Reduce the heat to low; simmer, partially covered, 20 minutes.

4 Divide each leg into thigh and drumstick pieces at the joint. Add to the soup and simmer for 20 minutes. Strain the soup through a sieve; skim off the fat from the surface and return the liquid to the casserole. Set the duck pieces aside until cool enough to handle. Remove the skin, pull the meat off the bones, and return the meat to the strained soup. *(The recipe can be prepared to this point up to 1 hour in advance.)*

5 About 10 minutes before serving, whisk the egg yolks with vinegar in a small bowl until thoroughly blended. Over very low heat and stirring constantly, slowly pour the egg yolk mixture into the soup, stirring until slightly thickened. Do not allow the soup to boil. Remove from the heat; let stand, covered, a few minutes before serving. Taste and correct the seasoning. Spread the slices of bread with a thin layer of confit fat and sprinkle with freshly ground pepper. Toast the bread in a preheated 450°F oven until glistening, about 3 minutes. Place a slice in each warmed individual soup bowl and pour soup over. Serve immediately.

VARIATION At the last minute, toast the bread in a toaster and spread with confit fat; sprinkle with pepper and serve at once.

Inspired by a recipe from Zette Guinaudeau-Franc's Les Secrets des Fermes en Périgord Noir.

EVENING GARLIC SOUP IN THE MANNER OF THE CORRÈZE

→ *Tourain à l'Ail Comme en Corrèze*   SERVES 4 TO 5

IN THE REGION of the Corrèze, a typical evening meal would consist of a simple soup like this, followed by slices of pâté, some pickled fruits, crusty bread, and a salad. Serve the soup with crusty round of toasted French bread, dabbed with goose fat and sprinkled lightly with black pepper.

2 medium onions, finely chopped

¼ cup thinly sliced garlic

2½ tablespoons rendered duck fat or 3 tablespoons unsalted butter

1 tablespoon all-purpose flour

4½ cups poultry or meat stock, degreased and heated to lukewarm

2 eggs, separated

4 teaspoons red wine vinegar

Salt and freshly ground pepper to taste

1 In a heavy 3- or 4-quart saucepan, cook the onions and garlic in the fat over moderately high heat, stirring often, until golden but not brown, 5 to 10 minutes. Reduce the heat to moderate, add the flour and cook, stirring, until it turns a straw-beige color, 2 to 3 minutes. Remove from the heat.

2 Gradually whisk in 4 cups of the stock. Return to moderate heat. Bring to a boil, reduce the heat, and simmer, uncovered, for 30 minutes. *(The recipe can be prepared to this point up to a day in advance; let cool, then refrigerate.)*

3 About 10 minutes before serving, lightly beat the egg whites with a fork in a small bowl or pitcher until frothy. Beat in the remaining ½ cup cold stock until blended.

4 Reheat the soup to boiling; reduce the heat to low. Beat the egg yolks in a small bowl with a fork to break them up; then beat in the vinegar. Gradually whisk in 1 cup of the hot soup.

5 Pour the egg white mixture into the pot of hot soup in a thin, steady stream, gently whisking to form strands. Stir in the egg yolk mixture with a spatula, and simmer gently, stirring, until the soup is creamy, about 1 minute. Do not allow the soup to boil, or the eggs will curdle and strands will harden. Adjust seasoning and serve at once.

OLD-FASHIONED RABBIT SOUP

➤ *Soupe de Lapin à l'Ancienne*   SERVES 4 TO 6

THIS IS A SIMPLE SOUP from the tiny village of Poudenas in the Lot-et-Garonne. It is delicious and worth making whenever you intend to cook rabbit. Since the front legs and rib cage of rabbits have little meat but are very flavorful, they are better used for soup. The saddle and hind legs should be reserved for sautés.

Rib sections as well as tail bone, loose skin and fat, spine, and forelegs of 2 young, tender rabbits, or 1 stewing rabbit (see Note, page 62)

Salt and freshly ground pepper

2 tablespoons rendered duck or goose fat

1 tablespoon olive oil

½ pound carrots, peeled, halved, and thinly sliced (about 1½ cups)

1 leek (white and pale green parts), well washed and thinly sliced

1 tablespoon finely chopped shallot

2 quarts unsalted chicken stock (storebought or homemade—page 405)

1 garlic clove, peeled

Herb bouquet: 4 sprigs parsley, 2 sprigs thyme, 1 small imported bay leaf, tied together in cheesecloth

1 cup heavy cream

1 tablespoon minced fresh chives

1 With a cleaver, chop the rabbit into 1-inch pieces. Season with salt and pepper.

2 In a large flameproof casserole, heat the duck fat and olive oil over moderately low heat. Add the carrots, leeks, and shallot. Stir once, then cover, and cook gently for 5 minutes so that the vegetables become soft but do not brown.

3 Add the rabbit pieces; cover and cook for 5 minutes. Uncover the casserole and cook, turning the rabbit occasionally, until the pieces are lightly browned on all sides, about 10 minutes.

4 Add the stock, garlic, and herb bouquet; bring to a boil. Cover with a round of buttered waxed paper set right on top and a lid and simmer very gently over low heat for 5 hours. (You can also cook the soup in a preheated 250°F oven.)

5 Let the soup cool slightly; skim off all the fat and strain the liquid into a bowl. Pick over the solids to remove the bones. Discard the herb bouquet. Press through the fine blade of a food mill to puree. Press on the rabbit meat to extract as much flavor as possible; discard the fibrous solids.

(continued)

Alternatively, puree in a blender or food processor, then press through a tamis or wire sieve. Rinse out the casserole and return the soup to it. *(The recipe can be prepared to this point up to a day in advance.)*

6 About 15 minutes before serving, bring the soup to a boil and cook until reduced to 5 cups. Stir in the cream and season with salt and pepper to taste. Garnish each serving with minced chives.

NOTE TO THE COOK

If using frozen cut-up rabbit, buy 2 boxes. Use bony pieces for soup; rewrap meaty portions and save for Rabbit Stew With Preserved Pears With Ginger (pages 216–219). If you have a whole, skinned rabbit, you can include the head for added richness.

Inspired by a recipe from Marie-Claude Gracia of Poudenas.

Oyster Velouté With Black Caviar

→ *Velouté aux Huîtres et au Caviar* SERVES 6 TO 8

CAVIAR HAS BEEN TAKEN from the Gironde River since the Russian Revolution. According to one of the many legends, it was the owner of the famous Parisian fish restaurant Prunier who employed Russian refugees to extract and preserve caviar from the Gironde sturgeon. The eggs obtained were of excellent quality, comparable to the best Iranian caviar. Sadly, in the 1950s parts of the Gironde became quite polluted, and caviar production declined; but now, happily, it's the cleanest estuary in Europe, and production is back up to its heyday in special sturgeon hatcheries. The Gironde sturgeon roe is black to lustrous grey, is nicely saline, and possesses a wonderfully delicate flavor with a long, lingering, buttery finish on the tongue. You can purchase Caviar d'Aquitaine from D'Artagnan or any good quality caviar dealer.

Fat, juicy oysters of Japanese origin are now raised in the bay of Arcachon, where oysters have been cultivated since Roman times. The oldest were flat, common European oysters, which were wiped out in the 1920s. Portuguese oysters, similar to our bluepoints, are still raised in the bay, but they are being replaced by the more resistant Japanese variety. In this recipe, the oysters are pureed and added near the end, so as not to overcook them and lose their natural taste.

If you garnish this velouté with a fine caviar, it becomes an extremely elegant soup course. Lumpfish eggs can be used, but they must be drained first. Whatever type of caviar you choose, be sure to add it at the last minute to avoid possible discoloration.

2 shallots, finely chopped

3 tablespoons unsalted butter

3 tablespoons all-purpose flour

3 cups unsalted fish stock (storebought or homemade—pages 411–412)

3 cups unsalted chicken stock (storebought or homemade—page 405)

¾ teaspoon sea salt

12 to 15 oysters, shucked, plus their liquor (or, if you buy them shucked, about 1⅓ cups, including liquor)

Pinch of cayenne

3 large egg yolks

¼ to 1 cup heavy cream

1 to 2 drops fresh lemon juice

2 tablespoons black caviar, preferably Caviar d'Aquitaine

(continued)

1 In a heavy 4-quart saucepan, preferably copper, soften the shallots in the butter without browning. Blend in the flour and cook over very low heat, stirring often, for 10 minutes. The mixture—called the roux—must be very smooth and not darken beyond the color of yellow straw. If necessary, use a metal simmer mat to control the heat. This mixture must cook slowly so that the flour proteins will absorb liquid and thicken properly.

2 In a second saucepan, combine the fish and chicken stocks (see Note below) and heat to lukewarm. Gradually pour this liquid into the roux, stirring constantly, and bring to a boil over moderate heat. Reduce the heat and simmer gently for 20 minutes, skimming off scum that rises to the surface. Add half the salt.

3 Strain the oyster liquor to remove any traces of shell and sand. Puree the oysters in a food processor or electric blender. Add the pureed oysters and strained liquor to the soup. Simmer, partially covered, for 5 minutes. Add the cayenne. Rub the soup through a fine strainer set over a large mixing bowl, pressing down hard with the back of a spoon to extract as much oyster pulp as possible. *(The recipe can be prepared to this point up to 2 hours in advance.)*

4 About 10 minutes before serving, slowly reheat the soup. Combine the egg yolks and ¾ cup heavy cream in a small mixing bowl; whisk them together. Gradually whisk in 1 cup of the hot soup in order to raise the temperature of the egg yolk–cream mixture and prevent curdling. Stir the egg-yolk mixture into the soup and cook over low heat, stirring constantly, until the soup thickens slightly; do not allow to boil. Immediately remove from the heat. Taste for seasonings and adjust. If necessary, add a bit more cream.

5 Sprinkle the lemon juice over the caviar. Ladle the soup into individual soup plates and top each with a teaspoon of the caviar. Serve at once.

NOTE TO THE COOK

The mixture of equal amounts of fish and chicken stocks is important to this dish. It provides good body and background taste without overpowering the flavor of the oysters.

VARIATION To serve the soup cold, chill quickly over cold water or ice, then refrigerate. Thin with half cream and half milk before serving.

Fish Soup Basquaise

➤➤ *Ttoro* SERVES 4

THIS IS A MODERN INTERPRETATION of the classic onion and pepper fish soup of Bayonne. It is moderately spicy on account of the hot red pepper flakes. The Basques have a fondness for their home-grown piment d'Espelette, which imparts a rounder, deeper pepper taste to the soup than ordinary cayenne or the common crushed hot red pepper.

I attended the pepper festival in the village of Espelette, where the peppers are grown. This festival is held each year in late October to celebrate their wonderful hot peppers—spicier, meatier, and richer in flavor than rival peppers from other towns. Peppers are everywhere—strings of them hang from buildings, and like everyone else, I wore a string of them around my neck!

Espelette isn't the only Pyrenees town that likes to promote its produce. Biarritz sets aside a day to celebrate its bounty of shellfish; Bayonne honors its ham; Hendaye (on the coast near Spain) boasts its delicious tiny eel; Saint-Gaudens fetes its excellent fat white beans served in *garbure*; and in Sainte-Croix-du-Mont the grape pickers toast the fruity wine called Irouléguy—so good that it makes the girls dance.

1 dozen large mussels

½ cup dry white wine

¼ cup extra virgin olive oil

½ cup chopped onion

½ cup finely chopped celery

1 large garlic clove, finely sliced

¼ teaspoon piment d'Espelette or other moderately hot red pepper, or 1 teaspoon crème de piment d'Espelette (see Mail Order Sources, pages 415–417)

Pinch of imported sweet paprika

½ cup diced (½ inch) red bell peppers

½ cup diced (½ inch) green bell peppers

¾ to 1 pound mixed boneless fish fillets (red snapper, halibut, monkfish, hake, or cod), cut into ¾-inch cubes

2½ tablespoons chopped fresh herbs: flat-leaf parsley, basil, chervil, a few leaves of rosemary or sage

½ cup peeled, cubed, and seeded plum tomatoes

3 cups hot fish stock (storebought or homemade—pages 411–412) or water

½ cup cooked crabmeat (optional)

Dash of fresh lemon juice

Salt and freshly ground pepper

(continued)

1 In a large pot, steam the mussels in the white wine over high heat until they just open, 3 to 5 minutes. Remove the mussels to a bowl and let cool. Strain the cooking liquid through several thicknesses of damp cheesecloth and reserve. Remove the mussels from their shells; discard the shells.

2 In a large skillet, heat the olive oil. Add the onion, celery, garlic, piment, paprika, and red and green peppers. Cook over moderate heat for 2 minutes, stirring occasionally.

3 Add the fish, herbs, tomatoes, and reserved mussel liquor. Bring to a boil. Add the hot stock or water and simmer for 5 to 7 minutes, swirling the pan often. Skim off foam that rises to the surface.

4 Add the mussels and the crabmeat, if using. Season with a dash of lemon juice, and salt and pepper to taste. Cook over low heat for 2 minutes.

5 With a slotted spoon, gently divide the fish and shellfish among individual soup plates.

6 Ladle the broth over the seafood and serve at once.

NOTE TO THE COOK

The fish must not be allowed to disintegrate, so avoid fluke, flounder, and sole. Stick to firm-fleshed, delicately flavored, white-meat fish, such as bass, red snapper, hake, halibut, cod, scrod, monkfish, and sea eel.

VARIATION To make the soup more substantial, garnish it with garlic croutons: slices of French bread browned in hot olive oil. While still hot, rub each slice with a cut piece of garlic and sprinkle with coarse salt. If making the croutons in advance, reheat in a warm oven before serving.

AUTUMN SQUASH SOUP WITH
COUNTRY HAM AND GARLIC CROUTES

→→ *Crème de Potiron*   SERVES 6

THIS FALL SOUP is served with hot crisp rounds of French baquette topped with a good rubbing of garlic. To enhance the flavor of the squash, I roast it in the oven to preserve its natural sweetness. This soup reheats well, retaining its velvety texture and great savor.

1½ to 2 pounds butternut, kabocha, or buttercup squash

2 tablespoons extra virgin olive oil

2 tablespoons rendered duck fat or butter

½ cup chopped onion

½ pound Yukon gold potatoes, peeled and cubed

3 garlic cloves, peeled and halved

4 cups unsalted chicken stock (storebought or homemade—page 405)

Salt and freshly ground pepper

Freshly grated nutmeg

1 cup heavy cream

Pinch of piment d'Espelette or any moderately hot red pepper (see Mail Order Sources, pages 415–417)

2½ ounces jambon de Bayonne, Serrano ham, or prosciutto, trimmed of fat and cut into thin ribbons

6 thin slices of stale baguette

2 tablespoons minced fresh chives

1 Preheat the oven to 400°F. Wash the squash, halve lengthwise, and lay cut side down on a foil-lined baking sheet. Bake about 30 minutes, until soft. Turn the squash over, turn off the heat, and let the squash finish cooking and browning in the hot, turned-off oven for 10 minutes longer. Remove the squash and let stand until cool enough to handle. Scoop out the seeds and cut away the skin; discard.

2 Meanwhile, heat the oil and half the duck fat in a heavy 4-quart pot over moderately low heat. Add the onion, potatoes, and 1 of the garlic cloves and slowly cook the vegetables until soft and pale golden, 10 to 15 minutes. Add the chicken broth and simmer for 30 minutes.

3 Scrape the roasted squash into a food processor or blender. Add a few tablespoons of the hot soup broth and puree until velvet-smooth. Working in batches, puree the contents of the pot. Or if you have an immersion blender, puree the soup directly in the pot. Season with salt, pepper, and nutmeg to taste. Add the cream and bring to a boil. Reduce the heat and simmer for 5 minutes to blend the flavors.

(continued)

4 In a medium skillet, heat the remaining duck fat with a pinch each of black pepper and piment d'Espelette. Add the ribbons of ham and the rounds of bread and sauté over moderately high heat until slightly crisp, about 2 minutes. Generously rub the bread with the remaining garlic. Serve the soup garnished with the ham, toasted bread, and chives.

Cabbage and Dumpling Soup
➤➤ *Soupe aux Miques et aux Choux* SERVES 6 TO 8

IT WAS IN THE OLD CAPITAL of the Black Périgord, in the town of Sarlat, that I first heard about *miques*—enormous dumplings poached in soup to give added substance to a meal. *Miques* are traditional peasant fare in the Périgord, Quercy, and Corrèze and are, therefore, considered a homey accompaniment to soup.

These dumplings can be made with stale bread, with a mixture of cornmeal and flour leavened with yeast, or with a type of brioche dough flavored with garlic, parsley, and pork cracklings. Like bread, *mique* is served after the first helping of broth, along with the meat and vegetable portion of the soup. In the Périgord, it is usually moistened with broth, while in the Corrèze the brioche-style *mique* is generally served dry. Leftover *mique* is saved, sliced, and fried the following day, either with bacon and eggs or sprinkled with sugar and served as dessert.

I've eaten brioche-style *mique* with chicken in red wine, with a civet of rabbit, and even, in one home, simply doused with tomato sauce. My hostess, rather than cut the *mique* with a knife or with a string the way you might cut polenta, actually broke up the dumpling with two forks to show how light it was.

The *mique* is a good way to approach an understanding of the earthy country cooking of Southwest France, a perfect example of its purpose, which is, of course, to fill the diner up. The *mique* of Sarlat, fondly nicknamed *nuages pesants* (heavy clouds), is made from stale bread, bacon bits, and eggs and leavened with baking powder. It is served with a sparerib soup and assorted vegetables, and if the pot is big enough and the family prosperous enough, a veal knuckle or a chicken may be added, too.

I asked a friend who was born in Saint-Cyprien (a neighboring town to Sarlat) to find someone who could teach me a typical *mique*. She took me to a woman who taught local cooking to city people who owned vacation houses in the region, and here I confronted the classic difficulty of a food writer conducting field research in provincial France.

Madame X had a pointed chin and pointed ears, a tiny mouth, short-cropped hair, high cheekbones, and a typical square Périgourdin face. She was a quintessential peasant woman who loved to talk about cooking, worked hard for very little money, and was fiercely loyal to her family. On the other hand, she was obsessed with the notion that she must guard her "culinary secrets," suspicious of my interest in her knowledge, and totally confident in her ability to deceive. She did try to hide the "secret" of her *mique* and got caught in her own trap. Though her soup was delicious, her *mique* barely rose (*miques* generally double in volume). Her own family, sitting there at the table, complained about its size and less than marvelous good taste. She pretended not to hear one word and gobbled up her portion.

Still, the experience was fascinating, an insight into the cult of recipe secrets and into the lifestyle of a peasant family. The kitchen was in a wonderful stone building with a fireplace in the center. While we waited for the soup to cook and the *mique* to rise, we grilled chestnuts over the fire. Her husband came in and washed up; he had just finished force-feeding a dozen geese. One by one, the children returned home from school, changed their clothes, and proceeded to do chores around the house. During this time, while we were together, Madame X bombarded me with a confusion of advice, all sorts of theories about temperatures and cooking times, her subterfuge sprinkled with a little bit of peasant feminism. Actually, it was fun to fence with her and to watch her cook—she was really very good.

When the dough was ready to be cooked, she removed the chicken from the soup, explaining she had to make room for the *mique*, give it space to expand. I liked the way she slipped the *mique* into the pot along with the floured tea towel in which it was wrapped. She then pulled the towel out gently, covered the pot, and let the dough cook in the simmering liquid. After about 25 minutes, she turned the *mique* over and let it cook some more.

The recipe presented here is not Madame X's, since her *mique* did not turn out particularly well. My friend from Saint-Cyprien went about finding another teacher for me. This time it was a lovely lady in her late seventies, Madame Marthou, who quietly prepared this wonderful cabbage, sparerib, and *mique* soup. The *mique* in this recipe is a stale-bread dumpling with bacon, garlic, and herbs, flavored as is the custom in Saint-Cyprien.

(continued)

1½ pounds meaty salt pork

2 pounds meaty spareribs

1 small veal knuckle

1 onion, halved, 1 half stuck with a clove

Herb bouquet: 6 sprigs parsley, 2 sprigs fresh thyme, and 1 small imported bay leaf, tied together with string

The *Mique* (at right)

1 pound savoy or green cabbage, halved and cored

5 carrots, trimmed, peeled, and left whole

4 medium turnips, peeled and left whole

3 leeks (whites and pale green parts), rinsed well and tied in a bundle

1 garlic clove, halved

1 tablespoon rendered goose or duck fat

Grainy mustard and cornichons

1 About 4 hours before serving, put the meats in a stockpot and cover with cold water. Bring to a boil over high heat; boil for 5 minutes; then drain, rinse under cold running water and drain well. Return to the stockpot.

2 Add fresh water to cover and slowly bring to a boil. Skim off any scum that rises to the surface, then partially cover and simmer for 1½ hours. Remove from the heat and let the meats cool in the soup so that excess fat can be removed easily; if this is not done, the soup will be too greasy.

3 Meanwhile, prepare and refrigerate the mique as described in the recipe that follows.

4 Bring the soup with the meats to a boil. Add the cabbage, carrots, turnips, leeks, and garlic. Reduce the heat and simmer, partially covered, for 1 hour.

5 Remove 1 cooked carrot and 1 turnip from the pot. Slice them and brown in the fat in a small skillet over moderately high heat for about 5 minutes. Return this fricassee to the soup.

6 Slide the chilled mique, still loosely wrapped in cheesecloth, into the soup. It should be submerged; if necessary, add a little boiling water. Cover and simmer over moderately low heat for 45 minutes. Do not uncover while the mique is cooking.

7 Transfer the mique to a plate. Drain off any cooking liquid and let rest for 10 minutes. Remove the cheesecloth. Halve the mique, then cut it into slices.

8 Slice the meats and vegetables and divide them among heated soup plates. Add a thick slice of mique to each plate and moisten with a ladleful of cooking broth. Serve at once, with a grainy mustard and French cornichons.

NOTE TO THE COOK

In this recipe, the leftover cooking liquid is not served as a separate soup.

THE MIQUE

½ cup soup liquid (from Step 2 at left)

4 eggs

Coarse kosher salt

4 strips of bacon, chopped

3 tablespoons milk

2 tablespoons mixed chopped fresh herbs, such as flat-leaf parsley and chives

¼ teaspoon minced fresh garlic

Freshly ground pepper

½ pound stale French, Italian, or country-style bread, torn into small pieces by hand or cut into small cubes (crusts are included) to make 3 loosely packed cups

1 cup all-purpose flour

1½ teaspoons baking powder

Vegetable oil

1 Boil the soup until reduced to 3 tablespoons. Remove from the heat and let cool.

2 Break the eggs into a shallow bowl. Sprinkle just enough salt over the yolks to create a thin veil, about ½ teaspoon. (This is Madame Marthou's truc for adding just enough salt to a stuffing.) Beat the eggs to combine.

3 In a medium skillet, cook the chopped bacon with 2 tablespoons water over moderately low heat until all the water has evaporated and the bacon is half crisped, about 5 minutes.

4 Remove the bacon with a slotted spoon; reserve the warm bacon fat separately. Deglaze the skillet with the milk and reduced soup liquid and gradually whisk into the beaten eggs. Add the still-warm bacon fat and beat lightly to combine. Mix in the herbs, garlic, and pepper to taste.

5 Gently and thoroughly blend the egg mixture with the bread cubes in a large bowl.

6 Put the flour and baking powder in a strainer set over a plate. Shake one third of the flour mixture over the moistened bread cubes. Swirl the bowl so cubes are tossed with the flour and become coated evenly. Repeat with half the remaining flour and baking powder and swirl to combine. Sprinkle the bacon into the bowl. Add remaining flour mixture and swirl again to keep the mixture as light as possible.

7 Fold a large piece of cheesecloth (about 24 by 36 inches) in half to 24 by 18 inches. Lightly brush with oil. Gently press the mique mixture into a mound and place on the oiled cheesecloth. Wrap loosely to allow for expansion, because the mique almost doubles in size when cooked. Tie the ends of the cheesecloth with string. Set the mique on a plate and refrigerate for at least 30 minutes to allow the bread and flour to absorb the moisture.

Appetizers and Small Plates

Asparagus With Asparagus Sauce

➤➤ *Asperges Avec Sauce Coulis d'Asperges*   SERVES 6

THIS RECIPE WAS INSPIRED by an asparagus sauce served with grilled duck foie gras that I ate in Michel Guérard's restaurant at Eugénie-les-Bains. Guérard's sauce was made with lukewarm asparagus, mounted with vinegar and oil, and pureed in an electric blender. My sauce, a puree of asparagus skins mounted with butter, is served warm over freshly cooked large asparagus spears. It can also be used to coat a mixture of other springtime vegetables, such as baby carrots, turnips, mushroom caps, and, of course, the tips of young asparagus. The fresher the asparagus, the better the dish.

To peel or not to peel—that is the question. Many people discard the bottom halves of large asparagus spears because they find them tough and stringy. The solution, of course, is to peel off the skins, but some cooks think this is too much work. I hope this dish will inspire them to peel, since it gives them something to do with the peelings that will marvelously enhance the taste of asparagus, and at the same time salvage the good vitamins concentrated in the peels.

A vegetable peeler isn't the best tool for this, since, due to the tapering of the asparagus spears, you must remove more skin from the bottoms than from the tops. There are two solutions: You can invest fifteen or so dollars in an asparagus peeler, or make an inexpensive guide for your paring knife, which will help cut off just the right amount of peel. I'm grateful to André Soltner, former chef-owner at New York City's legendary restaurant Lutèce, for teaching me how to make one.

To make a wire knife guide that can easily slip onto any thin-bladed knife, purchase a 15-inch length of 16-gauge wire. The wire should just bend under a small amount of pressure. Using both your index fingers, twirl each end toward the center, leaving about 1¼ inches of straight wire between two concentric circles. If you're right-handed, slip the circles onto the blade so that the straight wire is above and in front of its sharp side. (There should be an ⅛-inch or so margin between blade and wire, to be adjusted as necessary according to the thickness of the asparagus stalk.) Lefties can fasten the circles so that the wire is below and in front of the blade.

2 bunches of fat, fresh green asparagus, about 30 to 36 spears

8 tablespoons (1 stick) unsalted butter, cut into small pieces (see Note below)

Coarse kosher salt and freshly ground pepper

Juice of ½ lemon

Pinch of sugar

1 Line up the asparagus and cut away about 1 inch of the tough bottoms. (Breaking at the tender part of the asparagus is for pencil-thin types, which are not peeled.) Place one asparagus on a work surface and, starting at the thick end, using the knife and guide, peel toward the tip. (Some people find it easier to work from the tip to the base of the spear.) The guide should just skim the top surface while the knife cuts away the thick peel; be sure to reserve all the peels. You will notice that the knife takes less peel as you near the tip. Drop into a bowl of water. Tie into bunches when all are peeled and wrap in a moist towel until ready to cook. (If you prepare the asparagus in advance, soak in ice water with 1 teaspoon salt and 1 teaspoon sugar to each 4 cups.)

2 To make the sauce, cook the reserved peels in a small saucepan of boiling salted water until very soft, about 10 minutes. Drain and rinse under cold running water. Puree until perfectly smooth in an electric blender, or pass through the fine blade of a food mill. *(The recipe can be prepared to this point up to 2 hours in advance.)*

3 In another small saucepan, bring 3 tablespoons water to a boil and reduce by half. Quickly whisk in the butter, piece by piece over moderately high heat. The butter will appear foamy. It must not turn to oil. When all the butter has been added, bring to a fast boil, whisking constantly, let it boil for 5 seconds, and immediately pour into a small bowl. Stir in the pureed asparagus peels and season with salt, pepper, and lemon juice to taste. A pinch of sugar will intensify the flavor and counteract any bitterness. The sauce can stand for about 15 minutes. Reheat very gently.

4 To cook the asparagus, bring 1½ inches of salted water to a boil in a large, deep skillet. Slip in the bundles of asparagus and simmer for 3 to 5 minutes, or until the asparagus are just cooked. To test if they are done, lift out one bunch with a pair of tongs; if the ends fall slightly limp, they are ready. Drain on a clean kitchen towel and remove the strings. Serve the asparagus with the asparagus sauce.

NOTE TO THE COOK

To ensure success when making the sauce, be sure to use AA quality or low water content butter, such as Plugra.

(continued)

VARIATION Substitute thick white asparagus: Use a few green asparagus to make the sauce for a more attractive presentation and different flavor. Please note that you need to cook white asparagus until completely tender. Alternatively, serve white asparagus with a light walnut oil and *verjus* dressing.

Other Southwest French Ways of Cooking Asparagus

→>─<←

In the Périgord, scrambled eggs cooked in goose fat are served with the thin asparagus that grow wild in the spring. The cultivated purple spears are cooked and served lukewarm with a walnut oil vinaigrette dressing. After cooking the spears, dry on towels, pressing lightly to extract excess water. Let marinate 10 to 15 minutes before serving.

In the Languedoc, cooked but still crunchy spears are served with a lovely and very simple dipping sauce held in an eggshell set in an eggcup. It is made with 3½-minute eggs. For each serving, a freshly cooked egg is broken up and mixed with 1 tablespoon melted (but not cooked) fresh butter and seasoned with salt and pepper. Small warmed porcelain ramekins can easily be substituted for the eggshell.

TOMATO AND ARTICHOKE SALAD WITH ROASTED HERB BREAD, ANCHOVY-OLIVE DIP, AND SALMON RILLETTES

➤➤ *Salade de Tomates et d'Artichauts à la Rôtie et*
à la Tapenade de Toulouse, et aux Rillettes de Saumon

THE FOUR RECIPES that make up this salad can all be completed in advance. This isn't a composed salad but an informal assembly of good things to eat together. Each of the elements can be enjoyed by itself, or in combination with other dishes. Robert Courtine, a French food writer, recently wrote, "There is no new cuisine; there are no inventions, but there is research and the discovery of natural affinities among different foods." This dish was popular at Lucien Vanel's restaurant in Toulouse.

To serve, let your guests arrange their own plates with a sampling of the Tomato and Artichoke Salad and a scoop each of the Salmon Rillettes (pages 80–81) and Anchovy-Olive Dip (pages 78–79) to accompany the hot bread.

TOMATO AND ARTICHOKE SALAD

Salade de Tomates et d'Artichauts   SERVES 8

5 large globe artichokes, trimmed to their bottoms (see To Prepare Artichoke Bottoms, page 327)

1 lemon, halved, plus 3 tablespoons fresh lemon juice

1 medium onion, sliced

1 carrot, sliced

½ cup extra virgin olive oil

3 tablespoons milk

1¼ teaspoons salt

⅛ teaspoon freshly ground pepper

5 large ripe tomatoes, peeled

Sugar

2 tablespoons red wine vinegar

1 tablespoon Dijon mustard

⅓ cup crème fraîche or heavy cream

3 tablespoons minced fresh chives

1 tablespoon finely chopped shallots

1 In a large nonreactive saucepan or flameproof casserole, combine the artichoke bottoms with the onion, carrot, 2 tablespoons of the oil, the lemon juice, milk, ½ teaspoon of the salt, the pepper, and 2 cups of water. Heat to boiling, cover with crumpled wet parchment paper and a tight-fitting lid. Reduce the heat to low and simmer until the artichoke bottoms are tender when pierced with a knife, 20 to 30 minutes. Drain the artichoke bottoms and pat dry. Let cool, then cut into ½-inch cubes, cover with plastic wrap, and set aside.

2 Meanwhile, quarter the tomatoes, stem to tail. Remove the entire inside of each quarter; save for stock or juice. There will be 4 "petals" from each tomato. Sprinkle each petal with a pinch of salt and sugar; let drain for 30 minutes, cut side down, on a plate lined with paper towels. Cut the drained tomatoes into ½-inch cubes.

3 Shortly before serving, make the creamy vinaigrette: Whisk together the vinegar, mustard, and salt. Gradually beat in the remaining 6 tablespoons oil. Whisk in the crème fraîche, chives, and shallots into the vinaigrette. Add the tomatoes and artichokes and gently toss to coat with dressing. Serve at room temperature.

ANCHOVY-OLIVE DIP

Tapenade de Toulouse   MAKES ABOUT ¾ CUP

This is a mixture of Provençal tapenade, a black olive–based spread, and the Languedoc version of *anchoïde*, a savory paste that uses anchovies as its base. It is perfect on crusty roasted bread.

1 can (2 ounces) flat anchovy fillets packed in oil, drained

18 pitted oil-cured black olives

⅔ cup plus 3 tablespoons fruity extra virgin olive oil

1 garlic clove, slivered

1 tablespoon Dijon mustard

1 egg yolk

1 tablespoon fresh lemon juice

Cayenne

1 Place the anchovies in a small bowl with cold water to cover. Soak for 20 minutes; drain.

2 Meanwhile, soak the olives in 3 tablespoons of the olive oil with the slivered garlic for 15 to 20 minutes; drain.

3 Combine the anchovies, olives, garlic, and mustard in a food processor or electric blender and pulse until coarsely chopped. Add the egg yolk and blend thoroughly until smooth. With the machine on, add the remaining ⅔ cup oil in a slow, steady stream. Season with the lemon juice and cayenne to taste.

4 Spoon the tapenade into a 1-cup crock. Serve at once or refrigerate, covered, for up to 3 days.

NOTE TO THE COOK

If you wish to substitute salted anchovies, soak them in cold water for 2 hours. With a small knife, remove the four fillets from each fish; rinse thoroughly and pat dry.

ROASTED HERB BREAD

La Rôtie

I'm sure you will make this bread often to serve with goat cheese, grilled red peppers, and, of course, with this salad. Note that in this recipe, the toasted bread is seasoned with a mixture of dried herbs called *herbes de la garrigue*, which is commonly used in some parts of the Languedoc, principally in Gard. Made from wild herbs such as lavender, sage, savory, thyme, and fennel, as well as rosemary and mint, the blend is similar to the more familiar herbes de Provence, which can be substituted.

8 stale ½-inch-thick slices of coarse country-style bread

3 tablespoons fruity extra virgin olive oil

1 tablespoon Herbes de la Garrigue (page 80) or herbes de Provence

1 Preheat the oven to 450°F.

2 Brush both sides of the bread slices with the olive oil and set on an ungreased baking sheet. Season the top with a sprinkling of the herbs.

3 Roast in the oven until the bread is golden brown and crisp, 5 to 6 minutes.

(continued)

Herbes de la Garrigue

This fragrant herb blend imparts a captivating, robust flavor to grilled meats and chicken as well as to slices of roasted bread.

1 tablespoon dried thyme leaves	¾ teaspoon dried rosemary
2 teaspoons dried summer savory	¾ teaspoon dried mint
2 teaspoons dried marjoram	½ teaspoon dried lavender
1½ teaspoons fennel seed	¼ teaspoon rubbed sage
1 teaspoon dried sweet basil	1 imported bay leaf

Coarsely crumble the herbs into a small bowl and toss to blend well. Store the mixture in a tightly capped jar. Measure the amount needed, then just before using, crush finely in a mortar or electric spice mill.

SALMON RILLETTES

Rillettes de Saumon   MAKES 2 CUPS; SERVES 8

This dish improves with a little age; keep it for up to 1 week under a layer of clarified butter. It is perfect starting on the third day. Try it also with mixtures of fresh and smoked eel, trout, or mackerel. These rillettes also go well with a salad of roasted red peppers, thin green beans, and tender lettuce leaves.

½ pound skinned fresh salmon fillet, preferably wild, cut into 4 pieces	2 tablespoons mild olive oil
¼ teaspoon fine sea salt	1 egg yolk
9 tablespoons unsalted butter, at room temperature	1 tablespoon fresh lemon juice
1 large shallot, minced	⅛ teaspoon freshly ground pepper
1 tablespoon dry white wine	Pinch of freshly grated nutmeg
¼ pound lightly smoked salmon, cut into ¼-inch dice	¼ cup clarified butter

1 Sprinkle the fresh salmon with the salt and let stand at room temperature for 20 minutes. Then pat dry with paper towels.

2 In a medium skillet, slowly cook the shallot in 1 tablespoon of the butter until soft but not brown, 2 to 3 minutes. Add the wine and arrange the fresh salmon pieces in a single layer. Cover with a tight-fitting lid and cook over low heat, turning once, until the center of fish is just opaque, 3 to 4 minutes.

3 Remove the salmon to a bowl. Reduce the pan juices to syrup and pour over the fish, along with any shallots left in the pan. Flake the salmon with a fork, mixing well with cooked shallot.

4 Cut the remaining butter into small pieces and place in a food processor fitted with the plastic blade, along with the cool flaked salmon and smoked salmon cubes. Pulse once or twice to combine. With the machine on, quickly add the olive oil, egg yolk, and lemon juice. Do not process to a paste; the mixture should have a coarse texture. Season with the pepper, nutmeg, and additional salt to taste.

5 Pack the rillettes into a 2½- to 3-cup crock; pour the clarified butter over the surface to seal. Refrigerate at least 3 and up to 7 days before serving. Serve at room temperature. If the rillettes are partially used, reseal with clarified butter.

YELLOWFIN TUNA WITH AVOCADO AND PIMENT D'ESPELETTE

⤜ *Thon aux Avocats et Piment d'Espelette*   SERVES 2 TO 4

"I GREW UP with a little pepper in my food," chef Laurent Manrique told me, describing his early life in a small village in the section of Gascony where duck, foie gras, and confit are best known. In fact, he lived close enough to the Basque country where the medium-hot paprika, piment d'Espelette reigns supreme.

Laurent gave me two recipes for the revised edition of this book: a beef short ribs version of his grandmother's recipe for duck legs (Braised Short Ribs in Cèpe-Prune Sauce, pages 261–263) and this brilliant starter. Thinly sliced, quickly seared tuna is served with meltingly soft slices of avocado and a peppery grapefruit vinaigrette.

(continued)

½ pound sushi-grade yellowfin or ahi tuna, in one piece

2½ tablespoons extra virgin olive oil, preferably Spanish

1 ruby red grapefruit, peeled, sectioned and diced

Juice of ½ lime

1 pinch of sea salt

1 good pinch of ground piment d'Espelette or other moderately hot red pepper

1 teaspoon toasted pine nuts

1 ripe avocado, peeled

2 large opal basil leaves (see Note below)

1 Dry the tuna with paper towels. Heat a nonstick skillet over high heat with a drop of the olive oil. When hot, sear the tuna for 1 minute on each side. With a wide spatula, transfer the tuna to a cutting board and let rest while preparing the vinaigrette.

2 Gently toss the grapefruit, lime juice, salt, piment d'Espelette, remaining oil, and toasted pine nuts without breaking the grapefruit chunks.

3 Quarter the avocado or, if desired, thinly slice. Tear basil into small pieces. Thinly slice the tuna. Arrange the avocado and tuna on 2 plates. Spoon the citrus vinaigrette with the chunks of grapefruit over the tuna, scatter basil on top, and serve at once.

NOTES TO THE COOK

⇥ Store the piment d'Espelette in the refrigerator.

⇥ Opal basil is intensely flavored and colored deep purple. It is available in Asian markets.

HOME-CURED DUCK HAM

⇥ *"Jambon" de Magret*   MAKES 3 TO 4 DOZEN SLICES; SERVES 12

FRESH—NOT DEFROSTED—duck breasts may be cured the same way one cures a ham: The meat is rubbed with salt and pepper, then left to hang until firm and dry but not hard, about 12 to 15 days. (The salt draws out the moisture that might harbor bacteria, and the air-drying keeps the meat from deteriorating.)

The resulting "ham" is very flavorful, with a prosciutto-like texture. It is delicious intertwined with very thinly sliced fresh figs, melon wedges, or along with a platter of pickled wild leeks. Or serve as part of an antipasto, thinly sliced in a cold consommé with cubed melon balls, or with warm asparagus dressed with a light walnut oil vinaigrette. Odds and ends of the "ham" can be chunked and used like bacon or duck cracklings in a green salad.

A Catalan friend makes a spicier version, combining paprika, cayenne, pepper, oil, and vinegar into a thick paste, which he then rubs into the flesh.

You will need one package of cheesecloth.

1 whole large, fresh boneless moulard or Muscovy duck breast, with skin on, about 1½ pounds	2 teaspoons coarsely cracked black pepper
½ cup coarse kosher salt	½ teaspoon fresh thyme leaves or ½ teaspoon herbes de Provence
	2 tablespoons red wine vinegar

1 Shave off the duck skin leaving the fat underneath intact. Score the fat almost but not quite all the way through to the meat in crosshatch lines.

2 Gently rub the salt, pepper, and thyme into both sides of the duck breasts. Place on a paper towel-lined plate, cover with more paper towels and refrigerate without further wrapping for 24 hours.

3 The following day, wipe the duck to remove the seasonings. Dip the meat side of one breast in the vinegar for 10 seconds and dry well. Place skin side down on a double layer of cheesecloth that measures 18 inches by 18 inches. Press and roll to create a nice tight cylinder with no air pockets. Tie both ends to seal. Repeat with the second breast.

4 Hang the duck "hams" in a cool, dry place for 2 weeks; reverse the top and bottom after 1 week. If you have a frost-free refrigerator you can suspend them in it. Otherwise, hang the "hams" in a wine cellar or cool basement or garage. The duck hams are ready when the fleshy sides feel very firm and the skin sides feel firm but there is some "give" when they are pressed.

5 If not serving right away, suspend in your refrigerate for up to 1 week. To serve, unwrap and thinly slice on the diagonal, like smoked salmon.

VARIATION If you're working with Pekin ducks, substitute one whole fresh boneless 5-ounce breast with skin on, reduce the salt to 1½ teaspoons, reduce the pepper and thyme, and reduce the curing time to 8 to 10 days.

(continued)

→► I particularly like D'Artagnan's duck prosciutto as a substitute for home-cured ham.

→► A tip from Southwestern cooks: If you only use part of the cured duck breast, wipe the cut end with vinegar to keep it fresh.

With thanks to the late, great chef Jean-Louis Palladin for sharing this recipe with me.

HOME-CURED DUCK HAM WITH MIXED MELON SALAD

→► *Melon au Jambon de Canard*   SERVES 6

YOU CAN SUBSTITUTE smoked duck breast available at upscale food shops or by mail order from D'Artagnan (see Mail Order Sources, pages 415–417). Either way, this salad makes a great appetizer, a play on the Italian classic prosciutto and melon.

½ recipe Home-Cured Duck Ham (pages 82–84) or ½ duck breast prosciutto (about ¼ pound)

6 cups mixed melon cubes, cut into ¾-inch cubes

3 tablespoons fresh lemon juice

2 tablespoons fresh orange juice

2 tablespoons French walnut oil

Salt and freshly ground pepper

1 Thinly slice the duck ham crosswise on the diagonal; trim off the fat if you wish. Cover the slices with plastic wrap to keep moist.

2 In a large bowl, toss the melon gently with the lemon juice, orange juice, and walnut oil. Season with salt and pepper to taste.

3 Add half the duck ham slices and toss. Add the remaining slices attractively on top and generously sprinkle with pepper.

Salad of Home-Cured Duck Ham
With Chestnuts and Walnuts

➤➤ *Salade Campagnarde*   SERVES 4

CHESTNUTS ARE SERVED WARM in this country-style salad from the Périgord, which also includes thin slices of tender, juicy duck ham, crisp ventrèche or pancetta, and chopped walnuts. If curing the duck breast yourself, prepare about 2 weeks in advance, or substitute duck prosciutto or smoked duck breast.

½ recipe Home-Cured Duck Ham (pages 82–84)

3 tablespoons French walnut oil

2 teaspoons red wine vinegar, preferably aged

Salt and freshly ground pepper

3 tablespoons unsalted butter

4 slices of firm country-style bread, crust removed, cut into ½-inch cubes

1 garlic clove, crushed

¼ pound ventrèche or pancetta, cut into thin strips

1½ cups cooked chestnuts (jarred or packed *sous vide*), or 1 pound freshly cooked chestnuts

4 cups field greens, rinsed and dried

¼ cup chopped walnuts

1 Thinly slice the duck ham crosswise on the diagonal; trim off the fat, if desired. Cover with plastic wrap to keep moist.

2 In a small bowl, whisk together the walnut oil, vinegar, and a pinch each of salt and pepper. Set the vinaigrette aside.

3 In a large skillet, melt 2 tablespoons of the butter over moderately high heat. Add the bread cubes and fry, tossing, until golden on all sides, 1 to 2 minutes. Add the garlic and toss for an instant. Remove from the pan.

4 In the same skillet without added fat, fry the ventrèche over moderate heat until almost crisp, 4 to 5 minutes. Add the remaining 1 tablespoon butter and the chestnuts and season lightly with salt and pepper. Gently cook, shaking the pan, for 30 seconds or until the chestnuts are glistening. Remove from the heat.

5 In a salad bowl, quickly toss the greens with the vinaigrette. Add the hot chestnuts, chopped walnuts, croutons, and ventrèche; toss gently to mix. Arrange the slices of duck ham on top and serve the salad while the chestnuts are still warm.

CARPACCIO OF PIG'S FEET, CELERY, AND BLACK TRUFFLES

➤➤ *La Carpaccio de Pieds de Porc et de Truffes*   SERVES 6 TO 8

SOMETIMES YOU FALL so in love with the presentation of a dish, you decide then and there to make it. This is exactly what happened to me when I first tasted this dish, a creation of the brothers Jacques and Laurent Pourcel of the restaurant Le Jardin des Sens in Montpellier.

Their dish consists of thinly sliced boned pig's feet smothered with fresh favas, lots of thin sliced black truffles, a truffle vinaigrette, bits of tomato, and a few sprigs of fresh chervil. It was a stunning presentation.

In my adapted version, I cook the pig's feet slowly in an aromatic broth, then bone them, roll them into a long cylinder, wrap well, and return them to the still simmering broth to cook to a congealed state (akin to that of a sausage). I then allow the "sausage" to cool, and finally slice it into very thin rounds, which the *frères* Pourcel call "carpaccio." Because all this requires a lot of work, I decided to forgo the fresh favas, replacing them with small chunks of cooked celery, which, being bright green, look good and goes so well with truffles.

Deciding that truffle vinaigrette and smothering a dish with true Périgord truffles was more than I could afford, I opted for Chinese truffles, and adding literally a single drop of black truffle oil to the vinaigrette. It's kind of cheating, but it works really well.

You can prepare the roll of pig's feet well in advance and refrigerate or freeze.

2 pig's feet, split lengthwise, about 4 pounds

1 tablespoon white vinegar

2 carrots, washed and cut into chunks

2 garlic cloves, peeled and bruised

1 onion, halved, stuck with 2 cloves

2 imported bay leaves

1 tablespoon coarse kosher salt

½ teaspoon black peppercorns

Salt and freshly ground pepper

12 bright green celery ribs

1 small black truffle, fresh or canned, trimmed and thinly sliced (trimmings reserved)

Truffle Vinaigrette (page 88)

Diced tomato, sprigs of parsley, and fleur de sel, for garnish

1 Soak the pig's feet in a bowl of water with the vinegar for 5 minutes; drain. Place the feet in a deep pot. Cover with 2 quarts fresh water and bring to a boil, skimming. Add the carrots, garlic, onion, bay leaves, salt, and peppercorns. Simmer for 3 hours, or until the pig's feet are very tender.

2 Remove the pig's feet to a cutting board; set the pot of cooking liquid aside. As soon as the pig's feet are cool enough to handle, bone them using a small sharp knife and a pair of scissors. Cut out all the small bones and gristle. Spread the pig's feet, skin side down, on a long sheet of foil or parchment paper to form a narrow rectangle about 15 inches long. Scatter any loose chunks of pork on top. Season generously with salt and pepper. Using the foil or paper as an aid, roll the pig's feet into a cylinder and wrap tightly. Be sure that the shape is even, and squeeze gently to press out any air pockets. Tightly double-wrap the roll in heatproof plastic wrap or seal in a boilable pouch.

3 Bring the cooking liquid in the pot to a boil. Add the roll of pig's feet and boil for 10 minutes. Immediately slip the roll into a bowl filled with cold water to quickly cool it down. Refrigerate the roll overnight. *(The recipe can be prepared to this point up to 3 days in advance and refrigerated, or frozen for serving at a later date.)*

4 When ready to serve, string the celery; cut into ½-inch dice. Steam the celery until tender, 5 to 8 minutes. Cool under cold running water; drain well. Season lightly with salt.

5 Unwrap the pig's foot roll and use a narrow-bladed knife to cut the roll into about 36 very thin slices. Arrange in concentric circles on a heatproof serving platter. Set in a cold oven and turn the oven temperature on to 350°F. Bake for 15 minutes, or until just warm to the touch.

6 Drizzle half of the Truffle Vinaigrette over the pig's feet, scatter the celery and sliced truffles on top, and moisten with the remaining vinaigrette. Garnish with diced tomato, fresh herbs, and a nice pinch of fleur de sel.

NOTE TO THE COOK

The pig's feet poaching liquid can be saved and used for soups, bean dishes, or cooking more pig's feet.

(continued)

TRUFFLE VINAIGRETTE

2 tablespoons fresh lemon juice

Coarse sea salt

3 tablespoons extra virgin olive oil

¼ teaspoon black truffle oil, preferably French

Truffle trimmings (reserved above; optional)

Stir together the lemon juice and salt to dissolve the salt. Mix in the olive oil. Stir in the truffle oil and trimmings.

CÈPE AND WALNUT CREAM TARTS

➤ *Tarte aux Cèpes et aux Noix* — SERVES 8

TWENTY YEARS AGO, when self-taught chef Michel Bras was relatively unknown, this was his signature dish, and I loved it. Today, Bras is a Michelin three-star chef working in his home town, Laguiole, in the Aveyron, a magnificently savage rural area in the high pasturelands of the Aubrac Mountains. He gathers almost all his ingredients from the local countryside: crayfish and trout in the streams, lambs and calves on the farms; mushrooms and nuts, apples, raspberries, and wild herbs.

A perfect example of Michel Bras's style are these irresistible tarts of wild mushrooms with a creamy walnut filling, a dish that conveys to me the essence of the forest. They make a great first course. Michel's wife, Ginette, who acts as sommelier in his restaurant, suggested I accompany the tarts with a Gaillac Premières Côtes of Robert Plageoles. This is a curious wine, called a *vin de voile*, on account of the way its vines are trained to grow low on very soft sandy soil, so that they spread themselves over the earth almost like a sheet. I found this tawny-colored wine smooth, fragrant, and rather sweet—excellent with the tart. Since vin de voile is virtually unobtainable in this country, I suggest you accompany the dish with a fine dry sherry.

You will need eight 4½-inch flan rings or tart molds.

Pâte Brisée (page 92)

2 pounds very small, firm, fresh cèpes, porcini, boletes, or small mushrooms

2 ounces shelled walnuts

1⅓ packed cups toasted or fried bread cubes

½ cup milk or water

1 large egg, lightly beaten

2 ounces cured ham, such as jambon de Bayonne, Serrano ham, or prosciutto, finely diced

1 large shallot, chopped

2½ tablespoons butter, melted

½ cup heavy cream, chilled

Salt and freshly ground pepper

1 garlic clove, crushed

1 to 2 tablespoons French walnut oil

1 Make the Pâte Brisée (pastry dough) the day before or bring it to room temperature if premade. Trim the cèpes' stems and wipe the caps with a damp paper towel. Blanch the mushrooms for 5 minutes in plenty of salted boiling water. Drain and rinse quickly under cold running water to stop the cooking and remove the excess salt; drain and press in kitchen towels until thoroughly dry.

2 In a nut grinder or with the shredding disk of a food processor, grate the walnuts; there will be about ⅔ cup.

3 Soak the bread in the milk for 5 to 10 minutes, until completely softened. Squeeze dry and place the bread in a food processor. Add the egg, ham, walnuts, and shallot and grind to a smooth paste. Scrape into a bowl, cover, and refrigerate for 45 minutes.

4 Using a fork, gradually work small amounts of the cold heavy cream into the walnut mixture. Each portion of cream must be blended in before the next is added. Season to taste with salt and pepper.

5 Meanwhile, roll out the dough to about ⅛-inch thickness between sheets of plastic wrap to make a large rectangle. Fold the pastry dough into thirds like an envelope. Rotate the dough one quarter turn and repeat the rolling and folding. Chill the dough for 20 minutes, then cut it into 8 equal pieces.

6 Roll out each portion of dough between plastic wrap to a paper-thin round and fit into the flan rings or tart molds. If necessary, patch with odd pieces of dough. Cover with plastic wrap and refrigerate while you repeat with the remaining pieces of dough. Set all the molds on a baking sheet; use a dark-finish baking sheet for a crisper crust.

(continued)

7 Preheat the oven to 400°F. Spread a thin, even layer of the walnut filling over the dough in each mold. Cut the cèpe caps into very thin slices; fan out the slices slightly and place on top of the filling. Brush the sliced mushrooms with a little melted butter mixed with the crushed garlic, salt, and pepper.

8 Bake the tarts on the middle rack of the oven for 30 minutes. Sprinkle a few drops of walnut oil over the mushrooms. Serve hot.

WILD LEEK AND MUSHROOM TORTE

➤➤ *Tourte de Poireaux de Vignes et Champignons*   SERVES 6 TO 8

THIS RUSTIC PIE, perfect for a light supper or a light luncheon entree, comes from the French town of Poudenas, a lovely village set amid the rolling hills of Lot-et-Garonne. Poudenas, with its pink houses, eleventh-century château up on a hill, and wonderful food tradition, is a town you can fall in love with.

In the Southwest of France, wild leeks are called *baragnes*; they are foraged in vineyards in the month of May. Since the garlicky flavor of these is best preserved with gentle cooking, they are most frequently found in omelets, soups, and savory pies, like this one. French wild leeks are almost the same as our American ramps. If you don't live along the North American "ramp trail," which runs all the way from Quebec and Minnesota to the Carolinas, you can mail order them in the spring.

Pâte Brisée (page 92)

1 pound ramp bulbs (3½ cups), or 7 to 8 young green garlic shoots, about 1½ pounds

Coarse sea salt

1½ tablespoons unsalted butter

⅔ cup crème fraîche or 1 cup heavy cream reduced to ⅔ cup

½ pound small, very firm white mushrooms, wiped clean but not washed

Finely ground white pepper

Flour, for dusting

1 egg yolk beaten with 1 tablespoon heavy cream to make a glaze

1 Up to two days in advance, make the Pâte Brisée (pastry dough).

2 Wash the ramps and trim away hairy roots. Halve each ramp lengthwise, then cut crosswise on the diagonal into ¼-inch slices. (Quarter each leek lengthwise, and then cut crosswise into ¼-inch pieces.) There will be about 2 packed cups. Dump the ramps or leeks into a large sieve, rinse thoroughly, and drain. Soften the ramps or leeks by sprinkling them with 1½ teaspoons of the salt, tossing, and rubbing well through your fingertips. Leave in the colander for at least 1 hour. Rinse the ramps or leeks under running water and working in small batches, squeeze to extract as much moisture as possible.

3 In a large skillet, melt the butter over moderate heat. Add the ramps or leeks and cook, partially covered, until they are tender and the butter has been absorbed, about 2 minutes. Remove from the heat and let cool.

4 Divide the dough in half. Roll out one piece of the dough between sheets of floured waxed paper to make a large, thin round, less than ⅛ inch thick. Flip the dough over an 11-inch buttered and floured tart pan. Fit the pastry into the pan without stretching. (If the pastry is too soft at this point, simply let it chill in the refrigerator 10 minutes before lifting off paper.) Repair cracks or tears with overhanging pieces of pastry; trim off the excess with a thin bladed knife or by rolling the rolling pin over the edge. Prick the bottom of the pastry in 6 or 7 places with the tines of a fork.

5 Spread the leeks evenly over the dough. Slice the mushrooms paper-thin and scatter them over the leeks. Spread the crème fraîche evenly on top. Season with salt and white pepper. To make sure the filling is "light and delicate," do not press down.

6 Brush the egg glaze over rim of the pastry at the edge of pan. Roll out the second piece of dough as thin as possible and place it over the top. With the tines of a fork, crimp all around to seal the edges. Trim away any excess dough. Brush the top with the remaining glaze. With the point of a knife, make shallow lines crisscrossing the pastry.

7 Preheat the oven to 425°F. Bake the torte on the lowest oven shelf for 15 minutes. Reduce the oven temperature to 375°F, shift to a higher shelf, and finish baking for 20 minutes longer, or until golden brown and crisp. Remove the torte from the oven, let stand for about 20 minutes before cutting into wedges. Serve warm.

Inspired by a recipe from Marie-Claude Gracia.

PÂTE BRISÉE

½ pound whole-wheat pastry flour and ¼ pound all purpose flour, or ¾ pound pastry flour, about 2⅓ cups

½ teaspoon fine salt

Pinch of sugar

7 ounces AA grade unsalted butter with low water content, such as Plugra, cut into small pieces

⅓ cup cold water or degreased mild unsalted chicken stock (storebought or homemade—page 405), plus more if necessary

1 tablespoon *verjus* or cider or rice vinegar

In a food processor, combine the flour (or flours), salt, and sugar. Pulse once to sift. Scatter half the butter over the flour. Pulse 5 or 6 times. Repeat with remaining butter and pulse until the mixture resembles coarse oatmeal. Add ⅓ cup cold water or stock and the verjus or vinegar and pulse once or twice. Do not process to a ball. Turn out onto a lightly floured work surface and press into a smooth ball, adding a few drops of cold water as necessary to make supple smooth dough. Do not let the dough become too damp. Cover with plastic wrap and let rest in a cool place for at least 1 hour or up to 2 days in the refrigerator. The pastry dough can be frozen.

SUMMER FRICASSEE OF CHANTERELLES AND CONFIT OF GIZZARDS

⇢➤ *Fricassée de Girolles aux Gésiers Confits*

SERVES 4 AS A FIRST COURSE
OR 2 AS A LUNCHEON DISH

IN THE PÉRIGORD, the rainy summer mushroom of choice is the apricot-colored chanterelle. These wonderful tasting fungi are blanched, dried, seared on high heat, then cooked with a mixture called *hachis*: pancetta and garlic chopped to a fine puree, and stored in a jar in the refrigerator. As in so many dishes in Southwest France, this one relies on the mellowing effect to improve flavor.

1 cup Confit of Duck Gizzards (pages 209–210), at room temperature

8 ounces very small fresh chanterelles or girolles

1 tablespoon *verjus* or cider vinegar

1 tablespoon fat from the confit

1¼ tablespoons Hachis (page 94)

1 teaspoon fresh thyme leaves

2 tablespoons chopped fresh flat-leaf parsley

Salt and freshly ground pepper

4 rounds of baguette, toasted and rubbed with garlic

1 Wipe excess fat off the gizzards with paper towels. Cut the gizzards into very thin slices, cover, and set aside.

2 Quickly and carefully rinse the chanterelles in a bowl of 3 cups of water mixed with the verjus or vinegar. Squeeze the mushrooms dry and wrap in paper towels. If the mushrooms are a little "tired" or dried out, drop them into a pot of salted boiling water for 2 to 3 minutes. Drain and squeeze dry when cool enough to handle. Spread out on paper towels.

3 Put 1 teaspoon of the confit fat in a medium-sized skillet and set over moderately high heat. Add the chanterelles and cook, stirring, until you hear them squeak, about 1 minute. Reduce the heat to moderately low and continue cooking for 5 minutes. Stir in the Hachis, cover the pan, and cook for 10 minutes longer.

4 Add the sliced gizzards to the pan and the remaining 2 teaspoons confit fat and sauté, stirring, until heated through. Toss with the thyme and parsley and season with salt, pepper, and a few drops of additional verjus or vinegar to taste. Serve at once, with rounds of garlic toast.

HACHIS

Use 1 to 2 tablespoons of this puree to flavor pork or veal, soups, beans, and mushrooms, or as an individual recipe dictates.

6 large garlic cloves, unpeeled

Salt and freshly ground pepper

2 tablespoons finely chopped lean ventrèche or pancetta

2 tablespoons rendered duck or goose fat

1 In a small pot of water, boil the garlic cloves in their skins for 20 minutes. Drain, let cool, then peel. Wipe the cloves completely dry.

2 Place the cooked garlic in a food processor with a pinch each of salt and pepper, the ventrèche, and the rendered fat. Grind to a puree.

3 Pack the hachis into a small jar with a tight lid. Store in the refrigerator; use within 2 weeks or freeze for up to 2 months.

Duck Liver Flans With Caramel Vinegar Sauce

➜➤ *Flans aux Foies de Volailles,*
Sauce de Vinaigre Caramélisée

SERVES 5 TO 6

THIS DISH, which I've learned from the late Jean-Louis Palladin, is one of the most popular I have presented in my classes. Many other versions have cropped up elsewhere since I began teaching it in 1978, but this is the original.

You can substitute chicken livers for duck livers, or mix duck, goose, and chicken livers together. Do not be tempted to mix the eggs, milk, and cream in a food processor; the resulting flans will not be as silky and tender.

For mildness, the livers are soaked in milk for at least several hours, so plan your time accordingly.

4 duck livers or 5 blond chicken livers (see Note, page 97), trimmed

1 cup milk

1 teaspoon Armagnac or Madeira

Salt and freshly ground white pepper

1½ teaspoons unsalted butter

1 tablespoon Duck Demi-Glace (page 409)

1 small garlic clove, peeled

Pinch of freshly grated nutmeg

2 whole eggs, at room temperature

1 egg yolk, at room temperature

1½ cups milk, heated and kept warm

½ cup heavy cream

Caramel Vinegar Sauce (page 96)

Red wine vinegar

1 Trim the livers to remove any green bile, fat, and sinews. Soak them in the milk in the refrigerator for at least 3 hours. Drain the livers and rinse under cold running water until the water runs clear; pat dry.

2 Marinate the livers in the Armagnac seasoned with ¼ teaspoon salt and ⅛ teaspoon pepper for 1 to 2 hours.

3 Lightly butter 5 or 6 four-ounce porcelain ramekins or molds. Arrange them in a shallow roasting pan lined with 2 or 3 layers of newspaper (slit the newspaper in the center to avoid swelling when wet). Set aside.

(continued)

4 Preheat the oven to 325°F. In a food processor, combine the duck livers, demi-glace, garlic, 1 teaspoon salt, ¾ teaspoon pepper, and a sprinkling of nutmeg. Process for 2 minutes. Transfer to a strainer set over a bowl; add the whole eggs, egg yolk, warm milk, and cream. Strain, pressing with a rubber spatula; discard stringy egg albumen and any liver strands.

5 Carefully ladle equal amounts of the flan mixture into the ramekins, stirring the contents in the bowl; the molds should be not quite filled. Place the roasting pan in the center oven rack. Carefully pour enough boiling water into the roasting pan to reach halfway up the sides of the molds.

6 Bake for 20 minutes, or until the flans feel firm when lightly prodded with two fingers. If the flans are not set, turn off the heat and let stand in the oven for 5 to 10 minutes longer. Remove the water bath from the oven and let the molds stand in the water for 10 minutes longer before turning out.

7 While the flans are baking, make the Caramel Vinegar Sauce. Season the sauce to taste with pepper and an extra shot or two of red wine vinegar, if necessary; the balance should be more acidic and peppery than sweet. Spoon the hot sauce around the turned-out flans and serve at once.

CARAMEL VINEGAR SAUCE   MAKES ABOUT 1¾ CUPS

This piquant sauce is excellent on Broiled Duck Breasts (page 175).

1 cup red wine vinegar

3½ tablespoons sugar

1¼ cups Duck Demi-Glace (page 409) or 4 cups brown duck stock reduced to 1¼ cups

½ cup heavy cream

1 In a heavy, nonreactive 2½-quart saucepan, combine the vinegar and sugar. Bring to a boil, stirring to dissolve the sugar. Continue to cook over moderate heat until the vinegar is reduced to a thick syrup.

2 Swirl in the demi-glace and bring to a boil. Add the cream but do not stir; the cream will be "swallowed up" by the sauce. Boil vigorously for 5 minutes, or until the surface is full of tight bubbles.

3 Then stir gently until you can catch a glimpse of the bottom of the pan. Remove from the heat at once.

→→ Chinese and Hungarian markets sell duck livers loose. Look for the palest ones, since color indicates how they were fed. I was once shown a chicken that had been fed only rice; its liver was almost white. In the Southwest, where chickens and ducks are fed primarily on corn, their livers are "blond."

→→ To turn out all the molds onto a single warmed serving platter, place a wide spatula over the first mold; with spatula holding the flan in place, invert the mold over serving dish. Slip the spatula from underneath, leaving the flan and mold in place. Lift off the mold. Repeat with remaining molds. Serve warm.

→→ The sauce can be made ahead and warmed gently in a double boiler.

Making Sauces by Stratification

→→ ←←

The concept of stratification was developed by the late brilliant teacher-chef André Guillot. Stratification is easy, and with it you can make sauces without the usual thickening agents (flour, arrowroot, or egg yolk) by a series of rapid reductions.

You start off with an acid—as, for example, the red wine vinegar in the Caramel Vinegar Sauce—which you reduce in a deep saucepan to intensify flavor. Then you add a protein-rich stock, deep in flavor, that will harmonize with the acid. In the case of the caramelized vinegar, you add a duck-flavored demi-glace with a background hint of red wine. Next you add heavy cream and, without whisking, allow the sauce to boil vigorously until lots of bubbles appear on the surface. From time to time you stir this bubbling mixture with a wooden spoon until you catch a glimpse of the bottom of the pan. When you see the bottom, your sauce is finished and will adhere lightly to meat or fish (in this case to duck liver flans).

Basically, what has happened is this: The water in the cream has evaporated, allowing the remaining butterfat, in the presence of protein and acid, to bind the sauce and make it silky.

"The faster the evaporation, the better the emulsification" is the rule for creating a sauce by stratification. It takes less than 10 minutes to complete the entire process in a heavy-bottomed pan, and the sauce will hold for quite a while.

SNAILS WITH WALNUTS

➻ *Escargots aux Noix*   SERVES 4

WALNUTS CAN BE A PROBLEM, because so often they're either dry or old. French housewives have two tricks for reviving them: They soak them in sugared water or hot milk overnight or gently toast them in a skillet to release their natural oils.

1 cup crème fraîche or heavy cream	2 tablespoons fresh lemon juice
1 can (7½ ounces) snails (24 large snails)	¾ teaspoon salt
3 tablespoons dry white wine	⅛ teaspoon freshly ground pepper
4 tablespoons unsalted butter, softened	Pinch of freshly grated nutmeg
2 tablespoons chopped fines herbes (see Note at right)	½ cup coarsely chopped walnuts

1 Place the crème fraîche in a funnel lined with a paper coffee filter and let drain until reduced to ¾ cup, about 3 hours. Or boil the heavy cream until reduced to ¾ cup. Refrigerate until ready to use.

2 Drain the snails and toss with the wine in a small bowl. Cover and refrigerate until ready to cook. Remove from the refrigerate about 30 minutes before you plan to cook them.

3 Place 3 tablespoons of the softened butter in a shallow bowl; cream with a wooden spoon. Gradually work in the fines herbes, lemon juice, salt, pepper, and nutmeg. Cover and refrigerate the seasoned butter. *(The recipe can be prepared to this point up to 2 hours in advance.)*

4 Shortly before serving, melt the remaining butter in medium skillet over moderate heat; stir in the walnuts and reduce the heat to low. Cook, tossing, until the walnuts until aromatic, about 3 minutes. Stir in the crème fraîche or heavy cream. Raise the heat and bring to a boil, stirring constantly. Add the snails and wine; heat through. Do not allow to boil, or the snails will toughen. Remove from the heat.

5 Swirl in the seasoned butter, 1 tablespoon at a time, until the sauce is thick and well blended. Return the skillet to low heat to reheat gently, 15 to 20 seconds; overheating will cause the sauce to separate. Season with salt and pepper to taste.

6 Spoon 6 snails into each of 4 hot ramekins; divide the sauce equally among them. Serve immediately.

NOTE TO THE COOK

Fines herbes is a mixture of fresh parsley, chives, tarragon, and chervil. At least 2 of the herbs should be fresh and the others can be dried if fresh are not available.

Inspired by a recipe from Lucien Vanel.

SNAILS WITH COUNTRY HAM AND GARLIC

↦ *Escargots à la Caudéran* SERVES 4 TO 6

THIS IS A SUPERB DISH, happily free of all the problems usually associated with snails: heaviness, toughness, and the excuse to eat garlic, since, the myth goes, snails have no taste of their own. Snails do have flavor, though they do also need seasoning. But they needn't be overwhelmed, and they should certainly not be boiled in garlic butter; boiling toughens them, butter makes the dish too heavy, and too much garlic obscures the flavor of the snails instead of enhancing it.

This recipe from Bordeaux takes all these problems into account. The result is a tender, succulent dish of snails enrobed in a gentle garlic-shallot sauce, lightened with uncooked butter, scented with Pernod, and garnished with bits of country ham. You'll want plenty of good French bread for mopping up the buttery juices.

1 can (7½ ounces) snails (24 large snails)

2 teaspoons rendered pork fat or butter

1½ tablespoons finely chopped jambon de Bayonne, Serrano ham, or prosciutto

2 tablespoons finely chopped shallots

½ cup dry white wine

½ cup well-reduced (thick) meat or poultry stock

1 teaspoon fresh thyme leaves or ¼ teaspoon dried thyme

1 tablespoon finely chopped fresh garlic

1 tablespoon chopped fresh flat-leaf parsley

1 large plum tomato, peeled, seeded, and finely diced

2 teaspoons Pernod

6 tablespoons unsalted butter, at room temperature

Salt and freshly ground pepper

(continued)

1 Drain the snails; rinse in fresh water and set aside to drain.

2 Heat the fat in a large skillet. Add the ham and the shallots and cook over moderately low heat for 5 minutes without browning. Tilt the pan; press on the ham and shallots with a slotted spoon and mop up the exuded fat with a paper towel. Deglaze the pan with the white wine and boil down to a glaze.

3 Add the stock, thyme, and garlic; simmer, covered, for 10 minutes.

4 Add the snails, parsley, tomato, and Pernod to the hot broth; cover and cook for about 1 minute to heat through. Do not allow the liquid to boil, or the snails will toughen.

5 Adjust the seasoning with salt and pepper, keeping in mind that "snails like salt," but that the ham can be salty. Swirl in the butter both on and off the heat, to create a sauce thick enough to coat a spoon. Serve at once.

FISH AND SHELLFISH

Mussels

TO CLEAN MUSSELS

Scrub each mussel under cool running water. Pull off the beard if there is one. Soak the mussels in a bowl of fresh cold water for 30 minutes. (Many mussel farms are selling these mollusks already cleaned and soaked. To repeat the soaking may result in a loss of flavor so consult your fishmonger.)

TO COOK MUSSELS

Rinse again, steam open, remove shells, cut away any remaining beards, and use as directed in the recipe. If the mussels are unusually large, remove and discard the dark brown rubbery strip around them.

Éclade

→►◄←

Mussels are popular along the entire Atlantic coast of Southwest France, where they are served in a number of unusual and delicious ways. I could not imagine a better preparation than the Normandy classic *moules à la marinière* until I tasted the little-known regional specialty *éclade de moules*, particularly famous in the town of Rochefort in the Charente-Maritime.

To prepare *éclade,* the cooks of the region arrange tightly closed mussels hinge side up on a wooden plank; the mussels are crammed together so they won't open easily despite the pressure of the steam within their shells. The idea here, as opposed to the normal procedure, is to keep the juices inside, where they will swell up the mussels and make them succulent. A thick layer of partly dried pine needles, about 5 inches deep, is placed above the shells and set aflame. When the flames have died, in about 3 minutes, the ashes are brushed away, and the mussels are eaten with ash-blackened fingertips. The taste is intense and the experience a delight, as is any eating experience requiring bare hands.

In the Landes, I found a home version of *éclade.* Pack your mussels together hinge side up in a deep cast-iron skillet or an enameled cast-iron casserole with a tight-fitting lid (36 medium-size mussels fit perfectly into a 3-quart casserole) so that none of them can move. Lay a bed of partially dried pine needles 4 inches thick on top, cover, and set the skillet or saucepan over moderate heat for 3 to 4 minutes. The mussels will plump up from their own steam as they try to force open their shells; the pine needles will impart a delicate flavor and aroma, though it will not be the smoky flavor of the Charente version. Some juices may escape, but they are not lost and can be used later for stocks and soups, or simply boiled down to a tablespoon and used to flavor an accompanying bowl of lemon butter, if there is one.

Steamed Mussels With
Ham, Shallots, and Garlic

→► *Moules Paysanne*

THIS IS A VERY SIMPLE and quickly made dish. I first tasted this dish in the city of Pau, the capital of the Béarn. What impressed me most, I think, is how well mussels and ham go together, despite the fact that both are rather salty. The soft fresh white bread crumbs seemed to swallow up the excess salt and kept the dish light.

3 tablespoons unsalted butter

1 ounce jambon de Bayonne, prosciutto, or Serrano ham, cut into thin matchsticks

1½ teaspoons minced shallots

2 pounds fresh mussels, debearded and soaked if necessary (see page 102)

¼ cup dry white wine

½ teaspoon finely minced fresh garlic

1 tablespoon chopped fresh flat-leaf parsley

Freshly ground pepper

2 to 3 tablespoons fresh white bread crumbs

1 Preheat the oven to 250°F. In a large nonreactive skillet, melt 1 tablespoon of the butter over moderately low heat. Add the ham and shallots and cook for 4 to 5 minutes without browning. Remove from the heat and set aside.

2 In a 3-quart covered pot, steam the mussels in their own juices over moderately high heat until they just open, 3 to 5 minutes, depending on size. With a wide slotted skimmer, remove the mussels to a bowl. Quickly remove the upper shell of each mussel and discard. Place the mussels in their half-shells on a shallow heatproof platter. Cover loosely with foil and set in the preheated oven to keep warm.

3 Strain the mussel liquor in the pot through several layers of dampened cheesecloth and add to the skillet with the ham. Pour the wine into the skillet and boil over moderately high heat until reduced by one-fourth, 2 to 3 minutes. Add the garlic, parsley, a few grinds of pepper, and the bread crumbs and reduce the heat to moderate. Cut the remaining 2 tablespoons butter into small chunks and add to the skillet. Swirl over the heat just until the butter binds with the bread crumbs to make a sauce, about 20 seconds. Spoon over the mussels and serve at once.

(continued)

VARIATION: STEAMED MUSSELS WITH TOMATOES, PERNOD, AND PIMENT D'ESPELETTE *(Moules à la Bordelaise)*

In step 1, add 2 ripe tomatoes, peeled, seeded, and cubed, a drop of Pernod, and a pinch of piment d'Espelette or other moderately hot red pepper to the shallots and ham.

HOT MUSSEL SALAD WITH CURLY ENDIVE AND CREAM

⤳ *Salade de Moules Chaudes*

SERVES 4 TO 6 AS A FIRST COURSE

THIS WARM SALAD of mussels, carrots, and shredded wild greens makes a very pretty first course or luncheon salad. The method of cooking the mussels is a variation on the famous *mouclade* of the Charente, a dish often tinted with a pinch of saffron or curry. These Eastern spices are more common that you might think in this area—especially along the coast where ships from India stopped in at Bordeaux en route to England.

4 pounds fresh mussels (about 3½ quarts)	Pinch of saffron threads
Salt	Pinch of curry powder
4 tender carrots, peeled and cut into thin julienne strips	½ cup heavy cream
2 tablespoons finely chopped shallots	5 tablespoons unsalted butter
5 or 6 sprigs of parsley	3 tablespoons minced fresh chives
½ cup dry white wine	1 head of tender chicory (curly endive), rolled up and cut into thin strips (about 1¾ cups)
½ lemon	
Freshly ground white pepper	

1 Pick over and discard any mussels that are cracked. If the mussels are not cultivated, clean and soak them as directed on page 102.

2 Preheat the oven to 500°F. Cook the carrot strips in boiling water for 30 seconds. Rinse in cold water and drain.

3 Place the mussels side by side on a rack in a large roasting pan. Sprinkle the shallots, parsley sprigs, and ½ cup white wine over the mussels. Cover tightly with foil or a cover and set in the hot oven. Roast for 8 minutes for average-size mussels; overcooking will make them tough. The only way to check doneness is to take a peek: If the shells are just beginning to open, leave them 1 minute longer. If they are open and the mussels could easily be removed from their shells, they are done.

4 Remove the mussels from their shells over the roasting pan in order to catch their juices. As they are shelled, put the mussels in a bowl. Season the mussels lightly with a grinding of pepper and a few drops of lemon juice. Cover the bowl with foil to keep moist and warm.

5 Strain the mussel cooking liquid from the roasting pan through several thicknesses of dampened cheesecloth directly into a wide nonreactive saucepan. If the liquid is extremely salty, replace up to half of it with water. Add the saffron threads and curry powder. Bring to a boil and reduce by half. Add the cream and simmer until the sauce barely coats a spoon, about 5 minutes.

6 Swirl in the butter to thicken the sauce. Throw in the mussels, carrots, chives, and shredded chicory. Swirl over very low heat for up to 1 minute to blend the flavors and heat the ingredients. Do not allow the sauce to boil; you don't want to overcook the mussels at this point. Adjust the seasoning, adding a few drops of lemon juice if necessary. Serve in warmed soup plates as a first course.

Inspired by a recipe from Bordeaux chef Francis Garcia.

Squid

Squid is at its best in the warmer months, when it's succulent, tender, and full of flavor. In the United States, we have two main types of edible squid: West Coast, found off Monterey, California, and East Coast, found off Nantucket, Massachusetts. Either variety will work here.

TO CLEAN SQUID

Wash squid under cool running water. Peel off the outer mottled skin. Pull the head and viscera from the body. (If the transparent quill bone comes out easily, the squid is very fresh.) Collect the thin, elongated ink sacs and set them aside in a small cup. Remove the tentacles by cutting just below the eyes, then turn the head over and press out the tough round beak. Discard the beak, the viscera, and the transparent quill bone. Rinse the inside of the body well. Leave the pouch whole for stuffing. Store the pouch and tentacles in a small amount of icy water until you are ready to cook them.

BASQUE STUFFED SQUID IN ITS INK

➤➤ *Chipirons Farcie à l'Encre*   SERVES 4 AS A MAIN COURSE

TO EXTRACT THE INK from fresh squid, carefully place all the long, silvery ink sacs in a small bowl and crush with the back of a wooden spoon. Add a tablespoon of water and let stand at least one hour. The liquid will become thick and very black; strain before using. Two pounds of baby squid will supply about ½ teaspoon ink. To augment this, small packets of ink—an extract of all sorts of squid and octopus inks—are sold in some upscale fish markets or by mail order. This product should be used very sparingly, as it is considerably more potent than plain squid ink.

Another inexpensive way to achieve the distinctive color and correct taste of squid ink is to use tinned imported *calamares en su tinta* (squid ink). This is a good alternative if you can only buy cleaned squid. Open up two tins, spoon off the surface oil, and add the sauce and solids to the bowl with the reserved squid ink; let stand 1 hour. Strain before using.

This recipe for squid in its own ink is traditionally served with a bowl of white rice and roasted Piquillo peppers.

2 pounds baby squid (about 16), cleaned and skinned, ink sacs removed and reserved

½ cup extra virgin olive oil

1½ cups chopped onions

1 scant tablespoon chopped fresh garlic, plus 1 garlic clove, peeled

2 mild green frying peppers (see page 353): 1 finely chopped, 1 sliced

2-inch piece of stale Italian bread, crust removed

¼ cup milk

1 egg, beaten

Salt and freshly ground white pepper

¼ teaspoon ground piment d'Espelette (see Mail Order Sources, pages 415–417) or moderately hot paprika

2 medium tomatoes, peeled, seeded, and finely chopped

½ cups Squid Stock (page 108)

1 Early in the day, prepare the squid as described in section To Clean Squid (at left): Leave the pouches whole. Chop the tentacles. Wrap separately in paper towels, place in a covered dish, refrigerate.

2 In a large, heavy skillet heat set over moderate heat, combine 2 tablespoons of the olive oil, 1 cup of the chopped onions, and 1 cup of water. Bring to a boil and cook, stirring occasionally, until the water has evaporated and the onions are soft and golden brown, about 25 minutes.

3 Add the chopped garlic and chopped mild frying pepper. Cover, reduce the heat to low, and cook for 5 minutes. Remove half the contents of the skillet to a side dish. Add the chopped tentacles to the skillet, raise the heat to moderately high, and sauté, tossing, until all moisture has evaporated, 4 to 5 minutes. Remove from the heat and let cool completely.

4 Tear the bread into a bowl. Add the milk and let soak for 5 to 10 minutes. Squeeze the bread to remove as much liquid as you can and crumble it into the reserved onion-pepper mixture. Add the beaten egg and blend well. Season with salt, white pepper, and piment d'Espelette. Fill the squid pouches without overstuffing and fasten the openings with toothpicks.

5 Thoroughly dry the stuffed squid pouches. In a large skillet, fry them in the remaining 6 tablespoons olive oil along with the whole garlic clove over moderate heat, turning, until the squid is lightly browned all over, about 2 minutes. With a slotted spoon, remove the squid to a side dish and cover to keep moist.

(continued)

6 Remove all but 2 tablespoons oil from the skillet. Add the remaining ½ cup chopped onion, the sliced mild frying pepper, and the chopped tomatoes. Cook over moderate heat, stirring, until the mixture is thick and just beginning to fry. Stir in the Squid Stock. Cover with a sheet of crumpled wet parchment paper and a lid, and simmer for 1 hour.

7 With a slotted spoon, transfer the stuffed squid to a shallow serving dish, cover, and keep hot in a warm oven. Strain the sauce; return to the skillet and boil down until thick enough to coat a spoon. Adjust the seasoning. Remove the toothpicks from the pouches. Pour the sauce over the squid and serve.

SQUID STOCK
MAKES 1¼ CUPS

4 grams squid ink extract or 2 cans (4 ounces each) squid in ink *(calamares en su tinta)*, oil removed

1 carrot, sliced

1 leek, sliced

Herb bouquet: 4 sprigs parsley, 2 sprigs of thyme, and 1 imported bay leaf tied together with string

In a medium saucepan, combine the squid ink extract or the contents of the can (without oil) of the canned squid, the carrot, leek, bouquet garni, and 1½ quarts water. If you have any skins or trimmings from your squid, add those as well. Bring to a boil; skimming. Reduce the heat to a simmer, cover, and cook for 30 minutes. Strain, return the liquid to the pan, and boil until reduced to 1¼ cups.

Scallops

Roasted Sea Scallops on a Bed of Chestnuts and Mushrooms

↣ *Coquilles St. Jacques Rôti sur Son Ragoût de Châtaignes et Champignons*   SERVES 4 AS A MAIN COURSE OR 6 AS A LUNCH DISH

THE UNUSUAL ROASTING METHOD is extremely useful if you want really tender scallops, hot with a "just cooked" quality, while still giving yourself time to prepare a luscious sauce and a glazed chestnut garnish. After a quick sauté, the scallops are finished in a low oven, which dries their exteriors while leaving their interiors moist and tender.

16 to 18 jumbo sea scallops, about 1¾ pounds

¼ pound fresh cèpes or small cremini mushrooms

4 tablespoons rendered duck fat

2 ounces sliced jambon de Bayonne, Serrano ham, or lean pancetta, finely diced

¼ cup chopped carrot

¼ cup chopped onion

¼ cup chopped celery leaves or 3 tablespoons chopped fresh lovage

1 garlic clove, sliced

2 tablespoons crumbled dried cèpes or porcini

Herb bouquet: 3 sprigs thyme, 1 imported bay leaf, 2 inches leek greens, and 5 sprigs parsley wrapped in cheesecloth or tied together with string

2 tablespoons Armagnac or Cognac

⅓ cup dry white wine

1½ cups unsalted chicken stock (storebought or homemade—page 405), plus more for the sauce, if necessary

Coarse sea salt and freshly ground pepper

7 to 8 ounces shelled cooked chestnuts, jarred or *sous vide*

⅓ cup heavy cream

1 teaspoon chopped parsley

1 teaspoon chopped garlic

2 tablespoons fresh lemon juice, or more to taste

1 teaspoon chestnut liqueur, optional

(continued)

1 Rinse the scallops and pat dry with paper towels. Cut away the small tab of tough connective tissue on the side of each scallop and reserve for Step 3. Wrap the scallops in paper towels to keep dry and store in the refrigerator.

2 Prepare the mushrooms by wiping each with a damp cloth; separate the stems from the caps. Quarter the mushroom caps and chop the stems.

3 In a heavy medium skillet, heat 1 tablespoon of the duck fat over moderate heat. Add the ham and cook, stirring, until golden and slightly crisp, 2 to 3 minutes. Use a slotted spoon to remove half the ham to paper towels and reserve for garnish. Add the carrot, onion, celery, garlic, crumbled dried cèpes, herb bouquet, scallop trimmings, and chopped mushroom stems to the remaining ham in the skillet. Cook until all the moisture has evaporated and the contents begin to caramelize, about 5 minutes.

4 Add the Armagnac and carefully ignite with a long match, averting your face; as soon as the flames subside, add the wine, chicken stock, and pinches of salt and pepper. Cover the skillet, reduce the heat to moderately low and simmer for 45 minutes.

5 Strain the contents of the skillet through a fine-mesh sieve; discard the solids. Return the liquid to the skillet and boil until reduced to about 1 cup; set the reduced broth aside.

6 Place 12 of the chestnuts in an electric blender or food processor. Add the cream and ¼ cup water and puree until smooth. Add the reduced broth and blend well. Season the sauce with salt and pepper to taste plus a few drops of the lemon juice. *(The recipe can be prepared to this point early in the day. Let cool, then cover and refrigerate.)*

7 About half an hour before serving, preheat the oven to 225°F. Warm the sauce over low heat. Season half the scallops lightly with salt and pepper. Heat a large stainless-steel skillet over high heat until very hot. Add 1½ tablespoons of the duck fat. Just before the fat begins to smoke, add the seasoned scallops and sauté until well browned, 1 minute to a side. Transfer the scallops to a rack set over a baking sheet; repeat with the remaining duck fat and scallops. Still on the rack, transfer to the oven and finish cooking, 15 to 20 minutes.

8 Wipe out the skillet. Add the remaining duck fat to the skillet and heat over moderate heat. Add the mushrooms and sauté until tender, 7 to 10 minutes. Add the reserved crisped ham and the remaining whole chestnuts and sauté until nicely glazed, 1 to 2 minutes. Add ½ cup of the creamy chestnut sauce and a little water to thin, if necessary, and cook over moderately high heat,

stirring, for a minute or two. Add the parsley, garlic, and remaining lemon juice. Correct the seasoning with salt and pepper to taste.

9 To serve, arrange the ragout of chestnuts and mushrooms on a heated platter. Top with the scallops and spoon a few tablespoons of the chestnut sauce around the ragout; serve at once. Pass the remaining sauce in a small bowl.

NOTE TO THE COOK

Try dressing the glazed chestnuts with just a few drops of sweet chestnut liqueur; it will contrast with the mildly dusky flavor of the chestnuts.

Inspired by a recipe from Hélène Darroze.

SCALLOPS IN TANGERINE SAUCE
⇢ *Coquilles St. Jacques, Sauce Mandarine*   SERVES 4

ANOTHER LOVELY DISH created by the late Gascon chef Jean-Louis Palladin. The sweetness of the scallops is counter pointed by the astringent taste of the sauce, which is so intense, very little is needed.

16 large fresh sea scallops, preferably all the same size (about 1½ ounces each; 1½ pounds total)

3 tablespoons fruity olive oil

1 tablespoon coarsely chopped fresh flat-leaf parsley

1 tablespoon coarsely chopped celery leaves

2 pinches of crumbled fresh thyme leaves

Coarse sea salt and freshly ground pepper

1½ cups fresh tangerine juice

¼ cup fish glaze (storebought or homemade—page 412) or 1¼ cups unsalted fish stock (storebought or homemade—pages 411–412) reduced by boiling to ¼ cup

2 tablespoons demi-glace (storebought or homemade—page 406) or ¾ cup unsalted chicken stock (storebought or homemade—page 405) reduced by boiling to 2 tablespoons

½ cup heavy cream

Fresh lemon juice

(continued)

1 Rinse the scallops; pat dry and toss with the olive oil, parsley, celery, and thyme. Season lightly with salt and pepper; marinate in the refrigerator for 2 to 3 hours.

2 In a small nonreactive saucepan, boil the tangerine juice until reduced to ⅓ cup.

3 Add the fish glaze and demi-glace. Bring to a boil; add the cream and boil vigorously without stirring for 5 to 7 minutes, until large bubbles appear on the surface and the sauce begins to bind. From time to time, test by stirring with a wooden spoon to see if the sauce has thickened. You should be able to glimpse the bottom of the saucepan for an instant. If the sauce is too sweet, adjust with a few drops of lemon juice and freshly ground pepper to taste. If the sauce turns oily, you have reduced it too much; in this case, add a tablespoon of water, and it will immediately smooth out. (At this point, the sauce can be held over warm water [such as in a double boiler] for up to 1 hour and reheated gently.)

4 About 15 minutes before serving, preheat the broiler. Reheat the sauce, if necessary. Remove the scallops from the refrigerator and arrange them on a broiling rack. Broil the scallops about 4 inches from the heat for 2 minutes on each side, or until lightly browned and just cooked through.

5 Spoon about 2 tablespoons hot sauce onto 4 warmed plates. Tilt the plates to coat the bottom evenly. Set 4 scallops on each plate and serve at once.

NOTES TO THE COOK

➻ If sauce is too strong tasting or too thin, swirl in bits of butter, on and off the heat.

➻ The rule for creating sauces is "the faster the evaporation, the better the coagulation" by stratification, as in Step 3. It takes less than 10 minutes to complete the entire process in a heavy-bottomed pan.

Salmon

SALMON SLICES WITH FRESH OYSTERS

→ *Escalope de Saumon au Fumet d'Huîtres*   SERVES 4 AS A FIRST COURSE

THE TRADITIONAL WAY to eat oysters in Bordeaux is to follow each one with a piece of spicy, warm sausage and a glass of dry white wine. In this refined adaptation, chef Christian Clément "plays back" this Bordeaux tradition with cool irony by pairing the oysters with fresh salmon: Each part works to create a whole greater than the sum of the parts.

Christian's combination brings a wonderful briny taste of the sea to freshly caught river salmon. It is easy and elegant, light and tasty, and goes well with a crisp acidic white wine with a long, lingering finish. Try a Pinot Gris, Riesling, Roussanne, or Sauvignon Blanc.

1¼ pounds fresh center-cut fillet of salmon, preferably wild, in 1 piece

4 large white firm mushrooms

1 teaspoon fresh lemon juice

7 tablespoons unsalted butter, preferably low water content butter, such as Plugra

12 shucked large oysters, with their liquor reserved

3 tablespoons crème fraîche or heavy cream

Salt and freshly ground white pepper

3 tablespoons minced fresh chives

1 Preheat the oven to 300°F. Lay the salmon fillet on your work surface, skin side down. With a very sharp, thin, flexible knife, cut the fillet crosswise on an angle (as you would slice a side of smoked salmon) into 4 equal "scallops," about 4 ounces each; discard the skin.

2 One by one, place each mushroom sideways on your work surface; holding it by the stem with one hand, slice the cap into thin rounds, stopping when you reach the gills. Stack the rounds and cut them into thin julienne strips. Sprinkle the lemon juice over the mushroom strips and gently toss. Wrap tightly in plastic wrap. *(The recipe can be prepared to this point up to 3 hours in advance. Refrigerate the salmon and mushrooms.)*

(continued)

3 Lightly oil a baking sheet. Place a large skillet, preferably nonstick, over moderately high heat. When the pan is hot, add 2 teaspoons of the butter. When the foam subsides, add the salmon scallops and cook on one side only for 30 seconds, or until edges are opaque and the center still raw. Season with a light grinding of white pepper and invert, raw side down, onto the oiled baking sheet. Set the skillet aside.

4 Top each piece of salmon with 3 oysters. Sprinkle with white pepper and place in the oven. Cook for 3 to 5 minutes, or until the oysters are warm and salmon is just cooked through.

5 Meanwhile, quickly prepare the sauce. Add the reserved oyster liquor to the skillet in which the salmon was sautéed; swirl to pick up any pieces stuck to the pan. Add the slivered mushrooms and boil over high heat until reduced to a thick mass, 1 to 2 minutes. Add the cream, return to a boil, and continue to cook until liquid is reduced by half, about 1 minute. Swirl in the remaining butter 1 tablespoon at a time. Season with salt and freshly ground white pepper to taste.

6 Use a wide spatula to transfer the salmon and oysters to heated plates. Spoon the sauce over the seafood. Sprinkle with the chives and serve at once.

SALMON WITH CRACKLING WAFERS

➤➤ *Le Filet de Saumon aux Croustillants de Lard*   SERVES 4

MICHEL BRAS'S FISH RECIPES are sophisticated and unorthodox for the way they reveal natural flavors and yield rich moist texture. This recipe is a perfect example of what Bras calls the "trilogy" of the main ingredient, the accompanying vegetables, and the condiment.

The salmon fillet is cooked slowly in a steamy low-temperature oven. It is served with crackling wafers made from crisped fatback, and a combination of bright leafy greens, soft stewed onions, and shelled fresh peas. After watching Michel Bras make this dish juggling a heavy cast-iron skillet to weigh down and crisp the fatback, I purchased a good, old fashioned, American bacon press for him, and sent it to him as a gift. I like to think he's still using it!

Steps 1 and 2 can be prepared one day in advance.

4½ tablespoons unsalted butter

2 medium onions, thinly sliced

Salt and freshly ground pepper

1 pound fatback, cut into 8 thin slices (leaves) about 5 inches square

12 large Swiss chard leaves, stemmed

½ cup shelled fresh or thawed frozen peas

1¼ pounds center-cut fresh wild salmon fillet, cut into 4 equal portions, about 1 inch thick

1 Melt 1½ tablespoons of the butter in a heavy 9-inch skillet over moderate heat. Add the onions and cook them, stirring often, until softened, golden, and reduced to about ⅔ cup, 25 to 30 minutes. Season lightly with salt and pepper. Remove from the heat and set aside.

2 Heat a large, heavy skillet over moderate heat until hot. Rinse the fatback leaves in water and shake off the excess. Add 1 slice to the skillet. Weight the leaf with a bacon press or the bottom of a cast-iron skillet. Cook until golden brown, turning twice, about 1 minute to a side. Transfer to paper towels. Pour off the fat from the skillet. Repeat with the remaining fatback leaves. *(The fatback wafers can be prepared 1 day ahead. Let them cool them completely, then refrigerate in an airtight container.)*

3 About 30 minutes before serving, position one rack in the lower third of the oven and a second rack in the upper third. Preheat the oven to 225°F. Place a skillet on the lower oven shelf and fill with boiling water.

4 Meanwhile in a medium saucepan of boiling water, cook the chard leaves until just tender, 2 to 3 minutes. Remove them with a slotted spoon; drain and rinse under cool running water. Add the peas to the same boiling water and cook for 1 minute; drain and rinse under cool running water. Combine the green leaves and peas in a small saucepan with 2 tablespoons fresh water and the 3 remaining tablespoons butter. Cover and finish cooking over very low heat, about 2 minutes. Season with salt and freshly ground pepper to taste.

5 While the green vegetables finish cooking, arrange the salmon pieces on a large baking sheet and place it on the upper rack of the oven. Bake for 10 minutes. Turn the salmon over and cook for 1 minute longer. Note that the salmon retains its color and remains very juicy. Season lightly with salt and pepper.

6 Meanwhile, reheat the onions over low heat, stirring occasionally. Crisp the fatback wafers in the oven while the salmon cooks, or in a nonstick skillet over low heat. To serve, place a crisp fatback wafer on each plate. Cover with the onions. Top each with a salmon fillet and another wafer. Spoon the chard and peas alongside.

(continued)

Paper-thin slices of firm white fatback (or lard leaves or barding strips) are the best choice for these wafers, but in some places it can be hard to come by. To substitute salted fatback, soak it overnight in water, drain, pat dry, chill, and slice. If you do use salted fatback, be careful not to salt the salmon or onions.

STEAMED SALMON WITH COOKED EGG SAUCE

➵➤ *Saumon Cuit à la Vapeur, Sauce de Sorges*   SERVES 4

THIS LUSCIOUS SAUCE, created by Lucien Vanel, is based on cooked eggs and oil, and uses the same techniques as hollandaise and mayonnaise. Though the Sorges of the title is a village in the Dordogne, the sauce is quite common beyond the area, where it is generally served with boiled chicken. Traditionally, the eggs are dipped in hot water, dried, and then tucked under the embers of a fire, where they finish cooking and take on a smoky flavor.

Here the sauce is served with salmon that has been seasoned, buttered, and wrapped airtight in heatproof plastic wrap or a boiling pouch before steaming. This technique enhances the moist, fresh flavor of the fish.

2 salmon steaks, preferably wild, cut ¾ to 1 inch thick (about 10 ounces each)

Salt and freshly ground pepper

4 teaspoons unsalted butter, cut into 4 even pieces, softened

2 extra large eggs

¾ teaspoon Dijon mustard

2 to 3 tablespoons fresh lemon juice

¼ cup mild olive oil

¼ cup peanut oil

3 tablespoons heavy cream

1 large plum tomato, peeled, seeded, finely diced, and drained

2 tablespoons chopped fresh flat-leaf parsley

1 tablespoon tiny nonpareil capers, rinsed and dried

2 tablespoons minced fresh chives

1½ teaspoons finely slivered fresh basil leaves (optional)

1 Cut the salmon off the bones, dividing each steak in half. Remove the skin. Season the salmon lightly with salt and pepper. Paint with the softened butter. Wrap each steak in a small piece of parchment paper and then seal with 3 or 4 layers of heatproof plastic wrap, or wrap airtight using a vacuum-packing appliance (see Notes below). Refrigerate for up to 3 hours until ready to cook.

2 To make the sauce: Run the eggs under warm water for a full minute. Then simmer in a small saucepan of water for 5 minutes. Remove and rinse under cold running water for 1 minute to cool. Carefully scoop out the yolks into a small mixing bowl or the top of double boiler. Set the whites aside.

3 Set the bowl or top of double boiler over hot—but not simmering—water. Crush the egg yolks with a spoon to a smooth paste. Beat in the mustard and 1½ tablespoons of the lemon juice, whisking until the mixture thickens. Combine the olive and peanut oils and very gradually whisk into the yolks, several drops at a time, whisking constantly. An emulsion should form, just as it does when you make homemade mayonnaise. It takes about 5 minutes to add all the oil. Remove from heat and whisk in the cream.

4 Press the egg whites through a medium sieve with back of a spoon. Fold the sieved egg whites, tomato, parsley, capers, chives, and basil into the sauce. Season with salt and pepper to taste and add more lemon juice, if necessary. *(The sauce can be prepared early in the day and refrigerated. Reheat very gently.)*

5 To steam the fish: Set a steamer rack over 1½ inches boiling water in a large saucepan. Add the packets of fish and steam, turning once, for 4 minutes per side. Do not overcook; salmon continues to cook while waiting to be unwrapped. (The salmon can be cooked up to 10 minutes before serving.) Carefully unwrap and place on individual heated serving plates. Top with lukewarm egg sauce.

NOTES TO THE COOK

→ If the mixture at any time appears about to curdle, immediately remove from the heat and dip the bottom of the bowl or pan into cold water or quickly whisk in a spoonful of cold heavy cream. If the sauce begins to separate, cool it down as fast as possible by whisking it over a bowl of ice water. If that doesn't work, you will need to cook another egg and begin adding the curdled mixture in droplets, just as you do when attempting to save mayonnaise.

→ If you have a vacuum-pack sealer (an electrical appliance available in housewares stores), you can seal the salmon steaks airtight in their special packaging and drop them directly into simmering water to cook for 7 to 8 minutes. If the packages float to the top, weight them down with a plate so that the water covers them entirely.

Salt Cod

Morue

In inland areas, far from the fresh fish markets along the coast of Southwest France, the only saltwater fish to be found in the past were slabs of cod, either salted or wind dried. At local grocery stores, beside the barrels of lentils, beans, and other staples were huge tubs where these slabs were piled up on Thursdays. The salt cod would be sold that day to be soaked at home under slowly dripping water for 24 hours so it would be ready for the traditional Friday lunch.

In the southern part of the Languedoc, the great salt cod dish is the famous *brandade*, made with olive oil, rich milk, and garlic all crushed together to produce a light, creamy substance. Just a bit farther north, in the Rouergue, they have a variation I like even better; it's made with walnut oil, hard-boiled eggs, garlic, and herbs. In the Lot, you will find brandade prepared with potatoes and drizzled with fresh walnut oil. In Gascony, salt cod and beans is a dish to seek out, and in the Basque country, salt cod and hot peppers are delicious together.

Once acquired, the taste for salt cod can turn the most sedate individual into a gastronomic savage upon the mere mention of morue. The French have a particular way of wetting their lips and rolling their eyes up toward heaven with reverence when they think about the dishes made from this inexpensive, though very nourishing, highly digestible, humble food. Most appealing is its particularly succulent and briny taste. These qualities make salt cod especially popular in Southwest France, Italy, Spain, Portugal, and Greece.

You will find the dried fish in most Spanish, Portuguese, Greek, and Italian seafood markets as well as in large supermarkets. Buy about four ounces per person. Look for ivory-colored flesh with a tinge of green or yellow; salt cod should not be snowy white. It should be thick and supple—not hard as a rock. When pressed lightly, it should not give off flakes of salt. Cod from Gaspé in Canada is excellent, and so is Icelandic cod. When buying salt cod, do not confuse it with the yellow-hued, wind-dried cod called stockfish, which often has a strong fishy odor (the smell disappears after soaking, but the taste is still stronger than that of salt cod). Salt cod is sold whole, with skin and bones intact, which requires 24 to 36 hours soaking in several changes of water, and in fillets, which require less soaking time.

TO SOAK SALT COD

Place the pieces in a colander or pasta basket so that the salt that leaches out will run off. Ideally, boned salt cod should be rinsed under cold running water for 12 hours. Since this is impossible for most home cooks, the next best thing to do is to set your colander or pasta basket into a deep pot filled with cold water, and then change this water 3 or 4 times, or until the water no longer has a salty taste, about 18 to 24 hours. Salt cod is not evenly salted, and thus some pieces are more salty than others; this fact will affect the number of times you must change the water. A well-soaked piece of salt cod will sometimes actually require salt in the final dish. The type of salt used to preserve the fish is not particularly good for eating, though the Catalans sprinkle grated, unrinsed dried salt cod on fresh fava beans and radishes to give them a salty flavor.

When your piece of cod has swollen up from its soaking, it is ready to cook. Roasting, frying, and poaching are three popular methods.

TO POACH SOAKED SALT COD

Cover the pieces with cold water, or with a mixture of cold water and milk if you want the cod to come out white. Slowly bring it to a bare simmer. (This poaching water can be flavored with herbs or with a split, unpeeled whole head of garlic—an excellent idea when you intend to use the same water later to cook potatoes.) When the first white foam appears on the surface of the cooking liquid, remove the pot from the heat, cover, and let stand for 10 minutes or so, depending upon the thickness of the fish. (The reason for removing the pot completely from the fire and then letting the dish "cook" in the receding heat is to ensure that the cod never boils, thus preserving its succulence—if cod boils, it becomes leathery.) To tell when the fish is done, stick the point of a sharp knife into the thickest part; if there is little resistance, the cod is ready. Lift the pieces out and let them dry on a kitchen towel. When cool enough to handle, remove the fatty skin and all the bones. Save the poaching liquid if you are making Puree of Salt Cod, Potatoes, and Walnut Oil (pages 122–123), or for a fish soup.

SALT COD WITH HOT PEPPERS AND GARLIC

→→ *Morue Pil-Pil* SERVES 4

THE BASQUE EXPRESSION *pil-pil* means to cook slowly. In this recipe, salt cod is simmered and shaken in olive oil with garlic in a shallow earthenware *cazuela* until the pieces of fish begin to "float" in the resulting emulsification between the olive oil and the exuded white gelatinous juices of the fish. The dish is decorated with chopped fresh parsley and thin strips of red chili pepper. It is traditionally served right from the casserole.

When buying salt cod for this dish, try to get a thick center piece. If the salt cod is packaged, buy a little more than you need, choose the thickest pieces for this dish, and save the thin ends for the Rouergue version of *brandade,* Puree of Salt Cod, Potatoes, and Walnut Oil (pages 122–123).

1 pound boneless salt cod	1 small hot red pepper, cut into very thin rings
1 cup milk	
¼ cup olive oil	2 tablespoons chopped fresh flat-leaf parsley
4 garlic cloves, thinly sliced	

1 Soak the salt cod in cold water to cover for 18 to 24 hours, or until it is swollen. Change the water at least 3 times, adding milk for last soaking.

2 Rinse the cod; cut into 8 pieces of approximately equal size. Pick out any bones; remove the scales but not the skin. (The skin has much of the gelatin needed to enrich the sauce as well as to add flavor.) Lay each piece of fish on a kitchen towel–lined plate and keep refrigerated for up to 8 hours until ready to cook.

3 About half an hour before serving, place the pieces of cod, skin side down, in a shallow 10-inch round flameproof earthenware cooking dish, or substitute an enameled cast-iron skillet. Pour the olive oil over the cod, add the garlic, and set over low heat (if cooking in earthenware, use a flame tamer or trivet to protect the pot from cracking). Cook for 30 minutes. During this time shake the dish or skillet often so that juices exuded from the fish mix with the oil. Do not turn the fish pieces over, but do move them around a bit so that they do not stick to the bottom of the pan. From time to time tilt the pan and baste the fish with the simmering pan juices.

4 Just before serving, raise the heat and bring almost to a boil. Add the peppers and parsley and swirl the juices in the skillet to combine the flavors and lightly reduce the liquid. The result should be a smooth, blended sauce. Serve hot directly from the skillet or transfer to individual serving plates.

Puree of Salt Cod, Potatoes, and Walnut Oil

➤➤ *Morue à la Rouergate*   MAKES ABOUT 4½ TO 5 CUPS; SERVES 6 TO 8

ALL FOOD ENTHUSIASTS know about the famous *brandade* of Nimes, in which pounded salt cod moistened with olive oil is mixed with boiling milk and served warm with fried garlic croutons. Here is an unusual and heavenly version that uses a little mashed potato, sieved hard-boiled eggs, and fragrant walnut oil. In the original Rouergue version, wind-dried cod (stockfish) is used instead of salt cod.

1 pound boneless salt cod

1¾ cups milk

Herb bouquet: 3 sprigs parsley, 1 sprig thyme, and 1 imported bay leaf tied together with string

1 onion, quartered

1 large garlic clove, halved

2 to 3 black peppercorns, freshly cracked

¾ pound baking (russet) potatoes, peeled and cut into chunks

½ to ¾ cup imported walnut oil

3 eggs: 1 raw, 2 hard-boiled

1 teaspoon finely chopped fresh garlic

1 tablespoon finely chopped fresh flat-leaf parsley

Finely ground white pepper

White wine vinegar, sherry vinegar, or fresh lemon juice

24 triangles of crustless bread, toasted or fried in olive oil, then rubbed with garlic

1 A day in advance, soak the cod in a large basin of cold water to cover for 18 to 24 hours, or until the fish is swollen, changing the water at least 3 times and adding 1 cup of the milk for the last soaking.

2 Rinse the cod; cut into 3 or 4 pieces. Place in a large saucepan and cover with fresh cold water. Add the herb bouquet, onion, garlic clove, and peppercorns. Heat slowly until the first white foam appears. Remove from the heat at once; cover and let stand for 10 minutes.

3 Using a slotted spoon, remove the salt cod pieces to a paper towel–lined plate. Reserve the liquid for cooking the potatoes. Carefully remove the bones and hard skin; flake the flesh finely. Keep warm.

4 Meanwhile cook the potatoes in the poaching water. Drain off the cooking liquid. (This broth can be used for a soup.) Dry the potatoes over low heat, then immediately mash them until smooth, using a ricer, a potato masher, or the wire beaters of an electric mixer. Beat in 2 tablespoons of the walnut oil, the raw egg, and the chopped garlic. Beat until smooth. Keep warm.

5 Meanwhile, scald the remaining ¾ cup milk in a small saucepan and heat the remaining walnut oil in a second saucepan.

6 Place the flaked cod and a little of the warm milk in a food processor. Pulse on and off once. Gradually add the warmed oil and milk alternately, pulsing without overworking the salt cod. The mixture should feel light but slightly gritty.

7 Scrape the fish into the mashed potatoes. Sieve the hard-boiled eggs into the mixture, then add the parsley. Gently but thoroughly mix until well blended and light. Adjust the seasoning with white pepper and a few drops of vinegar or lemon juice to taste. Serve warm in a wide dish surrounded with the garlic toast triangles.

NOTE TO THE COOK

The spread can be made up to 6 hours in advance. If you do so, reserve a few tablespoons warm milk for reheating. Mix together over low heat.

Baby Eel
Pibales

------>-><-<------

Baby eel—called *pibales* in French, *angulas* in Spanish, *angulak* or *txitxardinac* in Basque, and sometimes called *elvers* in English—are soft, white, slippery little things 1½ to 2 inches long; heaped together, they resemble a mass of cut-up spaghetti. You should not be put off by their appearance. Baby eel is considered a delicacy along the coasts of Morocco, Spain, Portugal, and France from the Spanish border up to Bordeaux. For years, when I lived in Tangier, I'd anticipate them as I drove forty minutes down the coast to the town of Asilah to Pepe's Cafe, where they were a famous specialty. And whenever I am in Saint-Jean-de-Luz in early winter, I make a point to eat them at Pablo's Restaurant on rue Mlle. Etcheto, where they are served in a shallow earthenware casserole in sizzling hot olive oil flavored with the piquant piment d'Espelette and slivered garlic. At Pablo's, they are eaten the traditional way—with a wooden fork.

LA TUPINA'S SARDINE AND POTATO CAKE

→► *Gâteau de Sardines aux Pommes de Terre*   SERVES 4

AT THE RESTAURANT La Tupina in Bordeaux there's no closed season on giblets sizzling in a skillet, stuffed chicken roasting on a spit, beans simmering in an iron pot in the fireplace, and thick slices of jambon de Bayonne sautéing with glazed shallots (Cured Ham With Vinegar and Caramelized Shallots, pages 23–24). Jean-Pierre Xiradakis, the keeper of the Bordeaux culinary flame, provides numerous wonderful authentic local dishes prepared the traditional way. For the first edition of this book, he gave me a little known recipe that he didn't want forgotten (Confit of Pig's Tongue, page 282). And, indeed, it is a keeper.

For this edition, he wanted me to include the great seasonal combination of the Bordeaux–La Rochelle corridor: an assembled, perfectly balanced dish of nutty, thin-skinned potatoes interlaced with just-cooked fillets of the local sardines, called *royans*, voluptuously coated with Charentais butter and dotted with fresh chives.

12 very fresh, shiny, sardines (about 1⅓ pounds), cleaned and skinned (see Notes at right)	⅓ cup AA quality salted butter (see Note at right)
1 pound fingerling potatoes, scrubbed	Juice of 1 lemon
Coarse sea salt	Freshly ground pepper
2 imported bay leaves, halved	2 tablespoons minced fresh chives

1 Spread the sardines fillets out in a single layer in an ovenproof glass or ceramic dish. Season lightly with sea salt and scatter the bay leaves on top; cover with plastic wrap and refrigerate.

2 Preheat the oven to 450°F. Meanwhile, boil the unskinned potatoes until tender, 10 to 12 minutes. Drain and pat dry. Cut the potatoes lengthwise into slices ½ inch thick. Slowly fry in a large nonstick skillet over low heat, in batches if necessary, in 3 tablespoons of the butter until golden on both sides, about 5 minutes. Drain on paper towels.

3 Slip the fillets into the oven to bake for 2 minutes. Melt the remaining butter in a small saucepan. Season it with the lemon juice and salt and pepper to taste.

4 On 4 warmed plates, alternate slices of potatoes with sardine fillets. Drizzle the butter on top and garnish with a sprinkling of chives. Serve at once.

NOTES TO THE COOK

➤➤ Stay on the lookout for fresh sardines at your favorite fish market. They show up fairly regularly now on the east and west coasts. You can find them frozen imported from Portugal at some Latin markets.

➤➤ If your fishmonger does not clean the fish for you, here's how to prepare them: Rinse the fish under cold running water. Hold the first one between your thumb and forefinger and use your thumbnail to slit open the belly. With the other hand, pull the head toward the belly. Remove the guts and cut off the head. Use a rubbing motion with your thumb and forefinger and, beginning at the tail, slip off the skin. Rinse and pat dry with paper towels. Repeat with the remaining sardines.

➤➤ If you can find butter from the Charente (see Mail Order Sources, pages 415–417), said to be the best butter from France, and some domestic fingerling potatoes, all the better—you're in for a superb culinary treat!

FISH BAKED WITH BRAISED LEEKS AND PINEAU DE CHARENTES

➤➤ *Chaudrée au Pineau*   SERVES 6

THE COMBINATION OF SILKY, soft leeks and assorted juicy fresh fish is famous all along the western coast of France. What makes this recipe special is the addition of Pineau de Charentes, an aperitif from France's Cognac region made with Cognac and sweet unfermented grape juice. (Pineau also goes beautifully with poultry and desserts.) Here the strong sweet taste of the Pineau is balanced by a hint of soft green peppercorns. (I use peppercorns from France where they're subjected to a freeze-dried method that preserves their unusual zest and clear color.)

(continued)

Chef Serge Coulons, from the town of La Rochelle in the Charente-Maritime, taught me a good trick for handling fish fillets: "Since they usually curl up as they cook," he suggested, "I simply curl them myself, then set them into a bed of cooked leeks arranged side by side. The presentation's attractive, and portions are easy to lift and serve."

Following his advice, I suggest fish such as snapper and bass, which are best curled skin side out, or fillets of flat fish, such as of sole or flounder, which curl skinned side in.

3 pounds young leeks, about 8

6 tablespoons unsalted butter

Coarse salt and freshly ground pepper

½ cup dry white wine

½ cup Pineau de Charentes

1 pound unskinned fillets of mixed meaty white-fleshed fish, such as snapper, blackfish, grouper, haddock, pollock, or striped bass

½ pound sole, or any member of the flatfish family such as cod, haddock, and whiting

½ cup crème fraîche

1 teaspoon brined green peppercorns, rinsed and lightly bruised

6 large sea scallops

6 medium-sized mussels, preferably cultivated

2 teaspoons minced fresh flat-leaf parsley

2 teaspoons minced fresh tarragon

1 tablespoon minced fresh chives

1 Trim the root ends from the leeks, then remove all but 1 inch of the green leaves. Cut each leek crosswise into 3 equal parts. Rinse well and drain.

2 In a medium nonreactive saucepan, melt the butter over moderately low heat. Add the leeks, season with salt and pepper, cover the pan, and cook, stirring often, until the leeks and butter just turn golden, about 45 minutes. Add the white wine and Pineau de Charentes and bring to a boil over moderately high heat. Reduce the heat and simmer for 5 minutes *(The leeks can be prepared 1 day in advance. Cover them when cool and refrigerate.)*

3 About half an hour before serving, preheat the oven to 425°F. Spread the leeks and cooking juices over the bottom of a deep earthenware casserole or a 2½-quart soufflé dish. Curl the fish as described in the introduction and nestle each fillet in the bed of leeks. Cover the dish with a circle of parchment and a lid and set it in a larger pan with enough boiling water to reach halfway up the sides of the dish.

4 Bake for 10 minutes. Add the scallops and mussels, cover again, and bake for 10 minutes longer, or until the fish is milky-white but still firm to the touch.

5 Meanwhile, warm the cream in a small saucepan with the green peppercorns over low heat. As soon as the fish is done and out of the oven, remove the cover and parchment. Pour the hot cream and green peppercorns into the dish and sprinkle the parsley, tarragon, and chives on top. Grasp the dish with oven mitts and swirl it to blend the cream and herbs with the pan juices. Taste for seasoning and serve at once.

FISH FILLETS IN RED WINE AND COCOA SAUCE

➤➤ *Filets de Poisson au Vin Rouge et Cacao*   SERVES 4

FISH FROM THE Gironde River, such as lamprey, trout, and shad, are often served with a red wine sauce in Bordeaux. The sauce served with lamprey is thickened with its blood— a very popular spring dish served at the Brasserie de Noailles just across from the Grand Thèâtre. Out of season, the Bordelais will continue to order it, knowing it comes directly from a can. Many gastronomes prefer it aged in the can!

In the neighboring Landais region, eel is cooked with prunes and leeks, and the red wine sauce is thickened with bitter chocolate, which, though not evident to the taste, deepens its flavor and color. This modern version of that sauce can be used for fillets of any of the fish listed above, as well as for bass or mullet.

1½ cups full-bodied red wine (see Notes, page 128)

2 tablespoons minced shallots

1½ cups unsalted chicken stock (storebought or homemade—page 405), boiled until reduced to ½ cup

1½ cups Fish Fumet (page 413), made with red wine and reduced to ¼ cup glaze

4 leeks (white part and ½ inch of pale green), well washed and thinly sliced crosswise

¼ cup heavy cream

Coarse sea salt and freshly ground pepper

1 pound boneless fish fillets, such as trout, bass, or mullet

8 tablespoons (1 stick) unsalted butter

1 teaspoon unsweetened cocoa dissolved in 1½ teaspoons water

1 teaspoon red wine vinegar

2 tablespoons minced fresh chives

(continued)

1 In a nonreactive saucepan, slowly simmer the red wine with the shallots until reduced to ¼ cup, about 40 minutes. Add the reduced stock and boil over moderately high heat until reduced by half. Stir in the fish glaze. *(This fish sauce base can be prepared to this point up to 1 day in advance. Cover and refrigerate. Reheat before using.)*

2 In a steamer or the top half of a couscous cooker, steam the leeks until soft, 12 to 15 minutes. Shake off excess moisture; place in a wide saucepan and cook away all moisture. Add half the cream and cook, uncovered, until thick, about 2 minutes. Season with ¼ teaspoon salt and a pinch of pepper. Remove the leeks from the heat.

3 Cut the fish into 4 pieces of approximately equal size, slicing each slightly on the diagonal. Lightly season with salt and pepper.

4 In a wide, deep skillet, melt 1 tablespoon of the butter; add the fish in a single layer. For extra moisture, sprinkle with 1 tablespoon water. Cover the pan tightly and cook over low heat for 2 minutes. Spoon the reserved fish sauce base around the fish so that the flavors mix with the pan juices. Cover and cook, basting once over low heat, for 2 minutes longer, or until just cooked. With a slotted spatula, transfer the fish pieces to a warmed serving platter.

5 Quickly bring the pan juices to a boil, add the remaining 2 tablespoons cream, and boil until reduced by half. Gradually swirl in the remaining 7 tablespoons butter, cut into chunks, and allow the sauce to thicken without boiling.

6 Mix the cocoa paste and vinegar until smooth; stir into the sauce in the skillet. Season with salt and pepper to taste.

7 To serve, mound a bed of leeks on 4 warmed plates. Set a piece of fish on each. Coat with the sauce and sprinkle with chives. Serve at once.

NOTES TO THE COOK

↦ If a whole fish is purchased (about 2½ pounds), have the backbone and head cut up to use in making the fish fumet.

↦ It's important to use an intense red wine for this dish, because the sauce is mounted with butter, which dilutes the color. The best wines for this kind of sauce are a California Petite Sirah, a French Côtes-du-Rhône, or Cahors.

↦ The initial reduction of the wine should be slow so that it has a chance to mellow; and the shallots need the long cooking to soften. If the wine evaporates before the 40-minute cooking time, add a little water and cook down slowly until the shallots are soft, then let the water evaporate.

Pan-Fried Trout With Mountain-Cured Ham and Bacon

→→ *Truites Comme en Sare*   SERVES 2

THE COMBINATION OF TROUT and bacon is not unique to camping trips in Oregon; it is also found in Spain, Italy, and France. There is nothing so wonderful as a freshly caught trout from a clean, cold, swiftly running stream cooked in bacon fat over a slow-burning fire. In this lighter version, from the town of Sare in the Basque countryside, mountain trout about 10 inches long are pan-fried in bacon-flavored oil and garnished with ham, onions, and garlic.

The repertory of trout dishes is not large in the Southwest, but the dishes are quite wonderful. In the Dordogne, trout are wrapped in oiled parchment and slowly grilled over juniper berry–scented embers, then sprinkled with *verjus* just before serving. Larger trout are stuffed with cooked cèpes, herbs, and ham, then grilled. Other regional cooks simply stuff trout with fresh herbs and butter and cook them in a simple white wine–flavored broth.

2 trout (8 to 10 ounces each), cleaned but with head and tail left on	Cornmeal or flour, for dredging
¼ cup plus 2 tablespoons red wine vinegar	1 ounce jambon de Bayonne, prosciutto, or Serrano ham, finely diced
3 ounces thick-sliced, applewood-smoked bacon	2 tablespoons finely chopped onion
1 tablespoon extra virgin olive oil	½ teaspoon minced fresh garlic
Milk	1 tablespoon finely chopped fresh flat-leaf parsley
Coarse sea salt and freshly ground pepper	1 good pinch of fresh thyme leaves

1 Rinse the trout in a bowl of water combined with 2 tablespoons of the vinegar. Drain and dry well.

2 In a large skillet, preferably a 14-inch oval, slowly cook the bacon in the oil until the fat is rendered and the bacon is crisp, about 5 minutes. Set the bacon aside, leaving the fat in the skillet.

3 Dip the trout in the milk, then roll in cornmeal or flour seasoned with pepper and a tiny pinch of salt. Shake off excess coating.

(continued)

4 Fry the trout in the bacon fat in the skillet over moderately high heat for 4 minutes, or until crisp and brown on the first side. Using two spatulas, turn the trout over and fry for 2 minutes longer to brown the other side. Tilt the skillet, pour off the fat; quickly scatter the ham, onion, and garlic around the trout. Reduce the heat to moderately low and finish cooking the fish, about 1 to 2 minutes.

5 Carefully transfer the trout to warmed plates. Garnish with the ham, onion, and garlic in the skillet. Add the remaining ¼ cup vinegar to the skillet, bring to a boil, and pour over the trout. Sprinkle with the parsley and thyme and serve at once.

ESCABECHE OF FRESH WHITE FISH WITH ARTICHOKES

→→ *Escabèche de Poisson Frits aux Artichauts*   SERVES 5 TO 6

THIS IS ONE TERRIFIC DISH: strips of fried fish in a marinade flavored with walnut oil and orange zest. Oily fish—such as sardines, tinker mackerel, herring, or smelts—are traditionally used, but in Lucien Vanel's inspired version, I prefer a leaner, fine, white-fleshed fish, such as halibut. The combination with quick fried artichokes make for an unusual play of textures and tastes, brought together by the tangy sauce.

Because of all the marinating, begin this recipe a day or two in advance. Note that leftover vegetables and marinade make an excellent salad tossed with cooked white beans.

1 pound skinless thick white fish fillets, preferably fresh halibut

⅔ cup flour

Coarse sea salt and freshly ground pepper

½ cup olive or peanut oil, for frying

⅓ cup plus 2½ tablespoons extra virgin olive oil

½ pound small white or red onions, thinly sliced

½ pound small carrots, peeled and thinly sliced

12 whole small garlic cloves, unpeeled, plus 2 large cloves, peeled and mashed with a pinch of salt

12 sprigs of thyme

2 imported bay leaves

8 juniper berries

1 teaspoon black peppercorns

2 whole cloves

1 cup dry white wine

1 cup white wine vinegar

3 fresh medium artichokes, 5 to 6 ounces each

1 lemon, halved

1½ tablespoons French walnut oil

Grated zest of ½ orange

2 cups loosely packed arugula

1 Cut the fish into 30 thin strips about 1½ inches long and ¾ inch wide (goujonettes). Season the flour with ½ teaspoon salt and ¼ teaspoon pepper. Roll the fish strips in the seasoned flour; shake off any excess. Fry in hot oil in a large nonreactive skillet in batches without crowding over moderate heat until golden on both sides, 2 to 3 minutes. Remove with a skimmer or slotted spoon, drain on paper towels, and place in a deep serving dish. Discard the oil and wipe out the skillet.

2 Heat ⅓ cup of the extra virgin olive oil in the skillet. Add the onions and carrots and cook over moderate heat, stirring occasionally, until softened but not browned, about 5 minutes. Raise the heat, add the 12 unpeeled garlic cloves, 9 sprigs of the thyme, the bay leaves, juniper berries, peppercorns, and whole cloves; let the seasonings sizzle for 1 minute, stirring constantly. Add the wine, vinegar, 1 cup of water, and 1 teaspoon salt. Bring to a boil, reduce the heat to low, and simmer the marinade, partially covered, for 25 minutes.

3 Pour the hot marinade over the fried fish. Let cool, then refrigerate, covered, for 24 hours, turning the pieces in the marinade once or twice.

(continued)

4 Trim the artichokes by first snapping off the tough outer leaves near the base. Use a stainless-steel knife to cut off the stems, then trim the crowns to within 1½ inches of the base. Use a melon baller to scoop out the hairy chokes and scrape around the inner sides to widen the cavity. Use a small knife to carefully trim the leaves, then pare off any remaining dark green parts. As you work with each artichoke, rub it with lemon to prevent discoloration. Put the artichokes in a bowl of water mixed with lemon juice.

5 One to 2 hours before serving, remove the fish from the refrigerator. Use a slotted spatula to gently remove the fish and some of the marinated vegetables to a large platter; spoon a couple of tablespoons of the marinade over the fish to moisten. Garnish with the remaining thyme sprigs.

6 Measure 2 tablespoons of the marinade into a wooden salad bowl. Whisk in the walnut oil, a pinch of black pepper, and the orange zest; set the dressing aside. Reserve the remaining fish marinade and vegetables for some other meal.

7 About 15 minutes before serving, pat the artichokes dry with a kitchen towel. Halve them lengthwise, cut each half into ¼-inch-thick slices and place them in a large, heavy nonreactive skillet with the remaining 2½ tablespoons extra virgin olive oil, ⅓ cup of water, and the mashed garlic. Cook over high heat, tossing, until all the water has evaporated, about 2 minutes. Immediately, remove the skillet from the heat to avoid "frying," which would make the garlic turn bitter. Scrape the slightly crunchy artichoke slices onto the same platter with the fish.

8 Just before serving, toss the arugula with the dressing in the salad bowl. Serve the arugula with the fish and artichokes.

CHICKEN

Baby Chicken With Lemon-Garlic Sauce

➤ *Poussin Rôti à l'Ail et au Citron* SERVES 6

THE THOUGHT OF A SAUCE OF SWEET GARLIC and astringent lemon at first astounded me. It turned out to be one of the most wonderful blends of two ingredients that I have ever tasted. Almost any bird could be served with this sauce; André Daguin used guinea hen when he first demonstrated it to me. Since then I have switched to baby chickens *(poussins)*. You could also use Rock Cornish hens that have never been frozen. Any of these birds—or a chicken—make a succulent foil for the sauce.

Originally, this was a French Catalan dish that bore the nickname "the poultry dish for the bandits' hideout" *(repaire de bandits Catalans)*, perhaps because the garlic was cooked so long, it lost its strong aroma and thus could not give away the location of the hiding bandits!

The dish can be made in two stages: the sauce base the day before and the cooking of the bird and the assembling just before it is served. Daguin suggests serving it with a gratin of sliced summer vegetables: eggplants, tomatoes, and zucchini.

3 baby chickens or large fresh Cornish game hens (1¼ to 1½ pounds each)*

Coarse kosher salt and freshly ground pepper

6 heads of garlic

3 large lemons, preferably organic, well washed

½ teaspoon sugar

1½ cups light cream or half-and-half

3 tablespoons unsalted butter, at room temperature

¼ cup imported Port or dry Madeira

2 cups unsalted chicken stock (storebought or homemade—page 405), reduced to 1 cup

1 Rub the birds with salt and pepper. Cover loosely and refrigerate until 30 minutes before cooking.

2 Separate the garlic cloves. Blanch them in boiling water for 2 minutes; drain and peel.

3 Peel 1½ of the lemons with a swivel-bladed vegetable peeler to remove the yellow zest. Blanch the zest in a pan of boiling water for 1 minute; drain and set aside. Cut off and discard the inner white peel (pith) from the lemons. Cut the lemons into thin slices; remove any seeds.

4 In a heavy 3-quart saucepan, combine the garlic cloves, with the lemon zest, lemon slices, sugar, 1 teaspoon salt, and 4 cups cold water. Bring to a boil, reduce the heat, and simmer, uncovered, for 1 to 2 hours, or until the liquid in the pan has almost entirely evaporated and the garlic cloves are golden brown and meltingly tender. Stir from time to time to avoid burning. (This can be done in a 350°F oven, in a heatproof glass or earthenware bowl. If you do roast the garlic and lemon in the oven, transfer to a saucepan before proceeding.)

5 Add the cream to the pan and boil, stirring often, until reduced by half. Strain through a fine sieve, pushing down on the solids to extract as much liquid as possible; discard the solids. The garlic cream will be thick and will taste slightly acrid. Set it aside, uncovered, until cool, then refrigerate for up to 1 day until ready to use.

6 About 1¼ hours before serving, preheat the oven to 350°F. Cut the remaining 1½ lemons into quarters. Slip 1 or 2 quarters into the cavity of each chicken. Truss them and rub with butter. Arrange the birds on their sides in a buttered roasting pan.

7 Roast the chickens for 1 to 1¼ hours, turning and basting every 15 minutes, until they are browned and the temperature in the thickest part of the thigh registers 160°F. To test for doneness, prick the thighs—if the juices run clear, the hens are done. Remove the trussing strings and lemon quarters; arrange the hens on a platter. Cover loosely with foil and return to turned-off oven to keep warm.

8 Discard the fat in the roasting pan. Pour in the port and bring to a boil on top of the stove, stirring to dissolve all the brown particles that cling to the bottom of the pan. Add the stock and boil quickly over high heat until reduced by half. Pour into a small saucepan.

9 Halve the hens; add any new juices that have accumulated on the platter to the sauce. Let the juices stand for a few moments to allow the fat to rise to the surface. Skim off and discard the fat. Stir in the reserved garlic cream. Boil quickly until the sauce is thickened to about 1⅓ cups. Adjust the seasoning with salt and pepper, adding a few drops of lemon juice for perfect balance.

*Avoid frozen hens; when fresh they are closest to a baby chicken.

BABY CHICKENS IN RED WINE

➤➤ *Poussins au Vin Rouge*

A TRUE COQ AU VIN should be made with an old, flavorful bird and a strong red wine. The long cooking softens the flesh of the bird and mellows the wine. This dish of young chicken in red wine is a good example of the updating of classic French country cooking using a mixture of modern and traditional methods. The dark, very flavorful sauce results from a technique called *tomber à glace*; a series of reductions of liquid makes the sauce darker, shinier—almost syrupy.

2 baby chickens (1½ to 2 pounds each) or 2 fresh Cornish game hens, split*

Salt and freshly ground pepper

½ pound (12 to 18) small white onions, about 1 inch in diameter

6 ounces lean pancetta or ventrèche, cut into ¼-inch dice

2 teaspoons rendered duck fat or 1 tablespoon mixed oil and butter

1 tablespoon tomato paste

3 cups full-bodied red wine, such as Syrah

½ pound fresh mushrooms, halved or quartered depending upon size

3 cups unsalted chicken stock (storebought or homemade—page 405)

3 tablespoons grapeseed, peanut, or corn oil

¼ cup finely chopped shallots

Chopped fresh flat-leaf parsley

1 Season the chickens with salt and pepper. Loosely cover with plastic wrap and refrigerate until 30 minutes before cooking. Dry the chickens well.

2 Cut an X in the root end of each small onion. Drop the onions into boiling water and cook for 2 minutes; drain and under cool water. Peel, leaving on enough of the root and stem ends so onions will not fall apart. Dry thoroughly on paper towels.

3 Place the pancetta in a large nonreactive saucepan with the fat; cook, stirring, over moderate heat for 2 to 3 minutes. Add the peeled onions, cover and cook, shaking the pan occasionally, for 15 minutes, or until the onions are almost tender. Pour off any fat.

4 Add the tomato paste and stir until the onions take on a yellow-red tinge. Add ½ cup of the wine; bring to a boil, then reduce to a glaze. Add the mushrooms and cook over moderate heat, stirring from time to time, until most of the moisture in the pan evaporates, about 5 minutes. With a slotted spoon, transfer the mushrooms, onions, and pancetta to a side dish.

5 Pour 1 cup of the stock into the saucepan. Raise the heat and boil uncovered until the stock reduces to ¼ cup. Add another 1 cup of stock and repeat. Add the remaining 1 cup stock; reduce the heat to low and simmer, skimming from time to time, for 15 minutes, or the liquid is reduced to about ½ cup. Scrape the onions, mushrooms, and pancetta into the reduced stock. *(The recipe can be prepared to this point 2 to 3 hours in advance.)*

6 Place the 3 tablespoons oil in a large, heavy nonreactive skillet with a tight-fitting lid and set over high heat. Add the chickens, skin side down, cover, and cook for 5 minutes without lifting the lid. Uncover and wipe off the moisture on the lid. Replace the cover and continue cooking over high heat for 1 minute longer. (If your skillet is not large enough to handle all the chicken in 1 layer, brown in 2 batches in the same oil.)

7 Set the chickens aside. Discard the oil in the skillet. Pour in ½ cup of the wine and bring to a boil, scraping up any brown bits from the bottom of the pan. Boil until reduced to a glaze. Return the chicken, skin side up, to the skillet. Scatter the shallots around chicken, add the remaining 2 cups wine, and cook, uncovered, over moderately high heat for 20 minutes, or until the chickens are just cooked. Remove to a platter and cover to keep warm. Boil the wine in the skillet until reduced to a glaze.

8 Scrape the reserved onions, mushrooms, pancetta, and reduced stock into the skillet; reheat and quickly reduce, if necessary, to a thick and shiny sauce, skimming once or twice. Season with salt and pepper to taste. Pour over the chickens, sprinkle with parsley, and serve at once.

Inspired by a recipe from André Daguin.

*Avoid frozen hens; when fresh they are closest to a baby chicken.

CHICKEN WITH GARLIC PEARLS IN SAUTERNES

→ *Poulet aux Perles d'Ail Doux et au Sauternes*   SERVES 4

THE ORIGINAL WAY to prepare this old Gascon dish is to rub a tasty barnyard hen with garlic and then stuff it with many garlic cloves. The hen is then cooked slowly so that the cloves become soft but do not lose their shape. Later the pan is deglazed with Sauternes, which has a high concentration of sugar, and the garlic cloves are pulled out and left to caramelize in the pan juices. The following recipe is a sophisticated adaptation conceived by Alain Dutournier—more elegant, I think, than the original, and with a deep, rich flavor that is highly seductive.

The sauce base and the garlic cloves are prepared ahead of time, and the chicken, quartered, is broiled just before serving. Thus, one has an elegant dish with a minimum investment in last-minute work. The sauce is really the key: Chopped vegetables and bones are cooked in an open pan. A French Sauternes or American Sauterne is added gradually and allowed to boil away and caramelize before more is added, so that the color deepens as the taste of the vegetables and bones mellows; and the bouquet of the wine becomes intoxicatingly intense. The garlic cloves, cooked separately, are added at the last minute. This sauce can be made up in quantity and frozen, for use whenever you wish.

1 whole chicken, preferably organic free-range, about 3 pounds, with its neck and giblets

Salt and freshly ground pepper

⅔ cup crème fraîche

½ tablespoons olive oil or rendered poultry fat

1¾ cups thinly sliced onions

1⅔ cups thinly sliced carrots

1 leek, split, well washed, and thinly sliced

2 pounds meaty veal neck bones or riblets, cut into 1-inch pieces

1 bottle (750 ml) Sauterne(s), or other sweet white wine such as a Semillon blanc or Johannisberg Riesling

1½ cups unsalted chicken stock (storebought or homemade—page 405)

Herb bouquet: 3 sprigs parsley, 2 sprigs thyme, 1 leafy celery top, and 1 imported bay leaf tied together with string

2 good-sized heads of garlic, cloves separated but not peeled

1½ teaspoons unsalted butter

1½ teaspoons sugar

⅓ cup heavy cream

1 to 2 teaspoons fresh lemon juice, or more to taste

3 tablespoons unsalted butter (optional)

1 tablespoon chopped fresh flat-leaf parsley

1 Cut the chicken down the back along both sides of its backbone; remove and reserve the backbone. Cut the wings off at the second joint; set the wing tips aside. Quarter the chicken. Rub with salt, pepper, and crème fraîche. Refrigerate for at least 1 hour or overnight. Let return to room temperature before cooking.

2 Using a heavy cleaver, chop the chicken neck, backbone, and wing tips into small pieces. Slice the gizzard and set aside. To make the sauce, heat the olive oil in a large deep skillet, preferably copper or flameproof casserole over moderate heat. Add the onions, sliced carrots, and leek. Cover and cook for 5 minutes. Uncover and continue cooking, stirring frequently, until the vegetables are lightly browned around the edges, about 15 minutes.

3 Add the veal bones and chopped chicken bones. Raise the heat to moderately high and cook, stirring often, until the bones are browned all over, about 10 minutes. Drain off and discard the fat.

4 Pour 1 cup of the wine into the skillet and boil until the liquid is reduced to a glaze, about 20 minutes. Continue adding the wine, 1 cup at a time, reducing to a glaze after each addition; the bones and vegetables should begin to caramelize and turn orange-brown. Reduce the heat to low. Add the stock, herb bouquet, and reserved gizzard to the pan. Cover and cook for 1 hour.

5 Transfer the mixture to a sieve set over a deep bowl and strain, pressing down on the bones and vegetables with the back of a spoon to extract as much liquid as possible; discard the bones and vegetables. Strain the sauce through a fine-mesh sieve into a small saucepan. Skim off the fat that rises to the surface. Bring to a boil and set the saucepan half on and half off the heat. Simmer, skimming, for 10 to 15 minutes, or until reduced to 1 cup. Remove from the heat and set aside. *(The sauce can be prepared to this point up to several days in advance; refrigerate in a covered container.)*

6 Preheat the oven to 250°F. To make garlic pearls, bring 3 cups water to a boil in a small saucepan. Add the garlic cloves and boil for 3 minutes. Drain the garlic well; peel off the skins.

7 Melt 1½ teaspoons butter in a cast-iron skillet or other heavy ovenproof pan over very low heat. Add the garlic, sprinkle with the sugar, and cook in the oven, uncovered, until the garlic is very soft and golden—but not brown—about 2 hours, shaking the pan 2 or 3 times; do not stir, or the garlic will fall apart. *(The garlic can be prepared up to a day ahead.)*

8 Preheat the broiler. Lightly oil a broiler pan. Remove the chicken from the marinade and arrange the chicken, skin side down, on the pan. Broil about 6 inches from the heat for 10 minutes. Turn the chicken over, baste once with the crème fraîche marinade, and broil until the skin is crisp and the juices run clear when chicken is pierced with fork, about 5 to 7 minutes for the breasts, 10 to 12 minutes for the legs and thighs.

(continued)

9 Meanwhile, bring the reserved sauce to a boil over moderate heat. Add the heavy cream and continue boiling until the sauce is thick enough to coat a spoon, about 10 minutes. Reduce the heat to low and add the garlic pearls. Season with salt, pepper, and lemon juice to taste.

10 Cut chicken into smaller serving pieces and arrange attractively on a heated platter. Spoon the sauce on top. Garnish with parsley.

NOTE TO THE COOK

For a richer sauce, in Step 4, after seasoning the sauce, gently swirl in up to 3 tablespoons unsalted butter, ½ tablespoon at a time.

Chicken With Red Onion Sauce

➤➤ *Poulet aux Oignons de Trébous*   SERVES 4

IN THE FRENCH SOUTHWEST, you will find many dishes—chicken, veal, tuna, or duck—smothered in onions; a residue, possibly, of Moorish influence, since so many Moroccan dishes are structured this way. A Gascon friend told me I could not leave this dish out because it is a typical "mother's dish," as basic to Southwest cookery as beans and franks are to American.

I have spoken in the first introduction to this book of the role played by "Mother's cooking" in Southwest France. Pierre Veilletet, a journalist originally from the Landes, where this dish is much beloved, refers to this kind of matriarchal cooking as *la cuisine ombilicale*. Pierre speaks eloquently of the Southwest mothers and their total matriarchal power over everything that enters the mouth. For every problem, the mother-cook will offer a culinary solution: garlic bread for worms; soup for every ailment. Her great refrain is, "It's good for you, so eat!" Pierre refers to all this alleged knowledge as *la gastronostalgie*.

One thing I like about this dish is its utter simplicity. It requires no stock, just perfectly chosen ingredients: a fine, tasty chicken and a good-quality cured ham to complement the flavor of the red onions.

1 chicken (3½ pounds), quartered, at room temperature

Salt and freshly ground pepper

2 tablespoons rendered goose or duck fat

½ cup slivered jambon de Bayonne, prosciutto, or Serrano ham (2½ ounces)

2 pounds red onions, coarsely chopped

½ cup dry white wine

1 teaspoons chopped fresh flat-leaf parsley

2 teaspoons minced fresh chives

1 Season the chicken with salt and pepper. Heat the fat in a deep large heavy skillet over moderately high heat. Add the chicken quarters, skin side down, and cook until browned, 2 to 3 minutes per side, shaking the skillet to keep the chicken from sticking.

2 Add the diced ham, cover, and cook for 2 minutes. Add the red onions and cook, covered, over low heat for 5 minutes, or until they are soft but not brown.

3 Add the wine and bring to a boil, stirring. Cover tightly and cook over low heat for 20 minutes, turning the chicken once. *(The recipe can be prepared to this point up to 1 hour in advance.)*

4 About 15 minutes before serving, preheat the broiler. Arrange the cooked chicken quarters, skin side up, in a shallow flameproof baking dish. Run the chicken quarters under the broiler for 2 to 3 minutes to reheat and crisp the skin.

5 Meanwhile, boil the onions and cooking liquid in the skillet until the sauce is thick. Season with salt and pepper to taste. Pour the onion sauce over the chicken and broil for 30 seconds longer to glaze it. Decorate with the chopped parsley and chives and serve at once.

ROAST CHICKEN STUFFED WITH GARLIC CROUTONS IN THE STYLE OF THE CORRÈZE

→→ *Poularde Farcie en Chaponnade Comme en Corrèze*   SERVES 6

A PERFECTLY ROASTED chicken can be simplicity itself, elegant in concept and rustic in flavor. Basically, this is just a roasting chicken stuffed with slices of dry country bread (cut from large round loaves called *tourtes*) that have been rubbed with garlic and then sprinkled with salt, thyme, and walnut oil. The bread slices are called *la frotte* in the Corrèze. The special quality of this dish derives from the taste of the barding fat, which when melted is used as a basting medium, resulting in a rich, flavorful, crisp skin. After the chicken is roasted, the pieces of bread are pulled out and allowed to soak up the delicious juices in the pan.

1 whole roasting chicken, 5 to 5½ pounds

Salt and freshly ground pepper

2 tablespoons French walnut oil

1½ teaspoons finely chopped fresh garlic

1 sprig of fresh thyme or ¼ teaspoon dried thyme leaves

6 slices of country-style bread, cut ½ inch thick, crusts trimmed

2 to 3 thin slices of fatty pancetta

2 tablespoons rendered chicken, goose, or duck fat, or 2½ tablespoons unsalted butter

1 medium onion, chopped

1 large carrot, chopped

½ leek (white and tender green), thinly sliced

1 Position rack on lower oven shelf and preheat oven to 425°F. Remove all the fat from the chicken and reserve for rendering, if desired. Wipe out the cavity with a moistened paper towel. Season with salt and pepper. Trim the liver and heart. Peel the gizzard and chop it into small pieces. Discard the skin from neck. Chop the neck bone into 1- to 1½-inch pieces.

2 In small bowl, combine the oil, garlic, ¼ teaspoon salt, ⅛ teaspoon pepper, and the thyme; mix well. Brush each bread slice with the garlic oil. Stuff the cavity of the chicken with the bread slices; then tuck in the liver and heart. Truss the chicken loosely and pat dry with paper towels. Cover the breast with a thin layer of the pancetta and tie in place.

3 Melt the poultry fat or butter in a large flameproof casserole over low heat. Add the onion, carrot, and leek, cover, and cook until softened, about 5 minutes. Add the chopped gizzard and neck bones; cook, stirring, for 1 minute.

4 Roll the trussed chicken in the vegetable and bone mixture. Nestle the chicken upside down in the casserole, scattering some of the vegetables and bones on its back. Transfer to the oven and roast, uncovered, for 15 minutes.

5 Lower the oven temperature to 350°F. Turn the chicken onto its side. Cover with generously buttered parchment paper, then with a tight-fitting lid; roast for 20 minutes. Turn the chicken onto its other side, cover, and roast an additional 20 minutes. Set chicken breast side up and remove the pancetta. Continue roasting, uncovered, until golden brown, basting occasionally with the juices in the pan, about 20 minutes. The chicken is done if the juices run clear when the thickest part of the thigh is pierced or a meat thermometer registers 160°F.

6 Remove the chicken to a carving board, cover loosely with foil, and let rest. Quickly strain the cooking juices, pressing down on the vegetables and bones to extract all their flavor. Degrease the cooking juices. Deglaze the casserole with 1 cup water and bring to a boil, scraping up browned bits that cling to bottom and sides of pot. Return degreased cooking juices to the pot and boil down to about 1¼ cups. Taste the sauce and adjust seasoning.

7 Untie the chicken and spoon the stuffing onto a heated serving dish. Ladle about half the sauce over the stuffing to saturate it. Carve the chicken and arrange the pieces over the wet stuffing. Pass the remaining sauce separately.

CHICKEN IN A POT

→► *Poule au Pot à la Gasconne*   SERVES 4

CHARACTER AND FLAVOR are the best words to describe this culinary gem of the French Southwest. On farms where chickens still scratch the barnyard earth and are fed on maize, they stew in the pot for many hours before coming to table. I have rarely eaten such a bird since I lived in Morocco, where there was hardly anything else. We cooked these tough birds for at least 3½ hours, which resulted in tasty but still chewy flesh. I have adapted this recipe to work with the tender, quick-cooking roasting chickens that are easily available.

In the past, the vegetables simmered along with the chicken for hours. I like to freshly steam wedges of cabbage, chunks of carrots, turnips, and potatoes, then simmer them for about 10 minutes in the chicken broth. The flavors mingled, and the chicken, stuffing, stock, and vegetables had both character and old-fashioned good flavor. Serve with the accompanying tangy Green Sauce.

In the Périgord, a similar dish is served, but *sauce de Sorges* (Cooked Egg Sauce), as decribed on page 144, is the typical accompaniment. The true *poule au pot* from the Béarn, the ultimate "mother" version from which all other regional recipes have been derived, always includes a stuffing flavored with marjoram and thyme. Otherwise, the dish is exactly the same as one I present here. This Gascon version was taught to me by Roger Duffour.

1 whole chicken, 3½ to 4 pounds

5 quarts Stock for Chicken in a Pot (page 146)

1 egg

½ cup fresh bread crumbs

½ pound jambon de Bayonne, prosciutto, or Serrano ham

1 small onion, quartered

2 shallots, coarsely chopped

2 garlic cloves, chopped

3 chicken livers, trimmed

2 teaspoons chopped fresh flat-leaf parsley

1 teaspoon fresh thyme leaves

Pinch of sugar

Salt and freshly ground pepper

Green Sauce (at right)

Freshly steamed wedges of cabbage, chunks of carrots, turnips, and potatoes as garnish

1 Remove all excess fat from the cavity of the chicken; reserve for stock or rendering, if desired. Rinse the chicken well and pat dry. Slowly reheat the prepared stock.

2 Make the stuffing: In a medium bowl, lightly beat the egg with a fork. Add the bread crumbs and stir to mix. In a food processor, pulse the ham until coarsely ground. Add the onion, shallots, garlic, chicken livers, parsley, thyme, and sugar. Process until well blended. Add to the bread crumbs and blend with a fork or with your hands to mix. Season lightly with salt and pepper to taste. Stuff the chicken, sew up the openings carefully, and truss securely.

3 Slip the stuffed chicken into the simmering stock. Bring almost to a boil, then lower the heat and simmer, partially covered, for 1¼ hours, or until the internal temperature of the thigh reaches 160°F. Transfer the chicken to a carving board and let rest for at least 10 minutes.

4 To serve, remove the strings. Turn the chicken upside down and with poultry scissors, cut along either side of the backbone to remove it. Pry the chicken open and remove the stuffing on one piece. Quarter the chicken and slice the stuffing. Put the chicken in the center of a heated platter. Arrange the stuffing in overlapping slices around the chicken. Spoon a few tablespoons hot stock over the chicken to moisten. Serve with the steamed vegetables and the Green Sauce.

NOTE TO THE COOK

After the dish has been served, cool the stock, and degrease completely. Reduce to 2 quarts. Cool, cover, and refrigerate or freeze for use in other dishes.

GREEN SAUCE

MAKES ABOUT 1 CUP

3 hard-cooked egg yolks

4 teaspoons wine vinegar

½ cup extra virgin olive oil

2 tablespoons chopped fresh flat-leaf parsley

2 teaspoons chopped shallots

Salt and freshly ground pepper

In a food processor, combine the egg yolks and vinegar; whirl to blend. With the machine on, add the olive oil in a slow, steady stream. Scrape into a small bowl. Stir in the parsley and shallots. Season with salt and pepper to taste. The sauce is best prepared several hours in advance.

STOCK FOR CHICKEN IN A POT

2 medium onions, halved, with skin on

3 pounds veal bones

3 pounds inexpensive chicken parts (wings, neck, backs, and feet) plus any loose chicken fat

1 large leek, halved, well washed, and cut into 3-inch lengths

2 celery ribs, cut up

½ bunch of parsley stems

1 tablespoon tomato paste

1 imported bay leaf

¼ teaspoon dried thyme

2 tablespoons coarse kosher salt

⅛ teaspoon each: freshly grated nutmeg, freshly ground black pepper, ground cloves, ground ginger, and cayenne

6 garlic cloves, whole and unpeeled

1 Place onion halves cut sides down on an ungreased griddle or over an open flame until browned, about 5 minutes.

2 Place the veal bones and chicken parts in a deep 7- or 8-quart kettle, stockpot, or casserole. Add 5 quarts cold water and bring to a boil. Simmer, uncovered, for 10 minutes, skimming often. When the liquid is clear, add the browned onion, leek, celery, parsley, tomato paste, bay leaf, thyme, salt, and the nutmeg, pepper, cloves, ginger, cayenne, and garlic.

3 Return to a boil; lower the heat and allow the stock to simmer gently, partially covered, for 3 to 4 hours. When the stock is full flavored, strain to remove the vegetables and bones. Measure the stock back into the pot, adding enough cold water to make 5 quarts.

CHICKEN BREASTS WITH PINE NUTS, CÈPES, AND HAM GOUDALIÈRE

→ *Blanc de Volaille à la Goudalière*

THIS CHICKEN DISH, one of the best from the Landes, is garnished with pine nuts, cèpes, and country-cured ham. (*Goudalière* is a Landais word for a gastronomic society.) Today the Landes region is filled with pine trees, planted over a hundred years ago to hold back the erosion of marshy areas. It is not surprising, therefore, to find pine nuts in many local recipes. The tiny nuts are used in cookies and cakes, sautéed with grilled wild birds, and, as in this recipe, simply sprinkled over the dish.

The original version of this dish calls for a sturdy local wine, Tursan, which tasted to me like a mixture of vermouth and lemon juice—a combination I have employed for the base of the sauce. A well-reduced demi-glace is very important to the success of this dish: The richer it is, the less butter will be needed to thicken the sauce. The method of cooking chicken breasts in a reduced demi-glace is an unusual technique but one that results in an extremely succulent, silky piece of meat.

2 ounces dried French cèpes or Italian porcini, or, if available, 1 pound fresh or 1 can (10 ounces) whole or quartered cèpes (see Note, page 149)

3 tablespoons pine nuts

4 large chicken breast halves on the bone (about 10 to 12 ounces each), at room temperature

Salt and freshly ground pepper

8 tablespoons (1 stick) unsalted butter

1½ tablespoons chopped shallots

1½ tablespoons fresh lemon juice

1½ tablespoons dry vermouth or dry white wine

1 cup demi-glace (storebought or homemade—page 406) or 3 cups rich unsalted chicken stock (storebought or homemade—page 405) or duck stock (page 407) reduced to 1 cup

2 tablespoons rendered duck fat or extra virgin olive oil

12 ounces fresh white mushrooms, quartered

1½ tablespoons finely chopped fresh flat-leaf parsley

1 teaspoon minced fresh garlic

3 to 4 ounces jambon de Bayonne, prosciutto, or Serrano ham, cut into ½-inch cubes

1 tablespoon Cognac

(continued)

1 Set an oven rack on the lowest shelf and preheat the oven to 300°F. Cover the dried mushrooms with hot water. Let stand for 30 minutes to soften.

2 Put the pine nuts in a small baking dish and toast until golden and fragrant, about 10 minutes. Remove to a small dish and set aside. Leave the oven on.

3 Rinse the chicken breasts and pat dry with paper towels. Season generously with salt and place, skin side down, in a hot cast-iron or other ovenproof skillet with 3 tablespoons of the butter over moderately high heat. Cook until the skin begins to turn golden, about 3 minutes. Do not turn the chicken over. Tilt the skillet and remove excess fat. Add the shallots, lemon juice, and vermouth. Continue cooking over moderately high heat until the juices are reduced to a glaze.

4 Add ¼ cup of the demi-glace. Cover the skillet tightly and transfer to the oven. Roast until the chicken is just firm to the touch, 15 to 20 minutes. (The breasts are not turned over at any time.)

5 Meanwhile, drain the cèpes in a sieve set over a small bowl. Strain the soaking liquid through a paper coffee filter or several layers of damp cheesecloth; set aside. Rinse the cèpes with cold water to remove any remaining dirt or sand. Drain dry.

6 Heat the duck fat in a 10-inch skillet over moderate heat. Add the cèpes and fresh mushrooms and sauté for 5 minutes. Add the reserved soaking liquid and cook until reduced to a glaze, about 10 minutes. Add the parsley, garlic, and salt to taste. Toss lightly until well blended. Transfer the mushroom mixture to a small bowl.

7 Add the ham cubes to the same skillet. Place over low heat, cover, and cook for 2 to 3 minutes. Return the mushroom mixture to the skillet and toss. Remove from the heat.

8 Transfer the chicken breasts to a carving board; set the skillet aside. Use a thin-bladed knife to lift each breast off the bones in one piece. If the breasts are not fully cooked, return to the cooking liquid in the skillet to poach gently, for 1 to 2 minutes, or until done. Place the chicken skin side up on a work surface. Slice each breast into 4 slices diagonally against the grain. Arrange the chicken slices on a heated serving dish, overlapping them slightly.

9 Skim off the fat from the cooking liquid. Add the remaining demi-glace. Place the skillet over moderately high heat and boil until the liquid is reduced by half, about 5 minutes. Remove the sauce from heat and swirl in the remaining butter, 1 tablespoon at a time to thicken. (You may not need all of the butter.) Swirl in the Cognac and season with salt and pepper to taste. Do not heat further, or the sauce will separate.

10 Strain the sauce over the chicken. Reheat the mushroom and ham mixture over moderately high heat until warmed through and spoon over the chicken. Sprinkle the pine nuts on top and serve.

NOTE TO THE COOK

If using canned or fresh cèpes, omit Steps 1 and 5. Drain and dry the canned cèpes. Dice the stems and quarter the caps. For Step 6, heat 2 to 3 tablespoons duck fat in a skillet until very hot. Add the caps and stems; simmer for 5 minutes for canned or simmer, covered, 10 minutes for fresh cèpes. Uncover and cook until the oil is clear. Then add the parsley, garlic, and salt to taste.

Inspired by a recipe from Bernard Cousseau.

CHICKEN BREASTS WITH GARLIC WINE
Poulet au Vin d'Ail   SERVES 4

CHEF MICHEL TRAMA runs one of the French Southwest's culinary treasures, Les Loges de l'Aubergade, a stylish three-star restaurant in the region of the Agen. There he produces ethereal, flawlessly balanced dishes using local products. This deceptively simple recipe includes chicken breasts coated in a sweet nutty flavored sauce made with garlic-infused white wine.

¾ cup Garlic Wine (page 150)	2 tablespoons clarified butter
4 boneless chicken breast halves, skin on	1 tablespoon extra virgin olive oil
Coarse kosher salt and freshly ground pepper	2 teaspoons fresh tarragon, plus additional for seasoning
Flour, for dredging	⅓ cup heavy cream

1 Make the Garlic Wine 1 to 2 days in advance.

2 Trim the chicken breasts and cut away fat and sinews. Remove the thin fillet that looks like a long strip on the boned side (Save these strips in the refrigerator or freezer for use at some other time for a quick sauté.) Place the chicken breasts between sheets of plastic wrap and flatten lightly with a rolling pin. Season with salt and pepper. Dredge the breasts in flour, shaking off the excess.

(continued)

3 Heat the clarified butter and oil in a large skillet over moderately high heat until sizzling. Add the chicken breasts and on both sides, until lightly browned and just cooked through, about 5 minutes. Transfer the chicken to a platter and cover with foil to keep warm.

4 Discard all but 1 tablespoon fat from the skillet. Add the tarragon and cook over gentle heat for 10 seconds. Deglaze with the garlic wine and ⅓ cup water and bring to a boil. Add the cream and boil to reduce until thick enough to coat a spoon. Adjust the seasoning with salt, pepper, and more tarragon to taste. Pour the sauce over the chicken and serve at once.

GARLIC WINE

MAKES 1 CUP

9 garlic cloves

2 sprigs of thyme

2 sprigs of tarragon

¼ teaspoon freshly crushed peppercorns

1 cup dry white wine

1 Halve the garlic cloves. If you see any green shoots, remove them. Put the garlic, thyme, tarragon, and crushed peppercorns in a 1-pint canning jar.

2 Bring the wine to a boil in an enameled or stainless-steel saucepan. Pour over the garlic and seasonings in the jar. Let cool, then cover and refrigerate for 1 to 2 days.

3 Strain the wine through cheesecloth and return to a clean jar; discard the solids. Cover and refrigerate until ready to use.

POACHED CHICKEN BREAST, AUVERGNE STYLE

Le Blanc de Poulet Farci Comme en Auvergne   SERVES 6

I THINK THIS IS ONE of the gastronomic gems of the French Southwest—a poached chicken breast protected during slow cooking by a thick coating of herbal stuffing, all wrapped in cabbage leaves. The stuffing is exceptionally light because the moistened bread is mashed by hand with a fork instead of being pulverized in a food processor. Its wonderful aromatic flavor comes from the combination of Swiss chard and fresh herbs. Do not grind the greens in your food processor; instead, cut them with a knife so as not to "break" their special sweet flavor and to retain their character.

Taste the delicious bouillon after the chicken is removed; it is a culinary miracle. A slice of the thick breast will sit in a soup bowl on a bed of carrots, turnips, and leeks, all moistened by this incredible poultry bouillon. Freeze the rest for other soups and stews. The addition of fragrant walnut oil to a finished dish is particular to some parts of the French Southwest and especially in the Auvergne. Present the dish on very hot plates and pass plenty of crusty French bread.

Swiss Chard, Giblet, and Ham Stuffing (pages 152–153)	3 small leeks (white and tender green), halved lengthwise
12 large cabbage leaves from a fresh, crisp head	6 young carrots, peeled and sliced on the diagonal
6 large skinless, boneless chicken breast halves	6 small turnips, peeled and quartered
2½ quarts unsalted chicken stock (storebought or homemade—page 405)	Coarse sea salt, preferably fleur de sel
	1 tablespoon French walnut oil

1 Up to a day ahead, make the stuffing.

2 About 2 hours before serving, blanch the cabbage leaves for 5 minutes in boiling salted water. Rinse under cold running water and drain. If the ribs are very thick, shave them off with a knife.

3 Enclose each chicken breast in ⅓ cup of the stuffing. Wrap each breast in 2 cabbage leaves, rib sides out, and tie securely with string. (If desired, wrap each cabbage roll in a 12-inch square of cheesecloth and tie with string.)

(continued)

4 About 1 hour before serving, bring the stock to a boil in a 5-quart casserole. Add the leeks, carrots, and turnips and simmer until tender, about 20 minutes. Remove the vegetables and set aside.

5 Add the cabbage rolls to the simmering broth and poach them over low heat for 25 minutes. Remove the cabbage rolls to a work surface and let them rest for 5 minutes. Remove the strings (and cheesecloth, if used) from the cabbage rolls.

6 Meanwhile, reheat the vegetables in the stock; drain. Cut each cabbage roll into 4 slices slightly on the diagonal. Arrange the slices cut sides up, on warmed plates. Sprinkle the chicken with fleur de sel. Surround each serving with assorted vegetables; moisten with a few tablespoons of the cooking liquid. Drizzle a little walnut oil over the chicken and vegetables and serve at once.

SWISS CHARD, GIBLET, AND HAM STUFFING   MAKES 2 CUPS

2 chicken livers

2 cups cubed stale firm white bread, crustless

⅔ cup milk

½ teaspoon salt

4 medium-large Swiss chard leaves

3 chicken hearts, trimmed

3 chicken gizzards, trimmed

3 ounces jambon de Bayonne, Serrano ham, or prosciutto

2½ ounces ventrèche or pancetta

½ small onion, peeled and quartered

1 large shallot, peeled

4 teaspoons flour

1 large egg, lightly beaten

1½ tablespoons minced fresh chives

1½ tablespoons finely chopped fresh flat-leaf parsley

½ teaspoon salt

¼ teaspoon freshly ground pepper

⅛ teaspoon of freshly grated nutmeg or ground allspice

Pinch of sugar

1 Trim any yellow fat or green spots from the chicken livers. Soak them in ⅓ cup of the milk with the salt in the refrigerator for at least 3 hours. Drain, rinse, and pat dry.

2 In large saucepan of boiling salted water, blanch the Swiss chard leaves (save the stalks for another use) for 1 minute. Drain, rinse under cold running water until the water runs clear, and squeeze dry. Finely chop the Swiss chard.

3 In a food processor, combine the chicken livers, hearts, gizzards, ham, and ventrèche. Pulse until coarsely chopped. Add the onion, shallot, and flour and process until well blended.

4 In a mixing bowl, soak the bread in the remaining ⅓ cup milk for a few minutes to soften. Press out and discard the excess moisture; leave the bread in the bowl. Add the egg and mix with a fork until they are light and well combined. Mash in the chicken liver mixture, then add the Swiss chard, chives, and parsley. Season with the salt, pepper, nutmeg, and sugar. Cover and refrigerate the stuffing for at least 2 hours or overnight to mellow and firm up.

Inspired by a recipe from Michel Bras.

CHICKEN, POTATO, AND ARTICHOKE CAKE

*Gâteau de Cuisse de Poulette aux
Pommes de Terre et aux Artichauts*　　　　　SERVES 6

THIS IS A MODERN VERSION of a little-known nineteenth-century dish called *gâteau de Père Lathuile*, which was a very famous and loved dish at Lucien Vanel's restaurant in Toulouse. It may look long and difficult, but it isn't. It is a "cake" created with sautéed slices of potato layered into a round shape, the center filled with boned chicken and artichoke bottoms. Each individual serving is decorated with strands of fried onions and sprigs of parsley. Vanel used to add cubes of slow-fried eggplant.

Père Lathuile was a farmer who lived outside Paris in Barrière de Clichy in the early part of the nineteenth century. He had a little restaurant there where he served this dish, made from chickens he raised himself. In the spring of 1814, when imperial guardsmen of the Russian czar were skirmishing with the French in the suburbs of Paris, Maréchal Adrien Moncey installed his general quarters on Lathuile's property, at which time Père Lathuile offered all his provisions and wines to Moncey's troops. "Eat, drink, my children! Nothing must be left for the enemy!" he said. From that moment, his establishment became famous. People thronged there to eat his famous cake of chicken with potatoes and artichokes. Later, Manet would use the restaurant as a setting for one of his paintings.

(continued)

1 pound purple eggplant, peeled and cut into 1-inch chunks

Coarse kosher salt

6 skinned and boned chicken thighs, trimmed of excess fat, at room temperature

Freshly ground pepper

⅓ cup rendered duck fat or clarified butter

1 cup finely diced ventrèche or pancetta

1 cup cubed (½ inch) blanched fresh or thawed frozen artichoke bottoms

⅓ cup dry white wine

⅓ cup unsalted chicken stock (storebought or homemade—page 405)

3 tablespoons minced fresh chives

2 teaspoons fresh thyme leaves

Juice of ½ lemon

Pinch of sugar

1 tablespoon chopped fresh flat-leaf parsley

1 teaspoon finely chopped fresh garlic

2 pounds russet potatoes

2 tablespoons olive oil

Coarse sea salt

1 Sprinkle the eggplant with 1½ tablespoons coarse salt and let stand for at least 2 hours. Rinse the eggplant chunks under running water; squeeze out as much moisture as possible. Do not worry about maintaining the shape; you should have about 1 cup dry clumps of eggplant.

2 Season the chicken thighs with salt and pepper. Heat 2 tablespoons of the duck fat or clarified butter in a medium skillet, preferably nonstick, over moderate heat. Add the ventrèche and brown lightly. Raise the heat and, working in batches, add the chicken and sear 30 seconds to a side; transfer to a platter to cool. Then cut each thigh into 6 pieces.

3 Add the artichokes to the hot skillet and cook, stirring, with the pan juices until just golden around the edges, 1 to 2 minutes. Using a slotted spoon transfer the artichokes to a bowl. Pour off the fat. Deglaze the skillet with a little white wine and stock and boil down to a syrupy glaze. Scrape into the bowl with the artichokes. Add the chicken chunks, chives, thyme, and 1 tablespoon of the lemon juice. Season with 1 teaspoon salt and ½ teaspoon pepper and toss lightly to mix. Cover and set aside.

4 Preheat the oven to 450°F. Heat the remaining 2 tablespoons duck fat in a large nonstick skillet over moderate heat. Add the eggplant, cover, and cook, turning the clumps from time to time, until they begin to plump up, feel tender, and turn golden brown, about 10 minutes. At this point, reduce the heat to low, add a pinch of sugar, and slowly cook, uncovered, turning the pieces of eggplant often, for 5 minutes. Add the chopped parsley and garlic and continue to cook, turning often, for another 5 to 8 minutes, or until the eggplant has a glowing, bronzed, moist appearance. Set aside on paper towels to absorb any excess fat.

5 Peel the potatoes, halve lengthwise, and cut into long thin slices. Wash well to remove their starch and pat dry with paper towels. In the same skillet used to cook the eggplant, set the olive oil over moderate heat. Working in batches, add the potato slices and cook until just pliable, 2 to 3 minutes.

6 Arrange a generous third of the potatoes slices, overlapping, in the bottom of a buttered, 9-inch straight-sided cast-iron skillet, copper tart tatin pan, or 6- or 7-cup shallow ovenproof baking dish. Cover with the chicken, pancetta, artichokes, and eggplant. Arrange the remaining potatoes on top and cover with a sheet of foil. Crimp the foil against the edge of the pan to seal tightly.

7 Bake in the center of the oven for 20 minutes. Remove the foil, press the pie down, and continue baking, uncovered, for 30 minutes longer. Brush the top with the remaining duck fat and place under the broiler for a minute or two to brown. Serve in the pan with a sprinkling of sea salt.

CHICKEN THIGHS WITH PINEAU DE CHARENTES
Cuisses de Volaille au Pineau   SERVES 4

HERE'S A SUCCULENT, easy-to-prepare chicken dish from the Cognac region, the "greater" French Southwest, that combines the earthiness of bolete mushrooms with the fruity, floral taste and aroma of the distilled white liqueur Pineau des Charentes. According to legend, Pineau was "discovered" in the sixteenth century when a vintner accidentally added grape must into a barrel containing eau-de-vie made from Cognac.

The sauce here is "short," meaning there isn't much of it, but it's strong and aromatic, and every drop—just like the Pineau—is downright luscious.

(continued)

½ ounce dried French cèpes or Italian porcini

5 tablespoons unsalted butter

2 pounds chicken thighs, 6 to 8 pieces, preferably from free-range chickens

Salt and freshly ground pepper

1 cup Pineau de Charentes, or substitute 2 tablespoons Armagnac or Cognac mixed with 1 cup semisweet white wine

1 tablespoon finely chopped shallots

½ pound fresh cremini or white mushrooms, quartered

½ cup heavy cream

1 tablespoon minced fresh chives

2 teaspoons finely chopped fresh flat-leaf parsley

1 Crumble the cèpes or porcini into a strainer and rinse well under cold running water. Put in a bowl and cover with 1 cup hot water. Let stand for at least 30 minutes. Drain the cèpes into a sieve lined with a paper coffee filter or several layers of damp cheesecloth set over a small bowl; reserve the cèpes and soaking liquid separately.

2 Set a heavy 12-inch skillet over moderately high heat. Add 3 tablespoons of the butter; as soon as it sizzles, add the chicken thighs, skin side down. Season with salt and pepper and cook without turning just until browned, about 5 minutes. Tilt the skillet and remove almost all the fat. Add the Pineau and, using a long kitchen match and averting your face, carefully ignite the liquid while it is still warm; the flames will flare quite high. When the flames subside, add the shallots and continue cooking, stirring, for 1 minute. Turn the chicken over, cover the skillet, and continue cooking over moderate heat until the juices from the thighs run clear when pricked and the pan juices are reduced to a glaze, about 25 minutes. Turn the chicken over and glaze the skin, then transfer the contents of the skillet to a platter. Wipe out the skillet.

3 Melt the remaining 2 tablespoons butter in the skillet over moderate heat. Add the cèpes and fresh mushrooms and sauté for 5 minutes. Add the reserved soaking liquid and cook until reduced to a glaze, about 10 minutes. Add the heavy cream and boil until reduced to a sauce consistency, about 5 minutes.

4 Return the chicken thighs to the skillet, skin side up, partially cover, and gently reheat. Adjust the seasoning with salt and pepper. Serve at once with a dusting of parsley and chives.

Chicken Legs With Sour Grape Sauce in the Style of the Dordogne

→→ *Cuisses de Poulet au Verjus à la Dordogne*   SERVES 6

VERJUS IS MADE from sour green grapes. You can make it yourself and freeze it, as described on page 34, or purchase a bottle. Its tart, fruity flavor provides a refreshing balance to the garlic, which becomes very sweet after cooking. Sarlat Potatoes (pages 342–343) go wonderfully with this dish.

4 pounds meaty chicken legs, at room temperature

Salt and freshly ground pepper

4½ tablespoons unsalted butter

12 plump garlic cloves, whole but not peeled

⅓ cup dry white wine

6 to 7 tablespoons *verjus*

3 cups unsalted chicken stock (storebought or homemade—page 405), reduced to 1 cup

3 dozen sour green grapes

1½ tablespoons chopped fresh flat-leaf parsley

1 Trim away any excess fat from the chicken legs. Dry well and rub with salt and pepper.

2 Set a large, deep skillet, preferably a sauteuse, over moderately high heat. Add 2½ tablespoons of the butter, then the chicken, skin side down, and the garlic cloves. Brown for 1 minute each side, shaking the skillet to keep the chicken and garlic from sticking.

3 Reduce the heat to low, cover the skillet tightly, and cook for 10 minutes. Uncover the skillet, tilt, and skim the fat off the pan juices. Turn the chicken over. Add the white wine; cover again, and cook slowly for another 10 minutes.

4 Uncover the skillet; add 5 tablespoons of the verjus and quickly cover the pan so that chicken pieces absorb all the aroma and flavor. Cook slowly for 5 minutes longer.

5 Add ¾ cup of the stock and cook for 5 minutes. Raise the heat; add the butter and the remaining stock and verjus. Swirl over heat to combine. Add the grapes and just warm through. Season the sauce with salt and pepper to taste.

6 Arrange the chicken, garlic, and grapes on a warm platter. Pour the sauce over the chicken. Sprinkle with the parsley and serve hot.

Sauté of Chicken With Peppers, Ham, and Tomatoes

➤ *Poulet à la Basquaise*   SERVES 6

THERE ARE A HUNDRED interpretations of this classic dish; mine is easy to make and tastes especially good on account of the addition of Espelette pepper, now available dried and powdered or as a crème or puree (see Mail Order Sources, pages 415–417). With Espelette pepper, you taste flavor, not just heat. If for some reason you can't find Espelette, substitute a good spicy paprika or mildly hot New Mexican pepper around 4 on the Scoville scale. (Note that the Scoville number 10 is the hottest pepper.)

6 chicken legs (3 to 4 pounds), at room temperature

Salt and freshly ground pepper

Flour, for dusting

2 tablespoons rendered duck fat (see page 169) or olive oil

2 ounces ventrèche or pancetta, diced

1 cup coarsely chopped onion

1 cup coarsely chopped red bell peppers

4 garlic cloves, peeled and sliced

2 ounces jambon de Bayonne, prosciutto, or Serrano ham, diced or slivered

2 pounds ripe tomatoes, halved, seeded, and grated, or 1½ cups homemade tomato sauce

Pinch of sugar

1 teaspoon crème de piment d'Espelette or ½ teaspoon ground piment d'Espelette

1 tablespoon chopped fresh flat-leaf parsley

1 Generously season half the chicken with salt and pepper and lightly dust with flour, tapping off any excess. Heat a large enameled cast-iron skillet over moderately high heat. Add the duck fat and, when almost smoking, add the seasoned chicken, skin side down, and the ventrèche. Cook over moderately high heat until crusty and a deep golden brown, about 5 minutes. Turn over and brown the other side, about 5 minutes longer. Remove the chicken and ventrèche to a side dish. Repeat the seasoning, flouring, and frying of the remaining chicken.

2 Add the onion and brown lightly around the edges. Add the bell pepper, garlic, ham, tomatoes, sugar, and piment d'Espelette. Cover and cook over low heat for 15 minutes.

3 Lay the chicken pieces, skin side up, on top of the tomato sauce, cover, and cook for 10 minutes longer. Remove from the heat and let rest, covered, for 10 more minutes, or until the chicken is tender.

4 To serve, gently reheat the chicken and sauce. Spoon most of the sauce onto a deep platter, leaving a few tablespoons in the skillet. Over moderate heat, turn the chicken pieces in the remaining sauce to glaze. Garnish with parsley and serve.

Ragout of Chicken Wings in the Style of the Béarn

→→ *Alycot Béarnaise*   SERVES 4 TO 5

THIS DISH, SOMETIMES called *alicuit* or *alycou* (*aile* for wing; *cou* for neck), is made all over Southwest France. This particular recipe, from the town of Pau in the Béarn, is interesting because it uses cinnamon, an uncommon spice in French cooking. Here the cinnamon has a moderating influence on the garlic and onion in the sauce.

Although my version uses only chicken wings, it is more typical to include necks and gizzards as well. This dish is excellent with fresh noodles. The ragout can be made in advance and reheated.

12 chicken wings, tips removed at second joint and reserved for stock

Salt and freshly ground pepper

⅓ cup rendered chicken or duck fat

1 cup coarsely chopped onions

1½ ounces jambon de Bayonne, prosciutto, or Serrano ham, cubed

1½ cups unsalted chicken stock (storebought or homemade—page 405) or Dark, Rich Duck Stock (page 407)

¾ cup peeled, seeded, and cubed fresh tomatoes (about 1 large tomato) or drained canned Italian tomatoes

2 large garlic cloves, halved

¼ teaspoon ground piment d'Espelette or ½ teaspoon crème or purée d'Espelette

Pinch of ground cloves

Pinch of freshly grated nutmeg

1 cinnamon stick

2 bunches of scallions (white and about ¾ inch of green)

3 large carrots, peeled and cut into 1-inch chunks

1 tablespoon chopped fresh flat-leaf parsley

(continued)

1 Pat the wings dry with paper towels. Lightly season with salt and pepper. Heat the rendered fat in a 4-quart flameproof casserole or Dutch oven over moderately high heat. Add the chicken wings and cook, turning, until lightly browned, about 5 minutes.

2 Add the onions and cook until lightly browned, about 5 minutes. Reduce the heat to moderate, add the cubed ham, and cook for 2 to 3 minutes, tossing lightly. Remove excess fat by tilting the pan and pressing on the wings and onions with the back of a slotted spoon. Blot with paper towels. Add the stock to the casserole and bring to a boil. Reduce the heat to very low and simmer for 5 minutes, skimming the foam from the surface. Stir in the tomatoes, garlic, red pepper, cloves, nutmeg, and cinnamon stick. Cover and simmer for 1 hour.

3 Add the scallions and carrots to the casserole. Simmer very gently for 1 hour longer.

4 Using a slotted spoon, remove the chicken wings, scallions, and carrots from the saucepan. Arrange in a shallow serving dish. Cover to keep warm. Bring the sauce in the casserole to a boil over high heat and boil until reduced to 1½ cups, about 20 minutes. Taste and adjust the seasoning; the sauce should be peppery but still tempered by sweet spices. Remove and discard the cinnamon stick. Pour the sauce over the wings and garnish with the parsley.

NOTES TO THE COOK

→ Use 6 chicken wings plus 3 necks and 3 gizzards instead of 12 wings. Slip off the neck skin and discard. Cut each neck into 3 or 4 pieces. Clean the gizzard. Using a thin-bladed knife, cut away and discard the hard yellow peel as well as the white membrane. Discard any yellow-green parts. Toss wings, necks, and gizzards with salt and pepper. Refrigerate until ready to cook.

→ Substitute duck wings for the chicken wings.

CHICKEN WITH SALSIFY IN PASTRY

Tourtière du Périgord aux Salsifis

SERVES 6 TO 8

THIS IS A WONDERFUL RAGOUT of chicken thighs and salsify wrapped in pastry. It is a specialty served around Mardi Gras in the Corrèze, the Périgord, and the Quercy. Originally it was prepared in a special three-legged iron or unlined copper pot (called a *tourtière*) placed in the fireplace and surrounded by embers.

White salsify, also called oyster plant, tastes to some like oysters and to others somewhat like asparagus with lemon. It is sometimes available in farmers' markets in late winter and early spring. Frenchselections.com carries canned, cooked and cut, salsify imported from France. But other root vegetables can also be used. See the Note on (page 163) on how to substitute fresh parsnips. In the Périgord some cooks substitute quickly sautéed chanterelle mushrooms tossed with garlic and parsley or cubed ham and peas.

Begin 1 day in advance.

1 recipe Pâte Brisée (page 92)	1½ tablespoons balsamic vinegar
8 chicken thighs, fat removed, about 2 pounds	2½ cups unsalted chicken stock (storebought or homemade—page 405)
Salt and freshly ground pepper	¾ cup heavy cream
1 clove garlic, halved plus ¼ teaspoon finely chopped fresh garlic	2 bunches firm white salsify (about 1 pound), or 2 cans (8.81 ounces) cooked salsify
1½ lemons (3 to 4 tablespoons strained fresh juice)	4 tablespoons softened unsalted butter
Pinch of crumbled thyme leaves	1½ tablespoons chopped fresh flat-leaf parsley
Pinch of ground bay leaf	1½ tablespoons minced fresh chives
2 tablespoons rendered poultry fat	1 egg yolk beaten with 1 tablespoon heavy cream
3 ounces lean pancetta, cut into ¼-inch dice	
1 cup thinly sliced onions	

(continued)

1 Make the pastry dough.

2 Rub the chicken thighs with salt, pepper, and half a garlic clove. Sprinkle with the juice of ½ lemon (about 1½ tablespoons), the thyme, and bay leaf, and let marinate in the refrigerator at least 3 hours. Remove from refrigerator 30 minutes before cooking.

3 In a large skillet, heat the fat over medium-high heat. Add the pancetta and sauté 5 minutes, transferring the pieces to a 3-quart flameproof casserole or Dutch oven as they are browned.

4 Pat the chicken dry. In the same skillet, brown the chicken thighs, a few at a time, transferring them to the casserole as they are lightly browned, about 3 minutes per side.

5 Pour off half the fat from the skillet. Add the onions; cook over high heat 2 minutes, stirring constantly. Using a slotted spoon, transfer the onions to the casserole.

6 Deglaze the skillet with the vinegar. Add 2 cups of the stock and bring to a boil, skimming. Scrape up all the bits and pieces that cling to the bottom of the skillet. Pour the boiling stock over the chicken, onions, and salt pork and cook, covered, over medium-low heat 20 minutes. Set the skillet aside.

7 Remove the chicken from the casserole and remove all the bones and gristle (add to your stockpot if you have one on the fire).

8 Strain the liquid (reserving the pancetta and onions) and skim to remove fat. Mix the chicken, onions, and pancetta in a bowl. Return the liquid to the casserole; reduce to 1½ cups over high heat, if necessary. Add the cream and boil down to about 1 cup. Pour over the still-warm chicken mixture. Let cool, uncovered.

9 Sauté the salsify in the same skillet in which the chicken was browned, in 3 tablespoons of the butter, 1 to 2 minutes. Season to taste with pepper. Add the remaining ½ cup stock and boil down to a glaze, shaking the skillet often to glaze the salsify and prevent burning. Sprinkle with parsley, chives, and chopped garlic. Season with salt to taste. Fold the salsify into the chicken-sauce mixture. Adjust the seasoning, adding a teaspoon or more of strained lemon juice. Allow to cool, uncovered, then cover and refrigerate. *(The recipe can be prepared to this point up to 1 day in advance.)*

10 Preheat oven to 400°F. Butter a 9-inch pie pan. Between sheets of waxed paper, roll out half the dough into a thin 11-inch round. Fit into the prepared pie pan. Prick the bottom and sides with a fork; brush a sheet of waxed paper with the remaining tablespoon softened butter and place it buttered side down on pastry. Fill with rice, beans, or aluminum weights. Bake 10 minutes. Remove the weights and paper; lower the oven temperature to 375°F and bake 5 minutes longer. Cool the pastry in the pan on a rack.

11 Fill pastry-lined pan with the chicken mixture. Roll out the remaining dough to a 9½-inch circle. Moisten around the edges with water, cover the tourtière with dough, and crimp to seal. Chill at least 15 minutes before baking.

12 One hour before serving, position an oven rack on the lower-center oven shelf and line the rack with a baking stone, quarry tile, or heavy black baking sheet. Preheat the oven to 375°F. Make 3 small openings in the top of the tourtière and insert a funnel in each to allow steam to escape during baking. Make decorative lines on the pastry, brush the top with the beaten egg yolk and set on the tile or baking sheet in the oven; bake 15 minutes. Remove the funnels. Continue baking until the crust is brown, about 30 more minutes. Use a serrated knife to cut the tourtière into serving wedges. Serve hot or lukewarm.

NOTES TO THE COOK

→→ If using fresh salsify, wash well in several changes of water. Using a stainless-steel knife, peel and cut into 2-inch pieces. Immediately drop pieces into water with a little lemon juice added (in the proportion of 1 tablespoon lemon juice to 2 cups water) to keep them from darkening. Cook the salsify in 3 cups boiling salted water with the juice of ½ lemon until just tender, 8 to 10 minutes. Drain well and dry on a kitchen towel. (Makes about 2 cups.)

→→ If using canned salsify, drain, rinse, and drain dry on a kitchen towel.

→→ If substituting parsnips, cook 1 pound fresh parsnips, unpeeled, in boiling salted water until just tender—that is, until it is easy to pierce one with a skewer. Drain and refresh in cold water. Peel and cut into 2-inch pieces. Drain dry on a kitchen terry towel. Add a pinch of sugar to skillet in which chicken was browned before sautéing.

→→ Black salsify, black in color and called *scorzonera*, is the most flavorful variety but the least digestible. Many people describe the taste as faintly like the meat of a coconut.

Inspired by a recipe from Lucien Vanel.

DUCK, GOOSE, AND RABBIT

Ducks are to Southwest France what beef cattle are to Argentina: the favorite and most reliable source of food and industry in the region. The fattening up of so many ducks and geese for the production of foie gras has led to the invention of numerous dishes that use the rest of the bird.

There is no need to cook a whole duck. Here you'll find a slew of wonderful dishes to make with cut up duck parts. This is the method generally used throughout Southwest France, where thrift and culinary good sense are working mottos, and where ducks are truly understood. Duck is so versatile, so complementary to so many other foods, that it can be used to play off nearly every flavor combination—sweet, sour, salty, or acid. Duck goes well with vinegars, peppers, olives, and vegetables. You can serve a duck breast with citrus or mulberry sauce, or turnips and chestnuts, or celery root puree. The legs can be braised and served with onions or prunes and red wine or grilled and paired with a walnut-garlic sauce. Ducks go with nearly anything and are superb, too, simply grilled alone over dried grapevine cuttings, broiled, or slowly sautéed in a deep skillet.

Nearly every duck recipe in this book is essentially free of duck fat (or else the fat is so visible that it's easy to cut away if you want). What happens to all that fat? Here you'll learn how to render it completely from your ducks, then use it to flavor without ingesting large quantities. Duck fat, like goose fat and pork fat, is a tasty cooking medium, and is used throughout Southwest France to flavor food.

To Cut Up a Duck

When you've mastered the cutting up of ducks, you'll discover that they're economically competitive with other meats. You'll use the fat as a cooking medium or preservative; the neck bone, wings, and carcass will provide excellent stock for soups and sauces; the neck skin, if you're skillful with a needle and string, can be stuffed (see Preserved Stuffed Duck Neck, pages 207–208); you'll be able to sauté, grill, or poach the breasts and braise, bake, or preserve the legs (see Traditional Confit of Duck, pages 201–203). Miscellaneous bits and pieces also can be used in pâtés and rillettes (these two dishes, of course, are not fat-free). And even the carcass can be brushed with duck fat and roasted as described below. The liver can go into flans, stuffings, or salads. You can even sauté the heart as a special treat for yourself. (It takes four hearts to make one serving, so in France duck hearts are usually reserved for the cook—see Sautéed Duck Hearts with Green Grapes, page 170). You can preserve the gizzards in duck fat and use them in all sorts of bean-based or soup recipes, or in stocks and soups. And if you want to truly embrace the spirit of the French Southwest, you can even use the duck feathers to apply fat to pastry.

1

>> Lay the duck breast side down on a cutting surface. Pull the neck skin away from the body and, using a sharp knife, remove it in one piece (Figure 1). Pull as much fat as possible from the body cavity and set it aside. Turn the duck over so that the breast side is up. Using a thin, sharp knife, loosen the wishbone surrounding the neck cavity. Pull the wishbone free of the body, cutting through the joint at each end if necessary (Figure 2).

2

>> Remove the wing tips at the second joint and set them aside for stock. If you wish to have the wings for *alycot* or confit, sever at the ball joint attaching wing to shoulder. To have a *magret*—boneless duck steak from the breast—sever the wing bone at the ball joint, attaching wing to shoulder. Then slice along the center line of the breast, cutting through the skin and the flesh down to breastbone (Figure 3).

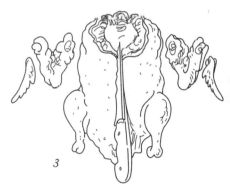

3

>> Slide the knife under one side of the breast. Holding the blade against the carcass, carefully separate the breast meat from the rib cage (Figure 4).

>> Cut the remaining flesh away from the carcass and lift off.

>> Trim off excess fat surrounding the flesh of this half breast. In the Gascon language this half breast is called a *magret*. (You may remove the skin. I only remove it for some recipes, such as Pekin Duck Cooked on a String, pages 181–182.) Repeat with the other half of the breast. If the breast is to be used for confit, the rib cage and wing joint should be left attached to the main part of the breast.

4

- Detach the tender or the "filet mignon," the narrow strip of delicate meat lying at the back of each half of the breast meat. Use it for a quick sauté for a salad or save it for a pâté. To remove it from the breast, slide a small knife blade under the white tendon running the length of the fillet and cut it free, keeping the meat intact. You can add it to the sauté pan when the *magret* is almost finished cooking; it cooks in less than a minute.

5

- Pull each thigh-leg portion away from the carcass and detach it in one piece. Trim off and reserve all excess fat. This portion can be used in ragouts, grills, salads, pâtés, sautés, and, of course, for confit (Figure 5).

- Cut the carcass into two portions: rib-cage front and back. The rib-cage portion, called *demoiselle* (young lady), can be roasted or grilled over hot coals and enjoyed as a snack with bread and wine. (In France, the carcass of the lobster is also called *demoiselle*.) And use the back and the rib cage if you're not going to try roasting it for stock, sauce bases, and soups.

- Remove and reserve, for various uses, all skin and fat from the carcass. Reserve the bones, gizzard, liver, and heart. Nothing is wasted on the duck but its quack.

- Wrap the duck parts in paper towels and set them in the refrigerator until needed. Or marinate as directed in some of the recipes.

- Render the fat as directed below if you plan to make confit or wish to cook with duck fat.

- Soak the liver in lightly salted milk to use it for pâtés, salads, or mousses.

- Chop up the bones and set them in a preheated 325°F oven to brown slowly to make a stock.

DUCK FAT AND CRACKLINGS

→ *Graisse de Canard Graisserons*

ONE OF THE BEST by-products of cutting up a duck is the fat you can render from it. It makes a superb cooking medium, a free dividend from your meat. The fat will keep 8 months in the refrigerator and up to a year in the freezer.

These crisp bits are wonderful sprinkled over a salad or an omelet or simply nibbled as a snack with drinks.

Reserved fat and fatty skin from 1 duck or
1 pound chunks of duck fat and fatty skin
from 1 duck

Coarse sea salt

1 Cut the skin of the duck into small pieces. Grind the fat and skin with ½ cup water in a food processor.

2 Scrape the puree into a heavy saucepan. Cook slowly for about 1 hour, or until the fat turns clear and pieces of skin have floated to the surface and are pale in color. (This can be done in a covered Pyrex bowl in the microwave in 15 minutes.)

3 Strain though a fine-mesh sieve into a container; reserve the bits of skin. Let the fat cool; then cover and refrigerate. It will keep well for up to 8 months.

4 The bits of skin can be made into savory cracklings; though a bit hard to digest, they are irresistible! Cook the reserved pieces of skin over moderately low heat for 10 minutes, or until golden brown, stirring from time to time. Cover the pan and continue cooking, stirring several times, for 10 minutes, or until the bits are crisp. Remove with a slotted spoon and drain well on paper towels. Sprinkle with salt and serve.

NOTES TO THE COOK

→ For perfect rendering of the skin and fat, melt it at a low temperature, preferably 170°F. At higher temperatures the surface would sear, sealing in the fat.

→ Moulard ducks are well endowed with fat; Muscovy ducks are not. You can purchase rendered duck fat in large quantities from D'Artagnan and other purveyors of duck products (see Mail Order Sources, pages 415–417).

Sautéed Duck Hearts With Green Grapes

➤➤ *Cœurs de Canard Poêlés aux Raisins Verts*   SERVES 1

IN AN EFFORT TO USE up every part of the duck, here is a quick meal for one, a special treat for the fatigued cook who has just cut up three or four ducks. Do not substitute chicken hearts. Serve with a thick slice of toasted crusty bread, lightly rubbed with garlic.

3 to 4 duck hearts

1 tablespoon duck fat or unsalted butter

Salt and freshly ground pepper

½ cup Dark, Rich Duck Stock (page 407) or 1 cup poultry stock boiled until reduced by half

20 green seedless grapes (peeled, if you like)

Red wine vinegar

1 Rinse the duck hearts; pat dry.

2 In a small skillet, gently sauté the duck hearts in hot fat about 1 minute, stirring occasionally. Sprinkle with salt and pepper. Blot away the fat.

3 Add the stock, cover, and simmer gently for 5 minutes. Boil, uncovered, until the pan juices are reduced by half. Add the grapes, toss, and cook for 3 or 4 seconds to heat through. Swirl in a few drops of vinegar and serve at once.

Grilled Duck Carcasses
Carcasses de Canard Grillées

➤➤ ◄◄

Chef André Daguin once invited me to dine in a private dining area off his kitchen. There was a small menu on the table with two words: *bones* and *beans*. The "bones" were duck carcasses baked in a hot oven, which were meant to be picked up and gnawed on. They were delicious. The "beans" that followed was a divine soup with beans and duck heads.

Duck Breasts

Magrets de Canard

The Southwestern *magret* is the boned breast from a fattened Moulard duck. Most often, the meaty breast is simply broiled or sautéed, then thinly sliced and served with a sauce, shallot vinaigrette, or *moutarde violette*. It is also delicious with a gratin of cooked cornmeal and fresh cheese, a sweet red wine sauce, a potato gratin, a fruit sauce, or a fricassee of mushrooms and chestnuts. In fact, the opportunities are endless.

Magret is not an old tradition. Years ago, the people who raised ducks for foie gras used the rest of the duck for confit, but in the 1970s, Chef André Daguin, in the Gascon town of Auch, came up with the idea of serving the breast grilled and rare, like a good steak. Today, it is hard to find breasts turned into confit. Instead, they are smoked, cured (see Home-Cured Duck Ham, page 84), or cooked in the various methods described in this chapter.

Pekin and Muscovy duck breasts can often substitute for the coveted Moulard on the following pages. Some duck breasts are so lean they can be dry even when rare. Moulards are not a problem; they can be cooked just like a steak. Muscovy duck breasts, however, are best if soaked in a salt brine for 1 to 2 days before cooking. In the recipes below I tell you which ducks I think are best to use and how to cook each of them.

MOULARD

Moulard ducks are fed fine corn, which results in fine flesh and a wonderfully assertive, gamey flavor that requires no marinade of any kind. A whole boneless Moulard breast is thick and weighs 1½ to 2 pounds. The whole duck is quite fatty, but its breast meat, or *magret*, is lean, though it is covered by a thick layer of fat under the skin, which must be scored thoroughly. Consequently, while the breast needs no brining, it does requires careful cooking. A *magret* from a Moulard is most delicious cooked rare or medium-rare, then left to rest for at least 10 minutes.

MUSCOVY

Muscovy ducks, the *canards de barbarie* in France, are more commonly available in markets in the United States than the Moulard. They are flavor packed, reduced in fat, and great for roasting.

A whole boneless Muscovy male (drake) breast weighs 2 to 2½ pounds. A female breast weighs much less. Both have a much thinner layer of fat under the skin than a Moulard magret. For grilling and sautéing, I like to soak these lean, thin-skinned breasts in a salt brine to avoid dryness and a chewy texture. You can use your favorite salt brine or the recipe below for 1 pound boneless Muscovy duck breasts. Soak overnight submerged in the brine. Since there's less fat on Muscovy ducks, it needs only light scoring before cooking.

BRINE FOR MUSCOVY DUCK BREAST
➤➤ *La Marinade Pour la Poitrine de Canard de Barbarie*

¼ cup Diamond Crystal kosher salt

1 tablespoon sugar

1 imported bay leaf

4 allspice berries

1 whole clove

1 teaspoon peppercorns

1 pound Muscovy duck breasts

Bring 1½ cups of water to a boil in a large saucepan. Add the salt and sugar and stir to dissolve. Add 4 cups cold water. Let cool, then stir in the bay leaf, allspice, clove, and peppercorns.

PEKIN

Long Island ducks are known as Pekin, and their size and quality varies greatly depending on the feed, water, and care. The top quality is called a Superior Pekin. Two sources I've tried are Liberty Ducks and Maple Leaf Farms (see Mail Order Sources, pages 415–417). You'll be amazed at the flavor, texture, and adaptability of a Superior Pekin. They have plenty of fat to make good confit with the legs, and their breasts are excellent broiled or sautéed. The technique for sautéing Pekin *magrets* is a little different from Moulards or Muscovies. After scoring the skin, the breast is sautéed skin side down in a heavy pan just to crisp it, about 2 minutes. Then it is left to rest for up to 10 minutes, after which it is turned over and finished in a very hot skillet or oven, followed by a 1- to 2-minute rest before slicing.

MOULARD DUCK BREASTS
GRILLED OVER CHARCOAL OR LAVA STONES

→→ *Magret à la Cheminée*   SERVES 4

I WOULD SUGGEST serving these gently cooked, delicious breasts with Michel Guérard's Pureed Celery Root with Apples (page 331) and Red Wine–Cooked Onions (page 348). In autumn, you can serve them with Cèpes in the Style of Gascony (page 337) and Potatoes in the Style of Quercy (page 341). And in summer, try the Baked Eggplant Studded With Garlic (pages 333–334), and a good dollop of *moutarde violette* (page 24) or Languedoc Walnut, Garlic, and Oil Liaison (pages 36–37).

2 boneless Moulard duck breast halves   Sea salt and freshly ground pepper
(magrets), 1 to 1¼ pounds each

1 About 1 hour before serving, remove the duck breasts from the refrigerator and while the fat is still cold, shave off the thinnest layer from the skin with a very thin, long bladed knife to remove the little "bumps," then score in very small crosshatch marks at a 45-degree angle all over the skin side. Remove the little fillet underneath, if desired, and reserve for some other purpose. Let the duck come to room temperature while you light a fire in a charcoal grill or heat your lava stones on low. If you are using a gas grill, preheat it to medium while the duck rests at the end of Step 2.

2 Set a cast-iron skillet over moderate heat until hot. Salt the fat side of the breast and place in the pan fat side down. Immediately, reduce the heat to moderately low and let the fat slowly melt in the skillet for 8 to 10 minutes, depending upon size. Five or six times tilt the skillet and spoon off all the expressed fat. (Save it for cooking.) You do not want the magret to cook too quickly; the goal is to extract as much fat as possible. At this point, the skin should be golden but not brown; it will crisp up when it is grilled. Do not turn the duck over to sear the flesh side. Simply remove the duck, skin side down, to a rack or a sheet of paper towels or crumpled brown paper and let rest for at least 10 minutes.

(continued)

3 When the coals are reduced to embers, salt and pepper the flesh side of the duck and set to grill, skin side facing the heat. Have long tongs ready to move the duck around to avoid flare-ups and burning fat. Grill for 2 minutes, or until the skin is nicely browned with some bits of black here and there. Flip over to the flesh side and cook 3 more minutes, or until the duck is done to your choice: With thumb and middle finger, pinch meat under the skin side. If the flesh springs back quickly, it is rare; if there is some give, it is medium. Transfer to a carving board and let rest for a few minutes. The flesh should be rare or pink. To serve, slice crosswise on the diagonal, sprinkle with a pinch of sea salt, and serve hot. One whole Moulard breast should yield about 18 to 24 slices.

NOTES TO THE COOK

- If you don't have a grill, the Moulard breast can be broiled. Set the broiler rack about 5 inches from the heat source and preheat the broiler while the duck is resting.
- A large Muscovy breast can be substituted for the Moulard. Make a few shallow incisions in the fat. Soak the duck breast in your favorite salt brine overnight or the Brine for Muscovy Duck Breast on pages 172–173. Since there is less fat to be expressed, you can completely grill the Muscovy duck breasts over the embers, for 8 to 10 minutes on the fat side, and 3 to 5 minutes on the flesh side. Watch for flare-ups and move the duck around accordingly. Allow to rest for 10 minutes before slicing and serving.

BROILED MARINATED DUCK BREASTS

➤➤ *Canard Grillé Dans Sa Peau* SERVES 4

THE FOLLOWING METHOD flatters Pekin and Muscovy ducks. Because the duck breasts in this recipe are marinated overnight, be sure to begin a day ahead.

2 whole fresh Pekin or Muscovy duck breasts, boned and halved with skin intact

GASCON MARINADE FOR THE PEKIN DUCK

1 tablespoon coarse kosher salt

1½ teaspoons minced shallots

1 teaspoon chopped fresh flat-leaf parsley

½ teaspoon crumbled imported bay leaf

¼ teaspoon fresh thyme leaves, crumbled

12 black peppercorns, lightly crushed

1 garlic clove, thinly sliced

OR

1 recipe Brine for Muscovy Duck Breast (pages 172–173)

Freshly ground pepper

1 One day before serving, trim off all excess fat from the duck breasts. In a bowl, combine the ingredients for the marinade or brine. Add the duck breasts, cover, and refrigerate overnight.

2 About 1 hour before serving, rinse the duck breasts to remove excess seasonings or any liquid that may have exuded during the marinating time. Discard the marinade or brine. Carefully dry the duck breasts with paper towels. Tightly score the skin and fat in close crosshatch lines without piercing the flesh. Let stand at room temperature for at least 30 minutes.

3 Preheat the broiler. Set the broiler rack about 5 inches from heat. About 15 minutes before serving, set the duck, skin side down, on a broiler rack. Broil for 1 minute to sear the flesh side. Quickly pour off any fat in the pan. Turn the breasts over, season lightly with salt and pepper, and broil for about 4 minutes longer for Pekin and a few minutes longer for Muscovy, depending on its size. The duck breasts will "tighten up " and become thicker. With your thumb and middle finger, pinch the meat under the skin side to test for doneness. If it springs back quickly, the meat is rare; if there is some give, it is medium. Transfer to a carving board and let rest for 1 to 2 minutes for the Pekin or 5 minutes for the Muscovy, tented loosely with foil. To serve, thinly slice the duck crosswise on the diagonal, then fan out each serving out on heated plates and sprinkle with freshly ground pepper. Serve at once.

PAN-SAUTÉED MOULARD DUCK BREASTS (MASTER RECIPE) WITH SHALLOT VINAIGRETTE

↠ *Magret de Canard Moulard Poêlé Dans Sa Peau,*
Vinaigrette à l'Échalote   SERVES 4

THIS CLASSIC DUCK BREAST dish of Gascony, called *lou magret* in Gascon, is sautéed and served rosy pink. After the breast is cooked, it is thinly sliced on the diagonal—much in the manner of a London broil; slices cut this way are much more tender. Many Gascons prefer theirs without any sauce. They twist a pepper mill over the slices, devouring them along with a pile of *frites* with the same gusto and delight as we devour a good steak. I enjoy it with a drizzle of a shallot vinaigrette.

2 boneless Moulard duck breast halves
(magrets), 1 to 1¼ pounds each

Sea salt and freshly ground black pepper

Shallot Vinaigrette (at right)

1 About 1 hour before serving, remove the duck breasts from the refrigerator and while the fat is still cold, use a thin long-bladed knife to shave off the thinnest layer from the skin to remove the little "bumps," then make very small crosshatch marks at a 45-degree angle all over the skin side. Peel away the tendon underneath and reserve for some other purpose. Wipe the breast dry; sprinkle with sea salt and pepper.

2 Heat a large heavy skillet over moderate heat. Add the duck breasts, skin side down, and immediately reduce the heat to moderately low. Sauté the breasts until crisp and brown, about 8 to 10 minutes, tilting the skillet and spooning off the fat 3 or 4 times. Flip the duck breasts over, sprinkle with salt and pepper, and finish cooking for 3 to 5 minutes to brown the flesh side and crisp the skin. With your thumb and middle finger, pinch the meat under the skin side to test for doneness. If it springs back quickly, the meat is rare; if there is some give, it is medium.

3 Remove the duck from the skillet to a paper towel–lined carving board, tent with foil, and leave to rest at least 10 minutes. Thinly slice meat crosswise on the diagonal and arrange overlapping on a serving platter. Sprinkle with sea salt and freshly ground pepper. Serve the Shallot Vinaigrette on the side.

SHALLOT VINAIGRETTE

MAKES ABOUT ⅓ CUP

2 large shallots, peeled and thinly sliced

1½ tablespoons Banyuls or sherry vinegar

¼ cup French walnut oil

1 teaspoon minced fresh chives

Pinch each of sugar, salt, and freshly ground pepper

Soak the shallots in the vinegar for 10 minutes. Mix in the rest of the ingredients and let stand until ready to use.

NOTES TO THE COOK

→ To substitute Muscovy duck breasts in this recipe: Brine 4 large Muscovy duck breast halves, 10 to 12 ounces each, in your favorite salt brine or in 1 recipe Brine for Muscovy Duck Breast (pages 172–173) overnight. The following day, score the fat in a crosshatch pattern without cutting into the flesh. Pat dry and place, skin side down, in a heated large skillet set over moderate heat and sauté for 7 minutes, tilting the skillet once or twice to remove fat. Flip over the breast and continue to sauté for 3 to 5 minutes, or until desired doneness. Let rest before slicing and serving.

→ To substitute Pekin duck breasts: Marinate 4 boneless Pekin duck breast halves, 6 to 8 ounces each, overnight in the Gascon Marinade (page 175). Score the skin, sauté the breasts skin side down in a heavy skillet until crisp, about 2 minutes; pour off the fat. Then remove the duck breasts from the pan and let them rest for up to 30 minutes before finishing the cooking, skin side up.

DUCK BREASTS WITH MOUTARDE VIOLETTE

➤➤ *Magret de Canard à la Moutarde Violette*   SERVES 4

2 boneless Moulard duck breast halves
(*magrets*), 1 to 1¼ pounds each

1½ tablespoons minced shallots

1 tablespoon rendered duck fat

¾ cup red wine

Pinch of fresh thyme leaves

1 tablespoon *moutarde violette*

1 tablespoon heavy cream

Salt and freshly ground pepper

1 Prepare and sauté the duck breasts as described in Steps 1 and 2 in the Master Recipe for Pan-Sautéed Moulard Duck Breast on page 177. Remove to a carving board, and let rest at least 10 minutes.

2 Meanwhile, add the shallots and duck fat to the skillet and cook over moderately low heat, stirring, until softened, about 2 minutes. Add the wine and herbs to the skillet and boil until reduced by half. Stir in the mustard and heavy cream. Adjust the seasoning. Thinly slice the meat crosswise on the diagonal and arrange overlapping on a serving platter. Spoon the sauce over the slices and serve at once.

DUCK BREASTS WITH PORT WINE SAUCE

➤➤ *Magret de Canard Poêlé au Porto*   SERVES 4

THIS IS AN IDEAL DISH for an elegant dinner.

2 boneless Moulard duck breast halves
(*magrets*), 1 to 1¼ pounds each

Salt and freshly ground pepper

1 cup imported ruby Port

Juice of 1 orange

3 cups unsalted chicken stock (storebought or homemade—page 405), reduced to 1⅓ cups

⅓ cup heavy cream

1 Prepare and sauté the duck breasts as described in Steps 1 and 2 of the master Recipe for Pan-Sautéed Moulard Duck Breast (page 177). Remove to a carving board, cover, and keep warm.

2 Pour off the fat from the skillet. Add the Port and orange juice to the skillet and bring to a boil over moderately high heat, scraping up any browned bits that cling to the bottom and

sides of the pan. Boil until reduced to a glaze. Add the reduced stock and boil until reduced by half, 2 to 3 minutes.

3 Transfer the sauce to a heavy 2-quart saucepan (see Note below). Return to a boil. Add the cream while the sauce is boiling hard, but do not stir. The cream will be "swallowed up" by the sauce. Boil vigorously for 5 minutes, or until you catch a glimpse of the bottom of the pan; remove from the heat. Season the sauce to taste with pepper and, if necessary, salt. Set aside and keep warm.

4 Slice the duck breast crosswise on the diagonal. Arrange the duck in overlapping slices on warm plates. Strain the sauce over the duck slices and serve at once.

NOTE TO THE COOK

The sauce can be completed in the skillet, but it is tricky—there is a tendency to overreduce the sauce (it becomes oily). If this happens, add a tablespoon of water and swirl to combine.

Inspired by a recipe from Lucien Vanel.

DUCK BREASTS WITH MULBERRY CREAM SAUCE
↣ *Magret de Canard Poêlé à la Crème de Mûres*   SERVES 4

THIS IS AN EASY DISH from the Périgord. Black mulberries have a luscious flavor, but alas they are the messy to work with. The Périgourdines turn them into a syrup, which is used to flavor sauces for duck and beef. Happily, I have discovered an excellent mulberry syrup from Lebanon, which is available at Middle Eastern stores (see Mail Order Sources, pages 415–417).

2 boneless Moulard duck breast halves *(magrets)*, 1 to 1¼ pounds each

Salt and freshly ground pepper

2 shallots, minced

2 tablespoons cider or Banyuls vinegar

2 tablespoons dry red wine

2 tablespoons mulberry syrup

3 cups unsalted chicken stock (storebought or homemade—page 405, reduced to 1⅓ cups

⅓ cup heavy cream

Follow the recipe at left for Duck Breasts With Port Wine Sauce, adding the shallots to the skillet after browning the duck breast and cook over moderately low heat, stirring until softened, about 2 minutes. Substitute the cider vinegar, red wine, and mulberry syrup for the Port and the orange juice.

Casserole of Moulard Duck Breasts With Potatoes as Prepared in the Region of the Bigorre

➤➤ *Magret de Canard en Cocotte Comme en Bigorre*   SERVES 4 OR 5

IN THE GORGEOUS REGION of Bigorre in the Pyrenees, the cooking is still very rustic. Here the Tarbais bean, a pyramid-shaped cake cooked on a spit in the fireplace *(gâteau à la broche)*, and an ancient breed of black-skinned pig are famous. Also celebrated is this recipe from the 150-year-old L'Hôtel-Restaurant Dupont in Castelnau-Magnoac. The duck is cooked in a very interesting manner: The breast is quickly seared and finishes cooking off the heat; it is served over the potatoes when they are finished. This savory dish features potatoes interlaced with ribbons of sweet onions and crisp ventrèche. When ready, the hot covered *cocotte*, or casserole, is brought directly to the table.

2 boneless Moulard duck breast halves *(magrets)*, 1 to 1¼ pounds each

Salt and freshly ground pepper

2 tablespoons rendered duck fat

1 large sweet onion, halved and thinly sliced

2 ounces finely diced ventrèche or pancetta

2 pounds red potatoes

1 imported bay leaf

½ teaspoon finely chopped fresh garlic

1 tablespoon chopped fresh flat-leaf parsley

1 Score the skin of each duck breast in crosshatch lines without piercing the flesh. Season with salt and pepper. Place the breast halves, skin side down, in a 3- to 4-quart flameproof casserole set over moderately high heat. Brown the skin side to a beautiful caramel in about 4 minutes while continually removing the fat from the skillet using a bulb baster or tilting the casserole and spooning off the fat. Turn the duck breasts over and quickly sear the other side. Transfer to a plate lined with paper towels, tent with foil, and let the meat rest for about 30 minutes. Discard the fat and wipe out the casserole.

2 While the duck is resting, heat the rendered duck fat in the casserole over moderately low heat. Add the onion and ventrèche, cover, and cook for 10 minutes, or until the onions are silky and the ventrèche is crisp.

3 Meanwhile, slice the potatoes ⅛ inch thick and pat each slice dry with paper towels. Raise the heat under the casserole to high, add the potatoes, and turn them in the fat for 2 minutes, making sure all are coated before pressing down to form a disk. Continue to cook until some of the slices begin to brown. Again press the potatoes with a spatula to form a flat round cake. Reduce the heat to moderately low, cover, and cook for 10 minutes.

4 Lift the cover and wipe away any moisture on the inside of the lid. Add the bay leaf and toss the potatoes gently so that the crisp bottom pieces mix with the rest of the potatoes and onions; cover and continue to cook for 5 minutes. Gently press down with a spatula to reshape. Season with a little salt and pepper, cover, and cook for 5 more minutes, shaking the casserole to keep the potatoes from sticking. Uncover, toss with the garlic and parsley, reshape by pressing down, and cook a few more minutes.

5 Carve the duck breasts into ¼-inch-thick slices. The meat should be very rare. Spread the slices over the potatoes and season with salt and pepper. Cover the casserole tightly, raise heat to high and cook for 2 to 3 minutes to brown the bottom of the potato cake and finish cooking the duck. Bring the covered casserole to the table and serve hot.

PEKIN DUCK BREASTS COOKED ON A STRING

-+- *Canard à la Ficelle, Sauce Diable* SERVES 3 TO 4

THIS VARIATION OF THE FAMOUS *bœuf à la ficelle* (beef on a string) is made with boneless, skinless duck breasts. The duck breasts are suspended by string and are simply dropped into a boiling spicy broth and cooked until rare. They are served with a piquant sauce studded with capers and pickles. Note that this sauce is "short"—only about a tablespoon of sauce per portion—but it is full of flavor.

(continued)

2 boned and skinned Pekin duck breasts, plus the wings of the 2 ducks, trimmed of excess fat and chopped into 1-inch pieces

Coarse kosher or pickling salt

3 cups unsalted chicken stock (storebought or homemade—page 405) or duck stock (storebought or homemade—page 407)

1 tablespoon coarsely cracked black peppercorns

3 tablespoons unsalted butter

1½ tablespoons minced shallots

1 tablespoon plus 1 teaspoon tiny nonpareil capers, drained but not rinsed

1 tablespoon plus 1 teaspoon minced French cornichons

1 tablespoon plus 1 teaspoon finely diced fresh tomato

3 tablespoons red wine vinegar

1 tablespoon dry white wine

1 teaspoon Dijon mustard

1 Rub the duck breasts with 2 teaspoons coarse salt. Thread them loosely onto an 18-inch length of kitchen string and tie the ends together to make a loop. Set on a flat dish, cover loosely with plastic wrap, and refrigerate for 30 minutes.

2 Bring the stock with the peppercorns to a boil in a 2½-quart saucepan. Cover and simmer for 20 minutes.

3 Meanwhile, in a large nonreactive skillet, brown the chopped duck wings in 1 teaspoon of the butter over moderately high heat. Pour off any fat. Push the wing pieces to one side. Add 2 more teaspoons butter and the shallots to the skillet. Reduce the heat to moderately low and cook for 2 to 3 minutes to soften the shallots. Add 1 tablespoon each of the capers, cornichons, and tomatoes. Cook, stirring, for 1 minute.

4 Add the vinegar and white wine and boil down to a glaze. Stir in the mustard and 1 cup of the simmering stock. Simmer over low heat for 5 minutes. Strain the sauce through a sieve into a small saucepan, pressing on the solids to extract as much flavor as possible. The sauce should be very piquant. Keep warm over very low heat.

5 Rinse the salt off the duck and drop the string of chilled breasts into the boiling stock. Immediately reduce the heat to a simmer and cook for 3½ minutes for small duck breasts (weighing about 4½ ounces) and 4 minutes for larger (about 5 ounces). Quickly remove from the pot and let rest for 30 seconds. Remove the string and carve the duck breasts crosswise on the diagonal into thin slices. Arrange overlapping on a warmed serving platter.

6 Swirl the remaining 2 tablespoons butter into the sauce to thicken it slightly. Fold in the remaining 1 teaspoon each capers, tomato, and cornichons. Spoon the sauce over the breasts and serve at once.

DUCK BREASTS BAKED IN SALT

➤➤ *Magret de Canard Cuite Dans le Gros Sel* SERVES 4 TO 6

THIS METHOD OF COOKING produces moist, tender, pink duck breasts. It trades off crisp skin, which is lost, for an incredibly intense flavor. To obtain perfectly colored rosy flesh, cooking times should be followed exactly. A total of 40 to 45 minutes includes browning the skin to release excess fat, baking in salt, and the appropriate rest period.

Egg whites are mixed with the salt to form a "cooking jacket." It's this combination of coarse grains of salt *(gros sel)* and the egg whites that absorbs the fat from the duck and keeps the flesh so deliciously moist.

Personally, I like to serve these duck breasts thinly sliced at room temperature. One whole breast will produce about 26 slices. Arranged on a platter, they make a terrific summer dish served with a Shallot Vinaigrette (page 177). I like to garnish the platter with roasted red peppers and Anchovy-Olive Dip (pages 78–79). Pass garlic toast in a basket.

2 boneless Moulard duck breast halves *(magrets)*, about 1 to 1¼ pounds each	2 pounds coarse salt: rock, pickling, or kosher
Freshly ground pepper	4 egg whites
	Shallot Vinaigrette (page 177)

1 Pat the duck breasts dry with paper towels. Place the duck breasts skin side up on a cutting surface. Score the skin of the breasts in a crosshatch pattern at 1-inch intervals with a sharp, thin-bladed knife. Do not cut through to flesh. Season the breast with pepper.

2 Heat a large, heavy skillet over moderately high heat, and quickly brown the skin side of each breast. Remove the duck, drain on paper towels, and let cool completely. (To make a simple sauce, degrease and reserve juices.)

3 Preheat oven to 425°F. Slap the 2 breasts together, flesh to flesh, and tie together with string.

4 Combine the salt and egg whites, mixing with your hands until the salt is like damp sand. Make a layer of salt about ½ inch deep in the bottom of an oiled disposable loaf or cake pan. Place the tied duck breasts on the salt and spoon the remaining salt around sides and over the top of duck to enclose completely. Press firmly to seal the duck in the salt.

(continued)

5 Roast for exactly 30 minutes. Remove from the oven and let stand for 10 minutes. Crack open the salt shell and remove the duck. Wipe off as much salt as possible with paper towels Allow to cool completely before carving crosswise on a sharp diagonal into wide, thin slices. Arrange the slices on a platter, overlapping. Season with pepper and drizzle some of the vinaigrette over the duck. Pass the remaining sauce on the side.

NOTES TO THE COOK

→→ This method works equally well for duck legs: Press the legs and thighs together in pairs, flesh side in; tie loosely with string and roast for 1¼ hours. Serve the duck with a sauce made from the skillet juices or serve it alone, slightly warm, with just a sprinkling of coarsely ground pepper and accompanied in fall with a serving of Ragout of Forest Mushrooms (pages 335–336).

→→ What to do with all those egg yolks? Make a Crème Anglaise (pages 380–381) without bay leaves to serve over fresh berries or the Prune and Armagnac Ice Cream (pages 397–398), which has the illusion of seeming very rich in cream but is made mostly with milk.

Ragout of Duck Legs With White Onions and Prunes

→→ *Ragoût de Cuisses de Caneton aux Petits Oignons et aux Pruneaux*

SERVES 4

DUCK BREASTS HAVE BECOME so popular that people often wonder what to do with the legs. One solution is to use them in this excellent dish, which relies on a good hearty wine for background richness. The slow simmering and the degreasing make this version of the dish much lighter than others. The duck can be cooked in advance, then gently reheated. The addition of bread fried in olive oil actually rounds out the flavor of the dish; don't leave it out. This is one of my favorite duck recipes.

12 extra large pitted prunes

2 cups hot tea, preferably linden or orange pekoe

4 Pekin duck legs, drumsticks and thighs separated

5 ounces thickly sliced ventrèche or pancetta, cut into 2- by ⅛-inch strips (lardons) and blanched

3 garlic cloves, peeled

½ teaspoon salt

¼ teaspoon freshly ground pepper

Pinch of dried thyme leaves, crumbled

1 large red onion, thinly sliced

1 tablespoon red wine vinegar

1 tablespoon Dijon mustard

2¼ cups full-bodied red wine, such as California Petite Sirah or a French Côtes-du-Rhône

1½ cups unsalted chicken stock (storebought or homemade—page 405)

3 medium carrots, peeled, halved crosswise, then lengthwise

18 small white onions (about 1 inch in diameter)

2 tablespoons unsalted butter

1½ teaspoons sugar

8 thin baguette slices, toasted

Chopped fresh flat-leaf parsley

1 Soak the prunes in the hot tea for 2 hours. Drain, reserving the prunes and discarding the liquid.

2 Trim off the loose fat from the duck legs and render it with 2 tablespoons water. Strain, reserving 2 tablespoons for this dish. Keep the remainder for some other purpose. Score the skin of the duck with the point of a small knife. Wipe off excess moisture.

3 Heat the duck fat in a heavy nonreactive skillet over moderate heat. Add the blanched lardons and fry, turning occasionally, until light brown, about 4 minutes. Remove with a slotted spoon and drain on paper towels. Reserve the drippings in the skillet. Transfer the lardons to a 4-quart flameproof casserole.

4 Add the duck pieces to the reserved drippings in the skillet and cook over moderately high heat, turning occasionally, until well browned, about 10 minutes. Briefly drain the duck on paper towels and add to the lardons in the casserole. Add 2 of the garlic cloves, the salt, pepper, and thyme and toss to mix.

5 Pour off all but 2 tablespoons fat from the skillet. Add the red onion to the skillet and sauté over moderate heat, stirring frequently, until lightly browned, about 5 minutes. Remove the onion with a slotted spoon, drain thoroughly on paper towels, and add to the casserole.

(continued)

6 Pour off all the fat from skillet; whisk in the vinegar, mustard, and ⅓ cup of the wine. Bring to a boil, scraping up any brown bits clinging to the pan. Reduce to a glaze. Add another ⅓ cup wine and reduce again to develop a stronger, deeper color in the sauce.

7 Pour the deglazing liquid from the skillet, the remaining wine, and the stock into the casserole; heat to boiling. Reduce the heat and simmer, uncovered, for 5 minutes, skimming. Add the carrots. Cover the casserole and simmer over low heat until the duck is tender, about 1½ hours; or cook in a preheated 300°F oven. *(This recipe can be prepared up to this step. Cool, cover, and refrigerate.)*

8 Cut an X in root end of each small onion. Blanch for 2 minutes. Drain and rinse under cold water until cool enough to handle. Peel the onions, leaving on enough root and stem end so the onion won't fall apart.

9 Combine the onions, butter, sugar, and ½ cup water in a medium skillet. Bring to a simmer over moderate heat and cook, stirring occasionally, until the water has evaporated, about 6 minutes. Reduce the heat to low and continue to cook, shaking the pan occasionally, until the onions are tender and nicely browned, about 8 minutes.

10 About 20 minutes before serving, add the prunes to the ragout and gently reheat. Transfer the duck pieces to a warm platter; surround with the prunes, carrots, and onions. Sprinkle the lardons over the duck; tent loosely with foil. Strain the sauce from the casserole through a fine-mesh sieve into a small saucepan, pressing on the solids with the back of a spoon to extract as much liquid as possible. Skim off any fat from the sauce. Bring to a boil and set the saucepan half on and half off the heat. Cook at a slow boil, skimming, for 10 minutes, or until the liquid is reduced enough to coat a spoon lightly. Spoon the sauce over the duck and vegetables and serve at once with the toasted baguette slices.

NOTES TO THE COOK

→ To save time, defrosted frozen baby onions can be substituted for the fresh here. Skip Step 8 and glaze as directed in Step 9.

→ If substituting Muscovy or Moulard duck legs, please note they need to cook longer, as much as 1 hour.

Inspired by a recipe from Lucien Vanel.

SLOW-COOKED DUCK LEGS IN RED WINE

→ *Salmis de Cuisses de Canard*   SERVES 4

ACCORDING TO THE OLD Gascon cooks, the secret of a great *salmis* is in the reheating over a three- or four-day period. Each day the meat is slowly reheated, simmered, cooled, and degreased. The flavors mellow more each time. The flesh turns meltingly tender. Don't be put off by this small amount of extra work. This recipe is one of the finest renditions of *salmis* that I have tasted in the Southwest. The flour-based sauce is not to be scoffed at. It holds the wine flavor through all those reheatings and is sensational.

An absolute "must" accompaniment is the fried cornmeal cakes called *armottes* (see pages 357–358). The textures and flavors mingle perfectly, making this a very fine rustic dinner. This recipe doubles easily.

To achieve best flavor, you must begin this recipe three days before serving.

8 whole Muscovy duck legs

3 tablespoons Armagnac

5 ounces lean ventrèche or pancetta

5 large shallots

10 garlic cloves

6 tablespoons flour

1 bottle (750 ml) full-bodied red wine such as a California Petite Sirah or a French Côtes-du-Rhône

Herb bouquet: 3 sprigs parsley, 1 sprig thyme, and 1 imported bay leaf tied together with string

Pinch of sugar

Salt and freshly ground pepper

1 Three days before serving, trim the fat from all of the legs and render it. With a thin-bladed knife, score the fatty skin on the legs without piercing the flesh.

2 In a large skillet, heat 1 tablespoon of the rendered fat over low heat. In batches if necessary, add the legs, skin side down, and cook, turning once, until browned, about 3 minutes per side. Pour off all the fat in the skillet.

3 Add 2 tablespoons of the Armagnac and carefully ignite with a long match. When the flames subside, transfer the legs to a 3-quart earthenware or enameled cast-iron casserole.

4 In a food processor, finely chop the ventrèche, shallots, and garlic. Add to the skillet and cook over moderate heat, scraping up the bits and pieces clinging to bottom and sides of the pan, until all is lightly browned around the edges.

(continued)

5 Sprinkle on the flour and cook, stirring constantly, for about 1 minute, until the mixture masses into a ball. Reduce the heat to moderately low. Gradually add the red wine by cupfuls, stirring to smooth out the flour. This must be done very slowly so that the flour will completely absorb the wine and the sauce will thicken properly. When all the wine has been added and the sauce is smooth, bring to a boil and pour over the duck legs.

6 Add the herb bouquet, sugar, and salt and pepper to taste. Cover with a sheet of buttered waxed paper and then a lid. Cook over very low heat for 1 hour. The wine should just "shudder." (This can also be done in a preheated 275°F oven.) Uncover and let cool, then cover and refrigerate overnight.

7 The following day, remove all fat from the surface. Let come to room temperature. Cover again and place in a cold oven. Turn the heat on to 275°F and cook for 1½ hours. Let cool, uncovered; cover and refrigerate.

8 The third day, repeat procedure but cook at 225°F for 1½ hours.

9 Just before serving, stir in the remaining 1 tablespoon of Armagnac and check for salt and pepper.

Inspired by a recipe from Roger Duffour.

DUCK LEG RAGOUT WITH GREEN OLIVES AND EGGPLANT

>> *Ragoût de Cuisses de Canard Comme en Gironde*   SERVES 2

THIS GIRONDINE LATE SUMMER or early fall ragout is served with hot toasted French bread and eggplant prepared in a unique way.

2 large whole duck legs, Moulard, Muscovy, or Pekin

Salt and freshly ground pepper

1 medium onion, chopped

1 large tomato, peeled, seeded, and coarsely chopped

3 sprigs of thyme

1 imported bay leaf

⅓ cup poultry stock

⅓ cup dry white wine

1 recipe Sautéed Eggplant (pages 334–335)

½ cup pitted green olives, preferably Picholine, soaked in water if salty

4 rounds of French bread toasted in the oven, rubbed with garlic

1 Trim the fat from all of the legs and render it. Reserve 2 tablespoons for preparing this dish; save the rest for some other purpose. Score the fatty skin without piercing the flesh. In a large deep skillet over low heat, warm the rendered fat. Add the duck legs, skin side down, and cook, turning once, until browned, about 5 minutes per side. Pour off all the fat in the skillet. Season the legs with salt and pepper.

2 Add the onion, raise the heat to moderate, and cook, stirring, for 5 minutes, until softened and golden. Add the tomato, thyme, and bay leaf and cook for 1 minute. Add the stock and wine and bring to a boil. Reduce the heat and simmer for 10 minutes. Cover and simmer until the legs are tender, about 1½ hours, turning the duck legs from time to time. Note: Muscovy legs will take an additional 30 to 60 minutes to cook. *(The recipe can be prepared to this point up to 1 day in advance. If made ahead, reheat gently before proceeding.)*

3 When ready to serve, make the Sautéed Eggplant. Add the olives and the duck legs with their sauce and gently stir to combine. Correct the seasoning and serve at once garnished with garlic toasts.

DUCK-STUFFED CABBAGE ROLLS

➤➤ *Choux Farcis aux Cuisses de Canard*   SERVES 6

INCREDIBLY MOIST AND TENDER, with an herb stuffing and a sauce thickened with pureed tart apple, these rolls should be served the day they are made, since refrigeration tends to dry them out. You can make them a few hours in advance and keep them warm in their cooking juices.

1 large head of green cabbage, about 3 pounds

6 whole Pekin or Moulard duck legs (3 to 3½ pounds)

Coarse kosher salt and freshly ground pepper

2 medium onions, chopped

2 medium carrots, sliced

3 garlic cloves, smashed

1 cup dry white wine

3 plum tomatoes, halved, seeded, and coarsely chopped

Herb bouquet: 2 sprigs each parsley and thyme, 2 imported bay leaves, 1 celery leaf, and 2 scallions tied together with string

Bread and Pork Sausage Stuffing (page 192)

5 ounces lean pancetta or ventrèche, finely diced

1 large tart green apple, such as Granny Smith

Torn fresh flat-leaf parsley leaves

1 Discard the tough outer cabbage leaves and cut out the tough core. Slip the entire head into a large pot of boiling water for 5 minutes, or until the outer leaves are supple. Remove and rinse under cold running water until cool enough to handle. Carefully separate and reserve 12 to 15 large leaves; use the remaining cabbage for some other purpose. Drain the leaves on kitchen towels and pat dry.

2 Carefully trim excess fat from the duck legs and set aside 1 tablespoon for Step 3. (Save the remainder for rendering or some other purpose.) Score the skin. Separate the drumsticks and thighs, bone them (reserving bones), and remove as many tendons as possible. Season the duck meat with a little salt and pepper and refrigerate.

3 Make a tomato-duck sauce: Place the duck bones and any other trimmings and 1 tablespoon of the duck fat in a large saucepan. Brown slowly over moderate heat, about 5 minutes. Add the onions, carrots, and garlic and continue to cook until lightly browned, about 15 minutes. Pour in the wine and bring to a boil, scraping up the brown bits stuck to the pan. Add the chopped tomatoes, herb bouquet, and 3 cups water. Bring to a boil, reduce the heat to moderately low, cover, and cook for about 1 hour. Let cool slightly, then strain into a bowl, pressing on the solids to extract all their juices. Degrease, return to the saucepan, and boil until reduced to 1¼ cups of sauce.

4 While the tomato sauce is cooking, make the Bread and Pork Sausage Stuffing, as described in the recipe that follows.

5 In a large skillet, slowly brown the pancetta cubes until crisp; add to the tomato sauce. Add the boneless duck pieces from Step 2 to the skillet, skin side down. Brown gently for 1 to 2 minutes. Drain the duck on paper towels. Remove half the fat in the skillet and discard.

6 To stuff the cabbage, lay out a leaf on a work surface with the stem end nearest you, and lightly season with salt and pepper. Divide the stuffing in 12 portions. Mound 1 portion of the stuffing on the cabbage leaf and set a piece of duck, meat side down, on top of the stuffing. Using both hands, lift the entire edge nearest you over the mixture. Bring the left side of the leaf up and over, then right side. Roll the filled leaf to form a tight packet; fasten with a toothpick or tie with white string. Repeat with the remaining leaves, stuffing, and duck.

7 Reheat the skillet with the fat until sizzling. Add the stuffed cabbage rolls and brown over moderate heat, turning, about 5 minutes. Tilt the skillet and remove as much fat as possible. Add the tomato sauce. Cover with parchment paper to fit and a tight-fitting lid, and simmer over low heat for 1 hour, turning the cabbage rolls midway.

8 Meanwhile, cook the apple in a microwave or steam until very soft. Peel and core the apple and crush to a puree. Transfer the rolls to a serving platter; cut away the strings or remove the toothpicks. Boil the cooking liquid to reduce quickly to about 1 cup. Whisk in the pureed apple, adjust the seasoning, and pour over the cabbage. Serve hot with a garnish of torn parsley leaves.

BREAD AND PORK SAUSAGE STUFFING

1½ packed cups cubed, stale, firm bread, crusts removed

⅓ cup milk or cold stock

6 to 7 ounces Italian sweet pork sausage, skinned

2 garlic cloves, crushed

2 shallots, finely chopped

1 egg, lightly beaten

1 tablespoon chopped fresh flat-leaf parsley

1 tablespoon minced fresh chives

½ teaspoon salt

¼ teaspoon freshly ground pepper

Pinch of freshly grated nutmeg

1 Put the bread in a mixing bowl. Pour the milk over the bread and let stand for 2 minutes to soften. Press out and discard the milk.

2 With a fork, work in the sausage meat, garlic, and shallots, breaking up any large lumps of meat. Add the beaten egg, parsley, chives, salt, pepper, and nutmeg; blend well. Chill the stuffing to firm it up, about 30 minutes.

DUCK LEG AND SWEETBREAD RAGOUT
➤➤ *Ragoût de Cuisses de Canard aux Ris de Veau*   SERVES 6

HERE'S A LUCIEN VANEL dish for the "thrifty cook," though only a restaurant chef would consider this economical today. The dish derives from Vanel's mother's way with leftovers. I find it quite marvelous that he took this kind of simple home-cooking idea to the restaurant stage, gaining two Michelin stars in the process. I loved watching him work. The first thing he did every morning was look in the refrigerator and see what he could "use up" on that day's menu.

This fascinating ragout—two stews joined together after each has been fully cooked and degreased—has the contrapuntal quality of a great duet: tastes interweave, textures collide, and the whole is greater than the sum of its parts. This is one of those *plats des pauvres* (poor people's dishes) brought to a sophisticated and expensive level that might now be called a *plat du haut bourgeois*.

You'll find sweetbreads in a few supermarkets and specialty meat markets, and in stores in ethnic neighborhoods.

2 pounds whole duck legs, Moulard, Muscovy, or Pekin	2 cups dry white wine
Salt and freshly ground pepper	2 garlic cloves, halved
4 tablespoons unsalted butter	¼ teaspoon fresh thyme leaves
2 medium onions, coarsely chopped	2 cups unsalted chicken stock (storebought or homemeade—page 405
¼ cup red wine vinegar	Sweetbread Ragout (page 194)
1 tablespoon Dijon mustard	1 cup heavy cream

1 Preheat the oven to 350°F. Trim away excess skin and fat from the legs and thighs. Season liberally with salt and pepper.

2 Heat the butter in an ovenproof nonreactive skillet. Add the legs and brown briefly on both sides. Prick the fatty parts many times without piercing the flesh itself. Continue to sauté the duck for 5 minutes. Remove to a side dish lined with paper towels. Pour off all but 1½ tablespoons fat from skillet.

3 Add the onions to the skillet and sauté until limp, 3 to 5 minutes. Drain off the fat. Add the vinegar, mustard, and wine to the skillet, stirring. Over high heat, reduce rapidly by one third, scraping up all the little bits and pieces that cling to the bottom of the skillet, about 10 minutes. Stir in the garlic, thyme, and stock.

4 Return the duck legs to the skillet and bring to a boil, skimming. Cover with a sheet of buttered parchment or waxed paper and a lid. Set in the oven to cook until legs are just tender, about 45 minutes for the Pekin duck, 1 hour for the Moulard, and 1½ hours for the Muscovy. *(The recipe can be prepared ahead to this point; let cool, then cover and refrigerate overnight.)*

5 The following day, make the Sweetbread Ragout up to 2 hours before serving. Cut the sweetbreads on a diagonal into 1-inch pieces. Skim the fat and reserve the sweetbread juices.

6 About 45 minutes before serving, preheat the oven to 300°F. Scrape off the chilled fat that has formed over the duck legs and sauce. Remove the legs from the sauce and pull the meat off the bone. Remove the skin and trim off any gristle. Cut the meat into 1-inch chunks.

(continued)

7 Arrange the sweetbreads alternately with the chunks of duck in an ovenproof serving dish. Scrape the reserved duck sauce into the sweetbread pan juices. Add the cream and boil, stirring, until sauce has enough body to coat a wooden spoon, about 5 minutes. Adjust the seasoning and strain the sauce over the duck meat and sweetbreads. Transfer to the oven and gently heat until hot and ready to serve, 20 to 30 minutes.

SWEETBREAD RAGOUT

¾ to 1 pound fresh or frozen sweetbreads

1 tablespoon wine vinegar

4 tablespoons unsalted butter

3 tablespoons minced carrot

3 tablespoons minced onion

1½ tablespoons minced celery

2 tablespoons dry vermouth

¼ cup imported ruby Port

½ cup Demi-Glace (page 406), or 2 cups unsalted chicken stock (storebought or homemade— page 405) reduced to ½ cup

1 teaspoon tomato paste

Salt and freshly ground pepper

1 Soak the sweetbreads in the refrigerator for 2 hours in 2 or 3 changes of acidulated water (1 tablespoon vinegar to 2 cups water). If using frozen sweetbreads, defrost directly in water; add 1 to 2 hours to soaking time. (Sweetbreads are not blanched for this dish.) Drain, peel, and cut away connective tube, gristle, and any fatty parts.

2 In a 10-inch skillet, melt the butter over low heat. Stir in the minced vegetables, cover, and sweat the vegetables for 5 minutes.

3 Uncover the skillet, add the sweetbreads, and turn them in the pan juices to moisten. Add the vermouth, cover, and gently cook for 10 minutes, turning the sweetbreads midway. Add the Port and boil over moderate heat until reduced to a glaze. Allow the sweetbreads to brown slightly on both sides in the syrupy juices.

4 Add the demi-glace or reduced stock and the tomato paste. Season with salt and pepper to taste. Bring to a simmer, skimming. Swirl to combine pan juices and keep sweetbreads moist. Cover and cook over very low heat 7 to 8 minutes longer, turning sweetbreads once or twice. Let cool, uncovered. *(The sweetbread ragout can be prepared to this point up to 2 hours in advance.)*

All About Confit

In the French Southwest, confit (pronounced cón-fee) is a way of life. Before refrigeration, preserving meat for winter was a necessity on farms where whole animals were slaughtered, and the thrifty cook had to make the best of all the meat at one time so that it would last until spring. Luckily for the farmer and his family, the curing technique developed was unbelievably unctuous and delicious, which is why it is still so popular.

Preserving meat in this traditional fashion requires adaptation for cooks not blessed with a constant supply of the correct meats and good, home-rendered fats. On its home territory, confit was intended to last for months without refrigeration—in fact, meats preserved in this way were sometimes kept the year round, with occasional reheating to prevent spoiling.

As with other preserved meats, a certain amount of time is necessary to allow the chemical changes to take place that will produce the husky flavor of true confit. People on rushed schedules can taste their confit within a week or so or, for that matter, as soon as it finishes cooking. But what they are eating won't really be confit any more than freshly drained curds are ripe cheese. True confit requires at least 2 to 3 weeks to begin to develop its character.

Use confit in cassoulets, *garbures*, soups, and lentil and bean dishes. Add it hot or cold to a walnut oil–dressed salad of mixed greens, or, perhaps best of all, serve it hot and crispy as a main dish along with sautéed potatoes or a plate of pureed sorrel (page 340), with braised cabbage, with cèpes sautéed in oil in the style of Bordeau (page 338), with sarlat potatoes (pages 342–343), with potatoes in the style of the quercy (page 341), with fresh green peas cooked with jambon de Bayonne and baby white onions (page 205), with red cabbage, chestnuts and watercress (page 206), with marinated strips of roasted red bell peppers, or shredded and sautéed with rice and slices of spicy pork sausage.

TYPES OF DUCK FOR CONFIT

In Southwest France, the popular duck for confit is the Moulard, which has a unique flavor and is more than twice as heavy as the average American Long Island duck, known as the white Pekin. The Moulard is a hybrid cross of a Pekin and a Muscovy duck. Moulards are sterile (i.e., they cannot reproduce), and this makes them fairly expensive.

In preparing this revised edition, all the duck leg confit recipes were retested with the three duck breeds available: Moulard, Muscovy, and Pekin. After years of experimenting with confit in American kitchens, I've codified adjustments in the basic techniques to handle the various ducks available, and also made reasonable compromises to better suit our less leisurely household rhythms.

Muscovy duck legs have a wonderful flavor and can be used, though you need to cook them a little longer since their flesh is often tougher. Also, you will need more fat since they have very little of their own.

Some markets carry a top quality Pekin called a Superior Pekin; Maple Leaf Farms, Reichardt, Liberty Farms, Wild Acres, and Culver are several good brands (see Mail Order Sources, pages 415–417). These are truly superb, thanks to quality breeding, water, and feed. They are smaller than the Moulard and Muscovy drakes, but they have good tasty flesh and plenty of fat and produce a very fine confit.

DUCK PARTS IDEAL FOR CONFIT

In the Southwest of France, where large numbers of ducks and geese are raised for foie gras, and confit is put up in vast quantities at a time, there are always enough duck leg pieces—the most desirable part for preserving—to make huge pots of confit without using the breasts. Though the breasts can be used, they do not take as well as the rest of the duck to the confit-making process, and they are generally reserved for other purposes unconnected with confit-making—for example, sautéing and grilling. Luckily, nowadays, you can purchase legs separately from the breasts. (If you do buy whole ducks, see pages 166–168 for directions on how to cut up a duck.) Also, plan to use the gizzards, wings, and necks for confit if you have them on hand.

CURING THE DUCK

The amount of salt I suggest for 5 pounds of duck pieces, 3 tablespoons plus 1 teaspoon, corresponds to the traditionally used French formula of 22 grams, or 2 teaspoons, of coarse pure pickling or kosher salt to each pound of trimmed meat. Shallots, garlic, and herbs are also added for flavor. The curing time ranges from overnight to two days.

COOKING AND AGING CONFIT

I have found that the gentle heat of an electric slow cooker is ideal for making confit (see page 204). If you use another vessel on top of the stove or in the oven, be sure that it is heavy enough to conduct heat steadily and gently. Increase quantities if desired, cooking the confit in batches as necessary and putting it up in any convenient-sized sterilized containers; proportionally less fat will be necessary to cook increased amounts of duck. Any leftover fat that will not fit into the confit crocks will make a delicious medium for sautéing potatoes, apples, or cabbage; or it can be used in putting up additional confit of any type. Store the fat, refrigerated, in clean covered containers for up to 6 to 8 months, or freeze it for up to 1 year.

STEAMING AND CRISPING THE CONFIT

To use confit, set the storage crock in a warm room or place in a deep pan of warm water until the fat is softened, 2 to 4 hours. Take out as many pieces as you need and set aside. Make sure the remaining pieces are well covered with fat; add peanut oil or melted lard, if necessary.

For safety, all confit should be heated through before serving, even for dishes to be served cold or at room temperature. If your dish does not require a crisp skin, steam the pieces for 10 minutes over boiling water or heat slowly in the oven. This steaming, which softens the preserved duck, also removes excess fat.

If you do want crisp confit, each breed of duck must be treated in accordance with the thickness of its skin: Steam Moulard or Pekin confit for 10 minutes, then immediately remove any superfluous fat; place the duck, skin side down, in a heated skillet to brown and crisp. This method from the Landes guarantees a crispy skin and silky flesh.

Alain Loivel, the Bordeaux-born chef-owner of the Montreal bistro Le P'tit Plateau uses an entirely different method, which works perfectly. He places his Moulard confit duck legs skin side down on a nonstick or ceramic baking dish or skin side up on a rack, then bakes them in a 400°F oven for 20 minutes until crisp.

Since the skin of Muscovy duck confit is very thin, the methods above don't really work as well. I've found that the following method, inspired by James Villas's instructions in his *American Taste* on how to crisp Southern fried chicken, works best: Lift the Muscovy duck confit pieces from the crock; scrape the fat that clings to the pieces back into the crock. Cook

2 legs at a time: Heat 2 to 3 tablespoons confit fat in a skillet with a tight-fitting lid. Add 2 tablespoons peanut oil and heat the fat to sizzling but not smoking. (Adding oil allows the fat to "ripple" at a higher temperature.) Add the confit pieces skin side down. Cover tightly and cook over high heat.

You will hear much spattering and sizzling. Please don't uncover the pan! Cook for 2 minutes, remove the lid and carefully wipe off moisture clinging to the underside. Shake pan to make sure confit is not sticking and check crispness. Cover and continue cooking, shaking the pan to prevent sticking, for 1 to 3 minutes to finish browning. Remove from heat and uncover. Pour off the fat and turn each piece over. Cook, uncovered, over low heat, for 3 to 4 minutes to finish heating through. Remove the confit to wire racks or brown paper bags to drain.

DUCK LEGS CONFIT COOKED IN A POUCH (FOR CASSOULET)

➤➤ *"Confit" de Canard en Sous Vide*
    (Pour le Cassoulet)

SERVES 4 AS A MAIN COURSE,
OR 12 IF USED IN THE CASSOULET
IN THE STYLE OF TOULOUSE (PAGES 317–319)

TRADITIONAL DUCK CONFIT is not only cooked in fat but also preserved for a period of time (see pages 201–203). A true confit has a unique flavor developed as it ages in duck fat. You can make it the traditional way, buy ready-made confit, or use the cooking method described here, called *sous vide* (under vacuum).

It was in the French Southwest that I first learned about *sous vide*. The technique was developed by Chef George Pralus in the 1970s. Food is sealed in special boilable plastic pouches, then the pouches are poached in simmering water—a process that intensifies flavor and creates a silky texture, while preserving the natural shape of vegetables, fish, sausages, foie gras, etc. (See recipes for Steamed Salmon With Cooked Egg Sauce, pages 116–117, and Croustade With Apples and Prunes in Armagnac, pages 370–372, for examples.)

Recently, I learned how to use this method to make duck confit for use in cassoulet, where large succulent chunks of boned meat are set between layers of beans to bake for a second long cooking. *Sous vide*–prepared confit will survive this extra cooking and remain flavorful and moist. Additionally, this is the easiest and least messy way to prepare this essential cassoulet component.

First, you marinate the duck legs, rinse and completely dry them, then seal them in pairs with their attached fat in pouches using a vacuum packer such as a FoodSaver. Then you cook the pouches for many hours in a water bath at 180°F. As soon as the pouches come out of the simmering water, they are chilled down in an ice bath and kept refrigerated until ready to serve.

As opposed to the traditional confit process, you don't need extra duck fat because the tight vacuum pouch presses the melted fat around the meat. Moreover, this slow, low temperature cooking enhances flavor while developing a particularly tender, silky texture. The only down side of *sous vide* confit as compared to traditional aged confit is the lack of the special husky flavor of the latter.

The duck of choice for *sous vide* is Moulard with its dense, rich, fleshy, fatty legs. Large lean Muscovy ducks can be substituted, but you'll need to add ½ cup chilled rendered duck fat to each pouch. If Pekin ducks are substituted, you can reduce cooking time by 1 to 2 hours, depending on size.

4 Moulard or large Muscovy duck legs, or 6 Pekin or small Muscovy duck legs (about 3 pounds)	¼ cup Diamond Crystal kosher salt or 2 teaspoons per pound
	2 sprigs fresh thyme
	Freshly ground black pepper

1 Season duck legs with salt and a few thyme leaves. Wrap in paper toweling and refrigerate 24 hours.

2 The following day: Rinse off seasonings, blot very dry, and wrap in pairs in boilable pouches, then use a FoodSaver or professional vacuum packing device to seal airtight. Cover one stovetop burner with a Simmer Mat (see Note, page 200) or heat diffuser. Place the sealed pouches in a deep flameproof ceramic or cast-iron casserole and cover with hot water. Be sure the pouches are completely submerged; if necessary, weight them down. Place the casserole over the mat or heat diffuser set over medium-low heat. Cover the casserole and heat to 180°F (use an instant-read thermometer), then reduce heat to low and allow to simmer at a constant 180°F temperature for

(continued)

at least 8 hours for Moulard, 9 for Muscovy, or 5 to 6 hours for Pekin. (If you have an electric oven, alternatively, you can place the pouches in very hot water in a casserole and cook at 180°F overnight. (Because of the constant water temperature, the flesh won't cook beyond its stage of "doneness.")

3 The duck is ready when the flesh feels very tender, begins to separate from the bone, and the joint between leg and thigh cracks easily. When you remove the pouches from the casserole, immediately set the pouches in a bowl of ice water to chill until completely cold, about 30 minutes. The fat should congeal. Refrigerate until ready to use, within one week (see Note below).

4 When ready to serve: Place the pouches under warm running water until you can easily break the chunks of the fat away from the meat. Open each pouch and separate the fat and jelly-like juices from the flesh. Set the fat aside for some other purpose; use juices for sauces or add to the beans. If using for cassoulet, bone the legs and break the meat into large chunks. Brown the skin to a crisp in a skillet; season the flesh side with pepper. Add the meat chunks and skin to the cassoulet.

NOTES TO THE COOK

→ If you want to serve *sous vide* duck confit as a main course on the bone with a crispy skin, remove the duck legs from the pouches as directed in Step 4, arrange them skin side up on a rack set over a pan (to catch the melting fat) and brown them in a 400°F oven. Serve with sautéed potatoes, salad, or Pureed Sorrel (page 340).

→ If you're using a home vacuum packing system, such as FoodSaver, rather than a professional chefs' system, it's best to serve the duck within one week. (More sophisticated machines allow chefs to keep refrigerated confit in pouches in the refrigerator for many months.) If, for whatever reason, a refrigerated pouch begins to puff up, discard it at once. Bagged duck legs prepared with a home vacuum packing system can also be frozen for longer storage.

→ Don't be surprised if there is some ballooning during cooking. When the pouches are immersed in ice water they will contract.

→ Due to its unique design, a thin, metal Simmer Mat is superior to a heat diffuser to control cooking at a low temperature on a stovetop (see Mail Order Sources, pages 415–417).

With thanks to Nathan Myhrvold for helping to develop this recipe.

Salad of Duck Confit With Red Cabbage,
Chestnuts, and Watercress (page 206)

Salmon With Crackling Wafers (page 114)

Salt-Cured Pork Belly
With Fresh Fava Bean Ragout (page 301)

Carpaccio of Pig's Feet, Celery, and Black Truffles (page 86)

Autumn Squash Soup With Country Ham and Garlic Croutes (page 67)

Ragout of Duck Legs With White Onions and Prunes (page 184)

Wild Leek and Mushroom Torte (page 90)

*Hot Mussel Salad With
Curly Endive and Cream (page 104)*

TRADITIONAL CONFIT OF DUCK

5 pounds duck legs (Moulard, Muscovy, or Pekin) plus the gizzards, necks, and wings, if available

3 tablespoons plus 1 teaspoon coarse Diamond Crystal kosher salt or 2 teaspoons per pound

1½ tablespoons coarsely chopped shallots

1 teaspoon coarsely chopped fresh garlic plus 1 whole head of garlic, halved crosswise

1½ tablespoons chopped fresh flat-leaf parsley

2 teaspoons black peppercorns, lightly crushed

1 imported bay leaf, crumbled

1 sprig of fresh thyme, chopped, or a pinch of dried thyme

6 cups rendered duck or goose fat

2 whole cloves

Butcher's lard (optional, for longer storage)

1 Cure the duck: Rinse the duck pieces and dry thoroughly. In a large bowl, toss the duck with the salt, shallots, chopped garlic, parsley, peppercorns, bay leaf, and thyme. Cover with plastic wrap and refrigerate for 18 to 24 hours. Plan carefully because longer brining will cause your confit to be overly salty.

2 Rinse the marinated duck pieces under cold running water to rinse off the salt and seasonings. Drain briefly; it is not necessary to dry completely. Place the rendered duck fat in a large, very heavy pot, such as a stoneware crock or enameled cast-iron casserole, and melt over low heat.

3 Stick a whole clove into each half-head of garlic and add to the melted fat. Slip in the pieces of duck. Cook, uncovered, in the casserole, until the fat reaches 190°F. This should take about 1 hour; faster heating will result in stringy texture. Add additional rendered fat, if necessary, to cover the duck. Continue cooking at 192°F to 210°F, but no higher, adjusting the heat level as necessary, until for another 1 hour, or 2 hours for the Muscovy, until a toothpick pierces the thickest part of a thigh easily. Remove from the heat and let the duck cool in the fat for 1 hour.

4 Meanwhile, set out three 1-quart earthenware crocks or wide-mouthed glass jars. Pour boiling water into each; swirl and pour out. Thoroughly dry the inside of the containers with a clean towel. Immediately place ½ teaspoon salt in the bottom of each container; this prevents the meat juices (salarque) that may seep from the duck during ripening from turning sour.

(continued)

5 Using a slotted spoon, carefully transfer the duck legs to the containers, filling each about three quarters full without crowding.

6 Heat the fat, uncovered, over moderate heat until a few bubbles rise to the surface, skimming off the foam that rises to the top. Let bubble slowly for 5 to 10 minutes, or until any spattering stops and the surface of the fat is clear. Watch very carefully and reduce the heat if necessary to avoid burning or smoking; fat that reaches the smoking point will be ruined for reuse.

7 Carefully ladle the hot clear fat through a fine-mesh strainer directly onto the duck pieces to cover, allowing a generous inch of air space between the surface of the fat and the rim of the container. Do not include the more perishable cloudy fat and meat juices at the bottom of the pot. Rap the containers gently to tamp out any air pockets. Let cool, uncovered, to room temperature. Cover and refrigerate overnight or set in a cold cellar or other cool storage area to allow the fat to congeal.

8 The next day, seal the confit by spooning a 1-inch layer of melted lard over the surface; since lard is more impenetrable to air than duck fat, this protects against spoilage. (The exact amount of lard needed will vary with the dimensions of your vessels.) Cover with parchment paper secured with a rubber band or with a lid. Store in a 50°F wine or root cellar, or in the refrigerator for at least 1 week or up to 6 months before using. If planning to use the confit within a week, you do not need to seal the confit with lard.

NOTES TO THE COOK

⇥ Rendered duck fat is sold in many butcher shops throughout the country. You can mail order tubs or small containers from D'Artagnan.com, preferredmeats.com, or Frenchselections.com. You can also freeze any unused pieces of fresh fat and skin whenever you cook a duck or goose. When you have accumulated several cups' worth, render it according to the directions on page 169. (Fat before rendering will keep for up to 6 months in the freezer; rendered fat will keep for 6 to 8 months in refrigerator and up to a year in the freezer.) Rendered goose fat, available from some butchers, is also an excellent choice.

⇥ As the Moulard or Pekin ducks cook they will release a lot of fat, which will help cover the pieces of duck. Muscovy duck has less fat and will need extra fat to get to an amount that will cover the duck during the cooking.

→ For sealing the confit, good quality butcher's lard, purchased from a pork butcher or other reliable meat store, is ideal; do not use packaged commercial lard, which is too strong-tasting and will spoil your fat for further cooking. Another alternative is to make your own lard from pork leaf lard (see Rendered Pork Fat, page 295).

→ Instead of cooking the confit on top of the stove, it can be prepared in the oven, but you must use a digital thermometer to check the temperature: Place the duck, skin side down, in a deep baking dish and pour the melted fat over the pieces. Place uncovered in a cold oven. Turn the oven on to 275°F. After the temperature of the fat has reached 190°F (1 to 1½ hours, depending on your oven), reduce the setting to 200°F. Cook, adjusting the heat as necessary, to maintain the temperature of the fat at 190°F, until the duck pieces are tender, 1½ to 2 hours, depending on the variety of duck used. Turn off the heat and let the duck legs cool in the fat in the oven for 1 hour.

→ Although confit at this point will not have the excellent flavor of aged confit, it can be used at once in any confit recipe; follow directions on pages 197–198 for browning or steaming and serving.

→ The garlic cooked with the confit can be pressed through a sieve to obtain a small amount of an unusually flavorful spread.

A Word About Geese

→ ←

Geese can be prepared like duck for confit with an additional hour's cooking time. Confit of goose (page 213) has an extraordinary flavor, and you can use the breast as well as the legs.

→ The cloudy fat can be used as a flavorful sautéing fat; any juices left in pot after all fat has been removed can be saved and added to soups for flavor. Any debris on bottom of pan after fat and juices have been removed can be turned into rillettes, a delicious spread. Scrape up debris and mix well in a small bowl with an equal amount of confit fat or fresh unsalted butter. Season liberally with pepper; use as a spread on crackers or toast rounds.

Confit Prepared in a Slow Cooker

❖

I have found that the gentle heat of an electric slow cooker set on low is ideal for making confit. Use duck legs, gizzards, neck, and wings and marinate them as described on page 196 (see Curing the Duck). You will need at least 4 cups rendered duck fat; the exact amount will vary depending on the size and shape of your cooking vessel. Ideally, the fat should cover the pieces of duck; if there is not enough fat, you might have to make the confit in two batches. In that case, do not remove the salt and herbs from the prepared duck parts until ready to cook.

1 Cure the duck as directed in Step 1 of the traditional recipe (pages 201–203). Render the duck fat in a saucepan as directed in the Duck Fat and Cracklings recipe (page 169).

2 The following day, rinse the pieces of duck, wiping away all the seasonings, and dry well. Place the rendered duck fat, the pieces of duck, and the garlic stuck with cloves in a slow cooker and set on low. Check the temperature and hold it at 190°F, adjusting the cover and setting as necessary to help control temperature. Cook the gizzards, neck, and wings until tender enough to be pierced easily with a wooden toothpick, about 3 hours. Remove them with a slotted spoon as they are done; keep the pieces covered with foil to prevent drying out.

3 Continue to cook the duck legs and thighs another hour or until the thickest part of a duck thigh tests done by piercing with a wooden toothpick. Turn off the heat but allow the duck legs to cool in the fat for 1 more hour. Remove the duck thighs and garlic with a slotted spoon to a side dish.

4 Ladle the fat through a sieve into a large saucepan. Heat, uncovered, over moderately high heat to almost boiling, but do not allow to smoke. Skim off the foam that rises to surface. Let bubble for 5 to 10 minutes, or until spattering stops and the surface of the fat is nearly undisturbed. Watch carefully and adjust the heat if necessary to avoid burning or smoking; fat that is allowed to reach smoking point will be ruined for reuse. Remove from the heat and let cool slightly. Store as directed above.

DUCK CONFIT WITH GREEN PEAS AND HAM

Confit de Canard Landaise

THIS IS AN EXCELLENT supper dish for spring and early summer when fresh tender peas still in their moist pods are available.

In years past I thought I could taste the difference between frozen and fresh peas. Nowadays, there are some wonderful frozen peas in the supermarkets and I suggest you use them when fresh peas are out of season. Serve this dish in a shallow earthenware pot for a rustic presentation.

3 pounds fresh peas in their pods, or 2 cups frozen baby peas

4 Duck Legs Confit (pages 198–200), at room temperature

⅔ cup cubed jambon de Bayonne, prosciutto, or Serrano ham

8 frozen baby white onions, thawed

⅓ cup diced carrots

Pinch of sugar

Herb bouquet: 3 sprigs parsley, 1 sprig thyme, and ½ imported bay leaf tied together with string

Freshly ground pepper

1 Shell the fresh peas; there should be about 2 cups. Blanch the fresh peas in boiling salted water for 2 minutes; drain and rinse under cold running water.

2 Set aside 2 tablespoons fat from the confit. Steam and crisp the Duck Legs Confit as directed on pages 197–198.

3 Heat 1 tablespoon of the duck confit fat in a large skillet. Add the ham, onions, and carrots. Cover and cook over moderately low heat for 5 minutes. Uncover and cook, stirring, until the carrots and onions brown lightly around the edges. Add the drained or frozen peas, sugar, herb bouquet, and ⅓ cup water. Cover tightly and simmer until the peas are almost cooked, 3 to 5 minutes, depending on whether fresh or frozen.

4 When peas are almost cooked, nestle the confit in the peas. Add the remaining 1 tablespoon confit fat and simmer together, uncovered, for 5 minutes to blend the flavors. Remove and discard the herb bouquet. Season with pepper. Serve very hot.

SALAD OF DUCK CONFIT WITH RED CABBAGE, CHESTNUTS, AND WATERCRESS

→ *Salade Cévenole*   SERVES 4 TO 6

THIS MAKES FOR a very pretty presentation, but unlike a lot of so-called pretty dishes, it has more than a merely decorative effect. The flavors blend together brilliantly; the visual appeal is equally striking.

4 to 6 leg portions Duck Confit (pages 198–200)

3½ ounces walnut halves (1 scant cup)

1½ teaspoons sugar

4 to 5 tablespoons fat from confit

3 tablespoons grapeseed oil or peanut oil

¼ cup red wine vinegar, preferably a strong-flavored variety

2 tablespoons red wine

2 to 3 tablespoons fresh lemon juice

¼ cup French walnut oil

Salt and freshly ground pepper to taste

1 small head of red cabbage

8 ounces vacuum-packed roasted chestnuts, coarsely crumbled

2 bunches of watercress, tough stems removed, or a mixture of watercress and several large handfuls of tender chicory

2 small carrots, peeled and shredded

Duck Cracklings (page 169, optional)

1 Set the crock of confit in a warm place or in a deep pan of warm water to soften the fat, 2 to 3 hours.

2 Preheat the oven to 350°F. Spread walnuts in small baking pan; sprinkle with ½ teaspoon of the sugar. Toast until lightly browned, 5 to 8 minutes. Remove from oven; let cool. *(The walnuts can be prepared to this point ahead of time.)*

3 When fat has softened, remove 4 to 6 confit pieces; pull out any loose bones. Steam and crisp "aged" confit as directed on pages 197–198. Otherwise, carefully scrape 2 tablespoons of the confit fat into a large, heavy skillet with a tight-fitting lid; add 1½ tablespoons of the grapeseed oil. Heat over moderately high heat to rippling. Add 2 or 3 pieces of confit, skin side down. Cook, tightly covered, for 2 to 3 minutes, until the skin is crisp and well browned. During cooking, remove the lid twice and carefully wipe off the moisture on the underside. Shake the pan to make sure the confit is not sticking. Remove skillet from heat; let stand, tightly covered, 30 seconds. Uncover, pour off and discard the fat. Return to the heat and let the confit crisp for about 10 seconds longer,

then set each piece skin side up on a wire rack or brown paper bag to drain. Repeat with more fat, the remaining 1½ tablespoons oil, and confit. Let cool while you make the salad. (If the confit skin loses its crisp quality, return to a greased skillet and crisp for 30 seconds.)

4 Quarter, core, and slice the cabbage into thin ribbons. Make the dressing by combining vinegar, red wine, the remaining 1 teaspoon sugar, the lemon juice, walnut oil, and salt and pepper to taste in small mixing bowl. Toss the dressing with the sliced cabbage; let stand at room temperature 30 minutes to develop flavor.

5 At serving time, toss the marinated cabbage in a salad bowl with the chestnuts, watercress, and walnuts. Taste and correct seasoning, adding drops of lemon juice to taste. Sprinkle the shredded carrots on top. Plate the salad with the confit and garnish with the cracklings.

PRESERVED STUFFED DUCK NECK
➵➤ *Confit de Cou de Canard Farci*   SERVES 6

THIS IS MY OWN VERSION of a classic Southwest recipe for stuffed duck neck. I transform duck breast and some extra neck skin into savory sausages, which are cooked, like confit, by poaching in rendered goose or duck fat to cover. The time to make this dish is when you are cooking other duck confits (see pages 195–213).

Preserved stuffed duck neck can be used for pot-au-feu, in which it is sensational. Or it can be crisped in a skillet for 5 minutes, thickly sliced, and served with a bitter green salad dressed with walnut oil vinaigrette. Other accompaniments can be Pureed Sorrel (page 340), sautéed potatoes and tart apples, or a traditional Périgueux Sauce (pages 260–261).

(continued)

1 whole Pekin duck breast, 10 to 12 ounces, plus neck skin of 2 ducks

Coarse kosher salt and freshly ground pepper

Armagnac

6 ounces fatty boneless pork shoulder, cut into 1-inch cubes

1 medium shallot, thinly sliced

1 garlic clove, halved

Pinch of crumbled dried thyme leaves

¼ small imported bay leaf, crushed to a powder

1 egg

½ cup leftover foie gras terrine or cooked foie gras, or 1 can (4 to 5 ounces) puree of foie gras

4 to 5 cups rendered duck or goose fat

1 Remove the skin in large pieces from the breasts and cut away all excess fat. Sprinkle with the salt, pepper, and Armagnac.

2 Bone the duck breasts. Trim off all excess fat. Pulse the duck meat and pork cubes in a food processor to coarsely chop. Add the shallot, garlic, thyme, bay leaf, ¾ teaspoon salt, and ¼ teaspoon pepper. Process until the mixture is coarsely but evenly ground. Scrape into a mixing bowl, mix in the egg, 1 tablespoon Armagnac, and the foie gras, blending well with a spoon. *(The recipe can be prepared to this point up to a day in advance; cover the stuffing and refrigerate.)*

3 Spread out all the duck skins, outer side down, to form a large rectangle. Sew the pieces together with kitchen string. Pile the stuffing in a cylinder shape down the center. Wrap the stuffing completely in the duck skin to form a roll about 1¼ inches in diameter to simulate a duck neck. If the skin overlaps, cut away the excess. Sew up the ends and tie the roll at intervals with kitchen string to preserve the shape.

4 Melt 4 cups of the poultry fat to 190°F. Slip the stuffed roll into the fat. If it is not covered, add the remaining fat. Cook for 30 to 45 minutes, or until the roll rises to the surface. Remove and drain well. Use at once, within 3 days, or preserve as directed in the recipe for Traditional Confit of Duck (pages 201–203).

NOTE TO THE COOK

Traditionally in the Southwest, this dish is made with goose neck, plus any bits of meat left over from making confit. If using a goose neck, singe the skin over an open flame. Peel the skin from the neck in one piece without tearing. Fill with stuffing, sew, and cook in fat until the neck rises to the surface.

CONFIT OF DUCK GIZZARDS

→ *Confit de Gésiers de Canard*   MAKES ABOUT 3 CUPS

"HAVE YOU EVER NOTICED how in most families only one person really likes gizzards?" André Daguin, the famous Gascon chef, asked me as he was cutting up ducks in his restaurant kitchen. I nodded, wondering what he was driving at since he was standing in front of a huge pile of gizzards ready to be cured and preserved under duck fat. "Well," he added, smiling, "in our family, we all love them!!!"

Actually, nowadays I think there are more gizzard-loving families than there used to be. These little luscious morsels of flavor and texture have become increasingly popular, either eaten alone or added as hearty flavor enhancers to soups, lentil and bean dishes, salads, vegetable stews, and daubes. I offer three different confit of gizzard dishes: confit of duck gizzards with a fricassee of chanterelles tossed with a Périgord blend of pancetta and garlic (pages 93–94); confit of duck gizzards with a simple, Warm Lentil Salad (pages 212–213); and Confit of Duck Gizzards With a Salad of Mixed Greens and Walnut Vinaigrette (page 211). For each recipe, you'll need about ½ pound raw fresh duck gizzards. Multiply the seasonings proportionately if you use a larger amount.

The question is: How can you ever find enough gizzards to make any or all of these dishes? One way is simply to coax your butcher into selling you fresh extra duck gizzards. Another is to visit an Asian meat market that offers them already separated and ready for sale. Or, perhaps best of all, you can simply collect them as you prepare different duck dishes in this book and store your cache in the freezer until you have enough. Another way is to order them in large amounts either raw or already prepared as confit from D'Artagnan (see Mail Order Sources, pages 415–417).

Homemade confit of gizzards keeps for up to 2 weeks in the fridge and freezes well. You can preserve the gizzards longer by processing them in sterile mason jars. For making a small amount of duck gizzards for confit, cure them and cook along with other duck parts such as the legs as directed on pages 198–200.

(continued)

1½ pounds large fresh duck gizzards (If using thawed frozen, see Note below)

2 teaspoons coarse kosher salt

1 medium shallot, chopped

1 teaspoon minced fresh garlic

1½ teaspoons lightly crushed black peppercorns

1½ teaspoons dried thyme leaves or herbes de Provence

4 cups rendered duck fat (see page 169) or rendered goose fat

1 Rinse the gizzards; drain dry. Using a paring knife or a pair of sharp scissors, cut away and discard the gizzard membrane and cut each one in half. Wash again to remove any grit. Pat dry with paper towels.

2 Spread out the gizzards on a baking sheet lined with a double layer of paper towels. Sprinkle with the salt, shallot, garlic, peppercorns, and thyme. Roll the gizzard chunks around to coat evenly with the seasonings. Cover loosely with more paper towels and let cure in the refrigerator overnight.

3 The following day, fully rinse the gizzards, dry them thoroughly, and place in a small ceramic casserole or ovenproof glass bowl. Pour the poultry fat over the gizzards to cover. Cover the casserole with a sheet of foil or a lid, and place in a cold oven. Heat to 225°F and cook for 2 to 3 hours, or until the gizzards are fork tender.

4 Immediately remove the gizzards from the fat. Use at once, or store in three sterile 1½-cup glass canning jars or plastic tubs, topping off with enough fat to cover. The gizzards must be completely submerged in fat. If necessary, add more duck fat, lard, or olive oil to cover. Refrigerate, covered, until you are ready to use. The gizzards keep up to 2 weeks in the fat in the refrigerator. For longer storage, freeze in plastic tubs or bags.

5 To use: Bring the jar or container of gizzards to room temperature. Set jar in a pan of water, uncovered; simmer until the fat melts, 10 to 15 minutes (or set plastic container in a microwave and melt the fat on low for a few minutes). Drain gizzards; reserve the fat for cooking. If desired, place the gizzards in a steamer and steam a few minutes to remove all the fat and to plump.

NOTES TO THE COOK

➼ If using thawed frozen gizzards, increase the salt to 4 ounces. Let cure in the refrigerator for only 2 hours in Step 2.

➼ Confit of Duck Gizzards can be prepared in an electric slow cooker, partially covered, and set on low for approximately 6 hours.

Confit of Duck Gizzards
With a Salad of Mixed Greens

→→ *Salade aux Gésiers de Canard*   SERVES 4

IT'S THIS CONFIT of duck gizzards dish that turned me into a gizzards addict! I was traveling in the Périgord, on the southern bank of the Dordogne, just ten kilometers from the town of Saint-Cyprien, when a friend took me to a small home-restaurant. I ordered a stuffed duck that had slowly cooked the entire morning in a heavy black pot and would be embellished with sautéed mushrooms. But first I was served a mixture of garden greens with confit of gizzards, which lent the salad a wonderful warm and salty flavor.

1 cup homemade Confit of Duck Gizzards (pages 209–210) or storebought precooked gizzards

Freshly ground pepper

6 ounces (about 4 cups) mixed greens: arugula, radicchio, frisée, mâche

½ teaspoon Dijon mustard or *moutarde violette* (see Mail Order Sources, pages 415–417)

2 teaspoons red wine vinegar, or more to taste

Salt

3 tablespoons French walnut oil

1 tablespoon dry red wine

1 Thinly slice the gizzards and generously season with black pepper.

2 Rinse and dry the greens, and tear into bite-size pieces.

3 In a salad bowl, whisk together the mustard, vinegar, and a pinch each of salt and pepper until well blended. Whisk in the walnut oil.

4 Place the gizzards in a medium skillet with 2 teaspoons of the duck fat from the confit. Gently cook over moderately low heat until hot, 2 to 3 minutes.

5 Add the greens to the salad bowl and toss once. Pour the contents of the skillet over the greens. Add the wine to the skillet and bring to a boil; pour over the salad and toss. Serve at once.

Preserved Gizzards
With Warm Lentil Salad

→► *Les Gésiers Confits Avec la Salade de Lentilles*

OF ALL THE LENTILS you can buy, the green *lentille du Puy* is the finest in flavor and the least floury in texture. Lentils in the shades of dark green, brown, and dark blue have an extraordinary rustic, full flavor with a velvety, luxuriously rich texture. They used to be grown only in the volcanic soil of the Auvergne, but now they are grown in the United States and cost a lot less. Unlike other lentils, they are very light and don't become mushy when cooked. I simmer them slowly until they are tender, then add a little Armagnac or Cognac, which gives them a great taste.

Another flavor enhancer common in the French Southwest is large pieces of raw onion, used to stud the lentils as they cool. The onion is removed before serving, leaving a faint hint of its savor behind.

You can prepare Steps 1 through 4 early in the day. It will only get better.

1 cup French lentilles de Puy, rinsed and drained

½ onion stuck with 1 whole clove, plus the remaining half onion separated into layers

1 sprig of thyme

1 imported bay leaf

2 tablespoons Cognac or Armagnac

1 medium shallot, peeled and chopped

2 tablespoons aged red wine vinegar

1 teaspoon Dijon mustard or *moutarde violette*

½ cup imported walnut oil

Salt and freshly ground pepper

1 cup homemade Confit of Duck Gizzards (pages 209–210) or storebought precooked

3 tablespoons minced flat-leaf parsley

¼ pound arugula, rinsed and dried

1 Put the lentils in a saucepan, cover with 1 quart of cold water, bring to a boil, and skim. Add the onion half with the clove, thyme, and bay leaf. Reduce the heat and simmer for 20 minutes.

2 Add the Cognac and continue to cook until the lentils are tender but still hold their shape, about 10 minutes longer. Drain; pick out and discard the onion half and herbs.

3 In a mixing bowl, soak the shallots in the vinegar for about 10 minutes. Add the mustard and walnut oil and whisk to blend well. Season with salt and pepper to taste. Remove about half of this vinaigrette to a salad bowl.

4 Add the drained hot lentils to the remaining dressing in the mixing bowl and fold gently to coat. Stud the lentils with the onion leaves and set in a cool place for several hours, stirring from time. Remove the pieces of raw onion.

5 Shortly before serving, remove the duck gizzards from the confit container. Slice thinly and place in a medium skillet with 2 teaspoons of the duck fat from the confit. Gently cook over moderately low heat until hot, 2 to 3 minutes. Add the lentils to the skillet and cook over moderate heat, stirring gently, until they are just heated through, about 1 minute. Stir in the parsley and season with salt, pepper, and perhaps a little more vinegar to taste.

6 Toss the arugula with the reserved vinaigrette in the salad bowl and divide among 4 plates, setting the greens to one side. Spoon the warm lentils and gizzards next to the arugula and serve at once.

CONFIT OF GOOSE
→→ *Confit d'Oie*

THROUGHOUT SOUTHWEST FRANCE, goose is turned into confit as often as is duck. Unfortunately, it isn't easy to find geese in American markets except at Christmas. However, goose is particularly desirable as confit. Its taste is richer and rounder than duck, and its fat is even better for cooking. To make confit of goose, follow the steps for duck but marinate a 9-pound goose, cut up, for 24 hours. Cook it for 2 to 2½ hours, or until pieces are tender when pierced with a wooden pick. If your pot is not large enough to cook large pieces all at once, cut into smaller pieces or cook in batches. It may be necessary to remove larger bones after cooking to fit the confit into storage containers.

Confit of goose is best served in the following traditional ways: hot in *garbure*, in cassoulet, with sautéed potatoes, with pureed sorrel, and with sautéed wild mushrooms, or cold with a green salad.

GOOSE STEW WITH RADISHES

→ *Daube d'Oie aux Radis*   SERVES 6 TO 8

THIS IS A MODERN VERSION of a very old Gascon recipe for goose stew. For good reason, we associate geese with fat, but goose meat itself is lean, especially in the breast. In this recipe, the breast meat is actually larded to keep it juicy—the strips of fat are soaked first in Armagnac mixed with chopped garlic and herbs. The addition of radishes is new—they taste like peppery turnips when they are cooked. Salsify, turnips, carrots, and blanched baby onions can be prepared similarly and used as an alternative garnish for this daube. The daube requires long cooking, but the result is rich and satisfying. Noodles make a good accompaniment.

Like most good stews, this one is better reheated, so plan to make it 3 to 5 days in advance of serving.

1 goose (10 to 12 pounds), preferably fresh

3 tablespoons Armagnac

1 teaspoon minced shallot

1 teaspoon minced fresh flat-leaf parsley

¼ teaspoon dried thyme, crumbled

¼ teaspoon freshly grated nutmeg

1 garlic clove, thinly sliced

8 ounces pancetta, divided into 6 to 8 slices

Coarse kosher salt

Herb bouquet: 6 sprigs parsley, 1 sprig thyme, and 1 imported bay leaf tied together with string

1 bottle (750 ml) full-bodied dry red wine such as California Petite Sirah or French Côtes-du-Rhône, or see A Few Words About the Local Wines (pages 38–40) for other choices

2 medium onions, thinly sliced

1 medium carrot, thinly sliced

1 medium leek, white part, thinly sliced

8½ cups unsalted chicken stock (storebought or homemade—page 405)

4 tablespoons unsalted butter

2 teaspoons sugar

3 to 4 dozen radishes, trimmed

Salt and freshly ground pepper

Chopped fresh flat-leaf parsley

1 Three days before serving, trim all fat and skin from the goose. Render the fat, let cool, then store in a covered jar in refrigerator.

2 Combine the Armagnac, shallots, parsley, thyme, nutmeg, and garlic in large bowl; mix well. Add the slices of pancetta and toss to coat with the marinade.

3 Cut up the goose, using a boning knife. Cut down the center breast to the bone. Guiding the knife along the breast, pull the meat back and lift it from bone in one piece. Sever the legs and thighs at the joints. Cut the meat off the bone and trim off any fat or gristle. Cut the goose meat into 1½-inch chunks.

4 Remove the pancetta from the marinade; set the marinade aside. Cut the slices crosswise into thin strips. With a thin, sharp knife, pierce a hole in center of each chunk of meat. Fill the holes with the pieces of pancetta. Add the goose meat to the marinade. Add 1 tablespoon salt and toss lightly. Let marinate for 2 nights in the refrigerator.

5 Meanwhile, peel the goose gizzard. Rinse the gizzard and heart and place in a deep bowl. Crack the carcass, wings, and neck into very small pieces. Add the cracked bones and herb bouquet to gizzard and heart. Pour the wine over all and refrigerate overnight to marinate. Reserve the liver for pâté or some other use.

6 The following morning, heat 1½ tablespoons reserved rendered goose fat in a large deep pot over moderate heat. Add the onions and carrot and sauté until browned, 5 to 10 minutes. Tilt the pot and press lightly on the vegetables with a slotted spoon to release the fat. Blot the fat with paper towels. Return the pot to moderate heat. Add the leeks, marinated bones, herb bouquet, gizzard, and heart with the wine marinade. Slowly bring to a boil. Reduce the heat to low and cook until the liquid is reduced to ½ cup, 3 to 4 hours, skimming often. (This can also be done in a slow cooker or in the oven.)

7 Add 8 cups chicken stock to the pot. If necessary, add water to cover. Bring to a boil over moderate heat. Reduce the heat and simmer, skimming frequently, for 3 to 4 more hours, until the stock is reduced to 3 cups. Strain the stock through a sieve. Refrigerate until the fat hardens on the surface. Scrape off and discard the fat.

8 Early on the day you plan to serve the dish, pat the goose meat dry with paper towels. Heat a large, deep skillet over moderately high heat. Add 3 tablespoons of the rendered goose fat. Add half the goose meat and sauté, turning, until browned, about 10 minutes. Tilt the pan and blot all excess fat with paper towels. Repeat with more fat and the remaining goose meat. Pour out excess fat and return all the meat to the pan. Add the reduced stock and bring to a boil. Reduce the heat and simmer gently until the meat is very tender but not falling apart, 2 to 2½ hours.

(continued)

9 Remove the meat to a side dish. Degrease the stock and pour it into a saucepan. Bring to a boil, set the saucepan half on the heat and cook at a slow boil, skimming, for 10 to 15 minutes, or until the sauce is thick enough to coat the meat. Pour the sauce over the pieces of goose. *(The recipe can be prepared to this point up to 6 hours in advance and refrigerated.)*

10 About 30 minutes before serving, remove any fat from the surface of the stew. Place the goose and sauce in a large skillet. Slowly reheat to a simmer.

11 Meanwhile prepare vegetable garnish: In another large skillet, combine the remaining ½ cup chicken stock with the butter and sugar over high heat. Add the radishes, cover, and cook until crisp-tender, about 5 minutes; do not let the radishes burn. Uncover and shake the skillet to glaze the radishes. Drain, discarding any liquid.

12 Add the glazed radishes to the goose stew and simmer for 5 minutes. Season to taste with salt and pepper. Transfer to a large serving dish or platter. Sprinkle with parsley and serve.

Inspired by a recipe from the late Jean-Louis Palladin.

RABBIT STEW WITH PRESERVED PEARS WITH GINGER

➤➤ *Blanquette de Lapin au Confit de Poires et Gingembre*

SERVES 4 TO 6

THIS COMBINATION of mustard-flavored rabbit stew and gingered pears is most unusual and exciting to the palate. Though wild rabbits are particularly flavorful, this recipe will work very well with the farm-bred variety. I believe that rabbits, like duck, work best when cut up into parts then used in different ways. The front part of this animal has little meat, while the saddle and hind legs are abundantly meaty. When I buy frozen rabbit, I use only the meaty pieces for this dish, saving the ribs and front legs for a delicious Old-Fashioned Rabbit Soup (pages 61–62). Use a fryer (young) rabbit for this dish.

Because the rabbit needs to marinate, begin this recipe two or three days in advance.

3 large shallots, halved

2 garlic cloves, halved

4 tablespoons olive oil

3 cups dry white wine

1 or 2 fryer rabbits (4 pounds total dressed weight), fresh or frozen; all parts of 1 rabbit or 2 pair hindquarters and saddles cut up for stewing

⅓ cup rendered duck or goose fat

5 ounces lean salt pork, blanched in water for 5 minutes, rinsed, and cut into 1-inch cubes

½ teaspoon Herbes de la Garrigue (page 80) or herbes de Provence

Coarse kosher salt and freshly ground pepper

Scant ½ cup Dijon mustard

3 onions (about ¾ pound), thinly sliced

2 egg yolks

Pinch of freshly grated nutmeg

1 cup heavy cream

Juice of ½ lemon

3 tablespoons minced fresh chives

Preserved Pears With Ginger (pages 218–219)

1 Put the shallots, garlic, olive oil, and half the wine in a large bowl. Add the rabbit pieces and turn them over until well coated. Cover with plastic wrap and refrigerate for 2 to 3 days, turning the rabbit pieces once or twice a day. If the rabbit is frozen, defrost it directly in the marinade.

2 About 3 hours before serving, remove the rabbit pieces and pat dry with paper towels. Strain the marinade, reserving the garlic and shallots, and the liquid separately.

3 Preheat the oven to 300°F. In a large skillet, heat the fat. Sauté the salt pork, transferring the pieces to a 4-quart casserole as they are browned. In the same skillet, brown the rabbit pieces, a few at a time, on both sides, transferring them to the casserole as they are browned. Sprinkle the rabbit and the pork cubes with the herbs, very little salt, and pepper.

4 Pour off all but 2 tablespoons fat from the skillet. Add the onions to the skillet along with the reserved garlic and shallots. Sauté over moderately high heat, stirring to avoid burning, until soft and golden brown, 6 to 8 minutes. Stir in ⅓ cup of the mustard with the juices in the bottom of the casserole until well blended.

5 Using a slotted spoon, transfer the onions, shallots, and garlic to the casserole. Deglaze the skillet with the strained marinade liquid and bring to a boil, skimming off any scum that rises to the surface. Add the remaining 1½ cups white wine and return to a boil. Skim again and pour the boiling liquid over the rabbit and onions. Cover with crumbled wet parchment or waxed paper and a tight-fitting lid.

(continued)

6 Set the casserole in the oven to cook for 2 hours, or until the rabbit is meltingly tender. (To avoid stringy rabbit, do not rush cooking time; if the rabbit is not tender; let it slowly finish cooking in the oven.) Remove the pieces of rabbit to a warm bowl; cover and keep moist.

7 Strain the cooking liquid, pushing down on the vegetables to extract all their juices. Quickly cool the liquid and remove any fat that surfaces. Place the juices in a heavy saucepan over moderately high heat and bring to a boil. Shift the pan so that only half of it is over heat. Slowly boil down to 1 cup, skimming often.

8 About 5 minutes before serving, whisk together the egg yolks, nutmeg, remaining mustard, and cream in a small bowl until well blended. Whisk a few tablespoons of the hot reduced cooking juices into the egg yolk mixture; then whisk the mixture back into the saucepan. Heat gently, whisking until the sauce thickens. Do not allow the sauce to boil. Add the lemon juice and season with salt and pepper to taste. Stir in the chives. Spoon the sauce over the rabbit and serve hot with the Preserved Pears with Ginger.

NOTE TO THE COOK

You can cook the rabbit in the casserole through Step 6 in advance. Leave the rabbit pieces in the sauce. Gently reheat, then remove the pieces of rabbit to a warm bowl and continue to make the sauce as directed above.

PRESERVED PEARS WITH GINGER

Poires Confites au Gingembre   SERVES 6

2 tablespoons grated fresh ginger

¼ cup sugar

¾ cup dry white wine

1 cup unsalted chicken stock
(storebought or homemade—page 405)

3 large Bosc pears (about 1½ pounds)

1 tablespoon unsalted butter

3 tablespoons fresh lemon juice

1 Preheat the oven to 375°F. In a medium saucepan, combine the ginger, sugar, and wine. Bring to a boil, stirring to dissolve the sugar. Reduce the heat and simmer until the syrup is reduced to 3 tablespoons. Add the stock and bring to a boil, stirring.

2 Meanwhile, peel, halve, and core the pears. Arrange, cut sides down, in a single layer in a large buttered baking dish. Sprinkle with 1½ tablespoons of the lemon juice. Pour the syrup over the pears.

3. Bake, uncovered, for 45 minutes, or until golden brown and glazed. Baste often with the syrupy juices. Sprinkle with remaining lemon juice. If not used at once, set aside at room temperature for up to 8 hours and reheat gently before serving; do not refrigerate.

Inspired by a recipe from Lucien Vanel.

CIVET OF HARE

➤➤ *Civet de Lièvre*   SERVES 5 TO 6

IN 1983, I WAS ASKED by the *New York Times* Travel Section to describe my most memorable bistro meal in Paris. It wasn't difficult—the memory of one of the most famous dishes of the French Southwest had been with me for years, and it was a delight to share it. This is what I wrote:

> Basically my favorite bistro is L'Ami Louis. The floor is concave, as if thousands of people have trod back and forth. There are long tables, and the feeling is like a mess hall. The walls have a patina of aged dirt. To quote Gault and Millau, the kitchen is from the Paleolithic age and the toilets are Neanderthal.
>
> The 82-year-old Antoine Magnin has a long, white beard; he may at times appear hostile toward the customers, but he has the right attitude about food. Eat the foie gras; it comes out like thick slices of black bread. Then order the civet of hare, and out comes the whole pot. It is enough for four people—they give you the whole animal, and they even serve the shot in the sauce. And it's really thick sauce—there's nothing like it. You scoop up the sauce with your bread. Then you can have potatoes béarnaise, fried in goose fat, the walnuts flown in from the Périgord. Drink Jurançon with the foie gras, the house Fleurie with the hare.

The now-deceased Monsieur Magnin did not like to share his recipes, but my friend Aude Clément knew him well, had eaten the hare many times at the restaurant, and offered to teach me how to make it. With her advice and a recipe in *La Bonne Cuisine de Périgord* by La Mazille, one of my favorite female food writers from the 1920s, I worked up a version that's pretty close to what I ate in Paris that memorable day.

(continued)

The success of this civet relies on:

→ Cutting the hare properly so that the flesh will not dry out during cooking;

→ Slow cooking, which inhibits toughening of the flesh;

→ Using plenty of pork fat to lubricate the flesh;

→ Using a good, full-bodied red wine, solid enough to hold its flavor during the long, mostly unattended cooking; and

→ Enriching the sauce with the hare's blood and liver, which will give it a strong, earthy taste.

Hare is a wild rabbit. While domestic rabbit has white flesh and is very mild in flavor, wild hare has reddish-brown flesh and is gamy. For this recipe, I use Scottish hare, which is now imported to the United States. D'Artagnan sells Scottish brown hare in season (see Mail Order Sources, pages 415–417). American jackrabbit is in the same family and can be cooked in the same manner.

Since not many people have access to a freshly killed young hare, you can adjust the recipe and make it with large duck legs. A sumptuous dish like this is at its best with a simple salad, pureed lentils, or rounds of French baguette toasted in the oven and rubbed lightly with crushed garlic.

Because the hare is marinated, begin one to two days in advance.

1 hare, 5 to 6 pounds, cut into 10 to 12 portions, liver and blood reserved separately (See To Cut Up a Hare or a Rabbit, at right, and Notes on page 222 for handling the blood and liver)

5 medium onions, quartered

2 carrots, sliced

1 celery rib, sliced

Herb bouquet: 3 sprigs each of thyme, parsley, rosemary, and 1 imported bay leaf, tied together with string

1 teaspoon freshly cracked black peppercorns

6 cups hearty red wine, such as California Petite Sirah

2 tablespoons Armagnac or Cognac

2 tablespoons rendered duck fat

8 ounces salt pork with rind

Salt and freshly ground pepper

Flour, for dredging

3 whole cloves

4 ounces (1 cup) julienne strips of prosciutto

1½ teaspoons sugar

4 large garlic cloves

5 large shallots, peeled

Pinch of Quatre Épices (page 231) or ground allspice

¼ cup dried French cèpes or Italian porcini, crumbled

3 cups rich game or poultry stock

1 tablespoon heavy cream

1 Place the hare pieces in a large ceramic or glass mixing bowl. Add 2 of the quartered onions, the carrots, celery, herb bouquet, peppercorns, red wine, and Armagnac. Mix well, cover, and refrigerate for about 24 hours.

2 The following day, remove the pieces of hare to a rack set over a bowl to drain. Meanwhile, pour the marinade liquid and vegetables into a medium nonreactive saucepan. Bring to a boil, reduce the heat and simmer, covered, for 30 minutes. Strain the marinade through a fine sieve, pressing down on the solids.

To Cut Up a Hare or a Rabbit
→>-<←

Cut off the front legs. Separate the hind legs at the joint and chop each leg into 2 pieces. Cut the saddle across the backbone into 4 pieces. Remove the lungs and heart from the chest cavity and discard. Leave the kidneys in place. Remove and clean the liver; wrap it in plastic film, and refrigerate.

3 Cut the rind off the salt pork. Dice the salt pork; blanch the dice and rind for 3 minutes in boiling water; drain, and cool. Sliver the rind and scatter it over the bottom of a 5-quart earthenware daubière or enameled cast-iron casserole.

4 In a sauté pan, heat the duck fat and cook the cubes of salt pork over moderately low heat, stirring often, until they are golden brown and a great deal of their fat has rendered out, about 10 minutes. Transfer the salt pork to the casserole.

5 Preheat the oven to 300°F. Dry the hare with paper towels; rub it with salt and pepper and dust with flour. Over moderately high heat, reheat the fat and, working in batches, brown the hare on all sides, then add to the casserole.

(continued)

6 Stick the cloves into 1 of the remaining onion quarters. In the same fat, lightly brown the quartered onions and the julienne of prosciutto; add them to the casserole. Pour off all the fat in the skillet. Add 1 cup of the reserved marinade and bring to a boil, scraping up any browned bits from the bottom of the pan; pour the hot liquid over the hare. Add the remaining marinade, the sugar, garlic, shallots, quatre épices, and dried cèpes. Cover with stock. Bring to a boil, cover with a round of parchment paper, cover tightly with the lid, and cook in the oven for 3 hours without disturbing.

7 Remove the casserole from the oven; transfer the hare to a cutting board. Discard the rib-cage section, remove any loose bones, and cut the meat into generous serving pieces. Season the meat with salt and pepper and cover tightly with a sheet of foil. Skim all the fat from the cooking liquid. Puree the liquid and solids in a food processor and strain. Return to the casserole. Bring to a boil, set the casserole half over the heat, and cook at a slow boil, skimming on the cool side, for 20 minutes, or until the sauce is reduced to about 3 cups. Adjust the seasoning. *(The recipe can be prepared to this point up to 8 hours in advance. Refrigerate the hare and sauce separately.)*

8 About one hour before serving, preheat the oven to 300°F. Skim any congealed fat off the sauce. Combine the hare and sauce in a clean flameproof casserole. Place in the oven and reheat slowly until hot, about ¾ hour. Remove from the oven. Arrange the pieces of hare on a heated platter and cover to keep warm. Set the casserole on the stove over very low heat.

9 In a food processor or blender, combine the cream with the liver and the mixture of blood, wine, and vinegar if you're using it (see Note below); puree for 1 minute. Add ¼ cup of the hot sauce to the processor and blend well. Slide the casserole half off the heat. Scrape the liver mixture into the cooler part of the sauce. Stir carefully until all the sauce becomes thick and creamy, about 5 minutes, but do not allow it to boil, or it will curdle. Season with salt and pepper to taste. Pour the sauce over the hare. There will be a generous amount.

NOTES TO THE COOK

→→ Often hare is sold without blood and liver, both necessary to thicken the sauce of a true civet. One very fresh large chicken liver can substitute for the hare's liver. Omit any substitution for the blood. If the sauce does not thicken to the desired creaminess, combine 2 to 3 teaspoons arrowroot with cold water, add to the sauce, and cook gently until thickened.

→→ If you have a fresh hare with its blood available, put 1½ tablespoons aged red wine vinegar and 2 tablespoons red wine in a deep glass or ceramic bowl. Place a rack on top and set the hare on it. Let all the blood fall into the bowl below, then beat it with the wine and vinegar until well blended. Cover and keep refrigerated until needed.

Foie Gras, Terrines, and Rillettes

"Our cuisine does not begin in our kitchens," I was told by a young woman from the Landes. "It begins with our fathers and brothers hunting birds, our neighbors raising pigs, whole families gathering wild mushrooms in the fall, our mothers and sisters fattening up ducks and geese." An eloquent statement, and one, I assure you, that reflects the kind of passion heard in the Southwest of France whenever the subject turns to food. These people have an almost mystical appreciation of cooking and of the many ways it derives from the bounty of their land.

The term *foie gras* refers to the fattened liver of a force-fed goose, also called *foie gras d'oie*, while *foie gras de canard* refers to the fattened liver of a force-fed Moulard duck. Its production is one of the most important cottage industries of the rural Southwest. Raising and force-feeding geese is women's work, as caring for poultry traditionally has been in the region. The force-feeding is called *gavage*, and the women who do it are *gaveuses*.

It's not news that there's plenty of controversy surrounding this practice, and not only here in the United States. Force-feeding has been banned in Israel, and in Hungary it is being phased out. There are animal-rights people in many countries who would like to see this practice banned everywhere, and it may yet happen. Though when I spoke to the *gaveuses* in the Gascon market town of Mirande—not just the ruddy complexioned old women, whom I expected to see, but many young women as well—they gently ridiculed the notion that their work was cruel. In fact, they claimed to adore the birds they fattened. "It is their destiny to provide us with livers," one told me.

This book is about the gastronomy of Southwest France, and as such, foie gras must be included. You'll find marvelous foie gras recipes in this chapter, and lots of information about it. One chef in San Francisco whom I respect greatly used to cook foie gras as well as anyone I know. Now, on grounds of animal cruelty, she no longer wishes to serve it. Others do not agree. Recently, I mentioned to a newspaper reporter, "I would rather live my life as a force-fed duck than an industrial American chicken!" The way I see it, it's up to every cook to make his or her own decision.

To produce the meltingly soft, sweet livers, some *gaveuses* claim secret feeding formulas that use moist corn, dry corn, corn mixed with salt, and so on. And they talk amusingly of birds who don't take to force-feeding.

The people of the Périgord say that the corn they use in the force-feeding is a deeper shade of yellow and thus gives the livers a richer flavor. On the other hand, the Gascons force-feed with a whiter corn that they believe gives their livers a rounder flavor. Actually, I think the differences reside more in color than in taste; the Périgord livers do have a more yellowish hue.

Foie gras is expensive, worth more than ten times all of the rest of the bird. It is one of the gastronomic highlights of the world. The *paletot*, or the rest of the bird, does not go to waste. One finds the breasts sealed in vacuum-packed bags ready for grilling or frying, and the other parts on sale for preparing for confits or stews. The gizzard and other innards are sold separately for special confits, as is the blood, used in a Southwest specialty called *sanguette*, which is coagulated into a round cake, then fried in goose fat and served with garlic and parsley.

Foie d'oie, or fattened goose liver, is about twice the size of and softer than the flatter duck foie gras. The goose liver weighs about 2½ pounds; the duck liver, about 1½ pounds. Because these livers are perishable, they are usually subjected to some kind of preservation. On some farms in the Southwest, it is cooked and then preserved in cans or jars under a thick layer of fat. Commercially, foie gras is often barely cooked (*mi-cuit* or *semi-cuit*). The expression *mi-cuit* does not mean half-cooked in the sense that more cooking is necessary; it means the liver has been cooked sufficiently for eating within a month. Serve *mi-cuit* cold, cut into slices, with a glass of chilled Sauternes or other white sweet wines, such as Monbazillac, Jurançon, Vouvray, Coteaux du Layon, or Montlouis.

Each Christmas and New Year (the traditional time in France for those who can afford it to indulge their desire for foie gras), the sales of canned fall and those of *mi-cuit* or fresh start to rise. This is because the taste and color of fresh or *mi-cuit* are preferable to those of the canned varieties. But there are people who claim that foie gras aged in the jar (or can) achieves a special and desirable flavor, as do wine, confit, sardines, and pâtés when matured. A canned goose liver reaches its peak about six to eight months after canning. Formerly, packers aged their canned livers before sending them out to the stores. My own experience has been that canned preparations of foie gras are overcooked, and additional cooking detracts from their charm. I don't recommend using them unless otherwise noted.

When this book was first written, the only fresh foie gras available was packed into a chef's carry-on from a trip back from Europe. Today, there are two major producers of foie gras: Sonoma Saveurs in Northern California on the West Coast and Michael Ginor in the Hudson Valley on the East Coast (see Mail Order Sources, pages 415–417).

The ducks used to force-feed in the United States are Moulard. The Moulards are created by insemination between Pekin and Muscovy ducks, and they produce creamy, flavorful foie gras.

Nowadays, foie gras is most often sold raw and vacuum-packed, which will keep it fresh for about 10 days. Top-grade foie gras (known as Artisan, grade A, or "prime" liver) varies considerably in quality, even though any given piece is good enough to be used in terrines, mousses, or sautés. (A foie gras graded B may have some extra blood, and thus won't be suitable for braising, roasting, or poaching in goose fat.) On the average, an A grade duck liver (including Artisan, which is always A grade) will weigh approximately 1½ pounds, will be uniformly firm to the touch, smooth textured, and creamy in color, with few surface blood spots. The A is the perfect choice for slicing and sautéing.

If North American duck foie gras is well seasoned and well cooked, it can equal the best-fattened duck liver in France—and I write this on the authority of some of the greatest French chefs who have visited the United States and tasted our product. But to prepare foie gras successfully, you should order from a purveyor who knows the product. Selecting the proper raw liver is not easy, for you must be able to spot whether the livers are too fatty. Just as important is to know how to cook them so they won't fall apart or dissolve. Because of these difficulties, because proper handling of foie gras requires a great deal of experience, and because experimentation can turn out to be an incredibly expensive hobby, I asked Ariane Daguin to teach me how to choose, prepare, and cook foie gras.

Ariane is coproprietor of D'Artagnan, a commercial distributor of foie gras and game birds. She is also the daughter of great Gascon chef André Daguin—the most knowledgeable man I know on the subject—and she learned the art at her father's knee. She chooses the foie gras from both East and West Coast farms for many of the top restaurants and fine food outlets in the country, and consumers can order this same quality product through her company.

A foie gras is an extremely delicate piece of meat that can be totally destroyed if overcooked. If the fat runs out, the foie gras will nearly melt away; so it must be cooked carefully to minimize shrinkage and to insure the final result is not dry. Southwesterners talk endlessly about this. Some chefs and home cooks use the method of wrapping the foie gras in a towel before steaming it. Others, like Chef Escorbiac, previously of La Taverne Restaurant in Cahors, claim they poach theirs in a solution called *la mère*, a combination of sweet white wine, Madeira, herbs, and the fatty liquid from previous poachings, which endows the foie gras with a richness of flavor and a texture as fine as silk. (See Foie Gras Poached in Red Wine "la Mère," pages 244–255.)

Foie Gras Facts

→>→ ←<—

→>— A perfect foie gras smells sweet and has a shiny texture.

→>— One liver can serve 8 to 10 as a first course and 4 to 6 as a main course.

→>— Remember there can be up to a 20 percent loss in fat in some types of cooking, so follow directions carefully.

→>— Foie gras is wonderful with apples, grapes, and figs; in stuffings and pâtés; and with pigs feet, fish, and shellfish such as sea scallops and lobster.

→>— Please note that foie gras fat is precious, and you will want to use it for cooking omelets, chickens, mushrooms, and any other food that deserves the best fat.

→>— If there is a loose membrane on the outside of the liver, remove it; otherwise forget about it. The less you use a knife, the better it is to keep the foie gras intact.

→>— When really bloody ends of veins are exposed, use a pair of tweezers to remove them by gently pulling on the vein when the foie gras is at room temperature.

→>— Any leftover scraps of cooked foie gras should be seasoned with salt and pepper and saved for other uses. This will keep in the refrigerator for 2 to 3 days in plastic wrap. Since it is now cooked, it can be frozen as well.

→>— The enemies of foie gras are light, which discolors it; aluminum foil, which discolors it; and long periods of cooking at high temperatures, which dissolve it.

→>— Once you cut into foie gras, it will discolor rapidly. Be sure to wrap it in plastic wrap and then foil to keep it fresh.

Top-grade raw foie gras has a certain suppleness and a slight resistance when pressed gently with the thumb. Some experts say it should have the consistency of cool butter, that the thumb should leave a slight impression; a tiny amount of fat should ooze out, too.

Smaller livers, or Bs, are not as readily available, but when they are, they are mostly used in rillettes, sauces, butters, stuffings, and pâtés by restaurants and small charcuteries. (Some chefs use them in sautés and terrines as well.) B grade foie gras often has thick, dark, bloody veins throughout the flesh and needs very careful cleaning.

André Daguin is strongly against freezing raw foie gras that has not been treated to special cleaning and commercial vacuum packing. "Simply throwing it into the freezer will make it taste like soap, feel like soap, and the only thing it won't do is foam up like soap!" So if you freeze foie gras, freeze it in its original packing. It freezes very quickly, just like butter, and will keep for several months. Leftover foie gras should be seasoned and turned into a small terrine, which will keep for a week.

NOTE TO THE COOK
All the temperatures for duck foie gras doneness in this book are per Gascon preference—and mine as well—125°F. The FDA recommends cooking it to an internal temperature of 155°F.

The taste of goose liver is finer and the texture smoother than the taste and texture of livers from the duck. Goose livers feel exceptionally silky to the tongue; I prefer them slightly chilled, served with a chilled Sauternes. Duck livers taste more rustic and feel firmer, and I like them either hot or cold. There are more than a hundred hot and cold goose and duck foie gras preparations, including ones with sauerkraut, seaweed, and capers. I remember back in the 1970s and '80s, when two-star Gascon chef André Daguin, now retired, was the leading master matchmaker between foie gras and other foods. At his restaurant I have eaten foie gras with shallots (a luxurious version of liver and onions), garlic, Port, prunes, scallops, green peppercorn sauce, and celery root. I did observe one unusual method when he poached the liver for two minutes in very hot liquid, then placed it in a scooped-out elongated yellowish-green pumpkin, which he set in the oven to braise. The moistness inside the pumpkin and the thickness of its skin helped the foie gras to cook evenly. Later, served cool directly from its "terrine," it had a stunning flavor indeed.

Another exciting creation was his presentation of foie gras cooked five ways: salt-cured raw (Foie Gras Cured in Salt, page 246), poached (Torchon of Foie Gras Poached in Duck Fat, pages 242–243), sautéed (Foie Gras Sautéed With Green Grape, pages 229–231), steamed (Steamed Foie Gras With Onion Compote and Yellow Raisins, pages 232–233), cooked in terrine (Duck Foie Gras Terrine, pages 239–241), and smoked. The last, one of his greatest triumphs, involved sautéing some slices of lightly smoked foie gras de canard and serving it with lukewarm truffle vinaigrette. Of course, the most famous combination is foie gras and truffles. As the Bordelais say, "To put a truffle in a foie gras is to give it a soul." The fat of foie gras also enhances the taste of the truffles, but too often the portion of truffle used is so small it doesn't do all that much for the liver. For this reason, I usually prefer to eat my truffles and foie gras separately.

Preparation of Foie Gras

A foie gras is made of two lobes: one small and one large. All livers first should be rinsed briefly to remove any surface blood. They should also be trimmed of any extra fat or greenish spots. If the liver is to be cooked whole—steamed, poached, or turned into a terrine—it should be deveined. However, it is desirable to use only the Artisan brand, which does not need to be deveined because of special feeding and sophisticated production techniques.

Please don't be against the idea of using duck or foie gras fat; in the eyes of the French it is almost the same as olive oil. At least it is according to Dr. Serge Renaud, who made famous the "French paradox" on CBS's *60 Minutes* some years ago. In Southwest France, where the population consumes lots of duck fat, there is the lowest incidence of heart disease in the country.

FOIE GRAS SAUTÉED WITH GREEN GRAPES

➤➤ *Les Escalopes de Foie Gras*
    aux Grappes de Raisin Blanc

SERVES 4 AS A FIRST COURSE
OR 2 AS A LIGHT DINNER

IN THIS CLASSIC RECIPE, the buttery rich flavor of the foie gras pairs beautifully with the astringent taste of the tart grape sauce. If your grapes are too sweet, add a few extra drops of *verjus* or vinegar to reestablish the proper harmony. When you sauté slices of foie gras, you have complete control over its cooking: a quick sear in a hot pan, simple degreasing, followed by deglazing with a little bit of vinegar to restore the proper balance of flavors.

Sautéing can be tricky if you are cooking for a lot of people, because you must slice, cook, and serve everyone within minutes. I have written this recipe for only the small lobe, on the assumption that you will use the large lobe in one of the other preparations in this book. You can, of course, double the recipe and sauté both lobes, using 2 skillets.

In the French Southwest the grape of choice is Moissac de Chasselas, often nicknamed the grains of beauty due to their incredible translucency, milkiness, aroma, and flavor. They

(continued)

stay fresh on the vine until Christmas surrounded with paper to protect them from the cold. Use any tasty green grape available in the market.

In the Périgord, the slices of foie gras are dusted with potato flour; you can substitute an "instant" flour such as Wondra, which creates a thin crust on the outside, and of course a melting creamy inside when fried in a little bit of duck fat. In other parts of the French Southwest, nonstick pans have replaced the necessity of the flour and extra fat.

The grapes for the sauce must soak overnight.

1 cup seedless green grapes, washed and peeled

⅔ cup sweet white wine, such as late-harvest Riesling

1 tablespoon rendered duck fat or butter

1 tablespoon *verjus* or Banyuls or sherry vinegar, or more to taste

¾ cup poultry stock

½ teaspoon freshly crushed black peppercorns

Pinch of Quatre Épices (page 231)

1½ tablespoons heavy cream

Fine sea salt

Freshly ground pepper

Pinch of sugar (optional)

1 small lobe of fresh A quality duck foie gras, 7 to 9 ounces (see Mail Order Sources, pages 415–417)

Instant flour, such as Wondra (optional)

1 tablespoon duck fat (optional)

Fleur de sel

1 Soak the grapes in the sweet wine overnight.

2 The following day, strain the grapes, reserving the wine. Set a large nonstick skillet over moderately high heat. When the skillet is hot add the duck fat or butter and the grapes; sauté, shaking the pan, until they are shiny all over, about 1 minute. Remove to a side dish.

3 Pour the reserved wine into the hot skillet, bring it to a boil over high heat, and reduce to syrup, 3 to 4 tablespoons. Add the vinegar, stock, peppercorns, and quatre épices. Continue to boil until reduced by half. Add the cream and boil down to a napping consistency, about 3 tablespoons. Add the sauce to the grapes, season with salt and pepper to taste, and adjust the balance of sweet and sour with pinches of sugar or drops of verjus or vinegar.

4 Wash out the skillet and dry well. *(The recipe can be prepared to this point up to 1 hour in advance.)*

5 About 5 minutes before serving, cut the foie gras into 4 slices of approximately equal size, about 2 ounces per slice. Be sure to use a thin-bladed knife, dipped in warm water and wiped clean between each cut. Season each slice with a pinch of salt and pepper. If you like, dip each slice in the flour and shake off any excess.

6 Set the dry skillet over moderately high heat. When it is hot, add the foie gras slices; quickly lift the pan off the heat for a moment. Return to moderate heat and cook, turning once, for 1 minute on each side. Using a slotted spatula transfer the slices to warmed individual serving plates.

7 Working quickly, pour off any exuded fat and reserve for some other purpose. Reheat the grapes and sauce in the skillet along with a few tablespoons water or stock to keep the sauce fluid. Bring to a boil and spoon equal amounts of grapes and sauce over each plate of foie gras. Lightly dust each portion with a pinch of fleur de sel and serve at once.

Quatre Épices

→>-<+-

Despite its name, quatre épices is a mixture of more than four spices. It includes pepper, nutmeg, cinnamon, cloves, ginger, and other spices. You can create your own mixture to taste. I prefer to make up small batches of this seasoning, since ground spices lose their punch in a short time. MAKES ABOUT 1 TABLESPOON

10 whole cloves

1 tablespoon white peppercorns

1 cinnamon stick (preferably the thicker, more pungent cassia cinnamon)

⅔ teaspoon ground ginger

¾ teaspoon freshly grated nutmeg

Grind all the ingredients together in a spice mill until powdery. Sieve and store in a tightly capped jar.

Steamed Foie Gras With Onion Compote and Yellow Raisins

➤➤ *Foie Gras de Canard Cuit à la Vapeur et
Compote d'Oignons et Raisins Blancs*   SERVES 4 AS A FIRST COURSE

WATCHING ARIANE DAGUIN drop a whole foie gras into boiling liquid seemed to be breaking all the rules. "But," she explained, "if you have a perfect liver chosen by an expert purveyor, there is no better way to cook it."

Most likely you will be like me and not feel so fearless; therefore, I offer an alternative method: I steam it rather than boil it. As Ariane explained to me, "Boiling or steaming produces a buttery consistency with a more pronounced flavor than that yielded by sautéing." Now that I've made it a few times, I have to agree with her: It is one of the best ways to enjoy hot foie gras.

You do need to flash-grill the livers after steaming to give them an attractive browning.

Begin at least a day in advance to prepare the onion compote.

4 medium white onions, halved lengthwise and cut into ¾-inch dice

1 tablespoon rendered duck fat

1 small garlic clove

Salt and freshly ground pepper

Pinch of sugar

3 tablespoons yellow raisins

2 tablespoons French *verjus* or cider vinegar

½ cup dry white wine

1 cup chicken stock (storebought or homemade—page 405)

4 medium cabbage leaves

1 small lobe of fresh A quality duck foie gras (preferably Artisan), 7 to 9 ounces (see Mail Order Sources, pages 415–417)

1 Place the onions, duck fat, garlic, and a pinch each of salt and pepper in an electric slow cooker or heavy earthenware or enameled cast-iron casserole. Cover the slow cooker and cook on low for 12 hours or slow-bake the casserole, covered, in a 250°F oven for 2½ hours. The onions should break down and cook in their own moisture. Add the sugar, and cook, uncovered, for 30 minutes, stirring often. The onions should turn golden and be a little firm to the bite. Let cool, then cover and refrigerate for up to 5 days. (Note that in this recipe, the foie gras is not seasoned in advance, because it would draw out the moisture during the steaming.)

2 The day you plan to serve the dish, let the onions and foie gras return to room temperature. Soak the raisins in the verjus or vinegar for 10 minutes.

3 Reheat the onions and allow them to fry in their own juices until golden brown. Add the raisins with their verjus or vinegar and bring to a boil. Add the white wine and stock and cook over moderately high heat, stirring often, until a thick, rich sauce develops, about 10 minutes. Correct the seasoning with salt and pepper and set aside, covered to keep warm.

4 Preheat the broiler. Bring plenty of water to a full boil in the bottom of a deep steamer (a pasta pot with a steamer basket will work well here). Place the cabbage leaves on the rack and steam, covered, for 2 to 3 minutes, or until they are soft and pliable. Remove and chill under cold running water.

5 Wrap the whole foie gras in the cabbage leaves. Steam for 8 minutes, or until the internal temperature measures 120°F. Remove the packet to a flat surface, unwrap, and let cool slightly. Cut into 4 equal servings and place on a baking sheet; discard the cabbage.

6 Spoon some of the juices from the onion sauce over the foie gras, then run under the preheated broiler about 4 inches from the heat for about 1 minute, just to glaze the top of each slice. Divide the hot onion sauce among 4 warmed plates. Slide the pieces of foie gras on top. Season with a pinch of salt and pepper and serve at once.

NOTE TO THE COOK

A larger lobe, weighing about 1 pound, which will serve 6 to 8, will steam in 15 minutes.

ROASTED DUCK FOIE GRAS
WITH PORT WINE AND CAPER SAUCE

→→ *Foie Gras Bonne Maman*

ROASTING FOIE GRAS produces a special texture: The outside of the liver becomes slightly crunchy, but the interior remains creamy. For roasting, I prefer a perfect large lobe. (I save the smaller one for a quick light dinner for two the following day.)

Serve this dish with Michel Guérard's Pureed Celery Root With Apples (page 331). It should be accompanied by a chilled rich and golden Sauternes.

1 large lobe of fresh A quality foie gras, about 1 pound, rinsed and deveined, at room temperature

Coarse kosher salt and freshly ground white pepper

2 tablespoons chopped shallots

½ cup imported ruby Port

Pinch of sugar

1½ cups dark, rich veal or poultry stock (such as Chicken Stock, page 405) reduced to ½ cup

1 teaspoon arrowroot dissolved in 2 teaspoons water

2 teaspoons fresh lemon juice or *verjus*

1½ teaspoons tiny nonpareil capers, rinsed and drained

1 Rinse the foie gras and gently pat dry. Carefully trim away all surface fat, blood, and any green parts without damaging the liver. There is no need to devein the liver for this recipe. Let it return to room temperature before roasting.

2 About ¾ hour before serving, preheat the oven to 425°F. Be sure the liver is bone dry for roasting. Put it in a small to medium oval enameled cast-iron gratin dish or ovenproof skillet and season generously with coarse salt and white pepper. Let the seasoned foie gras stand at room temperature for 15 minutes.

3 Put the liver in the hot oven and roast for 5 minutes. Remove the liver and reduce the oven temperature to 300°F. Pour off all but 2 tablespoons of the rendered fat, reserving it for another use. Scatter the shallots around the liver.

4 When the temperature reaches 300°F, return the liver to the oven and roast for 10 minutes, basting with the rendered fat in the pan every 3 minutes, until the internal temperature registers

120°F on an instant-read thermometer. (The foie gras will be slightly undercooked, but it will finish cooking as it rests, and after slicing when the hot sauce is poured on top.)

5 Transfer the liver to a clean kitchen towel and pat it gently to remove the excess fat. Cover the liver loosely with the towel or tent with foil to keep warm. Pour off the fat from the gratin dish and reserve it for another use. Add the Port and sugar to the dish, set it on the stove, and bring to a boil over high heat, scraping up any browned bits from the bottom of the pan. Continue to boil until the liquid is reduced to a syrupy glaze, 3 to 4 minutes. Add the stock and bring to a boil. Cook for 1 minute. Stir in the dissolved arrowroot and cook, stirring, for 1 minute longer. Season with lemon juice or verjus to taste.

6 Slice the liver crosswise thinly on the diagonal and arrange the slices on warmed serving plates. Spoon the hot sauce over the slices (to finish the cooking) and top each portion with capers. Serve at once.

Inspired by a recipe given to me by the late Jean-Louis Palladin.

In Praise of Perfect Foie Gras

→>-<-

Back in 1980, I was sitting on the terrace of a restaurant in the Quercy, in Southwest France, beneath the leafy branches of a giant chestnut tree, gazing out at reflections in the lazy Ouysse River. Suddenly, the idyllic calm was shattered by a series of screams: "Idiot! Fool! You don't roast an entire foie gras like that! You are costing me a fortune! Fool!"

There was a crash, the sound of a slap, a shriek—and then a red-faced chef, shaking with fury, appeared at the kitchen door. He breathed heavily, rolled his eyes, regained control, and then rushed back inside. A long silence ensued, lasting perhaps fifteen minutes, while a second foie gras (an entire foie gras!) was lovingly and carefully roasted for my lunch.

The dish was called *foie gras bonne maman*, a whole duck liver roasted and then sauced with Port and capers. The chef's apprentice had initially botched the job by placing the costly liver in too hot an oven, which melted half of it away. When the second attempt finally came to the table, it proved sumptuous eating: a dish of sublime and delicate taste, a perfect harmony, too, of disparate ingredients. The acid-piquant capers provided an ideal foil for the delectably rich, silky-smooth moist liver, all balanced by the sweet Port. "Worth doing twice to get it right," said the chef, restored to his normal calm state.

GRILLED FIGS AND FOIE GRAS

➤➤ *Foie Gras Poêlé aux Figues Grillées*   SERVES 2

IF YOU FIND YOURSELF with some leftover chunks of raw foie gras, here is a nice little luxurious lunch dish for one or two you can enjoy the next day. I serve the foie gras on slices of bread that are sautéed in just the exuded fat from the sautéing of the foie gras itself.

8 fresh purple (black Mission) figs

½ teaspoon sugar

1 large shallot, finely slivered

1 tablespoon *verjus* or cider vinegar

1 small bunch of arugula

4 small slices of fresh A quality foie gras, about 2 ounces, at room temperature

Salt and freshly ground pepper

Thinly sliced dense country-style bread, stale or lightly toasted

1½ tablespoons French walnut oil

1 Set a rack in the center of the oven. Preheat the broiler. Halve the figs and place cut sides up in a shallow pan. Dust the figs with the sugar and grill under the broiler 6 to 8 inches from the heat until the sugar has melted and glazed the figs, about 10 minutes.

2 Meanwhile, soak the shallots in the vinegar for 10 minutes. Wash and dry the greens, and heat a large skillet over moderately high heat until hot. Lightly season the pieces of foie gras with salt and pepper and sauté for 30 seconds a side. Use a flat, slotted spatula to transfer to a side dish.

3 Add the bread to the hot skillet and fry on both sides until the fat from the foie gras is completely absorbed. Remove to a side dish. Add the shallots and vinegar and quickly bring to a boil. Stir in the walnut oil and remove from the heat. Season with a pinch of salt and pepper. Dress the arugula with the oil-vinegar mixture in the skillet and toss. Divide the foie gras among the bread slices. Serve with the greens and the grilled fig halves.

Braised Duck Foie Gras With Vegetables in the Manner of Old Périgord

→→ *Le Foie Gras Chaud Préparé Suivante la Vielle Périgord*

SERVES 6 TO 8 AS A MAIN COURSE

A WHOLE FOIE GRAS, perfectly cooked until soft and smooth, nestled in a shallow serving dish, accompanied by braised cabbage and a chunky sauce of chopped carrots, leeks, and onions, can be an understated but elegant choice for a dinner menu. Slice the liver at the table and accompany it with mashed potatoes.

Danielle Delpeuch, an expert and former private chef for President Mitterand, gave me this recipe. She told me how, when her grandfather made a four-hour round trip to market in a horse-and-buggy, her grandmother would sometimes prepare this dish in a closed iron pot in the embers in the fireplace, moving the pot around to keep the cooking even and slow. Danielle has updated her grandmother's recipe, using an enameled cast-iron casserole on a stove top. Still, I would gladly make a four-hour horse-and-buggy trip knowing I was coming home to a meal like this!

To make last-minute preparation easier, trim the foie gras, soak the caul fat, and prepare the cabbage about 4 hours before you plan on serving the dish.

¼ pound caul fat, about 1 foot square (see Caul Fat, page 238)

1 tablespoon *verjus* or cider vinegar

1 small head of savoy cabbage

¼ cup rendered duck fat or olive oil

1¾ cups unsalted chicken stock (storebought or homemade—page 405)

Coarse salt and freshly ground white pepper

1 fresh Artisan duck foie gras, about 1½ pounds (see Mail Order Sources, pages 415–417)

¼ teaspoon freshly grated nutmeg

3 medium carrots, finely diced

3 medium leeks (white part only), finely diced

1 medium onion, finely chopped

1½ tablespoons minced shallots

1 tablespoon imported Port

1 Place the caul fat in a small bowl. Add the vinegar and enough cold water to cover and soak the caul for 15 minutes; rinse and drain.

(continued)

Foie Gras, Terrines, and Rillettes 🌼 237

Caul Fat

→> <←

Caul fat, a lacy fatty membrane that melts as it cooks, must be ordered from a butcher shop that carries it fresh. You can usually find it in an Asian market. It is well worth looking for. When you order caul fat, buy several pounds, and then freeze it in ½-pound packets. (It will keep in the freezer for up to 1 year.) Use it for cooking lamb, sausages, salmon, and terrines. To prepare the caul fat for use, soak it in several changes of vinegary water (1 teaspoon vinegar for every 1 cup water) for 30 minutes. Drain it well and pat dry.

2 Bring a large pot of water to a boil. Meanwhile, remove and discard the outer leaves from the cabbage. Cut the cabbage into 8 wedges; cut out the core and remove the thick ribs. Drop the cabbage into boiling water, cover, and quickly return to a boil. Cook 3 for minutes. Drain and rinse under cold running water; repeat with fresh boiling water. Squeeze the cabbage dry in a kitchen towel.

3 Heat 1 tablespoon of the duck fat in a large skillet. Add the cabbage and sauté over high heat, stirring, for 1 minute. Add 1½ cups of the chicken stock, ½ teaspoon salt, and ¼ teaspoon white pepper. Cover, reduce the heat to moderate, and cook for 15 minutes. Uncover and boil over moderately high heat, stirring frequently, until the liquid evaporates and the cabbage begins to caramelize slightly, about 20 minutes. Remove the cabbage from the heat and set aside, partially covered. *(The recipe can be prepared to this point several hours in advance.)*

4 About 1 hour before serving, pat the foie gras dry. Season with ½ teaspoon salt, ¼ teaspoon of pepper, and ⅛ teaspoon of the nutmeg. Snuggle the smaller lobe into the large one. Gently press the two lobes together to form an egg shape. Wrap them in the prepared caul fat.

5 In a heavy 3-quart flameproof casserole, soften the carrots, leeks, onion, and shallots in 2 tablespoons of the duck fat over moderate heat for 5 minutes. Season with pinches of salt and pepper. Meanwhile, reheat the cabbage over low heat.

6 In a medium nonstick skillet, melt 1 tablespoon of the duck fat over moderate heat. Add the foie gras, season with pinches of salt and pepper and the remaining ⅛ teaspoon nutmeg, and cook until lightly browned on the bottom, about 3 minutes. Turn over and cook the second side until browned, about 2 minutes.

7 Carefully pour off the fat from the skillet. Add the Port and gently turn the foie gras in the liquid to coat it and form a glaze, about 1 minute. Place the foie gras on top of the vegetables in the casserole. Add the remaining chicken stock to the skillet and bring to a boil, scraping up any brown bits at the bottom with a wooden spatula; pour over the liver. Cover and braise over low heat for about 30 minutes, or until the internal temperature registers 120°F. Remove the casserole from the heat and let it stand, covered, for 10 minutes; the liver will continue to cook in the receding heat.

8　When the liver has rested for 10 minutes, carefully transfer it to a heated serving dish. Remove any caul fat that has not dissolved. Tip the pan and skim as much fat as possible from the pan juices. Surround the foie gras with the vegetables and the cabbage. Moisten with the pan juices and serve at once.

Duck Foie Gras Terrine

→→ *Foie Gras en Terrine*   SERVES 12 TO 16

A CLASSIC TERRINE of foie gras on the buffet is the height of Christmas luxury. Chilled and sliced, then served cool, pink-beige, and delicately veined, the buttery liver literally melts on the tongue. Richer than butter and cream together, smoother and silkier than any ordinary liver, it provides a flavor that once tasted, will never be forgotten.

In Gascony, foie gras is often cooked in a porcelain terrine in a water bath, then served in its terrine along with a serving spoon and a small bowl of hot water. Each person dips his spoon in the water to heat it so it will cut neatly through the liver. He then scoops out a portion and smears it on a slab of grilled coarse French bread.

A more elegant presentation is to slice the foie gras, then arrange the slices on a porcelain plate surrounded with chopped aspic and lightly toasted brioche. The foie gras can also be served with a variety of greens, flavored with a vinaigrette made with *verjus* and walnut oil.

The preparation and resting times for this terrine are 5 to 7 days, so plan accordingly. Begin about 1 week before serving.

(continued)

2 fresh Artisan duck foie gras, about 1½ pounds each (see Mail Order Sources, pages 415–417)

1 tablespoon fine sea salt

1¼ teaspoons sugar

1½ teaspoons finely ground white pepper

Pinches of freshly grated nutmeg or Quatre Épices (page 231)

Pinch of sugar, for good pink color

3 tablespoons Armagnac or Cognac

3 tablespoons duck or veal demi-glace (storebought or homemade—see page 409 for duck demi-glace and page 406 for veal) or 1 cup poultry stock (such as Chicken Stock, page 405) reduced to a syrup, lightly warmed

Flour and water paste (about ½ cup flour blended with enough water to make a thick paste)

1 Drain the livers on paper towels and pat dry. In a deep bowl, combine the salt, sugar, white pepper, and nutmeg; mix well. Add the livers and rub them all over with the seasoning mixture. Sprinkle with a pinch of sugar and add the Armagnac or Cognac. Cover the livers and refrigerate overnight.

2 The following day, about 2 hours before cooking, remove the livers from the refrigerator and let them return to room temperature.

3 Preheat the oven to 160°F. Fit the nicest lobe, smooth side down, on the bottom of a 5-cup porcelain terrine and press down lightly to remove any air. Scatter small pieces and the two smaller lobes in the center and top with the remaining large lobe, smooth side up. Press again into the mold. Pour the warm demi-glace over the livers. Flatten the livers to eliminate all air pockets. Put on the lid, if it has one, and seal airtight with a paste made from flour and water.

4 Put the sealed terrine in a small roasting pan and add warm water to reach halfway up the sides of the terrine. Set in the oven and cook for 55 to 60 minutes. Break the seal and check for doneness. Use a touch test to poke at the liver; as it cooks, it gets softer. It is done when it has a soft, elastic feel to it. Or insert a metal skewer into the thickest part of the terrine for 20 seconds; then test the skewer on your wrist. If the skewer feels warm and the juices are spurting from the liver where it was poked are pink, the foie gras is cooked. The internal temperature should register 120°F–125°F. If the foie gras is not yet ready, the lid does not need to be resealed. Simply return the covered terrine to the water bath in the oven and continue cooking for 5 minutes longer.

5 When the foie gras is done, remove the terrine from the water bath, place it in a baking dish or jelly-roll pan, and let cool for 10 minutes. The liver continues to cook as it cools down. Gently push down the foie gras with a flat board weighted with cans or a terrine of the same shape filled with cans, to press out most of the fat and blood, which will overflow into the baking pan. Pour

off and reserve the fat; discard any bloody juices (refrigerate if necessary to separate the two). When it is cool, double-wrap the weighted terrine in plastic wrap and foil and refrigerate for at least 4 hours or overnight, until thoroughly chilled.

6 Unmold the foie gras from the terrine (see Notes below) and wipe away any bloody juices from the bottom of the liver.

7 Wash and dry the terrine and return the congealed liver to it. In a small saucepan, melt the reserved fat just until it is liquid. Pour over the liver in the terrine to cover it completely. Cover the terrine with its lid, if it has one, then wrap it tightly in clean plastic wrap and aluminum foil and refrigerate for at least 3 and up to 5 days before serving to allow the flavors to develop.

8 Serve the terrine cool, not chilled. Unmold the liver onto a cutting board; cut with a knife dipped in hot water and dried before cutting each slice.

NOTES TO THE COOK

→ For detailed notes on purchasing and handling foie gras, see pages 223 to 229. If using a terrine smaller than 5 cups, save any extra foie gras for a quick sauté.

→ Allow about 3 ounces of foie gras per person.

→ The shape of the mold, the density of the liver, and the temperature of the water and the oven will affect the cooking time of foie gras. Some oval-shaped terrines require a longer cooking time.

→ If you don't have a porcelain terrine, you can use an earthenware or enameled cast-iron terrine, but you will need to place a double layer of newspapers or a folded kitchen towel in the bottom of the roasting pan holding the water to moderate the heat. Also, add 1 teaspoon vegetable oil to the flour and water paste so it doesn't stick.

→ Be sure to remove the terrine of foie gras from the refrigerator about 30 minutes before serving. The flavor is most pronounced at cool room temperature.

→ Weighting a foie gras as it cools helps it firm up into a solid mass and pushes up fat trapped between the layers. If there is any leftover terrine, wrap it airtight, first in plastic wrap and then in foil to keep it from discoloring.

→ Save all fat for sautéing poultry, eggs, potatoes, or meat.

→ A French trick for easily removing the foie gras from its mold is to dip the terrine for an instant into a pan of very hot water to help loosen the bottom.

TORCHON OF FOIE GRAS POACHED IN DUCK FAT

➤ *Terrine de Foie Gras de Canard Cuit*
"au Torchon"

SERVES 6 TO 8 AS A FIRST COURSE

FOIE GRAS COOKED in duck fat has an extraordinary taste that is surprisingly different from that of the preceding cold terrine. Submerged in duck fat, the liver cooks evenly and retains all its flavors. After cooking and cooling, it is packed in a small terrine, enveloped in fat, then left to ripen for about 5 days. Serve with thin slices of toasted baguette.

The preparation and resting times for this terrine are 5 to 7 days, so plan accordingly. Begin about 1 week before serving.

1½ teaspoons fine salt or 1 tablespoon per 2 pounds weight

½ teaspoon sugar

¼ teaspoon finely ground white pepper

Pinch of freshly grated nutmeg, Quatre Épices (page 231), or mixed spices

1½ tablespoons imported ruby Port

1 fresh Artisan duck foie gras, about 1½ pounds (see Mail Order Sources, pages 415–417)

3½ to 4½ cups rendered duck fat (see Note, page 202)

1 Mix the salt, sugar, pepper, and nutmeg in a small bowl. Sprinkle the seasonings and then the Port evenly over the foie gras. Place the liver on a square of fine cheesecloth; double the thickness if the cloth is coarsely woven. Roll up to wrap the liver in the cheesecloth; twist the ends to form a compact 7-inch log. Tie the ends with string. Let it stand in a cool place, but not in the refrigerator, for 1 to 2 hours.

2 Preheat the oven to 160°F. In a small saucepan, heat the rendered fat to 100°F and pour enough to measure ½ inch into the bottom of a 2-quart heatproof glass loaf pan or terrine. Place the liver in the pan and pour on enough of the remaining fat to completely cover the liver.

3 Set the dish on a baking sheet and cook in the oven until the center of the liver registers 120°F to 125°F. Very carefully transfer the liver in its cheesecloth to a side dish to drain. Strain the fat from the pan into a bowl and reserve.

4 Roll the still-wrapped foie gras in a kitchen towel and hold it over the bowl of fat. Twist the towel ends to shape the liver and to squeeze out a little more fat. Unwrap the liver and pack it into a 2- or 3-cup terrine or bowl. Press the liver into the mold with your hands or the back of a large spoon. Let it stand for 2 to 3 hours, until cooled to room temperature.

5 Cover the liver with a ¼-inch-thick layer of the reserved fat; if the fat has cooled too much, heat it gently until just pourable. When the entire terrine is completely covered, cover it with plastic wrap and then with aluminum foil to seal well. Refrigerate for 5 to 7 days to allow the flavor to develop. Let return to room temperature before unmolding and slicing. Or scoop it out with a warm spoon at the table.

NOTES TO THE COOK

⇥ If the cooked liver is completely enrobed in fat, it will keep up to a week under refrigeration.

⇥ The fat from a foie gras is precious and should be saved separately from other fat. I love it with scrambled eggs or omelets, but you can use it instead of duck fat in any of the recipes in this book.

⇥ Know your oven. Depending on the size and shape of the terrine, cooking times will vary, but the slower the better for the greatest liver terrines. And the longer you wait to serve it the better it is: The second day it is eatable, but it really becomes fabulous about day five.

⇥ Another French trick for easily removing the foie gras from the mold is to cover it tightly, turn it upside down, place on a rack in the sink and pour a cup of very hot water over the bottom to help loosen the inside.

FOIE GRAS POACHED IN RED WINE "LA MÈRE"

➤➤ *Foie Gras Poché au Vin Rouge "la Mère"*   SERVES 12

MY FRIEND AMERICAN CHEF Mary Dumont learned to cook foie gras from a Southwest French master, and she is constantly surprising me with her foie gras specialties: cured and smoked foie gras, double-roasted foie gras, and this easy-to-make foie gras preparation poached in red wine. Since Mary uses the poaching liquid over and over, she calls it *la mère* or "the mother." You can do the same, using the liquid as a cooking medium for duck legs, deglazing a sauté pan, or poaching fruit such as prunes or figs. And, of course, to cook more foie gras.

Mary poaches an entire liver in a deep pot, she treats it like a baby, using only her hands to turn it. "A spatula," she warns, "would break the foie."

This foie gras preparation will keep up to a week, improving every day. On day 5 it is just perfect. For a great first course, serve with a bitter green salad dressed with truffle vinaigrette (recipe follows), toasted pistachios, and the best-tasting red grapes you can find. Be sure to sprinkle a smidgen of fleur de sel over the foie gras at the last minute.

1 fresh Artisan duck foie gras, about 1½ pounds (see Mail Order Sources, pages 415–417)

2 bottles (750 ml each) dry red wine

1½ cup imported ruby Port

½ cup unsalted chicken stock (storebought or homemade—page 405)

1 cup sugar

½ cup coarse kosher salt

¼ cup whole black peppercorns

Salt and freshly ground pepper

Salad of Bitter Greens With Truffle Vinaigrette (at right)

Fleur de sel

1 pound seedless red grapes (optional)

1 About 5 or 6 days before serving, bring the whole foie gras to room temperature for 30 minutes. It should soften just a small amount on the surface flesh.

2 Meanwhile, combine the wine, Port, chicken stock, sugar, salt, and peppercorns in a nonreactive 3-quart saucepan. Bring to a boil and simmer for 30 minutes. Let the liquid cool to between 120° and 125°F.

3 Generously season the foie gras with salt and pepper and submerge it, round smooth side down, in the warm poaching liquid. Cover with a sheet of parchment and poach the liver for 11 to 13 minutes, being careful to maintain the poaching liquid at no more than 125°F. At intervals of

4 minutes, use your hands to carefully turn the foie gras over while gently loosening the two lobes. The foie gras is fully cooked when it feels soft to the touch yet firm on the inside. Remove the saucepan from the heat and let the foie gras cool in the poaching liquid, covered with the sheet of parchment paper. When cool, refrigerate the foie gras in the liquid in the saucepan for 24 hours.

4 Remove the liver from the poaching liquid and pat dry with a soft towel. Tighten the towel and gently squeeze out any surface fat or liquid. Press the liver to shape it into an even loaf. Wrap in parchment paper, then plastic wrap, and finally a sheet of foil, and refrigerate for 4 to 5 days to allow the flavors to develop before serving.

5 To save the poaching liquid (la mère), strain it through cheesecloth and return to a clean saucepan. Bring to a boil, reduce the heat, and simmer for 10 minutes. Let cool, then refrigerate or freeze in a tightly covered container.

6 When ready to serve the foie gras, thinly slice the liver and arrange on plates. Garnish with the Salad of Bitter Greens with Truffle Vinaigrette, fleur de sel, and the grapes.

SALAD OF BITTER GREENS WITH TRUFFLE VINAIGRETTE

SERVES 12 AS A GARNISH

4 cups young bitter greens, such as arugula, curly endive, young dandelions

2 teaspoons Champagne vinegar

3 tablespoons black truffle oil, preferably Plantin

Fleur de sel and freshly ground pepper

2 tablespoons toasted pistachio nuts

2 tablespoons minced fresh chives

1 Rinse and dry the greens. Tear into bite-size pieces and put in a bowl.

2 Sprinkle the Champagne vinegar and truffle oil over the greens. Season lightly with salt and pepper. Toss to mix.

3 Sprinkle the pistachio nuts and chives on top.

FOIE GRAS CURED IN SALT

→ *Foie Gras Cuit-Cru au Sel*   SERVES 4 AS AN APPETIZER

FOIE GRAS CURED IN SALT is not that different from turning salmon into gravlax. Only an exceptional and very fresh liver should be used to prepare this dish. In San Francisco, I tasted one of chef Laurent Manrique's brilliant innovations using Artisan foie gras: sea salt–cured foie gras and monkfish à la Basquaise with Serrano ham.

You serve these thin slices on grilled slices of hot country bread and the salt-cured liver simply melts onto it.

Begin at least 1 day before serving.

1 small lobe fresh Artisan foie gras, 7 to 9 ounces (see Mail Order Sources, pages 415–417)

½ cup milk

Quatre Épices (page 231)

Freshly ground pepper

Fleur de sel

¾ to 1 pound coarse kosher salt, or more as necessary

1½ tablespoons sugar

4 to 8 hot grilled slices of thin-cut baguette or country bread

1 Soak the foie gras in 2 cups of water with the milk for 15 to 20 minutes. Drain, rinse, and pat dry on kitchen towels.

2 Season the foie gras lobe with a pinch each Quatre Épices, pepper, and fleur de sel. Use a tripled large sheet of cheesecloth to roll the foie gras into a sausage shape as if you were making sushi with a bamboo sheet. Wrap up the liver with the cheesecloth and tie at each end.

3 Mix together the salt and sugar. Spread about ¾ inch of this mixture in a nonmetallic terrine just large enough to hold the liver lobe. Surround and cover with the remaining salt; top with a flat board weighted with bottles of wine or a heavy can of the same shape and store the terrine in the refrigerator for 24 to 48 hours.

4 To serve, unwrap the liver and rinse it quickly under cold water. Dry completely, then cut into very thin slices while still chilled. Serve on very hot crusty bread.

NOTE TO THE COOK

You can remove the salt and cheesecloth and wrap the foie gras in airtight plastic wrap and store 1 to 2 more days in the refrigerator.

COMPOTE OF RABBIT WITH PRUNES

~~>~~ *Compote de Lapin aux Pruneaux* SERVES 6 TO 8

THIS UNUSUAL AND HEAVENLY dish of shredded rabbit and plump prunes set in aspic is Lucien Vanel's version of an old French recipe. In the Southwest, the word *compote* can be applied to any sort of stewed shredded meat or poultry (rillettes).

One of the problems with rabbit is that it often comes out tasteless and dry. In this dish, however, the flesh is tender and moist. When shredded, it gives the compote the texture of rillettes. The main difference between this compote and rillettes is lightness—instead of enriching it with duck, goose, or pork fat, Vanel's recipe calls for a small amount of fresh cream. The tangy, piquant touch of sorrel rounds out the dish, and the rich, plump prunes make a sweet counterpoint and a textural impression of fat.

This dish must be made about 2 to 3 days in advance so the compote has time to mellow. It is wonderful on thin slices of lightly buttered toast.

1 mature stewing rabbit or fryer (young; about 3 pounds), fresh or frozen

2 cups dry white wine

⅔ cup plus 2½ tablespoons extra virgin olive oil

3 medium onions, thinly sliced

½ cup sliced carrots

1 shallot, sliced

1 garlic clove, halved

5 ounces pancetta, cut into 1-inch cubes

2 teaspoons Dijon mustard

4 cups unsalted chicken stock (storebought or homemade—page 405)

Herb bouquet: 3 sprigs parsley, ¼ teaspoon dried thyme or 3 fresh sprigs, ¼ teaspoon dried rosemary or 1 sprig fresh rosemary, and 1 imported bay leaf tied in cheesecloth

Salt and freshly ground pepper

½ cup heavy cream

12 to 18 fresh sorrel leaves, depending upon size and pungency, finely shredded

Fresh lemon juice

12 pitted prunes

1 cup brewed black tea, preferably linden

(continued)

Foie Gras, Terrines, and Rillettes 247

1 Have the butcher cut the rabbit into 7 or 8 pieces. Combine the wine, ⅔ cup of the olive oil, the onions, carrots, shallot, and garlic in a large ceramic or glass bowl; mix well. Add the rabbit pieces to the marinade and turn them over until well coated. Cover with plastic wrap and refrigerate overnight. (Frozen rabbit defrosts directly in the marinade; add 6 hours to the marination time.)

2 The following day, remove the rabbit and pat dry. Strain the marinade, reserving the vegetables and liquid separately.

3 Preheat the oven to 300°F. In a large skillet over moderately high heat, sauté the pancetta cubes in the remaining 2½ tablespoons olive oil, transferring them to a 4-quart casserole as they are browned.

4 In the same skillet over moderate heat, brown the rabbit pieces in the fat, a few at a time, on both sides. Transfer the rabbit pieces to the casserole as they are browned. Add the reserved vegetables to the skillet and sauté over moderately high heat, stirring, for 10 minutes, or until lightly browned. Using a slotted spoon, add the vegetables to the casserole.

5 Add the mustard to the casserole. Set over low heat and cook, stirring, to blend the mustard with the juices exuded from the rabbit, pork cubes, and vegetables.

6 Pour off the fat from the skillet and deglaze with the strained marinade. Bring to a boil, stirring, then immediately remove from the heat. Slowly stir the marinade into the casserole.

7 Add the chicken stock to the casserole and bring to a boil, skimming. Add the herb bouquet, and ¼ teaspoon each salt and pepper, and cover tightly. Transfer to the oven and bake, covered, for 4 hours, or until the rabbit meat is falling off the bones.

8 Carefully remove the rabbit pieces with a slotted spoon and set aside. Strain the liquid into a clean saucepan and skim off as much fat as possible. Bring to a boil. Set the pan half on and half off the heat and boil slowly for 20 minutes, skimming off any fat and other impurities frequently.

9 Meanwhile, bone each piece of rabbit, being sure to remove all the tiny bones with your fingers. Crush the meat with the back of a fork. Place in a wide bowl.

10 Add the cream to the reduced cooking liquid and boil until the sauce is reduced to 1 cup. Add the shredded sorrel and bring to a boil. Pour the hot sauce over the rabbit and let cool. The rabbit meat should absorb all the sauce. Season generously with salt and pepper, and, if you want extra piquancy, a few drops of lemon juice. Pack down in an oiled stainless-steel bowl and let cool. Cover with plastic wrap and refrigerate for at least 2 and up to 7 days.

11 The day the compote is to be served, soak the prunes in a small saucepan of hot tea until swollen. Then simmer for 10 minutes; drain. Set aside until ready to serve.

12 About 1 hour before serving, remove the compote from the refrigerator. To serve, unmold onto a round platter. Garnish with the prunes.

RILLETTES OF SHREDDED DUCK

↣ *Rillettes de Canard*   MAKES ABOUT 6 CUPS; SERVES 10 TO 12

THE FOLLOWING RECIPE comes from my friend Marie-Claude Gracia. When I first read her name in a letter published in a French culinary magazine, *Gault Millau*, I immediately recognized a voice full of charm and passion for good food and decided to seek her out.

Spending time with Marie-Claude, I learned that before she opened her restaurant, she and her partner Richard made their living selling duck rillettes. They'd buy duck carcasses from chefs and foie gras producers, pick off the wonderful tasty little bits of meat left near the bone, then use the meat to make their rillettes from Marie-Claude's mother's recipe.

Eventually, Marie-Claude and Richard opened a restaurant in the town of Poudenas, which became in the late 1970s one of the most famous in Gascony. Four years ago, after Richard died, Marie-Claude closed the restaurant, a sad loss for her friends and for lovers of good food. I heard recently that she has remarried a wonderful man and that, when they walked through the streets of Poudenas to the *mairie* for the civil ceremony, they were cheered by hundreds of friends.

Marie-Claude suggests that, if time permits, you marinate the duck and pork pieces with the seasonings and the white wine overnight in the refrigerator before cooking.

Serve these peppery rillettes with rounds of French bread, cornichons, and a glass of chilled Sauternes.

Prepare up to 1 week in advance.

(continued)

2 pair duck legs and thighs plus carcass, wings, and all fat and skin of the ducks (reserve breasts for another use)

¾ pound boneless pork shoulder, cut into 1-inch cubes

Salt and freshly ground pepper

¾ cup unsalted chicken stock (storebought or homemade—page 405)

¾ cup dry white wine

1 teaspoon fresh thyme leaves or ½ teaspoon dried thyme, plus additional to taste

½ imported bay leaf

1 large garlic clove, halved

2 shallots, peeled

½ teaspoon Quatre Épices (page 231), plus additional to taste

2 tablespoons Armagnac, flamed and cooled

1 Trim all fat and skin from the ducks and chop into small pieces. Place the chopped skin and fat in a heavy 3-quart flameproof casserole. Add 3 tablespoons water. Render the fat over very low heat; then strain. Measure 1½ cups liquid fat and reserve in the refrigerator. (This barely cooked fat is the secret to light and easily digestible rillettes.) Return remaining fat to the casserole.

2 Meanwhile, preheat the oven to 300°F. With a mallet or cleaver, chop the legs and thighs of the duck into 1-inch pieces. Chop up the carcasses, wings, and backs. Add all the duck to the casserole along with the pork. Season with 1 teaspoon each salt and pepper. Add the stock, wine, thyme, bay leaf, garlic, shallots, and quatre épices.

3 Set in the oven and cook, uncovered, for 4 to 5 hours, or until the meat is falling off the bones. Stir from time to time to prevent sticking. (The liquid in the pan will evaporate, and the meat will cook slowly in the fat remaining.)

4 Strain the pork and duck through a colander set over a deep bowl. Let cool for 10 minutes. Pick out the lean meat, including the sweet morsels of duck flesh on the carcass and around the wings; discard the skin, bones, and gristle. Set aside ½ cup of the flavorful fat.

5 Transfer the duck meat and pork to a food processor fitted with the plastic blade. Pulse 4 to 6 times, or just until the fibers are broken down. Add the reserved 1½ cups chilled fat, the cooked garlic and shallots, and the Armagnac; process for 10 seconds, stopping twice to scrape down bowl. The mixture should have a shredded texture; do not process to a paste. Season with more salt, plenty of pepper, additional thyme, and Quatre Épices to taste; the rillettes should be very peppery.

6 Lightly pile the rillettes into clean stoneware crocks, leaving about ½ inch at the top. Tap to settle. Cover the rillettes with the reserved flavorful fat. Refrigerate for at least 3 days or up to a week before serving.

Beef, Veal, Pork, and Lamb

STEAK BORDELAISE WITH MARROW AND SHALLOT GARNISH

➤➤ *Entrecôte à la Bordelaise*   SERVES 4

THIS IS, OF COURSE, the great specialty of Bordeaux. In his excellent book on Bordelaise cooking, *Traité de Cuisine Bourgeoise Bordelaise*, Alcide Bontou explains that the original version is simply a grilled rib steak garnished with a mixture of "four shallots, a nice piece of firm bone marrow, and a small amount of parsley all chopped together. This mixture is spread over the side of the steak that has been grilled first; then a large wide-bladed knife is heated to melt the marrow. When the second side has been grilled, care must be taken that the topping doesn't fall off."

Bontou goes on to explain that the steaks were grilled over burned old wood from chestnut wine barrels, which was said to impart an excellent flavor to the meat. Now it is more prevalent to use dried grapevine cuttings.

When I lunched at Château la Brède, about twenty kilometers outside of Bordeaux, the steak was prepared in the following way: The meat was cooked in an open fireplace over a fire of dried vine cuttings, then served with a cooked marrow and shallot garnish that was juicy enough to be called a sauce. The vine cuttings imparted a delicious flavor and aroma to the meat. You can buy these at Napageneralstore.com. Ask for Sam's vine chips.

A Salty Trick

➤➤ ◄◄

A little trick I learned from André Guillot: Lightly salt the meat the minute you bring it home. If you do this, you won't need to salt later, and in the end you'll use half as much salt as you would normally. Lightly salted meat will tenderize and mature in flavor when stored overnight in the refrigerator. Though some blood will run out, it is insignificant. Guillot also suggests that meat be coated lightly with grapeseed oil to keep it from drying out; he prefers grapeseed oil, because it smokes at a much higher temperature than other oils.

4 veal or beef marrow bones, cut into 1-inch lengths

2 boneless well-marbled rib-eye steaks, cut 2 inches thick (about 2 pounds), well trimmed

Salt and freshly ground pepper

2 tablespoons grapeseed, French peanut, or unflavored vegetable oil

36 small to medium shallots (about 6 ounces)

1 tablespoon red wine vinegar

¼ cup dry white wine

1 turn of the pepper mill

¼ imported bay leaf

¼ cup well-reduced meat or poultry stock or demi-glace (storebought or homemade—page 406)

1 tablespoon finely chopped fresh flat-leaf parsley mixed with some chives

Fleur de sel or coarse sea salt

1 Gently pry the marrow out of the bones. Soak it in the refrigerator in a bowl of salted ice water, for at least 8 hours, or overnight, until whitened. Drain just before using.

2 Lightly season meat with salt and pepper; rub with oil. Cover loosely with plastic wrap and refrigerate until 1 hour before cooking. Pat the meat dry with paper towels. Brush with fresh oil.

3 Blanch the shallots in saucepan of boiling water for 1 minute. Drain and refresh under cold running water; this makes them easier to peel and milder in flavor. Peel and coarsely chop the shallots. There should be about 1 cup.

4 In a small saucepan, simmer the wine vinegar, wine, salt, pepper, bay leaf, and stock or demi-glace for 5 minutes. Remove from the heat. Remove and discard the bay leaf. Fold in the chopped shallots and set aside until just before serving.

5 Grill the steaks about 5 inches over hot coals, preferably with vine cuttings added, for 8 minutes; turn over. Quickly, with a slotted spoon, remove 1 to 2 tablespoons of the chopped shallots from the sauce and spread over the steak; the flavor of the shallots penetrates the meat, giving it added flavor. Cover with a cold, heatproof plate or pot lid. Continue to grill on the second side for 6 minutes for rare. Remove the steaks to a rack and let stand 5 minutes to rest before slicing.

6 Meanwhile, reheat the shallot–red wine sauce. Cut the marrow into ⅜-inch dice and poach it separately in lightly salted simmering—not boiling—water until it turns pink-gray, 20 to 30 seconds. Immediately, remove with a slotted spoon and add to the warm sauce. Season the sauce with salt and pepper to taste. Spoon over the steak slices and garnish with the herbs and fleur de sel.

(continued)

VARIATION: GRILLED STEAK WITH WHITE BORDEAUX WINE SAUCE

(Sauce Bordelaise au Vin Blanc) MAKES ABOUT ¾ CUP; SERVES 4

J.-E. Progneaux in his *Recettes et Spécialités Gastronomiques Bordelaises et Girondines* gives seven versions of the famous wine and shallot combination known worldwide as *sauce bordelaise*. A true sauce bordelaise must be made of Bordeaux wine, but interestingly enough not all of the versions offered by Progneaux employ red wine. Since red wine recipes have been published so widely, I offer here my adaptation of a recipe by Curnonsky using a dry white Graves.

1½ cups white Bordeaux wine, such as Graves or Sauvignon Blanc

3 fresh white mushrooms

¼ cup dried cèpes, well washed

2 tablespoons thinly sliced shallots

½ teaspoon freshly ground pepper

Herb bouquet: 3 sprigs parsley, 1 sprig thyme, and ½ imported bay leaf tied together with string

2 cups unsalted meat stock

1 to 2 teaspoons arrowroot

1 tablespoon chopped mixed fresh herbs: parsley, tarragon, chives, and chervil

1 In a nonreactive saucepan, combine the wine, fresh mushrooms, dried cèpes, shallots, pepper, and herb bouquet. Simmer slowly until the liquid reduces to a glaze, about 30 minutes.

2 Add 1 cup of the stock and again reduce slowly to a glaze, about 15 minutes, skimming often.

3 Add the remaining stock and simmer slowly for 10 minutes, skimming often. Strain through a sieve lined with several layers of damp cheesecloth. Squeeze the cheesecloth to extract all the liquid. Return to a clean saucepan set half over the heat. Cook at a slow boil, skimming, for 5 minutes, or until the sauce is reduced to ¾ cup.

4 Grill the steaks as directed in the preceding recipe.

5 Mix the arrowroot with 1½ tablespoons water until smooth. Bring the sauce to a boil. Reduce the heat to moderately low, whisk in the arrowroot mixture, and cook until the sauce is thickened. Fold in the chopped fresh herbs.

Steak With Shallots in Red Wine Sauce in the Style of Albi

➵➵ *Entrecôte à l'Albigeoise* SERVES 4

THIS ALBIGEOISE VERSION of steak with red wine and shallots was given to me by the top gastronomic personality of Albi, Jacques Rieux, whose father, Louis, wrote the definitive book on Albigeoise cooking.

2 2-inch thick well-marbled boneless rib-eye steaks (about 1 pound each), well trimmed

Salt and freshly ground pepper

3 tablespoons grapeseed, French peanut, or unflavored vegetable oil

24 small to medium shallots (about 4 ounces), peeled

1 large head of garlic, halved crosswise

2 cups full bodied red wine, such as a Rhône wine

1 tablespoon sugar

Herb bouquet: 3 sprigs parsley, 1 sprig thyme, and ½ imported bay leaf tied together with string

1½ tablespoons sherry vinegar or red wine vinegar

1 cup rich unsalted meat stock, degreased

2 tablespoons unsalted butter

2 teaspoons chopped fresh flat-leaf parsley

2 teaspoons minced fresh chives

1 Season the steaks with salt and pepper; rub with 2 tablespoons of the oil. Cover loosely with plastic wrap and refrigerate until ready to cook. Remove from refrigerator 1 hour before cooking. Dry the steaks with paper towels.

2 In a 2-quart nonreactive saucepan, combine the whole shallots, halved garlic head, red wine, 1½ teaspoons of the sugar, ¼ teaspoon pepper, and the herb bouquet. Simmer for 1 hour, or until the liquid is reduced by three quarters. Remove from the heat; discard the herb bouquet and garlic. Scrape the liquid and shallots into a small bowl and hold until ready to finish the dish.

3 Sear the steaks in a very hot, lightly oiled well-seasoned heavy skillet, 2 minutes per side. Using tongs, transfer the steaks to a cake rack and let them rest while finishing the sauce. Blot out any fat in the skillet.

(continued)

4 Add the vinegar to the skillet and bring to a boil over high heat, scraping up any brown bits from the bottom of the pan. Boil until reduced to a glaze, 2 to 3 minutes. Add ½ cup of the stock and boil down to a syrupy glaze. Add the shallots and red-wine reduction. Stir in 1½ teaspoons of the sugar and cook for 1 minute, or until the sauce begins to glisten. Add the remaining stock and bring to a boil. Pour the sauce into a small saucepan; boil down to ¾ cup and set aside. Wipe out the skillet.

5 Heat the remaining 1 tablespoon oil in the skillet until hot. Return the steaks to the pan and cook over moderately high heat, turning once, to finish to the desired degree of doneness, about 3 minutes per side for medium-rare. Transfer the steaks to a cutting board and let rest for 3 to 5 minutes.

6 Reheat the sauce. Swirl in the butter, 1 tablespoon at a time. Season with salt and pepper to taste. Slice the steaks and arrange the meat on a heated platter. Spoon the shallots and sauce over the steak. Sprinkle with the chopped fresh herbs and serve at once.

NOTE TO THE COOK

You want to use a heavy red wine with a high alcoholic content here so that it will reduce to a rich consistency.

Pan-Sautéed Steak With Black Pepper, Armagnac, and Yellow Raisins

➤➤ *Steak au Poivre et aux Raisins Secs* SERVES 2

HERE'S MY VERSION of the old bistro favorite, *steak au poivre*, with the addition of Armagnac-soaked yellow raisins to soften the aggressiveness of the pepper.

2 boneless rib, strip, or shell steaks, cut ¾ inch thick, trimmed of fat, about 7 ounces each

Coarse kosher salt

1 tablespoon grapeseed, French peanut, or mild-flavored olive oil

1½ tablespoons yellow or golden raisins, softened in warm water and drained

2 tablespoons Armagnac or Cognac

4 teaspoons freshly crushed mixed black and white peppercorns

¼ cup meat stock or water

1 teaspoon Dijon mustard

1½ tablespoons heavy cream

1 tablespoon unsalted butter

1 Season the steaks with salt; rub with half the oil. Cover loosely with plastic wrap and refrigerate until 30 minutes before cooking. In a small bowl, macerate the raisins in the Armagnac for at least 30 minutes.

2 Dry the steaks with paper towels. Spread half the crushed peppercorns on a paper towel. Firmly press the steaks into the peppercorns. Spread the remainder on top of the meat and use your palm to press them down firmly.

3 Slowly, heat a heavy skillet until hot and add the remaining oil. Add the steaks and sear them for 2 minutes on each side. Regulate the heat so that you don't produce too many burned peppercorns. Using a wide spatula, carefully transfer the steaks to a cake rack set over a plate; tent with foil to keep warm.

4 Pour off the fat and any loose burnt peppercorns in the skillet. Add the raisins and Armagnac and, when heated, avert your face and carefully ignite. When the flames subside, add the stock and bring it to a boil over high heat, scraping up any browned bits from the bottom of the skillet. Whisk in the mustard and cream and any meat juices that have accumulated around the beef; bring to a boil. Add the butter and shake the skillet over moderate heat until a smooth sauce forms. Adjust the seasoning and pour over the steak and serve.

FILLET OF BEEF WITH ROQUEFORT SAUCE AND MIXED NUTS

➤➤ *Filet de Bœuf au Roquefort*   SERVES 4 TO 5

THIS COMBINATION is a specialty of the town of Saint-Juéry in the Tarn. The brilliant sauce is the creation of Gascon chef André Daguin. The method of cooking and racking the fillet is my way of handling roasts and thick steaks. I happened on this method while preparing twenty pounds of beef fillet for a benefit in La Jolla, California. I wanted to be able to present all the fillets at once, perfectly cooked, hot, and at just the moment when my sauce was right. At eleven in the morning, I started searing them, in pairs, in a mixture of near-smoking grapeseed oil and duck fat. Grapeseed oil takes a high temperature without burning and breaking down; duck fat gives wonderful flavor to beef.

So far I was following a normal professional kitchen procedure. The difference came when the fillets had been seared and I was looking for a place for them to rest before their final cooking in the oven two hours hence. Most cooks I know place the seared meat on an upside-down plate set atop a larger dish; any juices that run out collect in the lower dish and are used later in the sauce. The fallacy is that the side of the meat that rests on the plate tends to soften and the beef crust tends to crack, thus releasing quite a bit of juice. I found that when I placed fillets on wire racks, so that air could flow underneath them as well as above, their crusty exteriors remained intact. Out of my twenty pounds of seared fillets, less than half a teaspoon of meat juice was released!

Later, of course, I finished their cooking in the oven, and then, too, no juice was lost. In fact, all the juice remained suspended in the fibers of the beef, keeping it moist, tender, and delicious until the fillets were finally carved.

When ordering a fillet, ask the butcher to give you a center piece so that the thickness will be even from one end to the other. Have him remove all the fat and sinews. Do not have him bard the meat, but do ask him to tie the roast at one-inch intervals so it will keep its shape.

1 center-cut beef tenderloin (2 pounds; trimmed weight 1¾ pounds)

Salt and freshly ground pepper

Grapeseed or peanut oil

1 teaspoon rendered duck or goose fat or clarified butter

1 tablespoon minced shallots

3 tablespoons dry Madeira or imported ruby Port

½ cup demi-glace (storebought or homemade—page 406) or 1½ cups unsalted meat stock reduced to ½ cup

1½ ounces creamy Roquefort cheese

3 tablespoons unsalted butter, plus more if necessary

2 tablespoons crème fraîche or whipped heavy cream

2 tablespoons lightly toasted pine nuts

2 tablespoons lightly toasted walnut pieces

2 tablespoons lightly toasted sliced blanched almonds

1 tablespoon chopped fresh flat-leaf parsley

1 Lightly sprinkle meat with salt and pepper. Rub a little oil over the beef. Loosely cover with plastic wrap and refrigerate until 1 hour before cooking. Pat the roast dry with paper towels.

2 In a large heavy skillet, preferably enameled cast-iron, heat 2 teaspoons oil and the fat until very hot. Sear the meat over high heat, turning, until browned all over, about 4 minutes total. Transfer the roast to a wire rack; let rest for a minimum of 20 minutes.

3 Throw out the cooking fat. Add the chopped shallots and Madeira or Port to the skillet; boil until reduced to a glaze. Add the demi-glace or reduced stock and bring to a boil. Reduce to a syrupy consistency. Set aside.

4 Crush the Roquefort and the butter to a smooth, creamy paste. Taste the mixture; if it's too salty, add another ½ to 1 tablespoon butter. Cover and refrigerate.

5 About 30 minutes before serving, preheat the oven to 450°F. Roast the beef fillets to 120°F or for 17 minutes for "blue" (very rare); to 125°F or 18 minutes for rare; or to 135°F or 19 minutes for medium-rare.

6 Meanwhile, gently reheat the syrupy sauce in the skillet. Divide the Roquefort butter into 4 or 5 chunks and swirl into the sauce, one by one. Remove from the heat and fold the crème fraîche or whipped cream into the sauce.

7 Spoon the sauce onto a heated serving platter. Slice meat and arrange, overlapping, on the platter. Surround with the toasted nuts mixed with the parsley. Serve at once.

(continued)

NOTE TO THE COOK

Adding 2 tablespoons crème fraîche or whipped cream to a sauce to thicken it sounds rich, but compared to butter enrichment, it isn't. Two tablespoons of heavy cream or crème fraîche is equal in butterfat to about 1 tablespoon butter. It is the consistency of the cream that thickens the sauce. To beat up that small amount of whipping cream may sound ludicrous, but with the hand-held immersion blenders that fit into a small cup, it is a simple chore of 30 seconds.

VARIATION: FILLET OF BEEF WITH PÉRIGUEUX SAUCE *(Filet de Bœuf, Sauce Périgueux)*

Prepare the fillet as directed in the recipe above. Instead of the Roquefort sauce and toasted nuts, substitute this luscious sauce.

PÉRIGUEUX SAUCE

Sauce Périgueux

MAKES ABOUT 1½ CUPS SAUCE; SERVES 6

2 cups dry white wine

¼ cup finely chopped jambon de Bayonne, prosciutto, or Serrano ham

¼ cup crumbled dried cèpes, rinsed

2 tablespoons finely chopped shallots

⅔ cup dry Madeira

1½ cups demi-glace (storebought or homemade—page 406), prepared with the addition of 2 chopped plum tomatoes

1 medium canned truffle, finely diced, and the truffle liquor, optional

2 to 3 tablespoons unsalted butter, cut into small pieces

Salt and freshly ground pepper

1 In a nonreactive medium saucepan, combine the white wine, ham, cèpes, and shallots; bring to a boil. Lower the heat and reduce to a glaze, about 30 minutes.

2 Add ½ cup of the Madeira and boil down to a glaze. Add the demi-glace and simmer for 15 to 20 minutes to blend the flavors.

3 Strain through a sieve lined with several layers of cheesecloth, pressing down on the ingredients to release all their flavor. You should have about 1⅓ cups. *(The sauce can be refrigerated for 1 to 2 days or frozen at this point.)*

4 Reheat the sauce to a simmer. Add any juices from the roast. Add the truffle, if using, and the truffle liquor from the can. Stir in the remaining Madeira. Simmer for 1 to 2 minutes. Remove from the heat and swirl in the butter. Season with salt and pepper to taste and serve.

BRAISED SHORT RIBS IN CÈPE-PRUNE SAUCE

↠ *Daube de Bœuf aux Champignons et au Pruneaux*   SERVES 6

CHEF LAURENT MANRIQUE, from Gascony, now cooking in San Francisco works on two fronts: the "old" and the "new."

This dish is from his "old" repertory—a variation on his grandmother's favorite duck leg recipe, in which he substitutes beef short ribs. (For one of his innovative new recipes, see Yellowfin Tuna With Avocado and Piment d'Espelette, pages 81–82.)

For best results, start this dish two days before serving.

3 pounds beef short ribs, well trimmed and cut into 2½-inch lengths

3 medium yellow onions, cut into 1-inch chunks

3 medium carrots, cut into 1-inch lengths

3 celery ribs, cut into 1-inch lengths

3 heads of garlic: 2 cut crosswise in half and 1 left whole

Herb bouquet: 1 loosely packed cup thyme sprigs, 2 imported bay leaves, and 1 tablespoon black peppercorns tied together in cheesecloth

1 ounce dried French cèpes or Italian porcini, rinsed

6 cups spicy red wine, such as Zinfandel

Salt and freshly ground pepper

¼ cup rendered duck or pork fat

3 cups rich unsalated chicken stock (storebought or homemade—page 405)

¼ cup chopped Confit of Pork Rinds (page 17), or chopped blanched salt pork rind

1 cup tiny peeled fresh white onions, or thawed frozen baby onions

¼ pound fresh cèpe or porcini mushrooms, or substitute fresh white mushrooms

¼ pound prunes, pitted and halved

A few drops of *verjus* or lemon juice

Parsley sprigs, for garnish

(continued)

1 In a 5-quart bowl, combine the short ribs, yellow onion, carrots, celery, 2 split heads garlic, herb bouquet, and dried cèpes. Pour the wine over all and mix well. Put a plate upside down over the contents and press down to keep everything submerged. Refrigerate overnight.

2 Remove the short ribs from the marinade and drain well. Pat dry with paper towels; set aside. Strain the marinade into a bowl, reserving the vegetables and marinade separately. Set aside the herb bouquet. Season the ribs generously with salt and pepper.

3 Heat a large skillet over moderately high heat, add half the duck or pork fat, and half the meat. Sear the short ribs without crowding until well browned on all sides, about 5 minutes. Transfer the ribs to a large casserole, preferably enameled cast-iron or earthenware. Repeat with the remaining ribs. Add the confit of pork rind, reserved herb bouquet, and garlic halves to the casserole. Toss to coat all the ingredients in the casserole.

4 Remove all but 2 tablespoons fat from the skillet. Add the drained vegetables in batches to the skillet and sauté, stirring constantly, until lightly browned. Use a slotted spoon to transfer the vegetables to the casserole. Repeat with the remaining vegetables. Discard any fat in the skillet. Add 2 cups of the wine to the skillet and bring to a boil, scraping up any brown bits that cling to the bottom and sides of the skillet. Reduce to a glaze. Add another 2 cups of the wine and reduce again.

5 Add the deglazing liquid from the skillet, the remaining wine and marinade, and the stock to the casserole; heat to boiling. Reduce the heat and simmer, uncovered, for 5 minutes, skimming the surface. Place a round of crumpled wet parchment over the contents of the casserole, cover, and place in the oven. Turn the heat to 325°F. Braise in the oven until ribs are tender, about 3 hours. Set aside the skillet without washing for use in the next step.

6 Remove the casserole and let the meat rest in the sauce for an hour or two. Remove the meat to a container and cover with a plastic wrap to keep from drying out. Pour the vegetables and liquid through a fine strainer directly into the skillet. Discard the solids in the strainer. Bring the liquid to a boil over high heat and cook, skimming and removing the scum that rises to the surface, for 10 minutes. Then push the skillet half off the heat and let the sauce slowly reduce, skimming, for about 15 minutes, or until the sauce has reduced by two thirds. Adjust the seasoning to taste. Pour the sauce and the meat into separate containers, let cool, cover, and refrigerate overnight or for up to 2 days.

7 Combine the ribs and sauce in a casserole and set over moderately low heat. Meanwhile, in a medium skillet, sauté the baby onions in the remaining duck or pork fat until lightly browned all

over. Add to the casserole. Separate the cloves of the remaining head of garlic, peel, and thinly slice. Add to the skillet with the mushrooms and sauté until they throw off liquid, add a few tablespoons of hot water to keep the garlic from burning; sauté until dry. Sauté until the mushrooms are lightly brown but moist, about 8 minutes. Add the prunes and cook until glazed. Scrape into the casserole. Simmer for 10 minutes.

8 Using a large slotted spoon, gently transfer the ribs, prunes, onions, and mushrooms to a large warmed platter. Taste the cooking liquid for salt and pepper and add verjus to develop and balance the flavors. Scatter plumes of parsley on top and serve.

Oxtail Daube

➤➤ *Daube de Queue de Bœuf*

CONSIDER A PERFECTLY COOKED prime-grade porterhouse steak. We know it is the marbling in the meat, the streaks of fat, that make it so succulent and delicious. We know it isn't healthy to eat much meat fat, but for flavor's sake we do. Here is a dish that uses fat to enhance its flavor but which is served close to fat-free because it is double degreased. In fact, when you read the recipe, you will see that I have actually added fat for extra flavor, but that is eliminated, too, before the dish is served. The result is a very soft, fleshy oxtail daube of incredible lightness and flavor.

The secret is long, slow cooking in a closed pot. During this time, the meat is never moved, and the juices are never allowed to boil. (If they did boil, the fats would bind with the wine and the sauce would be muddy.) Through long, slow cooking the meat renders out all of its fat; the meat and sauce retain the flavor of fat, which is water-soluble, but not the fat itself.

This dish, like many stews and daubes, benefits from being made one day in advance. In fact, some of the *salmis* (stews of wild birds and domestic barnyard fowl) and daubes of tough cuts of meat of the Southwest are slowly reheated and cooled each day for a period of four or five days so that, with each reheating, the flavors grow stronger and deeper. For our cuts of meat this is not necessary—one would end up with a mushy, tasteless stew.

Serve with noodles, followed by a bitter green salad.

Begin 1 day in advance.

4½ to 5½ pounds oxtail, cut into pieces

1 calf's foot or pig's foot, split (optional; for extra body)

¾-pound slab of lean salt pork

1 tablespoon olive or peanut oil

Salt and freshly ground pepper

4 medium onions, coarsely chopped

1 bottle (750 ml) full-bodied red wine, such as Syrah

⅓ cup red wine vinegar

Herb bouquet: 3 sprigs parsley, 1 sprig thyme, and 1 imported bay leaf tied together with string

2 garlic cloves, peeled

2 ounces jambon de Bayonne, prosciutto, or Serrano ham, cut into ½-inch dice

¾ ounce dried French cèpes or Italian porcini, crumbled

1 The day before you plan to serve the daube, preheat the oven to 275°F. Trim off all excess fat from the pieces of oxtail.

2 Blanch the calf's foot and salt pork in a saucepan of boiling water for 3 minutes; drain. Slice the rind off the salt pork and reserve. Cube the salt pork and divide into 2 batches. In a heavy nonreactive skillet, heat the oil and slowly cook half the salt pork, stirring often, until the cubes turn golden brown and a great deal of their fat has rendered out, about 10 minutes. Line a flameproof earthenware or enameled cast-iron 5- or 6-quart casserole with the pork rind, fat side down. Transfer the browned salt pork to the casserole.

3 Season the oxtail pieces with salt and pepper. Brown the oxtail pieces over moderately high heat in batches without crowding in the skillet used to cook the salt pork, about 10 minutes per batch. As they brown, transfer the pieces to the casserole.

4 Remove and discard half the fat in the skillet. Cook the onions in the remaining hot fat until golden brown. Add the onions to the casserole.

5 Deglaze the skillet with 1 cup of the wine. Boil down to a glaze. Add another 1 cup of wine and repeat. Add the remaining wine, vinegar, and 1½ cups water. Bring just to a boil and skim carefully. Pour over the meats. Add the calf's foot, herb bouquet, and garlic. Cover tightly and place in the oven to cook very slowly for 3 hours without disturbing.

6 Carefully remove the oxtails to a deep bowl; cover and keep moist. Remove the meat from the calf's foot while still warm and place in a food processor. Add the remaining salt pork cubes, the cooked pork rind, cooked garlic, and the ham. Grind to a smooth paste.

7 Strain the cooking liquid, pushing down on the onions to extract all their juices. Remove as much fat as possible and pour the juices into a large saucepan. Bring to a boil, reduce the heat to moderate, and boil slowly, skimming from time to time, until reduced by one third.

8 Carefully return the pieces of oxtail to the casserole and spread the meat paste on top. Add the reduced liquid. Rinse the cèpes under running water, drain, and add to the casserole. Cover and bake in a 275°F oven for 2½ hours without disturbing.

9 Remove the casserole from the oven; transfer the oxtails to a work surface; discard any loose bones. Season with salt and pepper, pour into a bowl, and cover and refrigerate. Separately, cover and refrigerate the cooking liquid.

(continued)

10 About 2½ hours before serving, preheat the oven to 275°F. Remove the jellied liquid from the refrigerator and lift off all congealed fat. Combine liquid and add the meat in the casserole, cover and reheat the daube without stirring for 1½ hours.

11 To serve, remove the oxtails to a deep heatproof platter. Cover with foil and keep warm in the turned-off oven. Strain the sauce into a small saucepan, pressing down on the solids. Bring the sauce to a boil and cook at a slow boil, half over the heat, skimming, until sauce lightly coats a spoon, about 20 minutes. Adjust the seasoning. Pour over the meat and serve hot.

Inspired by a recipe from Lucien Vanel.

Double Degreasing for Added Flavor

If you remove absolutely all the fat from a dish, there will surely be a loss of flavor. To compensate, I will degrease, then add more fat for more flavor, cook the dish some more, then degrease again. I call this technique double degreasing. A good example of this technique is in the Oxtail Daube recipe (above). I use the natural fat of the oxtail to enhance the flavor of the stew; then I totally degrease the sauce, add some pork fat for more flavor, and finally degrease the dish a second time before serving. The result is a really tender, meaty, and flavorful daube of incredible lightness.

The best way to degrease thoroughly is to remove the meat from the sauce and refrigerate both separately overnight. The fat in the sauce will rise to the surface and congeal, which makes it easy to remove. Fortunately, most stews and soups improve with slow reheating the next day (and sometimes multiple reheating).

There is another way to degrease thoroughly, when a dish is to be served the same day it is cooked. Meat and sauce are separated. The sauce is left to stand for a short time, so that most of the fat rises to the surface and can be skimmed off. While the meat is kept warm in a very low-temperature oven, the sauce is placed in a heavy pan on the stove, set half on and half off the burner. The flame is adjusted so that the side over the heat boils slowly, and the fat and any other impurities in the sauce rise on the cooler side and can be skimmed off. This process takes about 20 to 30 minutes, with frequent skimming to remove all the fat and impurities from the sauce. The resulting sauce is clear and shiny.

DAUBE OF BEEF IN THE STYLE OF GASCONY

➤➤ *Daube de Bœuf à la Gasconne*   SERVES 6 TO 8

MAURICE COSCUELLA, a Gascon chef from the town of Plaisance-du-Gers, taught me the secret of this beef stew: "It should be made with a mixture of meats: Gelatinous pieces such as shin; deep, flavorful pieces such as short ribs; and firm pieces such as chuck or bottom round." All the pieces should be large chunks, lest you end up with a crushed meat stew like the Daube de la Saint-André (Crushed Beef Daube for Early September, pages 272–273).

This version of a Gascon dish traditionally served on All Souls' Day is always started at least four days in advance. Ideally, it is made with red wine produced that year—a violet-colored liquid called vin bourret—but you may substitute any young red wine.

Serve with Fried Cornmeal Porridge Cakes in the Style of Gascony (pages 357–358).

Because the meats need to marinate, begin this recipe 3 to 4 days in advance.

5 to 6 pounds mixed cuts of beef in large pieces: 2 pounds chuck roast or bottom round, trimmed of fat; 2½ pounds beef short ribs or short ribs for flanken; and 1 beef shin with marrow

4 small carrots, cut into thin rounds

3 medium onions, thinly sliced

1 head of garlic, halved crosswise

½ pound celery root, peeled and cut into thin slices, or substitute 1 celery heart, thinly sliced

1 teaspoon bruised peppercorns

½ teaspoon Quatre Épices (page 231), plus an extra grating of fresh nutmeg

1 bottle (750 ml) full-flavored red wine, such as Syrah or Zinfandel

¼ cup rendered duck fat

Salt and freshly ground pepper

¾ pound fresh or salted pork rind, blanched 5 minutes and cut into strips

Herb bouquet: 6 sprigs of parsley, 2 sprigs of thyme, 1 small imported bay leaf, and 2 celery leaves tied together with string

¼ cup Armagnac

1 Three or 4 days in advance, cut the chuck and bottom round into 12 or 16 pieces of approximately equal size. Place all the meat in a large bowl. Add the carrots, onions, garlic, celery root, bruised peppercorns and the quatre épices. Pour in the wine. Cover the bowl with plastic wrap and let the meat marinate in refrigerator for up to 3 days, stirring once a day.

(continued)

2 A day before serving, preheat the oven to 250°F. Remove the meat from the marinade and dry with paper towels. Reserve the vegetables and the wine marinade together.

3 Heat the duck fat in a large heavy skillet. Generously season the meat with salt and pepper. Deeply brown all the meat in batches in hot fat, about 5 minutes for each batch. Line a 6- or 8-quart enameled cast-iron casserole or daubière with the pork rind, fat side down. Place the browned meat on top of pork rind. Add the garlic from the marinade and the herb bouquet.

4 Strain the marinating liquid through a fine strainer into a bowl. Press down to extract all juices from the vegetables. Add the vegetables to the skillet, cover and cook over medium heat for 5 minutes. Uncover and allow to brown over high heat for 5 minutes, stirring. Using a slotted spoon, transfer the vegetables to the casserole.

5 Sprinkle the Armagnac over the meat and vegetables.

6 Wipe out the skillet. Pour in 1 cup of the marinating liquid and bring to a boil, scraping up all the bits and pieces clinging to the bottom of the skillet. Skim carefully. Boil down to a glaze. Add another 1 cup marinating liquid and reduce to a glaze. Add the remaining marinade and simmer, skimming, for 5 minutes. Add 3 cups water and bring to a boil. Pour over the meat and vegetables. Cover the meat and liquid with a sheet of crumpled parchment paper and a cover. Transfer to the oven and cook for 6 hours.

7 Carefully remove the meat to a large bowl. Puree one third of the vegetables and the marrow in a food processor. Press through a sieve over the meat in the bowl. The cooked pork rind and meat from the shin can be diced and added or discarded. Cover and refrigerate.

8 Strain the cooking liquid and discard the remaining vegetables. Skim off as much fat as possible. Pour the liquid into a heavy saucepan, bring to a boil, and set half over the heat. Cook at a slow boil, skimming, for 10 minutes, or until reduced and very flavorful, about 2 cups. Let cool, then cover and refrigerate.

9 On serving day, remove any additional fat that has surfaced. Place the meat and the sauce in a wide ovenproof serving casserole in a cold oven. Set the oven to 350°F and bake, uncovered, until bubbling and dark brown, about 30 minutes.

CHILLED BEEF TERRINE IN THE STYLE OF THE GIRONDE

➤➤ *Terrine de Bœuf à la Girondine*   SERVES 8 TO 12

THIS OLD RECIPE for jellied beef is a good dish for picnics and warm summer night buffets. A dry white wine is used, and the dish benefits from being made a few days in advance. Choose bottom round, sirloin tip, or the midsection of the rump. It must be larded with hard fatback flavored with herbs, brandy, and lots of chopped garlic so that while the beef cooks, it is nourished and flavored from within (see Note, page 271).

The meat is cooked in its marinade, then sliced and molded in a terrine. When chilled and set, it is sliced like a pâté. Creamy Shallot Vinaigrette (page 271) makes a good sauce. A salad of haricots verts and a platter of thinly sliced red-ripe tomatoes would make fine accompaniments.

Begin 2 or 3 days in advance.

8 ounces firm white pork fatback with rind

¼ cup chopped fresh flat-leaf parsley

1 teaspoon finely chopped fresh garlic

3 tablespoons Armagnac or brandy

¼ teaspoon Quatre Épices (page 231)

4½ to 5 pounds bottom round, sirloin tip, or midsection of the rump, trimmed of all fat

Salt and freshly ground pepper

1 cup thinly sliced carrots

1 cup thinly sliced onions

2 cups dry white wine, such as Sauvignon Blanc

¼ cup white wine vinegar

3 tablespoons extra virgin olive oil

Herb and spice bouquet: 4 sprigs parsley, 1 sprig thyme, 1 imported bay leave, 3 celery leaves, 2 whole cloves, 1 small cinnamon stick, and 2 cracked allspice berries, tied together in cheesecloth

½ tablespoon lightly cracked peppercorns

1 tablespoon rendered duck or pork fat

1 tablespoon grapeseed or corn oil

1 calf's foot or 2 small pig's feet, split

1 leek, split and well washed, or 6 shallots, peeled and sliced

1 medium tomato, peeled, seeded, and chopped, or ½ cup canned tomatoes, drained

2 garlic cloves, halved

3 cups unsalted chicken, veal, or beef stock, or a mixture

(continued)

1 Place the pork fatback in cold water; bring to a boil and simmer 3 minutes. Drain, rinse, and sever rind from fat. Reserve both. Cut the fat, while still warm, into thin strips. Toss with chopped parsley, chopped garlic, 1 tablespoon of the Armagnac, and the Quatre Épices (warm fat absorbs flavors better). Refrigerate until the fat hardens so that you can easily use it to lard the meat. Cut the pork rind into strips and set aside.

2 Meanwhile, rub the beef with 1 teaspoon salt and ½ teaspoon pepper. Use half the seasoned strips to lard the beef with the grain, keeping the spacing even. Use remaining strips to lard on the diagonal throughout the meat, like a porcupine's quills. (When fat melts during the cooking, it passes through the "capillaries" of the meat, keeping it moist and flavorful.) Tie meat to keep its solid shape.

3 Place the carrots, onions, wine, vinegar, olive oil, herb and spice bouquet, cracked peppercorns, and remaining 2 tablespoons Armagnac in a large bowl. Add the larded meat and marinate in the refrigerator, loosely covered with plastic wrap, for 24 hours, turning the meat 2 or 3 times.

4 The next day, preheat the oven to 250°F. In a large saucepan, blanch the calf's foot or pig's feet for 5 minutes. Drain, rinse, and drain again.

5 Remove the beef from the marinade; dry thoroughly. Pick out and reserve the herb bouquet. Strain the marinade, reserving the vegetables (and any fatback strips that have slipped out) and the liquid separately. In a large heavy skillet, heat the fat and oil until hot. Lightly brown the meat on all sides, about 10 minutes. Remove to a side dish. Spoon off the fat; add the marinade vegetables and cook them over moderate heat until lightly browned, about 10 minutes.

6 Line a 5-quart casserole with the strips of pork rind, fat side down. Place the meat on top of the rind. Add the calf's foot or pig's feet, the browned vegetables, herb bouquet, leek or shallots, tomato, halved garlic cloves, and peppercorns from the marinade. Pour in the stock.

7 Pour the strained marinade liquid into the skillet and bring to a boil. Simmer for 2 to 3 minutes. Strain over the meat. Cover the casserole with parchment paper and a tight-fitting lid. Cook in the low oven for 5 hours.

8 Let stand, uncovered, for 1 hour. Remove the calf's foot or pig's feet and bone while still warm; dice the meat. Skim the fat off the top of the liquid in the casserole. Lift out the meat and remove the strings. Strain the liquid and remove as much fat as possible. Boil down to 3 cups clear, jellylike liquid. Season with salt and pepper to taste. Strain through a sieve lined with dampened cheesecloth.

9 Slice the meat thickly and arrange overlapping slices in a 5- to 6-cup terrine. Scatter the diced calf's or pig's feet on top. Pour the strained cooking liquid over the meat and chill until set. Then wrap well. The terrine will keep for 3 to 4 days in the refrigerator. Serve from the terrine, cutting into ½-inch-thick slices.

NOTE TO THE COOK

There are many types of larding needles on the market, each of which requires a slightly different larding technique. Follow the manufacturer's instructions. Whichever you use, be sure the fat is well chilled for easier handling. If you do not have a larding needle, drill holes with a skewer in the meat and push cold strips into the incisions.

CREAMY SHALLOT VINAIGRETTE   MAKES ABOUT ¾ CUP

2 tablespoons white wine vinegar

½ teaspoon salt

1 teaspoon Dijon mustard

6 tablespoons extra virgin olive oil

¼ teaspoon freshly ground pepper

⅓ cup heavy cream

1 tablespoon minced shallots

1 tablespoon chopped fresh flat-leaf parsley

1 Whisk the vinegar, salt, and mustard until well blended. Slowly beat in the oil to make a smooth emulsion. Beat in the cream.

2 Just before serving, stir in the shallots and parsley.

CRUSHED BEEF DAUBE FOR EARLY SEPTEMBER

➼ *Daube de la Saint-André*   SERVES 6

THIS DAUBE, TRADITIONALLY EATEN in early September during the first cold days of autumn, employs farmhouse methods that result in a melting, delicious, flavorful stew that can be eaten hot or cold. The original recipe calls for very thin slices of beef cooked in a red wine sauce overnight in the fireplace, degreased, cooked again, and degreased again. Then the meat was crushed with a fork into the sauce so that the dish became, in effect, a very rich, thick meat sauce. Its appearance was similar to that of a Georgia Brunswick stew. I cut my meat into ½-inch-thick slices so they remain intact. Traditionally, wine at least five years old was used for this recipe, but these days, that would be prohibitively expensive, so use a soft red wine.

In the old days, this type of crushed meat stew was served with the cornmeal and flour–based fried cakes called *armottes*, for which I offer a recipe on pages 357–358 (Fried Cornmeal Porridge Cakes in the Style of Gascony.

Begin 1 day in advance.

3 pounds bottom or top round of beef, trimmed of all fat, cut against the grain into ½-inch-thick slices

Freshly ground pepper and salt

1 pound thick-sliced lean ventrèche or pancetta

¼ cup chopped fresh flat-leaf parsley

¼ cup chopped shallots

1½ tablespoons chopped fresh garlic

2 cups soft red wine, such as Merlot

½ onion stuck with 1 whole clove

1 imported bay leaf

1 sprig of thyme

½ teaspoon sugar

Pinch of Quatre Épices (page 231)

1 A day in advance, preheat the oven to 225°F. Rub the meat with pepper and very little salt

2 Make the ventrèche blend: Cut it into small pieces and pulse in a food processor or put through the medium blade of a meat grinder. Mix the ground ventrèche with the parsley, shallots, garlic, a little pepper, and a pinch of salt to make a loose paste.

3 Layer the beef slices with alternate layers of the ventrèche blend in a 3- or 4-quart casserole, preferably stoneware or enameled cast-iron. In a nonreactive saucepan, bring the wine to a boil, reduce the heat, and simmer for 15 minutes to evaporate the alcohol. Pour over the meat. Add the onion half stuck with clove, bay leaf, thyme, sugar, and Quatre Épices. Cover with a sheet of

parchment and a tight-fitting lid. Set in the middle of the oven to cook very slowly for 6 hours. Uncover and let cool, then cover and refrigerate overnight.

4 The following day, preheat the oven to 250°F. Carefully degrease the liquid in the casserole. Cover again and cook for 1 hour in the oven. Let cool completely, then skim off all the fat.

5 Lift out the slices of meat and arrange, overlapping, in a shallow baking dish. Strain the cooking juices to remove any debris. If there is too much cooking liquid, reduce by boiling until flavorful and lightly thickened, skimming often. Pour over the meat. *(The dish can be prepared to this point several hours in advance.)*

6 Reheat gently before serving. If desired, crush the meat slices in the cooking juices. Serve in a wide soup bowl with slices of cornmeal cake.

TRIPE AND PIG'S FEET STEW

→→ *Tripes au Safran*   SERVES 6

THIS EXTRAORDINARY DISH is popular in Albi, where it is alleged to have been invented for the famous Toulouse-Lautrec family. Two foods of superb and varying texture — succulent, gelatinous nuggets of pig's feet and moist, chewy slices of tripe—carry the perfume of saffron, the strong earthy flavor of garlic, the saltiness of country ham, and the piquant taste of capers.

As in so many recipes of the Southwest, slow cooking is the secret to its succulence. The tripe and its flavorings are sealed in a large pot and set in a very low oven to cook for at least 12 hours. The tripe softens, the liquid never boils, the flavors mingle, and the sauce base becomes highly aromatic. Since tripe is relatively tasteless (I like tripe for its texture and ability to carry other tastes), this is one of the few times when the sauce should dominate the meat.

When you buy tripe (beef stomach lining), it varies in texture enormously; choose a honeycomb or weave pattern with small holes. Pieces with a larger weave will need an extra hour or two of cooking time to soften. The tripe and the sauce base can be prepared days in advance. The dish can then be finished just before serving. Present on very hot plates with plenty of crusty French bread.

Begin at least 2 days in advance.

(continued)

4 fresh pig's feet

Coarse kosher salt

1 teaspoon Herbes de la Garrigue (page 8) or herbes de Provence

2 pounds cleaned tripe

3 tablespoons white wine vinegar

1½ cups sliced carrots

1½ cups sliced onions

¾ cup well-washed sliced leeks

¼ cup sliced celery

Herb bouquet: 3 sprigs parsley, 1 sprig thyme, and 1 imported bay leaf tied together with string

1 bottle (750 ml) dry white wine

1 tablespoon tomato paste

¼ teaspoon saffron threads

¾ cup flour

1 teaspoon vegetable oil

½ pound jambon de Bayonne, prosciutto, or Serrano ham, cut into ⅜-inch dice

1½ tablespoons finely chopped fresh garlic

3 tablespoons chopped fresh flat-leaf parsley

3 tablespoons drained nonpareil capers

¼ teaspoon Tabasco or more to taste

1 to 2 teaspoons arrowroot (optional)

1 Two days in advance, scrub the pig's feet and dry. Rub with 1 tablespoon salt and the mixed herbs. Cover loosely with plastic wrap and refrigerate overnight.

2 The following day, soak the tripe in 3 cups water with the vinegar for 1 hour. Rinse and drain. Place the tripe in a deep kettle, cover with cold water, and bring slowly to a boil. Simmer for 15 minutes; drain. As soon as the tripe is cool enough to handle, cut it into 1½-inch pieces.

3 Preheat oven to 210°F. Place the vegetables in a 7- to 9-quart casserole, preferably earthenware or enameled cast-iron. Add the tripe, herb bouquet, wine, tomato paste, and saffron. Rinse the pig's feet and add to the pot. Add enough water to cover and ½ teaspoon salt. Cover the pot with the lid. Mix together the flour, oil, and enough water to make a thick paste. Seal the pot with a ribbon of the paste. Place the pot on center oven shelf to cook for 12 hours.

4 Twelve hours later or the following morning, strain contents. Discard all bones, vegetables, and herb bouquet. Bone the pig's feet while still warm, making sure you catch all the little foot bones. Cut the meat into small pieces. Place the tripe and boned pig's feet in deep bowl.

5 Allow the fat to rise to the surface of cooking liquid. Skim off and discard all the fat. Place the degreased liquid in a deep saucepan and boil, skimming, until reduced to 3 cups. Pour the liquid over the tripe and pig's feet; set aside to cool. Cover and refrigerate until 45 minutes before serving. (The recipe can be prepared to this point up to 2 days in advance.)

6 About 45 minutes before serving, gently reheat the tripe and cooking liquid.

7 In a large, deep, covered skillet, cook the ham over low heat 10 minutes, shaking the skillet frequently. Add the garlic and parsley; cook, covered, 2 to 3 minutes longer. Add the tripe and cooking liquid. Simmer, uncovered, 30 minutes, stirring often. Add the capers and Tabasco. If the sauce is too thin, mix the arrowroot with 1½ tablespoons cold water until well blended. Stir into the sauce and bring to a boil. Simmer, stirring, until thickened. Ladle the meat and sauce into heated individual soup plates.

Veal Dishes

VEAL CUBES BRAISED WITH ONIONS IN THE STYLE OF THE BÉARN

→ *Veau à la Béarnaise*   SERVES 3 OR 4

THE SECRET OF THIS SIMPLE, tasty family dish is in the cutting of the onions: They must be halved lengthwise and then hand-diced. If they are chopped in any sort of machine, they will end up acrid and mushy. Diced by hand, they retain their body while slowly exuding their sweet moisture. It is this liquid that provides the cooking medium for the cubed lean veal.

The onions and ham slivers are first sweated in a small amount of fat on top of the stove; then the veal and crushed anchovies are stirred in, and the casserole tightly covered. Once the ingredients are hot they are placed in a slow oven to cook for two hours without further attention. This method is ideal for cooking lean tender veal: The morsels of meat turn succulent; the onions, soft but still distinguishable, provide the sauce; the anchovies and ham provide added flavor.

This dish is good with rice, scalloped potatoes, or noodles.

(continued)

1¼ to 1½ pounds large white onions (see Notes below)

1½ ounces jambon de Bayonne, prosciutto, or Serrano ham, slivered (about ⅓ cup)

1 tablespoon rendered ham, duck, or goose fat

1¾ to 2 pounds boneless rump of veal, trimmed and cut into 1-inch cubes

4 anchovy fillets, rinsed and crushed to a puree

Freshly ground pepper

Salt (optional)

1 tablespoon minced fresh chives

1 Preheat oven to 325°F. Sweat the onions and ham in the rendered fat in a 3-quart flameproof earthenware or enameled cast-iron casserole over moderately low heat, covered, for 10 minutes.

2 Add the veal, anchovies, and pepper to taste to the casserole. Cover tightly and return to the heat to cook for 5 minutes longer. Transfer to the middle of the oven and cook for 1 hour without disturbing. Reduce the oven temperature to 300°F and cook for 1 hour longer.

3 Strain the cooking juices into a saucepan. Return the meat and onions to the casserole and return the casserole, uncovered, to the oven to keep hot. Degrease the cooking liquid, boil down by one third. Season with salt to taste. Pour the sauce over the veal and onions. Serve at once with a sprinkling of chives.

NOTES TO THE COOK

➻ The best method I have found to avoid tears when chopping onions is to lightly sprinkle the sliced onions and the work surface with vinegar. Rinse the onions afterwards to remove the vinegar.

➻ To dice onions, halve them lengthwise and lay them cut side down. Make even vertical cuts from the root end. Make several horizontal cuts, then slice downward into ⅓-inch pieces.

RAGOUT OF VEAL WITH ORANGE

Ragoût de Veau à l'Orange

THIS DISH FROM TOULOUSE originally called for the bitter Seville orange, *bigarade*. To compensate for that special tanginess, I have used a combination of orange and plenty of strained lemon juice. For easy service, this ragout can be prepared entirely in advance and reheated. I like this dish with rice.

1 pounds veal riblets or 1½ pounds boneless veal shoulder, cut into 1½-inch chunks

⅓ cup diced pancetta or ventrèche

2 tablespoons vegetable oil

1 or 2 veal bones, cut into 1½-inch pieces (optional)

2 cups dry white wine

1½ cups rich veal or unsalted chicken stock (storebought or homemade—page 405)

2 medium onions, thinly sliced

4 garlic cloves, halved

Herb bouquet: 3 sprigs parsley, 1 sprig thyme, 1 imported bay leaf, 1 sprig celery leaves, and a few pieces leek greens tied together with string

1½ teaspoons tomato paste

Salt and freshly ground pepper to taste

½ to ⅔ cup fresh orange juice

¼ cup fresh lemon juice

⅔ cup heavy cream

Zest of 1 medium orange, cut into thin strips

2 teaspoons minced fresh chives

1 teaspoon minced fresh flat-leaf parsley

1 Trim excess fat from the veal. In a large skillet, sauté the pancetta in hot oil until golden and lightly crisp. With a slotted spoon, transfer to a 5-quart flameproof casserole. Add the veal to the skillet in batches without crowding and sauté over moderately high heat, turning, until browned all over, 5 to 7 minutes. As each piece browns, transfer it to the casserole. Lightly brown the veal bones in the remaining fat, if using.

2 Pour out the fat and deglaze the skillet with the white wine. Pour the pan juices over the veal bones. Add the stock, onions, garlic, herb bouquet, tomato paste, and salt and pepper to taste. Cover and simmer for 1½ to 2 hours, or until the veal is very tender when pierced with the tip of a sharp knife.

(continued)

3 Remove the meat and cover to keep moist. Discard the herb bouquet and bones. Strain the juices; chill quickly and degrease completely. Pour into a nonreactive saucepan. Add ½ cup of the orange juice and the ¼ cup lemon juice. Bring to a boil and reduce to 2 cups, skimming. Add the cream, return to a boil, and reduce to 1½ cups. Season with salt and pepper to taste. Add the remaining orange juice, if you think it needs it. Return the meat to the sauce and reheat slowly.

4 Meanwhile, blanch the orange zest in boiling water for 5 minutes. Drain and rinse under cold running water. Add the orange zest, chives, and parsley to the sauce and serve.

VEAL KIDNEYS GARNISHED WITH SHALLOT CONFIT

⤛ *Rognons de Veau Poêlés au Confit d'Échalotes*   SERVES 4 TO 6

BORDEAUX CHEF CHRISTIAN CLÉMENT introduced me to this unique way of treating shallots: cooked very slowly for a long time in rendered goose or duck fat, as if they were pieces of duck or goose confit. When the shallots have become soft and translucent, they are caramelized in a skillet over high heat or in a hot oven. The juicy kidneys are served not with a sauce but with the soft, sweet shallots. This dish is especially good with potatoes sautéed in goose fat.

1 cup rendered goose or duck fat	2 light-colored, very fresh veal kidneys (about 12 ounces each)
½ pound large shallots, about 1 inch in diameter, peeled	Freshly ground black pepper and coarse kosher salt

1 Reserve 3 tablespoons of the poultry fat for cooking the kidneys. In a small heavy saucepan, warm the remaining fat and 3 tablespoons water over very low heat to body temperature. Slip the shallots into the warm fat and simmer slowly for about 1½ hours, or until they become translucent and very soft. Gently remove with a slotted spoon and set aside; reserve 2 tablespoons of the fat. (Remaining fat can be used for potatoes or confit.)

2 With a sharp knife, remove as much of the fat and membrane covering the kidneys as possible, leaving them whole. Place the 3 tablespoons fat reserved at the beginning of Step 1 in a heavy medium skillet over moderately high heat. Add the kidneys and sauté for 4 minutes. Turn over and cook for 3 to 4 minutes, until the kidneys are firm but not too resistant to pressure; they should be very pink inside. (Kidneys that weigh 1 pound cook in 10 minutes, 4½ to 5 minutes per side.) Remove the kidneys to a wire rack set over a plate to catch any juices. Cover loosely with foil to keep warm.

3 Wipe out the skillet with paper towels. Add the 2 tablespoons reserved fat from the shallots and place over moderately high heat. Add the shallots and cook, tossing frequently, until browned and caramelized all over, about 5 minutes.

4 With a sharp knife, cut the kidneys slightly on the diagonal into thin slices; discard any extra juices. Arrange the slices, overlapping in a flowerlike ring, on warm plates. Season lavishly with freshly ground pepper and salt lightly. Place the shallots in the center of the kidneys and serve hot.

NOTE TO THE COOK

If a sauce is desired, make the White Bordeaux Wine Sauce (page 254).

Veal Kidneys in a Priest's Omelet

→ *L'Omelette du Curé aux Rognons de Veau*   SERVES 3 OR 4

THIS IS A WONDERFUL DISH to serve for a light supper with a strong green salad. In Southwest France, a "priest's omelet" is an omelet made from odds and ends, undoubtedly inspired by the austere lifestyle of the local priests. In Lucien Vanel's Toulouse kitchen, however, the odds and ends are cèpes, chicken livers, veal kidneys, and truffles, making this simple dish one of the most expensive on his menu. Because of the obvious expense involved, truffles are optional in this recipe. However, if you do happen to have a truffle but would rather not use it in an omelet, Vanel suggests placing the truffle with the eggs, in their shells, in an airtight sealed box overnight. The truffle flavor will permeate the egg, and your truffle will remain unscathed.

8 ounces veal kidney

2 duck livers or 3 chicken livers

⅓ cup milk

Sea salt

3 tablespoons olive oil

¾ cup diced (½ inch) fresh cèpes or other boletes, or shiitake caps

¼ teaspoon finely chopped fresh garlic

2 teaspoons finely chopped fresh flat-leaf parsley

3½ tablespoons unsalted butter

Freshly ground pepper

1½ tablespoons Madeira or imported white Port

½ cup unsalted chicken stock (storebought or homemade—page 405) reduced to 2 tablespoons

Freshly grated nutmeg

6 large fresh eggs, at room temperature

1 teaspoon French truffle oil

1 About 3 hours before serving, peel the membrane from the kidney and cut the kidney lengthwise into quarters. Remove as much of the fatty central core as possible. Cut each quarter into ¾-inch pieces. Refrigerate until ready to cook. Place the livers in a small bowl. Pour the milk over the livers, salt lightly, cover, and refrigerate for 2 to 3 hours.

2 Drain the livers, discarding the milk. Remove any tough connecting tissue with scissors or a small knife. Rinse the livers under cold water until it runs clear; pat dry with paper towels. Cut the livers into 1-inch pieces.

3 Heat 1 tablespoon of the oil in a medium skillet until very hot. Add the cèpes, stir once, cover, and immediately reduce the heat to very low. Cook, covered, for 10 minutes. Stir in the garlic and parsley; season with salt to taste and set aside.

4 Heat 1 tablespoon of the butter in the same skillet over moderately high heat. When the foam subsides, add the livers and sauté, stirring, until they are seared on all sides but remain pink inside, about 2 minutes. Scrape into the bowl with the mushrooms.

5 Heat another tablespoon of the butter in the same skillet over moderately high heat. When the butter "sings," add the kidney pieces and season with a pinch of salt and 2 grinds of pepper. Sauté over moderately high heat, tossing frequently, until the kidney pieces are seared outside but still pink inside, about 1½ minutes. Do not overcook. Drain the kidney pieces in a small sieve; discard their juices. Wipe the skillet dry with paper towels, but do not wash it.

6 Heat the Madeira or Port in the same skillet over moderate heat. Carefully ignite with a long match; as soon as the flames subside, add the 2 tablespoons reduced stock. Boil until the liquid is reduced to 3 tablespoons, about 4 minutes. Pour over the mushrooms and livers. Add the kidney pieces and toss to coat. Season with salt, pepper, and nutmeg to taste. *(The recipe can be prepared to this point up to 1 hour in advance.)*

7 Just before serving, beat the eggs in a mixing bowl with a fork until the white and yellow are just blended, about 30 seconds; do not overbeat. Sprinkle with the truffle oil. Fold eggs into kidney mixture.

8 Heat a heavy 10-inch, well-seasoned or nonstick skillet over moderately high heat. Add the remaining 2 tablespoons fat and heat to rippling. Pour in the egg mixture and shake the skillet back and forth to prevent sticking. Cook, stirring with a fork, for 15 seconds. Reduce the heat to moderate and continue to cook the omelet until the bottom and sides are set but the top remains moist, about 1 minute. Remove from the heat.

9 Quickly cut the remaining 1½ tablespoons butter into small pieces and scatter them on top of omelet; press in with the back of a fork. Fold the omelet in half and slip onto a large warm serving platter. Serve at once.

Confit of Calf's Tongue

→→ *Confit de Langue de Veau*   SERVES 4 TO 5 AS A FIRST COURSE

THIS IS A VARIATION on a family recipe from the town of Blaye near Bordeaux. There it is done with pig's tongue, but a very small calf's tongue works beautifully. The texture and taste of tongue cooked this way are sensational. Do not be put off by the amount of fat—you only cook with it, you don't eat it. Serve it warm, thinly sliced, with Sweet and Sour Prunes as a first course.

Begin preparations a day in advance to allow some curing time.

2 calf's tongues, about 10 ounces each

1 tablespoon coarse kosher salt

½ teaspoon crumbled thyme

3 cups rendered fat: preferably goose or duck (see Note, page 202), but pork fat can be included

½ head of garlic cut crosswise

1 A day in advance, wash and dry the tongues. Slit each tongue down the center, opening it slightly. Roll in the salt and thyme. Set in a bowl, loosely cover with plastic wrap, and refrigerate for 18 to 24 hours.

2 The following day, preheat the oven to 300°F. Rinse the tongues under running water to remove the salt. Place the fat in a deep ovenproof bowl or earthenware baking dish. Place in the oven to warm. When the fat is melted, add the tongues and garlic. Cover and cook for 1½ to 2 hours, or until the tongues are very tender. A thin skewer should enter easily. Remove from the oven and allow the tongues to cool in the fat.

3 When cool, peel off the skin, return to the fat, and store in the refrigerator completely covered with fat for up to 1 week, until ready to use.

4 To serve, bring to room temperature. Scrape off the fat and steam the tongues to warm and remove remaining fat. Serve hot, at room temperature, or cold, thinly sliced. (For longer storage, follow directions for storing in recipe for Confit of Duck, Steps 4 through 8, pages 201–203).

Inspired by a recipe from Jean-Pierre Xiradakis.

VARIATION: CONFIT OF PIG'S TONGUE

Substitute 2 pig's tongues for the calf's tongues.

Calf's Liver as Prepared in the Valley of Ossau

→ *Foie de Veau à la Vallée d'Ossau*

IT WAS THE LATE ROLAND CASAU, chef at Chez Pierre in Pau, who first showed me how the Ossalois (people from the valley of Ossau) prepare calf's liver. I was immediately enchanted; the recipe was intriguing. It uses a variant on the technique of confit to create a juicy liver with silky-smooth texture.

In cities like Bordeaux and Bayonne, large chunks of calf's liver are often roasted with delicious results. But the Ossalois apply two intermediate steps, first marinating the liver to enhance its flavor, then poaching it in a liquid that Casau called *la mère*. This expression—literally "the mother"—is used to describe a poaching liquor used over and over for many different items, picking up the flavor of each and imparting it to the next. It is the classic poaching liquor for foie gras in the Quercy, where I met a woman who used the same liquor for cooking pig's feet for over a year. In the Landes, Pepette Arbulo used the word to describe the base stock of her *garbure*, in which she poached her stuffed cabbage and her duck breasts.

The *mère* in this case is a stock filled with pork rinds that have rendered out all their fat and flavor. The liver is tightly wrapped in cheesecloth, allowing the flavors of the stock to enter the flesh but still holding the fragile meat together. The large amount of fat in the stock keeps the texture of the liver silky—the way poultry and pork cook in a confit. After poaching, the liver is allowed to firm up by cooling down. Then it is unwrapped, lightly rubbed with oil, and set in a very hot oven to brown just before serving. This is excellent with Sautéed Peppers in the Style of Béarn (page 353) or with Red Wine–Cooked Onions (page 348).

Begin a day in advance.

(continued)

2½ pounds center-cut calf's liver, in one piece

2 cups milk

½ pound fresh or salted fatback

Freshly ground pepper

1 tablespoon chopped fresh flat-leaf parsley

4 cups unsalted chicken stock (storebought or homemade—page 405)

½ onion, thinly sliced

1 sprig of fresh thyme

1 tablespoon chopped celery leaves

½ imported bay leaf

¼ teaspoon Quatre Épices (page 231)

¼ cup plus 2 tablespoons olive oil

½ pound thinly sliced jambon de Bayonne, prosciutto, or Serrano ham, cut into slivers

¼ cup wine vinegar or *verjus*

3 tablespoons *hachis*: 1 tablespoon finely chopped fresh garlic mixed with 2 tablespoons finely chopped fresh flat-leaf parsley

Fleur de sel

1 Have the butcher remove the thin membrane surrounding the liver, or do it yourself with a thin-bladed knife. Cut out all pieces of fat and any hard parts. Soak the liver in the milk overnight in the refrigerator.

2 Meanwhile, remove the rind from the fatback and reserve. Cut some of the fatback into 12 strips about 4 inches long and ½ inch wide. Sprinkle the strips with pepper and 1 teaspoon of the chopped parsley. Wrap and refrigerate. Cut the remaining fatback and the rind into ½-inch dice.

3 In a medium saucepan, combine the diced fatback and rind with the chicken stock. Simmer for 1 to 1½ hours, until the rind and fat are totally rendered. Let cool, then refrigerate the fatty stock until chilled. *(The recipe can be prepared ahead to this point up to 1 day in advance.)*

4 The next morning, remove the liver from the milk, rinse, and dry thoroughly. Use a larding needle to lard the liver with the chilled strips of fat at equal intervals (see Note at right). Marinate the liver in a mixture of the onion, thyme, celery leaves, bay leaf, Quatre Épices, and ¼ cup of the olive oil in the refrigerator for 4 to 6 hours.

5 About 1 hour before serving, bring the fatty stock to a bare simmer; it should measure 206°F. Tightly wrap the liver in a single layer of cheesecloth and slip into the stock. Simmer for 25 minutes—or exactly 10 minutes to the pound—for rosy liver. The temperature of the poaching liquid must remain at 206°F; use a thermometer to keep an eye on this. If the liver is allowed to boil, it will harden and overcook. Carefully remove the liver to a wire rack; unwrap and thoroughly pat dry.

6 About 25 minutes before serving, preheat the oven to 550°F. Grease a shallow 10-inch oval gratin or other flameproof baking dish with 1 tablespoon of the olive oil and scatter the ham over the bottom. Brush the "bone-dry" liver with the remaining 1 tablespoon oil and place it in the dish. Roast in the hot oven until the outside is brown and crisp, 6 minutes. Transfer the liver to a carving board.

7 Scrape the ham bits onto a warmed platter. Quickly deglaze the baking dish with the vinegar or verjus, then add ½ cup water and set over very low heat.

8 Carve the liver into 12 slices. Arrange the slices over the ham on the platter. Scatter the garlic and parsley hachis on top. Season lightly with fleur de sel and pepper. Spoon the pan juices over the liver. Serve at once.

NOTE TO THE COOK

Follow manufacturer's instructions for larding needle technique. I use a *bœuf à la mode* larding needle. If you do not have a larding needle, drill holes with a skewer in the meat and push cold strips into the incisions. Be sure the fat is well chilled and firm for easier handling.

Pork Dishes

Red Beans With Pork and Carrots

→→ *Glandoulat*   SERVES 4 TO 5

RED BEANS HAVE A RICH and smooth taste, especially if they are cooked very slowly. This is an old country dish from the Rouergue. The word *glandoulat* refers to the area around the neck and throat, where the pork is half fatty and half meaty. Serve this hearty dish with a simple salad and a country dessert, such as the Batter Cake With Fresh Pears From the Corrèze (pages 365–366).

Begin 1 day in advance.

2 cups small red beans or red kidney beans

1 cup full-bodied red wine, such as Côtes-du-Rhône

1 large onion, halved and stuck with 2 cloves, plus 1 medium onion, finely chopped

1 cinnamon stick

1 large carrot, chopped, plus ½ pound carrots, sliced into ½-inch-thick rounds

2 tablespoons rendered goose, duck, or pork fat

1 pound boneless pork butt or shoulder, cut into 4 or 5 pieces

¼ pound pancetta

5 peeled garlic cloves: 4 left whole and 1 finely chopped

4 sprigs of parsley plus 1 tablespoon chopped flat-leaf parsley

1 imported bay leaf

¼ teaspoon thyme leaves

2 tablespoons butter

Pinch of sugar

Salt and freshly ground pepper

1½ tablespoons Armagnac or brandy

1 tablespoon walnut or olive oil

1½ teaspoons red wine vinegar

1 A day in advance, place the beans in a colander and rinse well under cold running water. Drain the beans and place in a large bowl. Add water to cover by at least 2 inches and let soak overnight.

2 Early the following day, rinse and drain the beans. Place them in a 5-quart flameproof earthenware or enameled cast-iron casserole with the wine and enough water to cover by 1 inch. Slowly bring to a boil.

3 When the beans reach the boil, skim thoroughly; add the onion stuck with cloves and the cinnamon stick. Reduce the heat and simmer while preparing the vegetables and pork in Steps 5 and 6.

4 In a large skillet, brown the chopped carrots and onions in the fat over moderately high heat, 5 to 7 minutes. Add the pieces of pork and sauté, turning, until browned on all sides, 7 to 10 minutes. Add the contents of the skillet to the beans.

5 In a food processor, combine the pancetta with 4 cloves of the garlic, the parsley sprigs, bay leaf, and thyme. Grind to a puree. Add to the casserole.

6 Cook the beans, covered, over very low heat or in a preheated 275°F oven for 2½ hours. After 2½ hours, uncover the beans and cook until the liquid is thick, about 1½ hours.

7 Meanwhile, in a heavy medium saucepan, cook the sliced carrots with 1 tablespoon of the butter, covered, over moderately low heat for 5 minutes. Uncover, add the remaining 1 tablespoon butter, and swirl over moderately high heat for 1 to 2 minutes, or until the carrots take on a little color. Sprinkle with a pinch of sugar. Mix the carrots into the beans in the casserole. Season with salt and pepper. *(The recipe can be prepared to this point at least 4 hours in advance.)*

8 About 1 hour before serving, preheat the oven to 350°F. Bake the beans uncovered until the tops glaze slightly, 20 to 25 minutes. Gently stir from bottom to top to keep the surface moist. Bake until a light crust forms on the surface, about 30 minutes.

9 Sprinkle the Armagnac on top and let stand until ready to serve. Serve hot, with a light sprinkling of the walnut oil and vinegar and a dusting of the chopped parsley and garlic.

NOTE TO THE COOK

To avoid drying out and breaking the beans, be sure that they are always covered with the cooking liquid or enrobed in the sauce. If necessary, add boiling water. Cooking beans in wine keeps them from turning mushy. They need longer cooking but are able to absorb more flavor.

Adapted from Fernand Molinier's Promenade Culinaire en Occitanie.

Pork Cooked in Milk

➤ *Porc Frais au Lait*   SERVES 6

THERE IS A VENETIAN DISH called *arrosto di maiale al latte* (pork loin braised in milk), described by Elizabeth David, which is somewhat similar to this one. I'm not sure where the recipe originated, but it appears prominently in Maïté Escurignan's marvelous work on Basque cookery.

Though red meats become more succulent and tender when cooked slowly in liquid, white meats, such as pork or veal, sometimes end up stringy and without much taste. Here is a recipe that solves that problem: A pork loin is submerged in flavored milk and slowly cooked at a very low temperature. The small quantity of butterfat in the milk "swims" through the meat, and the milk keeps the loin totally moist. Only after the cooking do you brown the pork.

Begin 1 to 2 days in advance.

3 to 3½ pounds boneless center-cut pork loin, trimmed of excess fat	2 tablespoons unsalted butter
2 garlic cloves, cut into slivers	1 quart whole milk
Coarse kosher salt	¼ teaspoon ground white pepper
¼ cup finely chopped carrots	Herb bouquet: 3 sprigs parsley, 1 sprig thyme, and 1 imported bay leaf tied together with string
¼ cup finely chopped onions	
2 tablespoons finely sliced leek (white part only)	1 tablespoon chopped fresh flat-leaf parsley

1 A day or 2 in advance, stud the pork loin with slivers of garlic. Rub the surface with salt; cover loosely and keep refrigerated.

2 About 4 hours before serving, preheat the oven to 300°F. In a 3- or 4-quart flameproof casserole, cook the carrots, onions, and leek in the butter over moderately low heat until soft but not brown, about 5 minutes. Place the pork roast on top of the vegetables.

3 In a saucepan, heat the milk until bubbles appear around the edge of the pan; pour over the pork. Add the pepper and herb bouquet. Cover and place on the lowest rack of the oven to cook for 3 hours. Turn the meat every hour so that it cooks evenly.

4 Remove the casserole and raise the oven temperature to 375°F. Transfer the meat, fat side up, to a large baking dish and return to the oven. Roast uncovered until browned, about 20 minutes.

5 Meanwhile, strain the milk cooking juices, pushing down on the milk solids that have separated out in the cooking. Quickly chill in larger bowl of ice and water or put in the freezer so the fat rises to surface. Remove and discard fat.

6 Return the sauce to the casserole and bring to a boil with a metal spoon on the bottom to prevent boiling over. Reduce by two thirds, about 15 minutes. Season with salt and pepper to taste.

7 Slice the meat and arrange on a serving platter. Spoon the sauce over the slices and sprinkle with the chopped parsley.

BARBECUED SPARERIBS, LANGUEDOC STYLE

➤➤ *Coustelou au Feu de Bois* SERVES 4

WHEN YOU PREPARE these ribs in the oven, you will find them a unique eating experience and a welcome change from the sweet, glazed effects of standard Chinese rib barbecue. This is not minimalist pork but robust and pure tasting ribs, dressed with herbs and sizzling ham fat.

The old recipes for this dish call for a special implement, the *flambadou*, a perforated wrought-iron cup fastened to a long rod. (In Albi this instrument is called a *capucin*, the word for monk, a reference to the shape of the cup, which is similar to a monk's tonsure.) The *flambadou* is a basting instrument used in charcoal cookery. The cup is made red-hot in the coals; then a piece of country ham fat is placed inside. The fat instantly melts and drips through the perforations; the sizzling hot fat dropping onto the meat sears it and gives it a wonderful charred ham flavor. (Chicken is also grilled this way in the Southwest.) You can achieve the same effect by rendering some fat from an American Southern ham, such as a Smithfield ham. If you're cooking outdoors, use a heavy-bottomed small saucepan and a heat-resistant mitt. The recipe is also very good without the ham fat.

Serve the ribs with Sweet and Sour Onion and Raisin Relish (pages 290–291).

(continued)

3 pounds pork loin rib ends for barbecue, or 2 sides of meaty country-style spareribs (about 4 pounds), divided into 8 serving pieces (do not substitute ordinary spareribs), trimmed of fat

Salt and freshly ground pepper

½ cup finely diced ham fat, or substitute 3 ounces finely diced pancetta and 2 ounces dried country ham, cubed medium

HERB-FLAVORED OIL

1 teaspoon Herbes de la Garrigue (page 80) or herbes de Provence, or a mix of thyme, imported bay leaf, rosemary, and sage

2 sprigs of fresh mint

½ cup extra virgin olive oil

2 tablespoons sugar

1 tablespoons balsamic or Banyuls vinegar

Sweet and Sour Onion and Raisin Relish (below)

1 Combine all the ingredients to make make the herb-flavored oil and and set aside to mellow in flavor.

2 Preheat the oven to 350°F. Rub the pork with salt and pepper. Place overlapping in a large roasting pan, cover with foil, and bake for 2 hours. Meanwhile, slowly simmer the ham cubes or pancetta and country ham in 1½ cups water until there are only cubes of meat and rendered fat in the pan; set aside.

3 Uncover the ribs, brush with the flavored oil; change to broiler heating. Brush the ribs with the seasoned oil in the pan and broil for 10 minutes. Turn ribs over; brush with more oil and broil for 5 more minutes. Spread the prepared ham fat and any juices over the ribs and broil a few more minutes.

SWEET AND SOUR ONION AND RAISIN RELISH

Oignons aux Raisins Secs   MAKES ABOUT 2 CUPS

This is Lucien Vanel's version; it is an excellent relish to serve with rich meats. The natural flavor of the pearl onion is retained, but there's a wonderful marriage of flavors, and the final sprinkling of olive oil just before serving enhances the sweetness of the onions.

1 red bell pepper

Finely slivered zest of 2 oranges

2 tablespoons sugar, or more to taste

¼ cup red wine vinegar, or more to taste

1 package (1 pound) frozen tiny white pearl onions, thawed

2½ tablespoons extra virgin olive oil

1 cup canned chopped tomatoes

⅓ cup golden raisins

¼ cup currants

1 tablespoon tomato paste

¼ teaspoon cayenne

Salt

¾ cup dry white wine

1 Preheat broiler. Roast the red pepper as close to the heat as possible, turning frequently, until the skin is charred and blistered all over, about 10 minutes. Place in a paper bag until cool enough to handle, about 20 minutes. Peel off and discard the skin. Remove stem, seeds, and thick veins. Cut into ⅛-inch-wide strips.

2 Blanch the orange zest in a small saucepan of boiling water for 2 minutes. Drain; rinse under cold running water, and drain on paper towels.

3 Melt the sugar in small nonreactive saucepan over very low heat until light brown, about 5 minutes, immediately remove the from heat. Carefully stir in the vinegar. Return to low heat and stir until the caramel is dissolved.

4 Preheat the oven to 375°F. Roll the onions in paper towels to dry them well. Heat 1½ tablespoons of the oil in a 2-quart flameproof casserole. Add the onions and sauté over moderate heat, shaking the pan frequently, until onions are glazed, about 3 minutes. Add the roasted pepper, tomatoes, caramelized vinegar mixture, orange zest, raisins, currants, tomato paste, cayenne, and salt to taste. Pour in the wine and enough water to cover. Slowly bring to a boil; cover the pan.

5 Transfer to the oven and bake until the onions are very tender, about 30 minutes. To serve, you want just enough liquid to coat vegetables. If there is more, strain the liquid into a small saucepan and boil until reduced enough to coat spoon lightly. Adjust the seasoning, adding more vinegar or sugar to taste. Return the onions to the sauce. Let cool, then cover and refrigerate for up to 5 days.

6 Remove the onions from the refrigerator 2 to 3 hours before serving. Serve at room temperature, sprinkled with the remaining 1 tablespoon olive oil.

CONFIT OF PORK

-+> *Confit de Porc*   MAKES 3 QUARTS

-+> -<+-

Où il y a un beau cochon, il y a une bonne ménagère.
(Where there is a beautiful fat pig, there is a good home cook.)

Southwest French saying

"YOU MUSTN'T WRITE your book until you witness the ritual killing of a pig," chef Alain Dutournier told me. "That's how you'll understand how important pigs are to us. They're one of the pillars of our cuisine. When we kill a pig, we know we'll have food on our table for months: bacon, ham, salt pork, confits, sausages . . . so, please, go back to the countryside and see how we do the slaughter."

I did not take his suggestion. I couldn't bring myself to watch such a thing after so many years of witnessing the ritual slaughter of lambs in Morocco. But the process has been described to me in great detail, and Dutournier is absolutely right about its importance. There is a mystical feeling about these beasts on the farms of the Southwest, similar to the way bread is regarded in some other parts of France. The pig itself is held in high esteem. Zette Guinaudeau-Franc remarks that the word *porc* is rarely used: "We always refer to him [the pig] as *le cochon*, or, with respect, *le monsieur*, or in patois, *lou moussur*."

The cult of the pig is exemplified in numerous proverbs: "Where there is a beautiful pig, you will find a good soup." "Seven hours of sleep for a man, eight for a woman, and nine for a pig!" "Four legs—four seasons!" signifying that a single pig can provide a family's food for an entire year.

"Nothing is lost with me," says the pig in a fable. In fact, this is true; all its parts are used, from the snout to the tail, including the skin, the feet, the ears, and the blood. There are so many different preparations for the various parts of the pig that in the Southwest, the art of charcuterie is a vast study in itself, including not only sausages, hams, pâtés, rillettes, andouilles, and *boudins* (both black and white) but also a unique regional dish: "the glory of the Southwest," confit.

I believe confit of pork is one of the best ways to treat the lean pork we've developed in the United States. The confit process creates moist, tender, and flavorful pork simply through the use of good-tasting pork fat and slow cooking. Of course, if the pork has been raised outdoors on natural feed, it will only be better! Shoulder makes the best *confit*, but other pieces can be used as well. If you are not satisfied with your locally accessible pork, you might consider contacting Niman Ranch (see Mail Order Sources, pages 415–417) for the nearest butcher selling quality pork.

Cold confit of shoulder or butt works splendidly in a salad with green beans and cabbage. Snout, ear, and ham hock confits are generally used to flavor soups and *garbures*, while confit of pork rind is used in dishes of dried beans.

Even when you serve confit of pork cold, you should always brown it first in its own fat. When reheated this way, a subtle hazelnutlike flavor is developed on the exterior, while the interior remains moist and aromatic. In summer, the Basques serve lightly browned pork confit with pickled cabbage, or slice it thin to serve with vinegared grapes or Sweet and Sour Cherries (pages 398–399).

Begin 2 days in advance.

3½ pounds pork butt or boned pork shoulder or blade end (see Notes, below)	1 teaspoon whole peppercorns, lightly crushed
2 to 4 tablespoons coarse kosher salt	4 to 6 cups rendered duck or pork fat (see Notes, below)
Large pinch of dried thyme, crumbled, or 1 sprig fresh, leaves only	½ small head of garlic cut crosswise
	1 whole clove

1 Two days in advance, cut the meat into 7 portions, each weighing about ½ pound. Trim away any ragged bits. Roll the pork pieces in salt combined with the thyme and pepper. Place in a large bowl, cover with plastic wrap, and refrigerate for 36 hours.

2 Remove the marinated pork pieces from the bowl; wipe off the salt and exuded juices, and pat dry with paper towels. Tie each piece with string to preserve a compact shape during cooking.

(continued)

3 Place the rendered fat with 2 tablespoons water in a large, heavy pot, such as an enameled cast-iron casserole; the exact amount of fat will vary depending on the size and shape of the cooking vessel. Melt the fat over low heat; slip in the pieces of pork. The fat should cover the meat. However, if meat is almost completely covered, enough additional fat will render out in cooking to submerge it. Add the half head of garlic stuck with the clove. Simmer for 3 hours, adjusting the heat as necessary so that the temperature of the fat never exceeds 200°F to 205°F.

4 Remove from the heat. For better texture, let the pork cool in the fat for 1 hour; it can be removed at once, but there will be some loss of texture. Remove the pork pieces and garlic with a slotted spoon and set aside to cool slightly. The meat will become firmer as it cools.

5 Reheat the fat over moderately high heat to boiling, constantly skimming off foam that rises to surface. Slowly boil for 5 to 10 minutes, or until the spluttering stops and the surface of the fat is nearly undisturbed. Watch carefully and adjust the heat if necessary to avoid burning or smoking; fat that is allowed to reach smoking point will be ruined for confit. Remove the fat from the heat and let cool for a few minutes.

6 When the pieces of pork confit are still warm but have firmed up slightly, remove the strings. Proceed to Step 7 if you want to use the confit immediately, or for richer flavor, age the confit as follows: Have ready 2 or 3 sterilized wide-mouth canning jars. Follow the recipe for Traditional Confit of Duck (pages 201–203), Steps 4 through 8. Pork confit is best after at least a 2-week ripening; it can be kept in the refrigerator for up to 4 months.

7 To use, bring the container of confit to room temperature or microwave for 2 to 3 minutes to soften the fat. Take out as many pieces as you need. (Return the remaining confit to the refrigerator, making sure the pieces are covered with fat; plan on using it within 1 week once you start.) Scrape the fat clinging to the confit pieces into a heavy medium skillet; add another tablespoon if amount of fat looks insufficient for browning. Heat the fat over moderate heat to rippling, but do not let smoke. Add the confit pieces and sauté, turning, until lightly browned on all sides, 5 to 8 minutes. Remove to a wire rack or brown paper bag to drain. Serve hot, at room temperature, or cold.

NOTES TO THE COOK

→→ If using pork shoulder or blade end, request 4½ to 5 pounds before boning and have the meat boned in one piece.

→→ Rendered fat suitable for this recipe can be any desired combination of butcher's lard from a reliable source, duck or goose fat, or home-rendered lard. (Though it is possible to use all lard, the flavor will be somewhat inferior; for authentic flavor, include a good proportion of rendered duck or goose fat.) For preparation of home-rendered poultry fat or lard, see Duck Fat and Cracklings (page 169) and Rendered Pork Fat (below). Good storebought equivalents are available from D'Artagnan and Niman Ranch (see Mail Order Sources, pages 415–417).

VARIATION: SLOW-COOKER PORK CONFIT

Follow the recipe above for preparing the pork (Steps 1 and 2) and the Notes on page 000 for the fat. Place the rendered fat with 2 tablespoons water in a slow cooker. Heat the fat on high until it just begins to simmer, add the pork, partially cover, and cook until fork-tender, 4 to 5 hours. Maintain the temperature to keep it at a steady 200°F.

Cool the pork in the fat. Ladle the fat into a large, heavy saucepan, leaving any meat juices behind. Heat, uncovered, over moderately high heat to boiling, constantly skimming off foam that rises to the surface. Boil slowly for 5 to 10 minutes, or until the spluttering stops and the surface of fat is nearly undisturbed. Watch carefully and adjust the heat, if necessary, to avoid burning or smoking. Fat that reaches the smoking point is ruined for confit or any other use. Remove from the heat; let cool for a few minutes. Store the confit as described above.

RENDERED PORK FAT

➤➤ *La Graisse* MAKES 4 TO 6 CUPS

THE TERM LA GRAISSE refers to the rendered fat of ducks, geese, and pigs. Pork fat or lard is used in cooking and for storing confits, rillettes, pâtés, and stuffed goose necks. It takes longer to render pork fat than the fat of a goose or duck, but the same basic principles are employed. One difference: with the pork, sometimes a cheesecloth bag of cinnamon sticks, whole cloves, garlic, and pieces of nutmeg is added for flavor.

1 Preheat the oven to 225°F. In batches as necessary, finely chop 2½ to 3 pounds cubed, unsalted pork fat in a food processor. Leaf lard, the firm white fat that surrounds the kidneys, is good, too.

2 Place the fat in a deep, heavy ovenproof saucepan. Add ⅓ cup water. Place the saucepan in oven and allow fat to render slowly, about 3 hours. Strain carefully and keep refrigerated until needed.

CONFIT OF PORK SALAD
WITH GREEN BEANS AND CABBAGE

→→ *Salade de Confit de Porc*
   aux Haricots Verts et aux Choux   SERVES 4 TO 6

THIS RECIPE SHOWS OFF the special succulence of pork confit browned in a little of its own fat. The amount of pork confit can be increased as desired, depending on whether you plan to serve this salad as an appetizer or as a luncheon or supper dish. Confit of pork is much more aromatic and delicious than a simple cold roast pork and is definitely worth having on hand. It is extremely easy to make.

½ head of cabbage, finely shredded (about 5 cups)

1 pound thin fresh green beans, preferably haricots verts, trimmed

4 to 6 pieces Confit of Pork (pages 292–295)

Creamy Mustard Vinaigrette (at right)

1 tablespoon minced shallots

1 Soak the shredded cabbage in a bowl of ice water for 2 to 3 hours. Soak the green beans in ice water for at least 30 minutes (see Notes at right). Drain just before cooking.

2 Meanwhile, bring the crock of confit to room temperature or microwave it for 2 to 3 minutes, to soften the fat. Carefully remove the pork without breaking the pieces. Scrape off the fat. Sauté the pork slowly in a little fat, turning, to glaze on all sides, about 5 minutes. Drain briefly on paper towels, transfer to a plate, and let cool completely.

3 Boil the green beans in a large saucepan of boiling salted water until just tender, 3 to 6 minutes. Drain, rinse briefly under cold running water, and drain well on a kitchen towel. Drain the cabbage at this time.

4 Toss the beans with the cabbage. Add the dressing and toss lightly to coat. Let stand at room temperature for 1 hour.

5 Sprinkle the shallots over the beans and cabbage. Thinly slice the confit of pork on the diagonal. Arrange on plates and serve the salad on the side.

CREAMY MUSTARD VINAIGRETTE

1 tablespoon Dijon mustard

2 tablespoons tarragon-flavored white wine vinegar

¾ teaspoon salt

3 tablespoons olive oil

2½ tablespoons walnut oil

⅓ cup crème fraîche or heavy cream

3 tablespoons minced fresh chives

Put the mustard in a small bowl. Bring the vinegar and salt to a boil in a small nonreactive saucepan; stir to dissolve the salt. Whisk the hot vinegar into the mustard until the mustard completely dissolves. Gradually beat in the olive oil and walnut oil in a thin stream. Fold in the cream and chives.

NOTES TO THE COOK

➤ I believe that whenever shallots are used raw in a dish they must be hand-chopped at right angles. This method of chopping ensures that the shallots will be milder in flavor and less acrid to the taste buds. To hand-chop at right angles, use a small sharp paring knife. Peel the shallot, leaving the root end attached. Hold the shallot by the root end and lay it flat on the chopping surface; if necessary, halve the shallot so it will lie flat. With the knife pointing at the stem end, make small nicks downward about ⅛ inch apart. Then use the knife to make thin slices across the grain and finally to slice downward crosswise. The shallots will be in perfect tiny cubes, much "pinker" in color, and have a far more subtle flavor.

➤ The green beans are hardened by soaking them first in ice water so that they will "sear" when they hit the boiling water in batches; thus, no flavor will be lost to the pot. The raw cabbage is soaked in ice water so that it will remain crunchy, even after it has been marinated in a creamy dressing.

TOULOUSE SAUSAGES

→ *Saucisses de Toulouse*   MAKES ABOUT 1¼ POUNDS

COARSE IN TEXTURE and flavored with nutmeg, Toulouse sausages are wonderful in cassoulets and *garbures*. They're also delicious in Cabbage Cake With Sausage (pages 332–333) or with a dish of Sarlat Potatoes (pages 342–343). If desired, you can purchase Toulouse sausages online from Frenchselections.com. Or substitute thick country-style Italian sausages flavored with thyme and garlic.

Begin 1 to 2 days in advance.

12 ounces boneless pork tenderloin, trimmed of all fat

4 ounces pancetta, at room temperature

¼ cup dry white wine

¾ teaspoon fine sea salt

½ teaspoon freshly ground pepper

¾ teaspoon freshly cracked black peppercorns

¼ teaspoon freshly grated nutmeg or mace

¾ teaspoon sugar

1 large garlic clove, minced

Hog or sheep casings*

2 tablespoons rendered lard or goose fat

1 One or 2 days in advance, coarsely dice the pork tenderloin, fatback, and pancetta. Toss the salt, ground pepper, peppercorns, nutmeg, sugar, and garlic with the cubes and push everything through the coarse plate of a meat grinder. If you do not have a meat grinder, finely dice the meat and pancetta, and chop separately in batches by pulsing in a food processor. Then mix together the chopped meats, white wine, and the seasonings. Cover and refrigerate overnight.

2 The following day, unravel a few feet of casing. Soak in lukewarm water for 30 minutes. Slip one end of the casing over faucet nozzle and run cold water through it to rinse. Check that there are no holes in the casing. If you find a hole, sever at that point and tie a knot. Tie knots at one end of each length after washing and draining.

3 Using a sausage stuffer, push the meat mixture through to fill the casings loosely; if too tight, the skin may burst. Press out all the air pockets. Twist the filled skins at intervals to shape sausages. Secure with string. Brush with fat. If time allows, refrigerate the sausages overnight to allow the flavors to mellow.

*Available in Asian, Eastern European, Italian, and German meat markets.

CONFIT OF TOULOUSE SAUSAGES

➤ *Saucisses de Toulouse Confites*   SERVES 4 TO 6

THESE MAY BE SLICED, sautéed, and served with scrambled eggs; added to *garbure* or cassoulet; or simply eaten along with a sharp mustard. Country-style sausages can be preserved the same way.

3 cups rendered pork fat   1 to 1¼ pounds uncooked Toulouse
                                            sausages or other fresh pork sausages

1 Bring the fat to a simmer over medium heat in a wide saucepan; lower the heat and slip in the uncooked sausages to cook very slowly for 1 hour.

2 Pack sausages into clean dry jars with cooking fat to cover. Be sure they are well covered in fat. Cool completely before closing. Store in refrigerator until ready to use. Keep at least 1 week before using. Keeps 1 to 2 months in refrigerator.

3 To remove, gently warm the opened jar in a pan of warm water and pull out sausages.

Blood Sausage With Apples and Potatoes

➵➵ *Pommes de Terre et Pommes de l'Air*   SERVES 2

WHEN A PIG IS KILLED as on a French farm, part of the ritual is to catch the blood from its severed throat in a bowl, then add some vinegar to prevent coagulation. From this blood, along with pork snouts and pork tongues, the French Southwesterners make an excellent black sausage *(boudin noir)* perfumed with onions or raisins. It is often flavored with hot pepper, cloves, nutmeg, and cinnamon.

Completely cooked, then partially dried, these sausages are delicious sliced, fried in a little fat, drained, then folded into an omelet, or else cut into chunks then fried in a little butter along with some slices of tart green apple. In Bergerac, they make a dish called *croquignolles*: deep-fat–fried pastry rounds stuffed with plumped raisins and *boudin noir*.

From the famous Limousin chef Charlou Reynal I learned a good way to remove the thick skin from commercial black sausage: Place the sausage in the freezer for about 20 minutes, then simply peel off the skin, and cut the sausage as thin or thick as needed for the recipe.

1 black sausage, 7 or 8 ounces	2 tablespoons rendered duck fat or butter
1 large tart green apple	Salt and freshly ground pepper
½ pound small fine-flesh potatoes such as creamer, fingerling, or Yukon gold	1 tablespoon chopped fresh flat-leaf parsley

1 Preheat the oven to 400°F. Place the sausage in the freezer for 20 minutes; peel off the skin and thinly slice. Meanwhile, peel, core, quarter, and skin the apple. Peel and thinly slice the potatoes.

2 Heat ½ tablespoon of the fat in a 9- or 10-inch ovenproof skillet over moderate heat. Add the apple and sauté until the edges of the pieces begin to color, about 5 minutes. Transfer the skillet to the oven and bake until tender, about 15 minutes.

3 Meanwhile, in a second skillet melt the remaining 1½ tablespoons duck fat over moderately high heat. Add the potato slices and fry until golden on both sides, about 15 minutes. Sprinkle with salt and pepper and scrape them over the apples. Bake for 10 minutes.

4 Arrange the sausage slices over the potatoes and apples. Bake until lightly browned and crispy on top, about 5 minutes longer. Scatter the chopped parsley on top and serve at once.

You can find black sausages in Mexican, German, and Spanish butcher shops. Or see Mail Order Sources (pages 415–417) for exceptional French-style *boudin noir*.

SALT-CURED PORK BELLY WITH FRESH FAVA BEAN RAGOUT

➤➤ *Ragoût de Fèves au Petit Salé de Jean-Pierre Moullé*

SERVES 6, WITH LEFTOVER PORK BELLY FOR SALADS, SOUPS, AND STEWS

JEAN-PIERRE MOULLÉ, long-time chef at Alice Waters's Chez Panisse in Berkeley, California, is a native of France. Described as "brilliant," "one of California's culinary stars," and "adorable " to boot, Jean-Pierre is an easygoing and friendly man. Along with his wife, Denise, Moullé hosts seasonal cooking classes and culinary trips throughout Southwest France.

"He brought true French training to the restaurant," one of Alice's cooks told me. He taught charcuterie, how to handle game and wild fish, and much else besides. He also set an example of calm in what is one of the most stressful environments, a restaurant kitchen!

Jean-Pierre developed this beautifully cured pork belly over a long period, working until he got the curing time just right. "At Chez Panisse, we serve the braised belly as part of our pork plate, along with spit-roasted loin and grilled pork leg," Jean Pierre told me. "At home I serve it as a pavé [a thick slice] over a plate of warm green lentils or favas with a garden salad and a good mustard vinaigrette, all to balance the richness of the meat."

I chose to serve the pork belly with a fava bean ragout, one of my favorite accompaniments to confit of duck. Some food writers will tell you that favas and lima beans are interchangeable. This is not true; there is no similarity in texture or taste.

Begin 4 days in advance.

(continued)

3 pounds skinned pork belly, preferably Niman Ranch or other organic, in one piece

2 ounces Diamond Crystal kosher salt (6 tablespoons)

1¼ ounces sugar (1 tablespoon plus 2 teaspoons)

2 imported bay leaves

6 allspice berries

2 whole cloves

¼ teaspoon peppercorns

2 medium onions, thinly sliced

2 carrots, trimmed and cut in half

3 garlic cloves, thinly sliced

½ fennel bulb, thinly sliced

¾ cup sweet white wine, such as California Orange Muscat Essensia

Fresh Fava Bean Ragout (at right)

1 tablespoon chopped fresh flat-leaf parsley

1 tablespoon chopped fresh thyme

1 Brine the pork belly: Bring 7 cups water to a boil in a large saucepan. Add the salt and sugar and stir to dissolve. Let cool, then stir in the bay leaves, allspice, cloves, and peppercorns.

2 Pour the brine into a large bowl and put the pork belly in it. Use a heavy plate as a weight to keep the meat submerged. Refrigerate for 3 days, turning the pork belly once or twice.

3 The day you plan to serve, cook the pork belly: Preheat the oven to 350°F. Drain the pork belly and pick off any whole spices clinging to the meat. Pat the belly dry with paper towels. Spread the onions, carrots, garlic, and fennel in a roasting pan. Set the meat on top of the vegetables, pour in the wine, and snugly cover with a sheet of parchment paper or foil. Braise in the oven, covered, for 2 hours.

4 Uncover the pork and roast for 15 minutes. Turn the pork belly over and roast for 15 minutes longer, until the meat is fork tender and beautifully brown on both sides, about 30 minutes total. Remove the pork and let cool; wrap tightly, and refrigerate until well chilled and firm, at least 1 hour so it firms up. (Save all the fat in the roasting pan for cooking stews, soups, and confits.) Neatly cut off six 4-ounce portions from the chilled pork belly; wrap in paper towels and refrigerate. Freeze the rest for future use.

5 Make the Fava Bean Ragout through Step 1 as directed at right.

6 About 10 minutes before serving, preheat a stovetop grill pan over moderate heat. Set the pieces of pork belly in the hot pan. Weigh down with a bacon press or heavy skillet and grill until nicely browned, about 3 minutes. Turn over and brown the second side, 2 to 3 minutes longer.

7 Meanwhile, finish the Fava Bean Ragout. Arrange the ragout in a serving dish. Place the browned and crisp pork belly (petit salé) on top, garnish with the fresh herbs and serve at once.

NOTE TO THE COOK

If you purchase pork belly with the skin on, remove the skin and cut it into 3 by 8–inch pieces. Use them to make Confit of Pork Rinds (page 17); you'll be surprised how often this comes in handy. It makes an excellent addition to soups and lentil and bean dishes.

FRESH FAVA BEAN RAGOUT   SERVES 4 TO 6

For this dish, you must not only remove the fava beans from their pods but also must slip off their skins. I have two quick ways of doing this: Steam the favas in their pods, then run them under cold water as you double-peel them, removing both the pods and the thin skins. This necessitates cooking the beans immediately to avoid their turning slimy. Or shuck the beans and freeze them in their skins for up to 4 months; this makes final preparation much easier time-wise, and the skins will slip off without blanching. Using the second method, you can roll the peeled beans up in paper towels and hold for a couple of hours before beginning preparations.

½ cup thinly sliced shallots

½ cup finely diced pancetta or ventrèche

1 tablespoon rendered duck or pork fat

½ cup thinly sliced artichoke heart, fresh or thawed frozen

½ small fennel bulb, trimmed and thinly sliced lengthwise

1 teaspoon sugar

¾ cup unsalted chicken stock (storebought or homemade—page 405)

6 pounds fresh young fava beans in their pods, shelled and peeled

Salt and freshly ground pepper

1 In a medium covered skillet, cook the shallots and pancetta in the duck or pork fat over moderately low heat for 5 minutes. Uncover and continue cooking until the pancetta is light brown around the edges. Add the artichoke slices, fennel slices, and sugar and cook for a few more minutes, stirring. Raise the heat to high, add ¼ cup of water, and remove from the heat. *(The recipe can be prepared to this point up to 8 hours in advance. Cover and refrigerate.)*

2 Add the stock and fava beans to the skillet. Bring to a boil, cover tightly, reduce the heat to moderate, and cook until the favas are completely tender, 3 to 5 minutes. Adjust the seasoning with salt and pepper.

Lamb Dishes

Mutton or lamb is the most succulent meat of the whole range the butcher can offer. It is wholesome, strengthening, an aid to digestion, and even slightly aphrodisiac.

-+>- -<+-

There are very few that are not all the happier and healthier for having dined on it.

Fulbert-Dumonteil (a Périgordian writing in
Paris over one hundred years ago)

ROAST LEG OF LAMB
IN THE STYLE OF BORDEAUX

-+> *Gigot à la Bordelaise*   SERVES 6

THE FLAVOR OF SHALLOTS and vinegar makes this roast leg of lamb delicious. Artichokes and Potatoes au Gratin (pages 326–327) goes particularly well with the lamb.

1 whole leg of lamb (about 5½ pounds)	2 tablespoons grapeseed or French peanut oil
2 large garlic cloves, peeled and cut into thin slivers	¾ cup red wine vinegar
1 teaspoon coarse kosher salt	2 tablespoons finely chopped shallots
½ teaspoon freshly ground pepper	¾ cup unsalted chicken stock (storebought or homemade—page 405)
2 tablespoons rendered goose or duck fat	

1 Trim off excess fat and tough outer skin from the lamb, leaving a thin layer of fat. Make about 10 incisions near the leg bone and insert garlic slivers. Rub the meat with the salt and pepper, then coat with the fat and oil. Massage into the meat. Refrigerate, loosely covered with plastic wrap, for at least 3 hours or overnight. Remove from the refrigerator 2 to 3 hours before roasting.

2 About 2 hours before serving, preheat the oven to 500°F. Place the lamb on a rack in a large roasting pan. Set the pan in the top third of the oven and roast for 25 minutes. Remove from the oven and let the lamb rest at room temperature for 30 minutes. Reduce the oven temperature to 350°F.

3 Meanwhile, in a small nonreactive saucepan, combine the vinegar and shallots; bring to a boil. Reduce the heat and simmer until reduced to ⅓ cup, about 20 minutes. Strain, reserving the shallots and vinegar separately.

4 Pour the vinegar and ½ cup water into the roasting pan. Return the lamb and roast, basting with the pan juices every 5 minutes, for 30 minutes, or until the internal temperature reaches 135° to 140°F for medium-rare. (Total roasting time should be about 10 minutes to the pound.)

5 Remove the lamb to a carving board and let rest for 5 to 10 minutes. Meanwhile, make the shallot sauce: Add the stock and reserved shallots to the drippings in the roasting pan and bring to a boil on top of the stove, scraping up any brown bits from the bottom of the pan. Season lightly with salt and pepper. Slice the lamb and serve with the shallot sauce.

LAMB CHOPS WITH TARRAGON SAUCE
→→ *Côtelettes d'Agneau à la Sauce d'Estragon* SERVES 2

TARRAGON IS A WONDERFUL flavoring for lamb and a refreshing change from rosemary or mint. Chef Francis Garcia of Bordeaux freezes fresh tarragon with great success, then uses it in its frozen state. To prepare fresh tarragon for freezing, drop the sprigs into boiling water. Remove at once and refresh in a bowl of ice water. Drain, pat dry, and place the sprigs on sheets of paper towels. Roll up the towels into cylinders. Pack in plastic bags and freeze. Frozen tarragon will keep several months.

Garcia's method with lamb is interesting: He sears the chops to develop their flavor, then allows them a short rest off the heat while the sauce is being made. After a simple deglazing with port wine and meat stock, the sauce is finished with butter and flavored with fresh tarragon leaves. The chops are then finished over moderate heat.

(continued)

2 loin lamb chops, each about 1⅜ inches thick, trimmed of extra fat

1 garlic clove, halved

⅓ cup chopped onion

½ cup chopped carrot

⅓ cup chopped celery

4 tablespoons unsalted butter

Salt and freshly ground pepper

¼ cup imported ruby Port

2 teaspoons fresh or frozen tarragon leaves

¼ cup demi-glace (storebought or homemade—page 406) or 1 cup meat stock reduced to ¼ cup

1½ teaspoons grapeseed or French peanut oil

1 About 30 minutes before serving, rub the lamb chops with the cut garlic.

2 In a heavy 9- or 10-inch skillet, sweat the onions, carrots, and celery in 1 tablespoon of the butter, covered, over low heat for 5 minutes. Uncover, raise the heat to moderately high, and allow any moisture from the vegetables to evaporate. Push vegetables to one side.

3 Add the lamb chops to the skillet. Sear for 2 minutes to a side. Season at once with salt and pepper and remove to a plate. Let the chops rest for at least 5 minutes.

4 Meanwhile, blot the skillet and vegetables with paper towels to remove most of the fat. Add the Port and boil until reduced to a glaze, 2 to 3 minutes. Add 1 teaspoon of the tarragon leaves and the demi-glace. Simmer over low heat for 1 minute. Strain into a small saucepan, pushing down on the vegetables and tarragon to extract all the good flavor. Discard the solids. Cover the sauce to keep warm.

5 Reheat the skillet until hot, add the oil and, when smoking, finish the chops to desired degree of doneness, about 2 minutes more per side for medium-rare. Transfer the chops to warmed plates.

6 Swirl the remaining 3 tablespoons butter into the sauce. Adjust the seasoning and spoon over the lamb. Decorate with the remaining tarragon.

ROAST SHOULDER OF LAMB WITH ANCHOVIES

➤➤ *Épaule d'Agneau aux Anchois* SERVES 6 TO 8

THIS SHOULDER OF LAMB is stuffed with anchovies and garlic and left to marinate overnight. Despite the seemingly large amounts of anchovy in the dish, at the end, the taste of the fish is hardly perceptible, and the flavor of the lamb is haunting. Serve with Baked Eggplant Studded With Garlic (pages 333–334).

Begin 1 to 2 days in advance.

10 anchovy fillets (see Note, page 308)

5 tablespoons extra virgin olive oil

2 garlic cloves, halved

¼ teaspoon dried thyme leaves

1 shoulder of young spring lamb (about 4 pounds), boned, bones reserved and cracked into 2-inch pieces

2 cups unsalted chicken stock (storebought or homemade—page 405)

¼ cup red wine vinegar

1 tablespoon Dijon mustard

Salt and freshly ground pepper

1 A day in advance, rinse the anchovies under cold running water; pat dry with paper towels. Cut the fillets in half lengthwise and place them in a small bowl with 3 tablespoons of the olive oil, garlic, and thyme. Let stand at room temperature, covered, for 2 to 3 hours.

2 Place the lamb shoulder, fat side down, on a work surface. Use a small knife to remove any tendons and hard cartilage. Make shallow slits in the meat about 1 inch apart. Remove the anchovies from the oil, reserving the oil, and stuff the fillets into the slits. Place any remaining anchovy pieces in creases between large portions of flesh. Roll the shoulder tightly into a sausage shape. Tie securely with butcher's string at 1½-inch intervals. Rub the roast with the reserved oil and wrap in plastic wrap. Refrigerate for 6 hours or overnight.

3 Heat the remaining 2 tablespoons olive oil in a large heavy skillet over moderately low heat until rippling. Add the lamb bones and sauté, turning occasionally, until well browned, about 15 minutes. Pour off the fat from the skillet; add ½ cup of the stock, scraping up brown bits that cling to the pan. Add the remaining 1½ cups stock; heat to boiling. Reduce the heat, partially cover, and simmer, skimming often, until about 1½ cups of rich broth develops, 1 to 2 hours. Strain through a fine-mesh sieve into a bowl; discard the bones. Let the lamb stock cool; refrigerate, covered, overnight. Scrape off any congealed fat before using.

(continued)

4   About 2½ hours before serving, remove the lamb from refrigerator. Let stand for 1 hour to come to room temperature.

5   Preheat the oven to 500°F. Place the lamb on a rack in a flameproof roasting pan just large enough to hold it snugly. Roast in the top third of the oven for 15 minutes. Remove the lamb to a rack set over a plate to collect the juices; let rest for 30 to 45 minutes. Reduce the oven temperature to 425°F.

6   Meanwhile, skim the fat off the drippings in the roasting pan. Set the pan over moderate heat. Add the vinegar and bring to a boil, scraping up any brown bits that cling to the pan. Transfer to small heavy saucepan. Boil over moderate heat until reduced to 2 tablespoons. Whisk in the mustard and the reserved lamb stock. Add any juices that have accumulated under the roast. Set the sauce aside.

7   About half an hour before serving, return the lamb to the rack in the roasting pan. Roast until the thickest part of the lamb meat registers 135°F to 140°F for medium-rare, about 20 minutes. Transfer the roast to a carving board and let stand while finishing the sauce.

8   Degrease any roasting pan drippings and deglaze the roasting pan with 2 tablespoons water. Scrape into the sauce. Boil down to 1 cup, skimming. Season with salt and pepper to taste. Carve the lamb shoulder into ½-inch-thick slices. Arrange on heated plates. Spoon the sauce over and around lamb and serve.

NOTE TO THE COOK

If using salt-packed anchovies, rinse off the salt from 3 anchovies and divide into fillets. Soak in plenty of cold water for 2 hours; drain. Remove the fillets and cut in half lengthwise. Two and a half salt-packed anchovies equal 10 canned anchovy fillets packed in oil. If using the oil-packed fillets, simply rinse and blot dry.

Inspired by a recipe from Lucien Vanel.

CASSOULET

Cassoulet is one of those dishes over which there is endless drama. Like bouillabaisse in Marseilles, paella in Spain, chili in Texas, it is a dish for which there are innumerable recipes and about which discussions quickly turn fierce. It was over 30 years ago that I set out to explore this quintessential dish of Southwest France. As an outsider, I felt I might be able to settle some questions: Which regional version of the dish is really the best, and who serves the best restaurant cassoulet in France?

It did not seem too difficult a task. Waverley Root, *Larousse Gastronomique*, and the food critics Henri Gault and Christian Millau have all defined the war over the three "genuine" versions of this casserole dish of meats and haricots (dried white beans such as Tarbais, Lingots, and cocos), one from each of three towns in the Languedoc.

In Castelnaudary, the legend goes, the dish was invented, and therefore a "pure" version is served. The haricots are cooked with chunks of fresh pork, pork knuckle, ham, pork sausage, and fresh pork rind.

In Toulouse, the cooks add Toulouse sausage and either *confit d'oie* or *confit de canard* (preserved goose or duck—see pages 213 and 201–203); while in Carcassonne, chunks of mutton are added to the Castelnaudary formula, and during the hunting season, an occasional partridge, too.

There would be many variations, I knew, but it seemed a simple matter to travel to each of these towns, discover where the best cassoulets were served, taste them, and decide which one I liked the best. What I did not count on was that these regional distinctions have been completely blurred and that cassoulet is not as simple as it seems.

Take mutton. Not one person in any of the three towns would admit that mutton could go into a local cassoulet. Whether my expert was a chef, a waiter, or just a citizen on the street, he or she would point in some other direction and say: "Oh, they use mutton in Toulouse [or Carcassonne, or Castelnaudary, or some other town that came to mind]. They don't know any better."

Take partridge. Some people said they'd heard of putting partridge in cassoulet, but no one could say he'd actually seen it done.

Take bread crumbs. "Never! Impossible!" many people proclaimed, but the woman who cooked the best traditional cassoulet I ate used bread crumbs without a qualm.

And what about breaking the crust—seven times, as some cookbooks proclaim? People laughed, but some agreed the crust could be broken and reformed twice to get some texture into the sauce. No need to go on. These technical matters diverted me from my mission. When I found the best cassoulet, I'd find out how it was made.

After a few hours' recuperation from jet lag in Paris, I ventured out to Lamazère, a restaurant where cassoulet in the style of Toulouse is a specialty of the house. Though the portion of meat was parsimonious, the cassoulet was very good, the beans enveloped in a thick creamy sauce, the preserved goose superb, put up the traditional way in stoneware jars for a minimum of six months. I returned to my hotel happy at last to have the taste of a good cassoulet in my mouth. Alas, I had not counted on the aftereffects. Requiring heavy doses of Alka-Seltzer to get to sleep, I was reminded of the famous tale of Prosper Montagné—how one day he came upon a sign on the door of a bootmaker's shop in Carcassonne: "Closed on account of cassoulet."

A few days later, on a cold and rainy night in Toulouse, I tried one of that graceful town's better-known cassoulet establishments, called, not surprisingly, Le Cassoulet. Arriving early, I was intercepted by a friendly drunk. "Go someplace else," he warned me; "in ten years they haven't changed the menu here."

My first cassoulet of Toulouse was crusty and wonderful, bubbly and aromatic, very subtle in regard to garlic. The confit literally melted in my mouth, and the Toulouse sausage (actually made for the restaurant by a charcutier in Castelnaudary) was extraordinarily fine. The charming and opinionated owner, Monsieur Bonnamy, held forth while I ate: "I'm from Provence, and I tell you that there is more drama here concerning cassoulet than anything I ever saw over bouillabaisse. In Toulouse, everyone talks about cassoulet, everyone cooks it, everyone eats it, but very few make it well. They use canned confit, even canned beans, or sometimes, God help them, they eat the whole dish from a can. Bread crumbs? I never use them! Mutton? It has no place in the dish. Put mutton in a pot with some preserved goose, and the mutton eats the goose alive! You ask me about the cassoulet of Carcassonne? It's just beans with a load of charcuterie! You say Michel Guérard says mutton is 'indispensable'? A comment typical of a person who lives in the Landes—they have so many sheep there, they're always trying to think up things to do with them!"

Early the next morning I paid a call on the then most famous chef in Toulouse, the kind, brusque, estimable, inventive Lucien Vanel. His restaurant, which was called simply Vanel, was a magnet for all gastronomic travelers to Toulouse. But Vanel was adamant—he would not cook cassoulet.

"I'm from the Quercy," he told me. "This is my adopted town, so I leave cassoulet to the native chefs. There are restaurants here that specialize in it, and I have arranged for a friend to cook you a good homemade version [see Cassoulet in the Style of Toulouse, pages 317–319]. But I do have something for you today."

There then appeared a twinkle in his eye as he told me he'd prepared his *cassoulet de morue*, something I thought he'd dreamed up for journalists—his satire on the most famous dish of his adopted town. (I learned later that such a dish actually exists.) His conceit must be recounted: In a casserole of white beans, he cooked salted cod (his "preserved goose"), a seafood sausage (his "sausage of Toulouse"), and large juicy mussels (his "chunks of pork"). The stock is a saffron-flavored fish soup, bound with mustard, egg yolks, and cream. The dish was a marvelous spoof on a real cassoulet, and, like everything chez Vanel, a treat.

I tried more restaurant cassoulets in Toulouse, Castelnaudary, and Carcassonne, then returned to Toulouse for the homemade version arranged for by Vanel. My hostess was Madame Pierrette Lejanou, wife of a potato broker, descendant of an old Toulouse family, a gastronome, and an excellent cook who learned to make cassoulet at her grandmother's knee.

What can I say about her version except that it was the best traditional cassoulet I ever ate! Madame Lejanou was so precise in her choice of beans, so careful about her cooking, so firm in her commitment to *andouillettes* (chitterling sausages), so intent on achieving a crust, so particular about her pork fat being just ever-so-slightly rancid, and so careful in her selection of meats (she puts up her own confit, as a good Toulouse cook always does) that her cassoulet was simply great.

A charming woman, effervescent in her approach to food, generous in the tradition of the Languedoc, she feasted me and instructed me until I was overwhelmed. The secret of her cassoulet, I thought, was that it was made with love.

It was on account of Michel Guérard that I drove to Robert Garrapit's restaurant in Villeneuve-de-Marsan in the Landes. Guérard had told me of a cassoulet cook-off among the chefs of the Landes. Garrapit had won first prize, and Guérard recommended his cassoulet in the highest terms. I arranged to meet him a few weeks later at Garrapit's restaurant for a feast.

Now, three-star chef Michel Guérard is a modest man, a becoming trait in so renowned a chef, but on the subject of cassoulet he is as opinionated as anyone else: "Cassoulet," he told me, "was originally a ragout of beans, which was obviously improved by the addition of mutton. To make a cassoulet without mutton is to be banal and, in my opinion, to commit heresy. Mutton is indispensable in a cassoulet, as indispensable as the bony fish *rascasse* in a bouillabaisse. It is a sophistication of dubious value to add confit. Cassoulet becomes too refined when it has a crust. Chefs put a crust on it to make it look better, but in the process they make it heavy and obfuscate its peasant origins. One must keep in mind the history of cassoulet and cook it as the peasants did, with mutton and poor people's food, such things as gizzards and pork skin."

By this time, Garrapit has appeared with his chef d'oeuvre. There were carrots in it, and I asked him why. "They're pretty," he said, "and they sweeten the mutton, too."

Garrapit's cassoulet was light, his sauce good tasting and thin. I understood why he had won the cook-off in the Landes, where, on account of Guérard's influence, lightness in cooking is an important goal. And there were interesting things about his dish—his use of preserved gizzards and huge incredibly flavorful Tarbais beans, which he'd canned fresh so that, most particularly, he would not have to use them dried. It was all very good, but was it a cassoulet?

Guérard, of course, insisted that it was nothing less than an authentic version of the dish. I was not so sure. Those very refinements that Guérard deplored (crustiness, a thick creamy sauce) have become, in my opinion, indispensable to a great rendition of the dish. Two years later, I discussed this again with Guérard when we dined together in Auch. He told me that he had changed his mind totally, that he now makes his cassoulet with confit, and leaves the mutton out.

All right. I had dined in the best cassoulet establishments in Paris, in the three great cassoulet towns, and also in the Landes. Madame Lejanou's cassoulet was still dear to my heart, but was it the ultimate, or can the great dish of Southwest France reach an even higher, more heavenly sphere?

During this visit to the region I'd become friendly with the Gascon chefs, especially their spiritual leader, the handsome, generous, multitalented André Daguin, whose elegant Hôtel de France in Auch had long been a mecca for gastronomes.

When Daguin learned I was passionate about cassoulet, he offered to cook me three different kinds and serve them at a single lunch. Knowing the brilliance of this chef, my tongue quivered with anticipation, even though by this time my stomach had started to rebel.

"Don't worry," said Daguin. "You will taste, not eat." But this proved impossible. Who can merely taste delicious food?

I had come full circle now, from the parsimony of Lamazère in Paris to the plenitude and hospitality of a great Gascon chef. Tasting and cross-tasting, eyed by envious diners at other tables who could not believe the sight of a single woman surrounded by huge casseroles, I ate and ate while Daguin paced by, every so often eyeing me like a sly Gascon fox.

His "normal" cassoulet was robust. The taste of a strong garlic sausage permeated the beans. This was a real country cassoulet but touched by a light hand. Daguin had used broken old beans as a thickening agent, rather than an inordinate amount of pork fat, as is common practice in the Languedoc. There was a lot of confit in this casserole (steamed first, interestingly enough). And tomatoes broke up the usual golden champagne color; Daguin's cassoulet was creamy-red.

Next came his cassoulet of lentils—green lentils cooked with duck fat, pork confit, and Spanish chorizo sausages. It had subtlety and mellowness that did not at first announce themselves; it was a quiet, deceptively lazy dish that crept up on me until I could not stop replenishing my plate.

But the best was yet to come: Daguin's famous *cassoulet de fèves*, a concoction of preserved duck and fresh fava beans, crisp on the outside, soft and buttery-tender within. The contrast of flavors and textures, the beans so full of spring and the Mediterranean, beans that absorbed the taste of the other ingredients and yet, almost paradoxically, maintained a fresh taste of their own—I could not quite believe what I was eating. It seemed a miracle.

Suddenly all the controversy—Toulouse versus Carcassonne versus Castelnaudary; mutton versus preserved goose; the questions of bread crumbs and partridges and *andouillettes*—became irrelevant. For Daguin's cassoulet of fava beans transcended definitions. As far as I was concerned, the cassoulet war was won!

André Daguin's Fava Bean Cassoulet

→→ *Cassoulet de Fèves*

ACCORDING TO ROBERT COURTINE, the French food authority, before white beans were cultivated in France, fava beans were used to make this dish. The old name for the dish was *fevolade*. In effect, then, Daguin's version is the "original" cassoulet.

This cassoulet is excellent reheated later in the day, or even the next day.

4 confit of Pekin or Muscovy duck legs (such as Duck Legs Confit Cooked in a Pouch, pages 198–200) or 2 confit of Moulard duck legs, drumsticks and thighs separated

8 to 9 pounds fresh fava beans, in their pods (usually available starting in March)

2 pounds small white onions, peeled

1½ pounds ventrèche or pancetta, cut into ½-inch dice

Freshly ground pepper

1 tablespoon sugar

6 ounces fresh pork skin with ¼-inch layer of hard fat attached, or substitute Confit of Pork Rinds (page 17)

4 cups unsalted chicken stock (storebought or homemade—page 405)

1 leek, trimmed, well washed, and left whole

8 small celery ribs: 2 chopped, 6 tied in a bundle

5 firm garlic cloves, peeled

1 To soften the confit fat remove from the refrigerator 3 to 4 hours in advance and let stand in a warm place or in a deep pan of warm water.

2 Shuck the beans; you should have about 2 quarts. Slip off and discard the heavy skin covering 1 cup of the favas; set the skinned beans apart. Cut off the tiny shoots on remaining beans, if old. (Because not all the favas are skinned, the cassoulet will turn dark in color; this is as it should be.)

3 Scrape the fat off the duck confit legs into 5- or 6-quart flameproof casserole. Add the onions and sauté over moderate heat, stirring occasionally, for 4 to 5 minutes, until softened. Add the diced ventrèche and a light sprinkling of pepper and sauté over moderate heat, stirring often, for 5 minutes longer.

4 Stir in the 1 cup peeled fava beans and the sugar. (The peeled beans will break down, and their natural starchiness will act as a liaison for the cooking juices.) Cover the pan tightly and cook the beans slowly for 10 minutes.

(continued)

5 Meanwhile, simmer the fresh pork skin in water to cover until supple, 10 to 20 minutes. (There's no need to simmer confit of pork rind.) Drain the skin, roll it up, and tie it with a string.

6 Add the stock, the remaining favas, rolled pork skin, leek, all of the celery, and the garlic to the beans. Bring to a boil and skim carefully. Reduce the heat, cover with a sheet of crumpled wet parchment and simmer over low heat for 1½ hours.

7 Place the pieces of duck confit in a colander set snugly over a kettle of boiling water; or use a steamer or couscous cooker. Cover and steam for 10 minutes. Remove the duck, let cool slightly, then remove the skin and bones. Set the meat aside, covered with foil to keep moist.

8 Preheat the oven to 300°F. Remove the rolled pork skin from the bean ragout and cut into slices 2 inches wide. Unroll the slices and use them to line a 3- or 3½-quart ceramic baking dish fat side down. (The skin side sticks.) Place the pieces of duck confit on top.

9 Pick out and discard the leek and bundle of celery from the beans. With a slotted spoon, transfer the favas to the baking dish, leaving the cooking juices in the casserole. Skim the fat off the juices and taste for seasoning; there will probably be no need for salt. Pour enough of the juices over the duck and favas to cover. Reserve the remaining juices. Loosely cover the baking dish with foil and set in the preheated oven.

10 Bake for 20 minutes. Spoon off all the fat that rises to the top. Add enough of the reserved cooking juices to keep the favas moist. Bake for 40 minutes longer. Remove the foil and bake, uncovered, until a crust forms on top, about 30 minutes. Serve hot.

NOTES TO THE COOK

→ The confit is salty and will salt the dish sufficiently.

→ If you cannot obtain ventrèche or pancetta, substitute lean fresh pork side or belly; blanch it in a large pot of boiling water for 10 minutes. Rinse, drain, dry, and cut into small dice.

CASSOULET IN THE STYLE OF TOULOUSE

➤➤ *Cassoulet de Toulouse*

THIS IS THE RECIPE given to me by Pierrette Lejanou. The addition of walnut oil at the last moment brightens the taste of the beans.

Begin preparations two days before you plan to serve the cassoulet.

1 pound boneless pork shoulder, trimmed of excess fat and cut into 12 chunks

1½ pounds fresh ham hock or pig's knuckles, cracked by the butcher

¾ pound fresh pork skin with ¼-inch layer of hard fat attached

Salt and freshly ground pepper

2 pounds dried white beans, such as Tarbais, Lingots, or cannellini, rinsed and picked over to remove any grit

⅓ cup fat from confit or rendered duck fat

2 medium onions, chopped

3 small carrots, peeled and cut into thin rounds

½ pound ventrèche or pancetta, or blanched lean salt pork, in one piece, about 1¼ inches thick

1 whole head of garlic, unpeeled, plus 4 small cloves garlic, peeled

1 large plum tomato, peeled or 1 tablespoon sun-dried tomato paste

2 quarts unsalted chicken stock (storebought or homemade—page 405)

Herb bouquet: 4 sprigs parsley, 2 sprigs thyme, 1 imported bay leaf, and 3 small celery ribs tied together with string

6 confit of duck legs (such as Duck Legs Confit Cooked in a Pouch, pages 198–200), drumsticks and thighs separated, or substitute 12 confit of duck wings

¼ pound fresh hard pork fat or blanched fat salt pork

1 pound Toulouse sausages, fresh garlic-flavored pork sausages, or Confit of Toulouse Sausages (page 298)

2 tablespoons fresh bread crumbs

2 tablespoons French walnut oil

1 Two days in advance, season the pork shoulder, fresh ham hock or pig's knuckles, and the pork skin moderately with salt and pepper. Place in an earthenware or glass dish, cover, and refrigerate overnight. Soak the beans overnight in enough water to cover by at least 2 inches.

2 The following day, simmer the pork skin in water to cover until it is supple, 10 to 20 minutes. Drain, roll up the strip, and tie it with string.

(continued)

3 Dry the cubes of pork shoulder with paper towels. In an 8- or 9-quart flameproof casserole, heat the duck fat over moderately high heat. Add the pork shoulder and lightly brown on all sides. Add the onions and carrots and sauté, stirring, until the onions are soft and golden, about 5 minutes. Add the ham hock or pig's knuckles and the whole piece of ventrèche or pancetta. Allow these meats to brown a little around the edges, turning the pieces occasionally. Add the whole head of garlic, and the tomato or tomato paste; cook, stirring, for 1 minute. Add the stock, bundle of pork skin, and herb bouquet. Bring to a boil; cover, reduce the heat to low, and simmer the ragout for 1½ hours.

4 When the ragout has cooked for 1 hour, drain the beans and put them into a large saucepan, cover with fresh water, and slowly bring to a boil. Skim, and simmer for a few minutes, then drain and immediately add the beans to the simmering ragout. Continue simmering for up to 2 hours, or until the beans are tender. (You can tell when the beans are done by removing one or two beans with a spoon and blowing on them—the skins will burst.) Let cool, then skim off all the fat that has risen to the top; reserve 2 tablespoons of this fat for finishing the cassoulet. Cover the pork ragout and beans and refrigerate overnight to develop the flavors.

5 The next day, steam the duck confit for 10 minutes to soften. As soon as the meat is cool enough to handle, pull it off the bones in large chunks.

6 Remove the ragout and beans from the refrigerator and bring to room temperature. Pick out the ham hock or pig's knuckles, pancetta, garlic head, and herb bouquet. Cut the meat from the ham hock or pig's knuckles into bite-size pieces, discarding bones and fatty parts. Cut the pancetta into 1-inch pieces, discarding the extraneous fat. Set all the meats aside. Press on the garlic to extract the pulp and set aside. Discard the garlic skins and herb bouquet.

7 In a food processor or electric blender, puree the pork fat or salt pork with the cooked and raw garlic and 1 cup water. Add this garlic puree to the ragout and beans and simmer for 30 minutes. Remove from the heat. Fold reserved meats into the ragout and beans.

8 Preheat the oven to 325°F. To assemble the cassoulet, remove the roll of pork skin from the ragout. Untie, cut the skin into 2-inch pieces, and use to line a 5½- or 6-quart ovenproof casserole, preferably earthenware, fat side down—the skin side sticks (see Note at right). Using a large slotted spoon or skimmer, add one half of the beans and pork shoulder. Scatter the duck confit on top of the pork and beans. Cover with the remaining beans and pork ragout. Taste the ragout cooking liquid and adjust the seasoning; there will probably be no need for salt. Pour just enough of the ragout liquid over the beans to cover them. Be sure there is at least 1 inch of "growing space" between the beans and the rim of the dish. Drizzle with the 2 tablespoons fat reserved in Step 4. Place the casserole in the oven and let cook for 1½ hours.

9 Prick the sausages and brown them under a hot broiler or in a skillet. Drain; cut larger sausages into 3- or 4-inch pieces.

10 Reduce the oven heat to 275°F. Gently stir up the skin that has formed on the beans. Place the sausages on top of the beans. Dust the bread crumbs on top of the beans and sausage. Bake the cassoulet for 1 more hour. The top crust should become a beautiful golden brown; if it isn't, turn on the broiler and carefully "toast" the top layer of beans, about 2 minutes. Transfer the cassoulet from the oven to a cloth-lined surface and let it rest 20 minutes. Drizzle with the walnut oil just before serving.

NOTES TO THE COOK

➤➤ Fresh pork rind is essential to enrich and flavor the beans. If only salted rind is available, do not include it in the first day's marinade.

➤➤ If you don't have a large enough earthenware or stoneware serving dish, substitute 2 smaller ones, such as the insert from a slow cooker or an ovenproof mixing bowl.

CONFIT OF TOULOUSE SAUSAGES AND DUCK COOKED WITH RED WINE–FLAVORED BEANS

➤➤ *Confits Dans les Haricots au Madiran* SERVES 6 TO 8

MADIRAN IS A "BIG" red wine, deep in flavor and very dark in color. It is like a full-bodied hearty Syrah from the Rhône Valley or an earthy, old-vines Zinfandel. Although you may have heard that beans should not be cooked in wine or, for that matter, in any other acid, this unusual recipe given to me by André Daguin exploits that prohibition to great advantage. The beans cook very slowly and absorb the flavor of the wine, which loses its acidity on account of the long cooking, becoming mellow by the time the dish is fully cooked.

Be sure to note that the beans must soak overnight before you begin the recipe. A dish like this is better prepared ahead and reheated.

1 pound dried white beans such as Tarbais, Lingots, or cannellini, rinsed and picked over to remove any grit

6 pieces confit of Pekin or Muscovy duck (such as Duck Legs Confit Cooked in a Pouch, pages 198–200)

⅓ cup confit of duck fat or rendered duck fat

1 medium onions, chopped

6 garlic cloves, peeled

2 teaspoons tomato paste

4 cups full-bodied red wine, such as Madiran, Zindandel, or Syrah

Herb bouquet: 3 sprigs parsley, 1 sprig thyme, and 1 imported bay leaf tied together with string

4 cups unsalted chicken stock (storebought or homemade—page 405)

8 ounces unsmoked pork rind (can be cut from salt pork or fatback) or Confit of Pork Rinds (page 17)

Salt and freshly ground pepper

12 baby white onions (about ½ pound), peeled

1 tablespoon sugar

½ recipe Confit of Toulouse Sausages (page 298)

1 Put the beans in a large pot and cover with at least 2 inches of cold water. Let soak overnight.

2 Remove the confit from the refrigerator and let stand in a warm place to allow the fat to soften while you cook the beans.

3 In a 5-quart flameproof, nonreactive casserole, heat 1½ tablespoons of the duck fat from the confit. When very hot, add the chopped onions and whole garlic cloves. Stir in the tomato paste until the onions and garlic are a uniform pink color, then add the red wine and herb bouquet. Bring to a boil, reduce the heat to moderately low, and simmer for 15 minutes.

4 Meanwhile, drain the beans and put them in a saucepan with enough tepid water to cover. Slowly bring to a boil. Boil for 5 minutes. In another saucepan, bring the stock to a boil. Drain the beans and immediately add to the simmering red wine. Pour in the boiling stock. Simmer, skimming, for 3 to 4 minutes.

5 Preheat the oven to 275°F. Soften the pork rind by simmering in water for 10 minutes. Drain, roll up, and tie with a string. Add to the beans.

6 Cover the casserole tightly and place in the oven. Bake for 3½ hours, or until the beans are tender and the wine has lost its acid taste. Season with salt and pepper.

7 In a medium skillet, cook the baby white onions in ½ cup water, covered, until almost tender, 6 minutes. Add the sugar and 1 teaspoon duck confit fat. Continue cooking over moderately high heat, stirring often, until all the water has evaporated and the onions begin to brown, 2 to 3 minutes. Remove from the heat.

8 Pull the confit meat off the bone. Discard the skin and any gristle. Cut the meat into bite-size pieces. Cut the Toulouse sausage into 1-inch lengths.

9 Raise the oven temperature to 350°F. To assemble the dish, remove the pork rind from the beans, cut into 2-inch pieces, and use to line a 3½-quart casserole, fat side down. Using a slotted spoon, cover with half the beans. Scatter the duck confit and sausage pieces over the beans. Spoon the baby onions on top. Add another layer of beans. Scatter any leftover pieces of pork rind on top. Pour the bean cooking liquid over all.

10 Return the dish to oven and bake, basting 3 or 4 times with the remaining ¼ cup duck confit fat, until the top crust becomes a beautiful mahogany brown, about 45 minutes. Serve directly from the dish.

CATALAN-STYLE SHOULDER OF LAMB WITH GARLIC AND WHITE BEANS

➤➤ *Épaule d'Agneau à la Catalane (en Pistache)*   SERVES 8

THERE IS A SUPERB VERSION of cassoulet called *en pistache* in Catalan, as served in the central Pyrenees. If you like the combination of lamb and garlic—and who doesn't?—you will adore this dish.

Buy "choice" lamb rather than "prime"; it is less fatty, and lamb fat is not particularly appetizing. The method of cooking the lamb in its own juices with a small quantity of wine and aromatics was devised to bring out the true flavor of the meat. With the dish, pass a small bowl of pickled walnuts.

1 pound dried white beans, such as Tarbais or cannellini

3 to 3½ pounds boned lean shoulder of lamb, cut into 2-inch chunks

1 whole head of garlic plus 4 garlic cloves

Salt and freshly ground pepper

1 teaspoon sugar

2 tablespoons extra virgin olive oil

10 ounces thick slices fatty pancetta or ventrèche, cut into ½-inch dice, any rind reserved

2 medium onions, chopped, plus 1 whole onion stuck with 2 whole cloves

1 cup dry white wine

3 tomatoes, peeled, seeded, and chopped, or 1 can (14½ ounces) organic diced, peeled tomatoes

1 tablespoon tomato paste

½ ounce dried French cèpes, rinsed

1 wide strip of orange zest

2 carrots, sliced

Herb bouquet: 3 sprigs of parsley, 1 sprig of thyme, 1 imported bay leaf, and 2 celery leaves tied together with string

1 pound French or Italian garlic sausage or homemade Toulouse Sausage (page 298) flavored with a pinch each of ground cinnamon, ground cloves, dried marjoram, and ground cayenne

1 Put the beans in a large pot and cover with at least 2 inches of cold water. Let soak overnight.

2 The next day, trim off as much fat as possible from each cube of lamb. Peel the 4 cloves of garlic and cut each clove into slivers. With a small paring knife, make a slit in each piece of meat and insert a sliver of garlic. Rub the meat with a little salt and pepper and sprinkle very lightly with sugar so the lamb will have a nice brown glossy color when browned.

3 In a 3-quart flameproof casserole, heat the oil over high heat. Add the lamb in batches without crowding and brown lamb on all sides. Avoid too high a heat, but do sear the lamb cubes. As they are browned, transfer the pieces to a plate.

4 When all the lamb has been browned, wipe the fat out of the casserole and return to low heat. Add the pancetta cubes, cover, and cook for 5 minutes, shaking the casserole often to prevent sticking. Uncover, add the chopped onions, and cook gently, stirring once or twice, until soft and golden.

5 Pour in the wine and bring to a boil. Return the lamb pieces to the casserole along with any juices that have collected on the plate. Add the tomatoes, tomato paste, dried cèpes, and orange zest. Bring to a boil, then reduce the heat and simmer, tightly covered, for 2 hours, or until the lamb is tender. Set aside, uncovered, to cool slightly. Skim off any fat that rises to the surface.

6 Drain and rinse the soaked beans. Put them in a 4- or 5-quart flameproof casserole. Add the carrots, onion stuck with cloves, pancetta rind if you have it, and herb bouquet. Add enough water just to cover and bring to a boil. Reduce the heat to low, cover the pot and simmer for 1 hour. Season with 1 teaspoon salt and simmer for 30 minutes. Add the sausages, each pricked in several places, and simmer for 30 minutes longer. Remove and discard the onion stuck with cloves, and the herb bouquet.

7 Separate the head of garlic into cloves. Cook the garlic cloves in their skins in a small saucepan of water to cover for 10 minutes. Set aside and peel when cool enough to handle.

8 Preheat the oven to 325°F. Line a 5½-quart earthenware or stoneware bean pot with the rind, fat side down. Using a slotted spoon, transfer about one third of the beans to the pot, then add a layer of about half of the lamb. Cut the sausages into 8 slices and place them between the lamb chunks. Scatter the peeled garlic cloves on top. Cover with another layer of beans, add the remaining lamb, then the remaining beans. Pour all the meat cooking liquid over the beans and add enough of the bean cooking liquid just to cover. Bake, uncovered for 1 hour, or until a crust forms on the surface. Serve directly from the pot.

NOTES TO THE COOK

➝ Parboiling the garlic cloves, then peeling and tossing them with the beans, makes for a pleasant surprise, since the peeled cloves and the white beans look alike.

(continued)

→ You can make your own Catalan sausage for this dish by following the recipe for Toulouse Sausage and seasoning the meat with pinches of ground cinnamon, ground cloves, crumbled marjoram, and hot cayenne, while leaving out the nutmeg. Or substitute a mildly spicy Italian, Spanish, or Polish sausage.

→ This dish can be prepared 1 day in advance. When ready to serve, poke holes in the bean crust, add ½ cup water, and reheat in 350°F oven for 30 minutes, or until hot throughout.

VEGETABLES

ARTICHOKES AND POTATOES AU GRATIN

Artichauts et Pommes de Terre au Gratin SERVES 4

IN THE PYRENEES, this dish is made with churned raw milk, rarely found anymore. No matter—it works fine as I've adapted it and goes especially well with roast leg of lamb. The artichokes are cooked only partially before being layered with potatoes and baked. To avoid any loss of flavor or discoloration, cook them just before using.

4 large or 5 fresh medium artichokes

½ lemon

1 cup milk

3 tablespoons unsalted butter

½ cup chopped onion

½ teaspoon minced fresh garlic

2 baking (russet) potatoes (about 1 pound)

⅔ cup heavy cream

½ teaspoon meat glaze or ¼ cup meat stock reduced to a glaze (optional)

½ teaspoon salt

⅜ teaspoon freshly ground white pepper

Crumbled fresh thyme leaves

1 Trim the artichokes down to their bottoms, as described at right. In a large pot, bring 6 cups of salted water to a boil. Add the lemon half, ⅓ cup of the milk, and the artichoke bottoms. Cover the pot and boil over high heat for 3 minutes (see Notes at right).

2 Drain the artichoke bottoms well. With a small spoon, scoop out and discard the chokes. Cut the artichoke bottoms on a diagonal into thin slices; you can use the food processor fitted with a thin (3 mm) slicing disk.

3 Preheat oven to 350°F. Grease the bottom and sides of a shallow 10-inch pie plate or oval gratin with half the butter. In a small skillet, melt the remaining butter. Add the onion and garlic and cook over moderate heat until softened but not browned. Scatter the onion-garlic mixture over the bottom of the buttered pan.

4 Peel the potatoes and slice as thinly as the artichokes (see Note at right). Alternate the artichoke and potato slices in overlapping rows. In a bowl, combine ½ cup of the heavy cream, the remaining ⅔ cup milk, the meat glaze, salt, white pepper, and thyme; blend well. Pour over the potatoes and artichokes.

5 Bake for 1¼ hours. *(The recipe can be prepared to this point up to 1 hour in advance; set aside, uncovered, at room temperature.)*

6 About 15 minutes before serving, preheat the broiler. Spoon the remaining heavy cream over the potatoes and artichokes and run the dish under the broiler until hot and golden brown. Serve immediately.

NOTES TO THE COOK

→► Frozen artichoke hearts may be used, but the results are not as tasty.

→► The potatoes can be peeled in advance and kept covered in a bowl of salted water in the refrigerator. Do not slice until ready to assemble and bake.

→► The secret of this dish is not to wash the potato slices. Their starch thickens the liquid and creates a creamy texture until the crust is formed.

→► Remember that when you make gratins, you must use enough milk or cream to cover the vegetables; otherwise they will shrivel on top, and there won't be sufficient liquid to make them tender. Add more cream if necessary.

To Prepare Artichoke Bottoms

→► ‹ ‹‹

1 Twist or break off the stem from each artichoke. If the stem base is too thick or short, make a small incision around the base of the artichoke and it will twist off easily. This will remove the tough inner fibers of the base.

2 By hand, break off 2 rows of outer tough leaves. With a thin-bladed, very sharp knife, remove the leaves one by one, using a seesaw motion behind each leaf. The knife should cut off just the leaf, leaving the fleshy part attached to the artichoke bottom. Repeat all around the artichoke until the trimmed leaves are tender, cone-shaped, and pale green. Cut the top off this cone about one third of the way down.

3 Using a swivel vegetable parer, trim the bottom of each artichoke to remove any tough green exterior.

4 Rub the artichokes all over with half a lemon. As you prepare them, drop the artichoke bottoms into a bowl of acidulated water (the juice of 1 lemon mixed with 3 to 4 cups water).

Artichoke Hearts in Red Wine Sauce

➤➤ *Ragoût d'Artichauts au Vin Rouge*   SERVES 6

THIS IS A RICH, wonderful dish, but it takes time. The recipe is an old one from the Languedoc; the sauce has extraordinary depth and texture. I originally served the ragout as a first course in small, individual brioches, but now I prefer it as an accompaniment to grilled lamb or roast veal.

6 globe artichokes or 2 packages (9 ounces each) frozen artichoke hearts, thawed

1 cup finely diced pancetta

¼ cup French peanut oil or light olive oil

1 cup finely diced jambon de Bayonne, prosciutto, or Serrano ham

1½ cups chopped onions

½ cup chopped mushrooms

⅔ cup minced scallions

1 cup sliced carrots

2 teaspoons sliced fresh garlic

1 bottle (750 ml) full-bodied red wine, such as California Petite Sirah

2 teaspoons tomato paste

Herb bouquet: 3 sprigs of parsley, 1 sprig of thyme, and 1 imported bay leaf tied in a bundle with string

6 peppercorns, lightly cracked

Salt

1½ cups unsalted chicken stock (storebought or homemade—page 405), reduced to ¾ cup

Pinch of sugar

1½ tablespoons Armagnac or Cognac

2 tablespoons unsalted butter

1 to 2 teaspoons minced fresh flat-leaf parsley

1 If using fresh artichokes, prepare the bottoms as described on page 327. Quarter the bottoms and remove the chokes. Reserve 1 cup of the trimmings for the sauce base. If using thawed frozen artichokes, chop 2 or 3 hearts into small pieces and set aside separately from the others.

2 In a large nonreactive skillet, cook the pancetta in 2 tablespoons of the oil over moderate heat until lightly browned, 2 to 3 minutes. Add the artichoke trimmings, ham, onion, mushrooms, scallions, carrot, and garlic. Sauté for 1 minute, stirring. Pour in the red wine. Bring to a boil, stirring. Blend in the tomato paste and add the herb bouquet, peppercorns, and ½ teaspoon salt. Reduce the heat to low, cover, and simmer for 1½ hours.

3 Stir in the reduced stock and simmer for 5 minutes. Strain, pressing down on the solids to extract all their juices. Skim off as much fat as you can from the surface of the stock. You should

have about 2 cups. Adjust the seasoning, adding a pinch of sugar, if necessary. Set the red wine sauce aside.

4 In a large skillet, sauté the quartered artichoke bottoms in the remaining 2 tablespoons oil over moderately high heat until lightly browned around the edges, about 2 minutes. Pour off the oil. Add the Armagnac and reduce to a glaze.

5 Add the red wine sauce and simmer for 15 minutes for raw fresh artichokes or 5 minutes for defrosted artichoke hearts. Swirl in the butter to thicken the sauce. Garnish with the chopped parsley.

ASPARAGUS WITH MORELS

➤➤ *Asperges Violettes aux Morilles*   SERVES 4

THIS LANDAIS COMBINATION of asparagus and morels makes for an elegant, easy to prepare, and marvelous spring vegetable dish. Though excellent with fresh morels, this dish is even better made with dried ones, which have a deeper flavor.

Soaking the morels in milky water makes them more succulent, but be sure to strain through several layers of cheesecloth before using. The perfume of the sauce becomes intoxicatingly intense if they are prepared in advance and allowed to stand for a few hours. Serve alone, before or after a main course, so that the extraordinary flavor and aroma can be appreciated.

1 ounce dried black morels, stemmed, and halved if large

¼ cup milk mixed with 1 cup lukewarm water

1 tablespoon unsalted butter

1 to 2 teaspoons fresh lemon juice

Salt and freshly ground pepper

½ cup heavy cream

¼ cup unsalted chicken stock (storebought or homemade—page 405)

32 medium-thick asparagus spears

1 to 2 teaspoons fine imported Port

(continued)

1 In a bowl, soak the morels in the milky water until softened, about 30 minutes. Scoop out the morels, squeeze the liquid back into the bowl, and set the morels aside. Strain the soaking liquid through cheesecloth and reserve it. Rinse the morels thoroughly under running water to remove any sand. Combine the soaking liquid and morels in a small skillet and bring the liquid almost to a boil. Simmer for 5 minutes, or until the liquid has been absorbed by the morels.

2 Add the butter, ¼ cup water, 1 teaspoon lemon juice, and salt and pepper to taste. Cook, partially covered, for 5 more minutes, or until the morels are tender and the liquid in the skillet has once again evaporated. Add ¼ cup of the cream and the stock, return to a simmer, and remove from the heat. (Do not worry about the abundant amount of sauce; the morels will absorb most of it.) Makes about 1 cup sauce.

3 Wash the asparagus, snap off the tough bottom portion of each, and peel the spears (see page 327). Cook the asparagus in a large skillet of boiling salted water until just tender, 4 to 5 minutes; the exact time depends upon the thickness and age of the asparagus. Drain on paper towels, cover, and set aside. *(The dish can be prepared to this point several hours in advance.)*

4 Just before serving, reheat the morels and sauce in the skillet; add the Port and the remaining ¼ cup cream. Adjust the seasoning with salt, pepper, and a few drops of lemon juice. Reheat the asparagus over simmering water or in a microwave. Pour the sauce over the asparagus and serve at once.

NOTES TO THE COOK

➤➤ These strange and wonderful spring mushrooms are the cook's prize. Conical, wrinkled, and hollow inside, morels are usually no more than 2 inches tall, yet they exude a powerful fragrant aroma of maple or walnuts. Their taste is nutty and meaty, woodsy and musty, which makes them one of the most sought-after mushrooms. And it is one of the few foolproof types safe for the experienced gatherer. To learn more about fresh morels in your area, contact your local mycological society. And remember: Never eat a wild mushroom unless it has been positively identified as edible. Morels must not be eaten raw; they are toxic though not fatal. Five minutes cooking time removes their toxicity.

➤➤ Dried morels, when reconstituted, also make excellent eating. Morels do not lose their flavor when dried—they actually become more intense in taste and aroma. Dried French morels have a smoky aroma while American ones are earthy and meaty. Their texture is not as fluffy, but they are firmer and they work well in the above recipe.

Michel Guérard's Pureed Celery Root with Apples

➤ *Purée de Céleri-Rave aux Pommes*   SERVES 4 TO 6

THIS IS AN INCREDIBLY DELICIOUS pairing and, to my taste, the best of the purees. Serve with Broiled Marinated Duck Breasts (page 175) and deep-fried celery leaves.

1 pound celery root	2 to 3 tablespoons heavy cream
1 quart milk	Salt and freshly ground pepper
¾ pound Red Delicious apples	

1 Using a stainless-steel knife to prevent discoloration, peel the celery root and cut it into chunks. In a large nonreactive saucepan, simmer the celery root in the milk for 10 minutes.

2 Meanwhile, peel, core, and quarter the apples. Add to the celery root and simmer together for 10 minutes longer, or until celery root is tender; drain.

3 Puree the celery root and apple quarters in batches in a food processor until smooth. Add the cream if necessary to loosen the mixture. Season with salt and pepper to taste. *(The recipe can be prepared several hours ahead. Let cool, cover, and refrigerate. Reheat gently before serving.)*

NOTES TO THE COOK

➤ The apples replace the more commonly used potatoes, resulting in a more silky, moist puree. The flavor of the apples is hardly noticeable, yet it heightens the flavor of the celery root. The very moist quality of the apple eliminates the need for large quantities of butter and cream.

➤ For a perfectly textured puree, press the mixture through a fine-mesh sieve.

Adapted from a footnote in Michel Guerard's La Cuisine Gourmande.

CABBAGE CAKE WITH SAUSAGE

→← *El Trinxat Cerda* MAKES A 10-INCH CAKE; SERVES 6

THIS RECIPE IS FROM a Catalan cookbook—it's made with white *butifarra* sausage, composed of lean pork and fat pork belly, and flavored with cinnamon, nutmeg, cloves, marjoram, and cayenne. Toulouse sausage seasoned with the same aromatics substitutes well, and so does fresh sausage from the butcher. Double blanching makes the cabbage lighter and easier to digest. The cake is perfectly cooked when the outside is crusty and the inside soft, like a puree. Serve with thinly sliced country rye or whole wheat bread.

3 pounds savoy cabbage

1 imported bay leaf

1 tablespoon coarse kosher salt

¼ cup homemade rendered lard or clarified butter

¼ pound thick-sliced pancetta, cut into ½-inch cubes

8 ounces fresh sausage

½ to 1 teaspoon freshly ground pepper

Red wine vinegar

1 Discard the tough outer leaves of the cabbage. Quarter the cabbage and cut out the inner core. Bring plenty of water to a boil in a large saucepan over high heat. Add the cabbage, return the water to a boil, and cook for 5 minutes; drain.

2 Bring fresh water to a boil in the saucepan. Add the cabbage, bay leaf, and salt. Cook for 10 minutes, then drain. Rinse the cabbage under cold running water and drain again. Squeeze to remove as much excess water as possible. Chop the cabbage coarsely.

3 Heat half the fat in a large skillet over moderately high heat. Add the pancetta and cook until lightly browned, 3 to 4 minutes. Add the cabbage and toss to coat thoroughly. Set aside in the skillet.

4 Prick the sausage with a fork. Combine with ⅓ cup water in a medium saucepan over moderate heat. Cover and steam the sausage for 10 minutes. Drain well and let cool, then cut diagonally into 1⅓-inch slices. *(The recipe can be prepared ahead up to this point.)*

5 Place the cabbage and pancetta over moderate heat and cook until heated through, about 5 minutes. Add the sausage and plenty of freshly ground pepper and mix well. Press into a flat cake that fills the bottom of the skillet. Cover the pan and cook for 10 minutes, shaking the pan often to prevent sticking.

6 Lift off the cover, dry the inside, and grease it lightly with some of the reserved fat. Invert the cabbage cake onto the lid and hold for an instant. Meanwhile, add remaining the fat to the pan and raise the heat to medium high. Slide the cake, crisp side up, into the pan and fry, uncovered, until the bottom is crisp and golden, about 10 minutes. Lightly sprinkle with vinegar and serve.

BAKED EGGPLANT STUDDED WITH GARLIC

→→ *Aubergines au Four à l'Ail*   SERVES 6

USE THE YOUNGEST, most tender eggplants you can find, allowing one per person. Asian eggplants work beautifully here. Many recipes for eggplant call for sautéing them in oil— delicious, of course, but sometimes indigestible since the vegetable sops up oil like a sponge. In this dish from the Pyrenees, the eggplant is roasted and fresh olive oil is added at the last minute, so much less is needed.

The eggplants are seasoned with a mixture of crumbled dried herbs. You can mix your own Herbes de la Garrigue (page 80) or use the mixed herbs from France called herbes de Provence.

3 large or 6 small whole garlic cloves, peeled and halved, plus 1 to 1½ teaspoons minced fresh garlic

½ cup fruity extra virgin olive oil

½ teaspoon salt

¼ teaspoon freshly ground pepper

2 tablespoons Herbes de la Garrigue (pages 79–80) or herbes de Provence

6 small whole eggplants, each about 5 inches long

2 tablespoons chopped fresh flat-leaf parsley

1 Preheat the oven to 400°F. Marinate the garlic cloves in the olive oil for 10 minutes. Remove the garlic, reserving the oil. Dry the garlic on paper towels and cut the cloves into long, thin slivers. Season the olive oil with the salt, pepper, and herbs. Let steep at least 10 minutes.

(continued)

2 Make 4 or 5 slits in each eggplant at equal distances. Slip the garlic slivers into the holes. Brush the outside of the eggplants with the seasoned oil and wrap each one in a sheet of aluminum foil; crimp to enclose securely.

3 Set all the wrapped eggplants on a baking sheet. Bake for 30 minutes.

4 To serve, unwrap the eggplants, slit them open, and spoon a tablespoon of scented oil from the packages over each. Sprinkle the minced garlic and parsley over the eggplants. Serve warm or cold.

Sautéed Eggplant, the "Cèpes of the Poor"

>> *Les Cèpes du Pauvre*   SERVES 2

THE TEXTURE OF COOKED EGGPLANT is mushroomlike and its color and appearance, bright and alive, but, of course, it lacks the delicate flavor of the real thing. Try frying slices in duck fat as an accompaniment to duck, pork, or chicken, or as a substitute for cèpes in Lucien Vanel's Chicken, Potato, and Artichoke Cake (pages 153–155) or in the Duck Leg Ragout With Green Olives and Eggplant (page 189). Then, as French Southwest cooks suggest, just close your eyes.

3 small (5- to 6-ounce) very fresh, very firm purple Italian eggplant, preferably homegrown or farmers' market quality

1½ tablespoons coarse kosher or pickling salt

1½ tablespoons rendered duck fat or olive oil

Pinch of sugar

1½ tablespoons chopped flat-leaf parsley

1 teaspoon finely chopped fresh garlic

Salt and freshly ground pepper

1 Peel the eggplant and cut into 1-inch chunks. Toss with the coarse salt. Place in a sieve over a bowl and let stand for at least 1 hour.

2 Rinse the eggplant well. Then, working in batches, gently squeeze out as much moisture as possible between your hands.

3 In a large skillet, preferably nonstick, heat the duck fat over moderate heat. Add the eggplant, cover with a lid, and cook, turning the pieces from time to time, until they begin to plump up, feel tender, and turn golden brown on all sides, about 10 minutes.

4 Reduce the heat to low, add the sugar, and slowly cook, uncovered, turning the pieces of eggplant often, for another 5 to 8 minutes, until tender and glazed. Remove the skillet from the heat. *(The recipe can be prepared to this point up to 2 hours in advance.)*

5 Shortly before serving, add the parsley and garlic to the eggplant. Toss to mix. Cover and cook over low heat to rewarm. Season with salt and pepper to taste and serve.

RAGOUT OF FOREST MUSHROOMS

Sauce de Cèpes

SERVES 5 OR 6

THE LANDAIS RECIPE adapted here employs white wine and a mixture of dried cèpes and fresh cultivated mushrooms enriched with tomatoes and ham. It's a dish best made a day in advance, then gently reheated before serving. In the Landes, they serve the mushrooms alone as a first course, but I like the dish with roast chicken or grilled meats. Fresh garlic and parsley chopped together can be strewn on top, if desired.

A rich, particularly succulent *civet de cèpes au vin de Cahors* was described to me by Monsieur Pierre Escorbiac, formerly of the La Taverne restaurant in Cahors in Quercy. Shallots and onions are softened in duck fat, then beef marrowbones, blanched pork skins, and pig's feet are added along with the cèpes. The mixture is covered with the red wine of the region, the inky thick vin de Cahors, hermetically sealed in an earthenware casserole, and allowed to cook slowly in embers for 3 to 4 hours. The marrow is then removed from the bones, the pork skins are cubed, and the pig's feet boned, ground up, then returned to the casserole to thicken the sauce, a procedure similar to that used in my recipe for Oxtail Daube (pages 264–266). (If you do this version, be sure to make it one day in advance so that all fat can be removed. Reheating will only make it better.)

(continued)

1 to 1½ ounces dried French cèpes or Italian porcini

Coarse kosher salt

1½ pounds fresh, firm cultivated mushrooms, trimmed (halved if very large)

¼ cup rendered duck or goose fat or olive oil

2½ ounces jambon de Bayonne, prosciutto, or Serrano ham, chopped

2 large shallots, minced

2 garlic cloves, finely chopped

¾ cup soft and fruity white wine, such as Saumur or Chenin Blanc

¼ cup diced tomatoes

Freshly ground pepper

1 tablespoon finely chopped fresh flat-leaf parsley

Fresh lemon juice

5 or 6 rounds of toasted French bread rubbed with ½ garlic clove (optional)

1 Soak the dried cèpes in 2 cups lukewarm water with a pinch of salt for 30 minutes. Drain by lifting them out of the liquid without stirring up the sediment at the bottom of the bowl. Rinse the cèpes under cool running water. Drain well by pressing on them lightly. Ladle the soaking liquid through a paper coffee filter or several layers of fine damp cheesecloth. Wipe the fresh mushroom caps with a damp cloth and a little coarse salt.

2 Preheat the oven to 300°F. In a large skillet, heat the fat or oil over moderate heat. Add the cèpes and their soaking liquid and cook until all liquid in the pan has evaporated. Add the ham, shallots, and garlic, and cook, stirring, for 1 minute. Add the fresh mushrooms and cook, stirring, over high heat, until all moisture has evaporated. Pour the wine over the mixture and boil down to a glaze. Add ½ cup hot water and the tomatoes. Reduce the heat to moderately low and cook, stir for a moment, then add ½ teaspoon salt, ¼ teaspoon pepper, and the parsley.

3 Scrape into an earthenware or enameled cast-iron casserole with a tight-fitting lid. Cover with waxed paper and the lid. Set in the preheated oven and cook for 2 hours. Uncover and let cool completely, then cover and refrigerate overnight.

4 Reheat the cèpes slowly. Adjust seasoning with a few drops of lemon juice, salt, and pepper. Serve with toasted rounds of French bread, if desired.

Inspired by a recipe from Monique Veilletet.

CÈPES IN THE STYLE OF GASCONY

→ *Cèpes à la Gasconne* SERVES 4 TO 6

THIS RECIPE IS A PERFECT demonstration of how the addition of dried cèpes can greatly enhance a dish of ordinary mushrooms. It doesn't hurt to add some olive oil, garlic, and cured ham as well.

1 ounce dried French cèpes or Italian porcini

¼ cup French olive oil or a light Italian olive oil

1 teaspoon finely chopped fresh garlic

2 tablespoons jambon de Bayonne, prosciutto, or Serrano ham, finely chopped

1 pound fresh cultivated mushrooms, quartered or sliced

Salt and freshly ground pepper

1½ tablespoons fresh lemon juice

2 tablespoons chopped fresh flat-leaf parsley

1 Soak the dried cèpes in 2 cups lukewarm water for 30 minutes. Drain by lifting them out of the liquid without stirring up the sediment at the bottom of the bowl. Rinse the cèpes under cool running water. Drain well by pressing on them lightly. Ladle the soaking liquid through a paper coffee filter or several layers of fine damp cheesecloth.

2 In a large nonreactive skillet, preferably copper, heat the olive oil over high heat. Add the cèpes; let them "sing" for a second, then reduce the heat to moderately high. Add the garlic and ham; cook, stirring, for 2 to 3 minutes, until the garlic begins to color slightly. Immediately add all the strained soaking liquid and bring to a boil. Slowly cook down to a glaze, about 15 minutes.

3 Add the fresh mushrooms. Season with salt and pepper to taste and sprinkle with the lemon juice. Sauté, tossing over moderately high heat, until all the moisture in the pan has evaporated, about 7 minutes. Serve very hot with a sprinkling of parsley. *(This dish can be made ahead and gently reheated. After cooking, cool uncovered. Cover and refrigerate until ready to serve.)*

NOTE TO THE COOK

If you have fresh cèpes on hand, omit Step 1 and the addition of the soaking liquid. If they have been washed, dry them out in a moderately low oven for 10 to 15 minutes before cooking.

Cèpes Sautéed in Oil in the Style of Bordeaux

➺ *Cèpes à la Bordelaise*

SERVES 2

IT WAS A HUNDRED YEARS AGO that the fashionable Café Anglais first introduced *cèpes à la Bordelaise* to Paris, a dish in which these wild forest mushrooms and garlic were cooked in oil. This was before the interest in provincial cookery, and the special combination of cèpes and oil was not particularly appreciated by the gourmets of the capital. Instead, the chefs starting cooking the cèpes in butter, a tradition still carried on today.

Auguste Colombié, the great nineteenth-century cooking teacher, once said, "The gourmets eat cèpes with butter; the fanatics eat them with oil." His recipe calls for the cèpes to be cooked twice, first in oil and then in butter!

With as few as one or two fresh cèpes you can make this memorable dish for two people.

2 large fresh cèpes or other boletes	1 teaspoon fresh lemon juice
1 large garlic clove, chopped	2 teaspoons minced fresh flat-leaf parsley
3 tablespoons French peanut oil or mild-flavored olive oil	Salt and freshly ground pepper

1 Separate the stems and caps. Chop the mushrooms stems and mix with the chopped garlic. Heat the oil in a shallow medium enameled cast-iron or earthenware pan over low heat. Add the chopped stems and garlic and cook gently until soft, about 5 minutes.

2 Add the mushroom caps and cook slowly for 15 minutes, or until all the moisture has evaporated. Turn them over, add a few tablespoons of water, and cook over low heat for 5 to 10 minutes longer, until completely tender. Drain off any excess oil.

3 Just before serving, sprinkle with the lemon juice and parsley. A light sprinkling of salt and very little pepper will do for seasoning.

NOTE TO THE COOK

Cèpes cooked this way are even better the next day. To keep freshly cooked cèpes a few weeks, simply cook in oil without seasoning, then drain; pack the mushrooms in clean jars, sprinkle lightly with salt, and cover with fresh olive oil. Store covered in the refrigerator.

Leeks Cooked in Their Own Juices "Under a Bed of Ashes"

Poireaux Sous la Cendre

SERVES 4

THERE IS A TOWN CALLED Mirepoix in the Ariège, whose name will be familiar to students of French cooking, since it is also the name of the finely diced vegetable base of so many French sauces and stews. It was near there that I first tasted young leeks roasted in dying embers, then peeled and served with a garlic and herb vinaigrette. These succulent leeks were a revelation of simplicity and pleasure. Their flavor is very intense and a great improvement over leeks boiled or steamed. Serve lukewarm with a garlic, herb, and olive oil vinaigrette.

The recipe has been adapted to enable the reader without a bed of ashes to prepare the dish in the oven or under the broiler.

12 thin leeks	2 tablespoons olive oil
Salt	Salt and freshly ground pepper

1 Preheat the oven to 450°F or preheat your broiler with the rack set about 4 inches from the heat. If you have hot coals in a fireplace or outdoor grill, stoke the ashes for even, steady heat.

2 Trim off the roots and all but 1 inch of green leaves from the leeks. Remove any remaining tough outer leaves. Beginning about 1 inch from the base, split the leeks lengthwise, using a thin sharp knife. Wash the leeks thoroughly; if very sandy, soak in a bowl of cold water for about 10 minutes.

3 Drain the leeks and pat dry with paper towels. Arrange in a single layer on a large sheet of heavy-duty aluminum foil. Rub each leek with olive oil. Sprinkle with salt and pepper to taste. Enclose completely in foil, wrapping tightly. *(The recipe can be prepared to this point up to 3 hours in advance.)*

4 Transfer the packet of leeks to a broiler pan or baking sheet. Broil wrapped in foil or bake for 5 minutes; then turn the packet over and cook for 5 minutes longer. If roasting in embers, cook for 10 minutes on each side and shake the packet from time to time to prevent the leeks from sticking to the foil.

Pureed Sorrel

➻ *Purée d'Oseille*

ONE OF THE GREAT natural affinities of taste is a plate of rich duck confit and lemony sorrel. Sorrel naturally purees itself when cooked, so it is an easy vegetable to prepare. Finding and cleaning enough for large groups is the problem. One pound of fresh young sorrel leaves makes about 1¼ cups puree, enough for two servings.

1 pound fresh sorrel leaves	¼ teaspoon freshly ground pepper
3 tablespoons unsalted butter	1½ tablespoons heavy cream or crème fraîche
½ teaspoon salt	

1 Carefully wash the sorrel leaves and remove the stems; drain well. Tear the larger leaves into small pieces. Roll the leaves into neat small bunches and cut each roll with a stainless-steel knife into thin strips, a chiffonnade. There should be about 6 packed cups.

2 Melt the butter in a large nonreactive saucepan over moderately low heat. Add the sorrel and season with the salt and pepper. Cover and cook for 1 minute to steam the leaves. Uncover and cook down until all moisture evaporates and the sorrel is thick. With the back of a stainless-steel fork, mash the sorrel to a puree. Set aside until ready to serve.

3 Reheat gently with the cream.

NOTE TO THE COOK

If only a handful of sorrel is available, combine with ¾ pound of fresh spinach, but cook each separately. Drain the spinach, add to the cooked and creamed sorrel, puree with an immersion blender, and serve.

POTATOES IN THE STYLE OF THE QUERCY

→→ *Pommes de Terre à la Quercynoise*   SERVES 4

THESE CHUNKS OF baking potatoes cooked until crusty-brown in goose fat make a hearty but not heavy or greasy dish. You will notice, after you've cooked the potatoes, that when you pour off the fat and measure it, you have recaptured almost all that you've put in.

½ pounds baking (russet) potatoes, preferably Idaho

3 tablespoons rendered goose or duck fat

Coarse kosher salt

1 tablespoon chopped fresh flat-leaf parsley

2 teaspoons chopped fresh garlic

1 About 2½ hours before serving, preheat the oven to 300°F. Peel the potatoes and cut into 1¼-inch chunks. Bring a large saucepan of salted water to a boil. Add the potatoes and boil for 3 minutes. Drain and shake dry in a colander.

2 Melt the fat in a large baking dish and add the potatoes in a single layer. Bake for 2 hours, turning the potatoes in the fat with a spatula from time to time. Allow all sides to turn crusty-brown.

3 Raise the oven temperature to 375°F and continue baking for 15 minutes. Just before serving, sprinkle with salt, parsley, and garlic.

NOTE TO THE COOK

During the first hour of baking, the potatoes will remain colorless. Do not attempt to raise the oven temperature during this time.

SARLAT POTATOES

➤ *Pommes de Terre à la Sarladaise*   SERVES 4 TO 6

BELOVED AND FAMOUS in the French Southwest, *pommes de terre à la Sarladaise* is especially good with crisp duck or goose confit. Slices of potatoes are sautéed in duck or goose fat, seasoned with salt and freshly ground pepper, sometimes sprinkled with thin slices of black truffle, and served hot. This version does not require truffles, so you will be able to make it more often. It is a marvelous half-crisp, half-soft potato dish, served hot and sprinkled with an *hachis*, a mixture of chopped garlic and parsley (see page 94).

2 pounds red potatoes (waxy potatoes are best for this dish)

3 tablespoons rendered duck or goose fat, or fat scraped from duck confit

2 teaspoons finely minced fresh garlic

1½ tablespoons minced fresh flat-leaf parsley

Salt and freshly ground pepper

1 About 30 minutes before serving, peel and rinse the potatoes. Using a mandoline or food processor, cut into ⅛-inch slices. Do not wash the slices.

2 Heat the fat in a well-seasoned, 10-inch nonstick cast-iron skillet over moderately high heat. Add the potatoes and let them brown for an instant. Cook, turning with a spatula to coat well with the fat and to avoid sticking, for about 2 minutes. Reduce the heat to moderate. When some of the slices begin to brown, press down on the potatoes with a spatula to form a flat round cake. Reduce the heat to moderately low, cover the skillet with a tight-fitting lid, and cook for 7 minutes.

3 Raise the lid to allow steam to escape. Wipe away any moisture on the lid. Toss the potatoes gently so that the crisp bottom pieces mix with the rest of the potato slices. Gently press down again with the spatula to reshape; cover and cook for 7 minutes longer, shaking the skillet to keep the potatoes from sticking.

4 Uncover the pan; wipe away any moisture on the lid, toss, and reshape the slices again. Cover tightly a third time and cook for 7 minutes. Remove from the heat and let stand without uncovering for 30 seconds. Lift the cover off, moving it to the side quickly so that the moisture does not fall onto the potatoes. Wipe the inside of the cover dry. Tilt the skillet and spoon off and reserve any excess fat.

5 Cover the skillet with a plate and invert to unmold the potato cake. Return the reserved fat to the skillet and set over moderate heat. Slide the potatoes back into the skillet and cook,

uncovered, until the second side crisps, about 3 minutes. The potatoes should look somewhat like a cake and should be puffy, crisp, and golden. Transfer to a heated serving platter and sprinkle with the garlic and parsley, and season with salt and pepper to taste. Serve at once while still hot.

NOTES TO THE COOK

➤ If the cast-iron skillet is not seasoned properly, the potatoes may stick. To season, wash skillet, rinse and dry thoroughly. Wipe 2 tablespoons vegetable oil over inside the surface of the skillet. Heat over moderate heat until very hot, about 5 minutes. Let cool; wipe surface dry with paper towels and repeat once more. Never use detergents or a stiff brush on the skillet. Coarse salt and damp paper towels are all that is necessary to scrub a skillet clean.

➤ If good-quality waxy potatoes are unavailable, Idaho potatoes can be substituted. Carefully rinse off the starch and dry each slice before cooking.

POTATO, CELERY ROOT, AND CORN PANCAKES

➤ *Galettes de Pommes de Terre au Céleri-Rave et Maïs*   MAKES EIGHT 3-INCH CAKES; SERVES 4 TO 8

IF YOU VISIT the Basque country in the fall, you will see a spectacularly beautiful land carpeted with russet-colored ferns and seemingly endless fields of corn. Basque sailors brought corn to France from the Americas sometime in the sixteenth century, and the Basques have been eating it in a variety of ways ever since. Cornmeal has always been a staple, but it has only been in the past decade that chefs have started to use fresh sweet corn, too. Pierre Laporte of the Café de Paris in Biarritz serves these little fried cakes with mustard-coated veal chops. They go marvelously with beef or duck as well.

1 small celery root, about ¾ pound

½ pound Yukon gold potatoes

½ cup fresh or thawed frozen corn kernels, dried thoroughly

2 tablespoons minced fresh chives

1 teaspoon salt

¼ teaspoon freshly ground pepper

⅛ teaspoon freshly grated nutmeg

⅓ cup clarified butter

(continued)

1 Peel the celery root; shred using the grating blade of a food processor. Arrange 2 layers of paper towels on a baking sheet. Spread out the shredded celery root on the towels in a single layer, fold over, and press out extra moisture. Put in a large bowl.

2 Peel and shred the potatoes; squeeze gently to remove excess moisture. Add to the celery root along with the corn, chives, salt, pepper, and nutmeg; blend well.

3 To make individual cakes, butter 8 individual brioche or tartlet molds. Divide the vegetable mixture evenly among the prepared molds, pressing firmly to form cakes.

4 Melt the clarified butter in a very large skillet, preferably nonstick, over moderate heat. One by one, invert the molds onto a wide spatula and slide upside down into skillet, leaving the molds in place. Fry until the bottom of the cakes is golden and crisp, moving the molds around often to prevent sticking, about 10 to 12 minutes.

5 Slip the tip of a knife or fork between one mold and its cake; lift off the mold. Repeat with the remaining molds. Invert the cakes with the wide spatula and continue to fry, uncovered, until browned on the second side and cooked through, 5 to 7 minutes. Drain on paper towels. If not serving immediately, keep hot in a low oven, turned off. Do not stack.

STRAW POTATO CAKE
STUFFED WITH BRAISED LEEKS

➤ *Paillaisson de Pommes de Terre aux Poireaux*   SERVES 6

THIS GOLDEN, CRISP potato cake filled with creamed leeks is one of the best potato dishes I know. In the Southwest, leeks are always cooked until silky and soft, never crunchy like string beans or broccoli. The creamed leeks act as a glue to hold the potato cake together.

1 pound leeks (white part plus 1 inch of green), split lengthwise in half, washed well, and dried

5 tablespoons unsalted butter

½ cup heavy cream

Salt and freshly ground pepper

1¾ to 2 pounds red potatoes

¼ cup clarified butter

1 Slice the leeks by hand or in a food processor fitted with the medium (4 mm) slicing disk (makes 5 cups). In a heavy medium saucepan, melt 2 tablespoons of the butter over moderate heat. Add the leeks and cook, stirring, for 2 minutes. Add the remaining 3 tablespoons butter. Cover and cook, without browning, for 20 minutes.

2 Stir in the cream and boil until thickened, about 3 minutes. Season with salt and pepper to taste. *(The recipe can be prepared to this point up to 1 day in advance; let cool, cover, and refrigerate.)*

3 Peel the potatoes and cut them in half or quarter so they'll fit in the feed tube of the food processor. Using the julienne blade, cut the potatoes into julienne strips, or use a large knife to cut the potatoes into very thin matchsticks; there will be about 3 cups. Rinse the potatoes in several changes of cold water to rinse off the starch; drain well.

4 Spread out the potatoes on a kitchen towel. Roll up the towel and the potatoes and squeeze tightly to extrude all excess water. The potatoes will keep in this state for ½ hour.

5 About half an hour before serving, heat the clarified butter in a large, seasoned cast-iron or nonstick skillet. Spread half the potatoes over the bottom of the skillet, making sure they are spread evenly to the edges. Top with the braised leeks, leaving a 1-inch margin around the edge. Cover with the remaining potatoes and pat with a spatula to form a cake about 10 inches in diameter. Cover and cook over moderate heat for 5 minutes, shaking the pan often to prevent the potatoes from sticking. Lift the cover off to allow the steam to escape and wipe the inside of the cover dry. Return to the skillet and cook, covered, for 5 minutes longer, still shaking the skillet to keep the potatoes from sticking.

6 Carefully remove the cover so that the moisture on it does not drip back onto the potatoes. Again wipe the cover dry. Tilt the skillet and spoon off and reserve any excess butter.

7 Cover the skillet with the lid and invert so that the potatoes rest on the lid. Return the butter to the skillet and heat; slide the cake back into the skillet, golden-brown side up. Continue cooking, uncovered, over moderately low heat, for 10 to 15 minutes, or until the potatoes are tender and the bottom is browned. Slide onto a serving dish, sprinkle with salt, and serve at once.

Inspired by a recipe from Lucien Vanel.

GRATIN OF POTATOES
IN THE STYLE OF THE AUVERGNE

➤➤ *Gratin Auvergnat*   SERVES 6 TO 8

IN THE ORIGINAL EDITION of this book, I presented a recipe for a rustic dish called *le gatis*—a mixture of Cantal and Roquefort cheeses served melting hot in a crust of brioche. (You'll find the recipe on my website, paulawolfert.com.) Here's a recipe for a luscious gratin that uses the same combination of cheeses along with slices of potatoes.

You can substitute a nice English Cheddar or a Monterey Jack for the hard-to-find Cantal, but please use a good blue-veined cheese—real Roquefort or bleu d'Auvergne. This gratin goes especially well with grilled or roasted beef.

3 pounds firm red potatoes

1 quart whole milk

Coarse salt

3½ ounces Roquefort or bleu d'Auvergne

½ cup heavy cream

¼ cup shredded Cantal, English Cheddar, or Monterey Jack cheese (1 ounce)

Salt and freshly ground white pepper to taste

¼ teaspoon freshly grated nutmeg

¼ teaspoon ground red pepper

½ garlic clove, crushed

2 tablespoons butter

1 Peel the potatoes, rinse, and slice them as thinly as you can, using a mandoline or a food processor fitted with a thin (2 mm) slicing disk. Do not wash or dry the potatoes after slicing.

2 Rinse a large, heavy pot with cold water, but do not dry it inside; this helps prevent the milk and starchy potatoes from scorching. Place the potatoes in the pot and cover with 3 cups of the milk. Add ¼ teaspoon of salt. Cover the pot, bring it to a boil, reduce the heat to low and cook, stirring occasionally, until the potatoes are just cooked, about 15 minutes. Remove the pot from the heat.

3 While the potatoes are cooking, mash the blue cheese with the heavy cream until smooth and blended. Stir in the remaining milk, the shredded Cantal, a pinch of salt, some white pepper, nutmeg, and red pepper.

4 Rub a shallow 3-quart baking dish with the garlic. Using a slotted spoon, transfer layers of potatoes to the dish, alternating with the blue cheese mixture and ending with the potatoes. If

the milk remaining in the pot is not thick, reduce it, and spread it over the potatoes in an even layer. Dot with the butter *(The recipe can be prepared to this point up to 3 hours before serving. Cover loosely and set aside in a cool place.)*

5 About 2 hours before serving, preheat the oven to 400°F. Place the dish on a flat baking sheet to catch any overspill and set it in the oven to bake for 1½ hours, or until the gratin is bubbling and brown and the liquid is nearly absorbed. Serve directly from the baking dish.

NOTES TO THE COOK

- If not serving at once, reduce the oven temperature to 200°F. The cooked gratin can hold for 1 hour.

- The potatoes can be peeled 2 to 3 hours in advance and kept covered in salted water in the refrigerator. Do not slice them until you are ready to assemble and bake the dish.

RED WINE–COOKED ONIONS

→← *Compote d'Oignon au Vin Rouge* SERVES 6

A LONG, SLOW COOKING of thickly sliced onions results in a meltingly sweet, thick compote, wonderful with grilled duck breast or calf's liver, braised pork, or on toast rounds with drinks.

5 tablespoons unsalted butter

3 to 3½ pounds large white onions, halved lengthwise and thickly sliced

1 tablespoon sugar

1½ cups rich and full-bodied red wine, such as a Petite Sirah or Côtes du Roussillon

Salt and freshly ground pepper

1 teaspoon red wine vinegar, or more to taste

1 Melt 3 tablespoons of the butter in a heavy medium casserole over low heat. Add the onions, cover, and cook, stirring occasionally, for 45 minutes. Meanwhile, in a small skillet, boil down ½ cup of the wine to 1 tablespoon. Add another ½ cup and reduce again to 1 tablespoon. Add the remaining wine and reduce to ⅓ cup. (This develops a stronger, deeper color.) Set aside.

2 Uncover the onions, raise the heat to moderately high, and cook, stirring frequently, until the onions are glazed and golden brown, about 5 minutes. Sprinkle the sugar over the onions and boil, stirring, for 2 to 3 minutes to reduce to a glaze.

3 Reduce the heat to low, add the reduced wine, cover, and cook, stirring from time to time, until the onions are very soft and deep purple in color, about 2 hours.

4 Raise the heat to medium high, add 1 tablespoon of the butter, and continue to reduce the mixture until all the liquid has evaporated and the onion starts to fry in the released fat. At this point you must give the dish your full attention, turning the onions over and over in the pan to avoid scorching. This turning and frying will take about 10 minutes to produce a thick rich jam, about 1¼ cups.

5 Season with salt and freshly ground pepper. Add the remaining tablespoon butter and enough vinegar to counteract any sweetness. Serve hot, lukewarm, or cold. This onion compote will keep in the refrigerator for up to 5 days, or it can be frozen.

MICHEL BRAS'S STUFFED ONIONS

→ *Oignons Farcis à la Farce "Noire"*   SERVES 6

AFTER THE COOKING OF SOUTHWEST FRANCE was first published, I kept running into people who felt that I should have included a recipe from their favorite chef. One afternoon in the Languedoc, a very serious gourmet—a doctor and vintner whose opinion I greatly respected—told me about a brilliant new chef at work in a remote village in the mountains of Southwest France.

"This one," he told me, "Michel Bras [the "s" pronounced] is wildly undervalued. He should have more than one star."

The doctor was so rapturous and convincing, I decided to make the trek. And a real trek it was—for Michel cooked in the Aveyron, in a town called Laguiole, which is famous for its knives. Laguiole was not on the road to anywhere. The nearest railroad station, Rodez, was an hour and a half away. The roads into town were considered good for half the year, but driving was slow. I remember thinking I'd never traveled so far to eat the food of so obscure a chef.

Let me end the suspense right now: The journey in was arduous, but the rewards were immense. In my opinion, Michel Bras is one of the most exciting chefs in France. And, he is no longer obscure. Now he has three Michelin stars!

I found him a modest man. He referred to himself as a "cook." Bespectacled, slight, an avid jogger, he radiated confidence. He did not train under a famous chef nor did he make the usual round of starred "great" kitchens during the period of his apprenticeship. In fact, he worked with his mother in their family restaurant and hotel for many years until he married and he and his wife, Ginette, took over the business.

To understand Michel Bras's food, one must understand the region where he lives. It is rural, sparsely settled, economically poor but rich in ingredients. High pastureland on the edge of the Aubrac Mountains is a place of sheepherders, vegetable growers, and river fisherman. Michel's recipes have their roots in local peasant cooking. He adapts, changes, lightens, and raises culinary concepts of humble origin to an extraordinarily sophisticated level, but always retains the regional base.

(continued)

Bras turned out to be just the kind of cook I most admire. He made magic out of foraged mushrooms and other wild foods, produced silken sorbets from shrubby herbs and plant roots, and created delicious slow-cooked vegetable dishes, such as these divine onions, filled with not much more than ordinary bread and poultry giblets—a perfect accompaniment to Thanksgiving turkey.

In this dish, onion skins and stuffing are a study in contrasting and complementing textures and tastes. There are only a few special things you should know:

→→ Choose large, firm, sweet onions.

→→ Slit them halfway from top to bottom so you can extract as many "container-ovals" as possible.

→→ Use good sturdy bread that will stand up to a savory mix of giblets, herbs, greens, eggs, and ham. I like to combine rye and white bread.

2 very large onions (1 pound each), preferably large red onions, peeled

Coarse salt and freshly ground black pepper

¼ pound Swiss chard (6 medium-sized stalks)

⅓ cup diced jambon de Bayonne, prosciutto, or Serrano ham, about 3 ounces

1½ tablespoons finely chopped shallots

¼ cup poultry giblets (gizzard, liver, and heart), cleaned and trimmed

1 cup unsalted chicken stock (storebought or homemade—page 405)

2 teaspoons flour

1½ cups cubed stale, crustless dense bread

⅓ cup milk

2 eggs, lightly beaten

2 tablespoons coarsely chopped flat leaf parsley

2 tablespoons minced fresh chives

Freshly grated nutmeg

2 tablespoons butter or duck fat

3 tablespoons crème fraîche

Several drops of Banyuls vinegar or quality balsamic vinegar

1 Make a lengthwise slit in each onion, just halfway through from stem to root. Drop the onions into boiling salted water and cook them for 10 minutes. Drain and refresh them under cool running water. Discard the thickest outside layers. Separate the layers, reserving only the 4 or 5 largest from each onion. (Use the remainder for soup or a puree; see Note at right.) Place the onion cups on a work surface; season with pepper and a pinch of salt.

2 Separate the chard leaves from the stems; reserve the stems for another use. In a large saucepan of boiling salted water, blanch the chard leaves for 3 minutes. Drain and rinse under cold running water until cool. Squeeze dry in your hands to remove as much water as possible. Chop the chard.

3 In a small nonstick skillet, cook the ham and shallots over moderate heat, stirring, until the shallots are softened, 30 to 60 seconds; remove from the heat and scrape into a food processor. Combine the giblets, half the stock, and the flour in the food processor; process until they are finely ground.

4 Soak the bread in the milk and squeeze out excess moisture. With a fork, crush the eggs and bread until they are light and well combined. Mash in the ham-liver mixture, chopped Swiss chard, parsley, and chives; mix well. Season with salt, pepper, and nutmeg to taste. Makes about 1½ cups. Refrigerate to firm up the mixture. *(The recipe can be prepared to this point up to 8 hours in advance. Cover and refrigerate.)*

5 About 4 hours before serving, preheat the oven to 300°F. Divide the stuffing into 8 or 10 portions; fill each onion "cup" and roll up, jelly-roll style, into football shapes. Place the onions, seam side down, in a buttered 10 by 7–inch baking pan, preferably ceramic. Pour the remaining ½ cup stock over the onions, cover with foil, and bake for 1 hour.

6 Turn each onion over, spread the crème fraîche on top, and return to the oven. Continue to bake, uncovered, 3 more hours, basting once or twice with the pan juices.

7 Raise the oven temperature to 400°F. Baste again and allow the onions to continue roasting until glazed brown and turn meltingly tender, about 15 minutes longer. Drizzle a few drops of vinegar over the onions. Serve hot or warm.

NOTE TO THE COOK

A delicious onion puree to be served the following day can be made with the insides of the onions, which are not used for this dish. Boil the onion centers in fresh salted water until tender, about 10 minutes. Drain, let cool, and squeeze them dry with your hands. Puree the onions in a food processor with a few tablespoons of heavy cream. Place the puree in a saucepan and add 2 tablespoons of poultry or meat juices and reduce until thick. Season with salt and pepper. Serve garnished with small bread croutons fried in clarified butter until golden brown.

Sauté of Tomatoes, Red Peppers, and Zucchini

➤ *Fricassée de Jardinier*   SERVES 4

THIS BRIGHT SAUTÉ of tomatoes, sweet red peppers, and zucchini is light and easy to make. It goes well with any meat or with braised chicken breasts.

2 red bell peppers

6 tablespoons unsalted butter

1 cup coarsely chopped onions

½ teaspoon finely minced fresh garlic

3 large red-ripe tomatoes, peeled, seeded, and cut into 1-inch chunks

2 small firm zucchini, cut into ¾-inch chunks

Salt and freshly ground pepper

Piment d'Espelette or other moderately hot red pepper powder

2 tablespoons chopped fresh flat-leaf parsley

1 teaspoon chopped fresh basil

1 Broil the peppers, turning, until the skins are black and blistered all over, about 12 minutes. Let cool for 10 minutes under a kitchen towel or in a brown paper bag. Core, seed, and slip off the skins. Cut into thin strips 2 inches long.

2 About half an hour before serving, in a large heavy skillet, melt 3 tablespoons of the butter. Add the onions and garlic, cover tightly, and cook over low heat for 5 minutes.

3 Add the tomato and zucchini chunks and continue to cook, covered, for 10 minutes, stirring often. Raise the heat to moderately high, uncover the pan and boil rapidly, stirring often to prevent scorching, until most of the excess moisture evaporates, 4 to 5 minutes.

4 Fold in the roasted pepper strips and allow to heat through. Season with salt, pepper, and piment d'Espelette or red pepper to taste. Cut the remaining 3 tablespoons butter into small pieces and off heat, swirl into the pan. Mix together the parsley and basil and sprinkle over the top. Serve hot.

SAUTÉED PEPPERS IN THE STYLE OF BÉARN

→ *Piments à la Béarnaise*

SERVES 4

SERVE THESE PEPPERS with the Calf's Liver as Prepared in the Valley of Ossau (pages 283–285), or with thick slices of country-cured ham. In the Béarn they often garnish hot slices of foie gras with these fried peppers. Use thin-skinned green, Italian-style "frying peppers"—sometimes called Hungarian or sweet Gypsy peppers—for this dish; they do not need to be peeled. If unavailable, substitute farm-stand bell peppers and peel them.

1 pound Italian frying peppers	1 or 2 splashes of Banyuls or sherry vinegar
1½ tablespoons rendered duck fat	Salt and freshly ground pepper

1 Steam the peppers for 5 minutes. As soon as they are cool enough to handle, remove the stems, cores, and seeds. Cut the peppers into bite-size pieces. Pat dry on paper towels. (*The peppers can be prepared up to 8 hours in advance.*)

2 A few minutes before serving, heat the fat in a medium skillet over high heat. Add the peppers and sauté for 2 to 3 minutes, or until peppers brown slightly around the edges. Remove with a slotted spoon. Sprinkle with the vinegar and salt and pepper to taste. Serve at once.

SAUCE BASQUAISE WITH EGGS AND HAM

→ *Pipérade*

SERVES 10

PIPÉRADE HAS BEEN misunderstood in the United States. For years I've seen it pictured in food magazines as a plate of scrambled eggs served with a chunky sauce of diced green and red peppers with a twist of ham perched on the top. It makes for a pretty picture that way, but the picture gives a false impression. The real *pipérade* of the Basque country isn't chunky at all and is not poured like a sauce on top of the eggs but is blended with them.

(continued)

The great Southwest French chef X. Marcel Boulestin wrote a definitive description in his 1931 book *What Shall We Have Today?*: "It is a kind of egg dish, and some people make it either like scrambled eggs or like an omelet. But this is not right, and when finished it should be impossible to see which is egg and which is vegetable, the aspect being that of a rather frothy purée."

Pipérade is a creamy, soft egg-and-vegetable mixture better served in a shallow bowl than on a plate. The *sauce basquaise* that is combined with the eggs is ubiquitous in the Basque country, where it is served on top of nearly everything and is even thinned by some cooks who then serve it as a soup. It is a great supper dish for a crowd.

¼ cup extra virgin olive oil or rendered goose fat	1 tablespoon coarse sea salt
1 medium onion, chopped	1 teaspoon sugar
1½ tablespoons crushed fresh garlic	½ teaspoon piment d'Espelette or 1 teaspoon puree or crème de piment d'Espelette (see Mail Order Sources, pages 415–417)
3½ pounds red-ripe tomatoes, cored, seeded, and chopped	10 large eggs
12 Italian frying peppers, seeded and cut into 1-inch strips (about 4 cups)	10 thin slices of jambon de Bayonne, Serrano ham, or prosciutto

1 In a large flameproof casserole, heat the olive oil or fat over moderate heat. Add the onion and garlic and sauté until softened, 3 to 5 minutes.

2 Add the tomatoes and peppers and stew until the sauce has thickened, about 45 minutes. Stir in the salt, sugar, and piment d'Espelette. Let cool, then press through a food mill to make a smooth sauce. (*The* sauce basquaise *can be prepared up to 2 days in advance. Cover and refrigerate.*)

3 About 10 minutes before serving, bring the sauce basquaise to a boil in a 12-inch skillet over high heat, stirring constantly. Reduce the heat to a simmer.

4 In a large bowl, lightly beat the eggs. Gradually pour them into skillet in spiral motion, starting at the edge of the skillet and working toward the center. Cook, stirring with a wooden spoon, until the eggs are almost firm but still very creamy, about 7 minutes.

5 Meanwhile, in a second skillet fry the ham slices in their own rendered fat or in 1 tablespoon oil. Serve the eggs at once under a blanket of fried ham.

CORNMEAL PORRIDGE

→ *Las Pous*

CORNMEAL PORRIDGE, the Southwest French version of Italian polenta, is called *las pous* in the patois of the Périgord—also *rimotes* or *milhas* in the Languedoc, *cruchade* in the Landes, *armottes* in Gascony, *broye* in the Béarn, and, frequently throughout the region, simply *millas*. Until recently, it was the true starch of the countryside. White bread was a luxury eaten only on Sundays. Today, you'll often find this porridge fashionably served with grilled sardines, daubes, sauces, and Civet of Hare (pages 219–222) or other game, as well as sugared and fried for dessert in many restaurants.

Las pous can be made with any of the following additions: garlic, sautéed onions, melted ham fat, any kind of poultry fat, or lukewarm milk or butter. Allowed to cool, cut into pieces and fried, it makes a superb accompaniment to any of the wine-based beef, chicken, or duck stews and daubes in this book. In fact, I highly recommend it as the best possible starch accompaniment to these meat dishes.

Fulbert Dumonteil, in *La France Gourmande*, writes that the reason this porridge is called *las pous* is because when it is prepared over low heat, its surface sputters, then seems to break into a "smile," giving forth the sound "pou," like a person moving, smiling, and sighing in his sleep. I've tried to smile back at *las pous*, but usually to no avail, since it requires constant stirring. Sometimes, while preparing it, I've felt like sighing myself. Recently, I learned a Tuscan method, which I share below, that obviates the need for stirring. This new recipe is a lot easier to execute than the one I offered in the original edition.

One of the most delicious versions of *las pous* was made for me in the town of Cordes in the Tarn. The woman who demonstrated the dish had been showing me how to make goose confit. When she finished, there were some meat juices, bits of goose meat, and a tiny amount of goose fat left in the pot. To this, she added a few cups of water and some flour and cornmeal, then stirred the mixture to make it smooth. She then proceeded with the laborious stirring version. If I'd known then what I know now, I'd have shared the Tuscan method with her.

Another time, in the Pyrenees, on the road to Gavarnie (the local equivalent of the Grand Canyon), I observed a shepherd making a polenta-type porridge without stirring! He had spent the summer utterly alone, tending his sheep in the mountains. The day I met him

(continued)

he brought some rich sheep's milk down to the inn where I was staying. He put a quart of this milk into an iron pot set in the fireplace and let it come to a boil. Then he threw in a few handfuls of fine white cornmeal, stirred once in a secretive fashion, then pulled back from the fireplace to reveal a large skinlike bubble that had formed on top of the mixture, allowing the porridge to cook within it, in effect within its own steam. At a precisely chosen point, he stabbed this dome, then scooped out perfect tender cornmeal porridge. All the people watching with me were equally amazed. Later, a waitress told me that this shepherd refused to reveal his secret, so that when he died, it would surely be lost. "Unless," she added with a smile, "he will marry me and pass along the secret to our son!"

First comes the traditional method; a simpler method follows.

1⅓ cups finely ground yellow cornmeal

⅔ cup unbleached all-purpose flour

¾ teaspoon coarse kosher salt

3 to 4 tablespoons lukewarm milk, butter, rendered duck fat, pork fat, ham fat, or heavy cream

1 In a heavy, deep saucepan, combine the cornmeal and flour with 2 cups lukewarm water. Stir until completely smooth.

2 In another pan, bring 4 cups water to a boil with ¾ teaspoon salt. Slowly stir the boiling water into the cornmeal mixture. Cook over moderate heat, stirring without stopping with a long wooden spoon (called a toudeillo in Southwest France), for 15 minutes. There must be no lumps. Season with additional salt to taste.

3 Reduce the heat to as low as possible and let the mixture cook gently for 30 to 45 minutes, stirring from time to time. It is fully cooked when the porridge no longer "smiles" when a spoon is stirred through it, but rather packs itself around the spoon. Stir in the lukewarm milk, butter, fat, or cream to loosen the mixture, then pour into a greased serving bowl and serve at once.

4 To use in a recipe that fries or grills cornmeal porridge, use a wet spatula to spread out the porridge to a ¾-inch thickness on a greased flat surface and let cool.

Inspired by a recipe from Monique Darras.

Here is a simpler method borrowed from the Italians.

2 cups medium coarse cornmeal, preferably organic	2 tablespoons rendered duck fat or melted butter
8 to 10 cups cool water	2 teaspoons salt

1 Preheat the oven to 350°F. Grease a 12-inch cazuela or ovenproof casserole. Add the cornmeal, water, duck fat or butter, and salt, and stir with a fork until blended. It will separate, but don't worry; it will come together later.

2 Bake the polenta uncovered for 1 hour 20 minutes. Stir with a long-handled wooden spoon, season with additional salt to taste, and bake for 10 minutes longer. Remove from the oven and let rest for 5 minutes before pouring into a greased bowl.

FRIED CORNMEAL PORRIDGE CAKES IN THE STYLE OF GASCONY

➤➤ *Armottes*

CORNMEAL FIRST APPEARED in the Southwest in the sixteenth century, when corn was brought back from the New World by Basque sailors. It grew well in this region, as did other New World vegetables such as tomatoes, pumpkins, peppers, and beans. I was particularly struck by this dependence on American ingredients when a young Basque in the town of Espelette told me about a flat cornmeal and flour pancake that his mother used to make, called a *taloa*. This pancake, about five inches in diameter, was fried on both sides in a pan greased lightly with ham fat until it showed little black burn spots and puffs on its surface. His mother then filled it with crumbled fresh cheese or crumbled bacon and hot pepper sauce.

This Gascon version is my favorite accompaniment to all red wine–based stews and daubes.

1 recipe for traditional or new Cornmeal Porridge (pages 355–357)	½ cup rendered duck, goose, or pork fat, or a combination of oil and butter
Flour	*(continued)*

1 Up to 3 days in advance, prepare the Cornmeal Porridge, spread out to cool, cover, and refrigerate.

2 Cut the porridge into the desired shapes. I like 1¼-inch rounds or squares. Dust with flour.

3 Heat the fat in a large skillet until sizzling. Fry the cornmeal cakes, in batches as necessary, over moderately high heat turning once, until golden brown and crisp on both sides, about 5 minutes. Immediately remove from the skillet and drain on paper towels.

NOTES TO THE COOK

→ For best results, leave the cornmeal shapes in the refrigerator until just before frying. If the cakes are cold when placed in the hot skillet, they will not absorb as much of the fat but will gain the flavor of the fat.

→ If you are working in batches, let the fat regain its high temperature before continuing with the next batch, or it will be absorbed.

→ To prepare the cornmeal cakes up to half hour in advance, set a large baking sheet in the oven and preheat to 300°F. Set the fried cakes in a single layer on the hot baking sheet in the oven and hold until ready to serve.

DESSERTS

Skillet Desserts

While researching this book I came upon a great number of desserts that are made in a heavy, black cast-iron skillet—not just simple crêpes but crêpes flavored with tantalizing combinations of aromatics, as well as other sweets that I have collected and filed under the category "skillet desserts." In the French Southwest, the most common flavoring for crêpes is anise, but many skilled home cooks have their own secret preparations for "perfuming" crêpes, waffles *(gaufres)*, sponge-type cakes *(massepain)*, and the famous *gâteau basque*.

Two simple skillet desserts are: *les daudines*, as it is called in the Périgord (elsewhere known as *pain perdu*), which is nothing more than French toast—slices of stale bread bathed in sugared milk flavored with rum or orange-flower water, dipped in beaten eggs, then fried in butter, and served with currant jelly or honey. And a homey dessert, called *cruchades* in the Landes or *millas* in the Languedoc, which is leftover cornmeal porridge that is fried, then sprinkled with sugar.

But there are other, more esoteric skillet desserts, such as *pescajoun aux fruits*, a crêpe batter made with buckwheat and wheat flour and lightened with beaten egg whites, served with fresh diced fruit soaked in liqueur. Also *clafoutis*, a crêpe batter studded with wild black cherries, as in the Limousin, or in the neighboring regions with Italian plums mixed with muscat raisins and scented with rum or eau-de-vie or cubes of sugared pumpkin. In the old days, this dish was baked in a skillet that was placed, covered, in the embers, and the top covered with more embers; today it is baked in the oven in a baking pan or a skillet.

Casserole of Moulard Duck Breasts with Potatoes as Prepared in the Region of the Bigorre (page 180)

Cassoulet in the Style of Toulouse (page 317)

Michel Bras's Stuffed Onions (page 349)

Poached Chicken Breast,
Auvergne Style (page 151)

THIS PAGE: *Madeleines From Dax (page 384)*

OPPOSITE: *Custard and Cherries Baked in a Skillet (page 362)*

Pastry Cake Filled With Apples
and Prunes in Armagnac (page 370)

MIXED FRAGRANCES

→→ *Parfums Mélangés*

FOR THOSE WHO ENJOY mixing aromatic concoctions, I offer the following two formulas for use in crêpes, cakes, and pastry cream. The first is a family secret of a pharmacist who lived in the Lot-et-Garonne: a very delicate combination of Armagnac, anise, lemon essence, orange-flower water, and rum. Though the pharmacist gave me this recipe in cubic centimeters, the original required a special footed cone-shaped glass for use as a measure. It called for some of the ingredients to be placed in the glass, for sufficient rum to coat the insides of this glass, which was then to be filled to the top with orange-flower water, after which the mixture had to be stirred. The second combination is a simple, straightforward Basque mixture.

3 ounces French orange-flower water

3 tablespoons dark rum

1 tablespoon Armagnac

2 teaspoons vanilla extract

¼ teaspoon anise essence or 1 teaspoon anise extract

¼ teaspoon lemon essence or 1 teaspoon lemon extract

Mix all the ingredients in a clean jar, cover tightly, and keep in a cool cupboard or in the refrigerator.

BASQUE AROMATIC MIXTURE

¼ cup Armagnac

2 tablespoons orange-flower water

2 tablespoons anisette

2 tablespoons dark rum

1 teaspoon almond extract

1 strip of organic lemon or orange zest, 1 inch long by ¼ inch wide

Mix ingredients in a clean jar, cover tightly, and keep in a cool cupboard or refrigerator.

NOTE TO THE COOK

Much depends upon the right kind of brandy, the right brand of orange-flower water, and the right flavor and color of rum; so I must warn that some of these combinations, when made with inferior ingredients, are not as enchanting as they are in France.

Custard and Cherries Baked in a Skillet

>→ *Clafoutis aux Cerises*   SERVES 6

I THINK OF THIS CLAFOUTIS as pure therapy for the stressed-out home cook. It's easy and homey, and it can be served at any temperature—warm, cool, or at room temperature.

The cherry version of this clafoutis is a regional specialty of the Limousin, a region producing beautiful tart cherries. Traditionally, the local cooks don't pit their cherries. One reason is they know if they do, the juices will bleed out during baking and make the cake unsightly. Since I find most people prefer using pitted cherries, I've devised a *truc* to keep the juices from weeping: Roll your pitted cherries in sugar, then slip them into the freezer for a while to keep the juices in.

To avoid a heavy cake, please make sure your oven temperature is accurate. You'll need a hot oven to make this cake rise.

1 pound sweet cherries (about 3 cups), pitted	4½ tablespoons unsalted butter, at room temperature
Grated zest of ½ lemon, organic if available	3 eggs
¼ sugar	2 cups warm milk
½ cup (4 ounces) all-purpose flour, pastry flour or whole wheat pastry flour, plus 1 tablespoon for the skillet	2 tablespoons Armagnac or Cognac
	½ teaspoon vanilla extract
Pinch of salt	Confectioners' sugar

1 Early in the day, rinse and dry the cherries. Stem and, if desired, pit the fruit; traditionally this dessert is made with the pits in. Line a 1-quart freezer container with paper towels and pile in the cherries. Sprinkle with the lemon zest and 3 tablespoons of the sugar. Cover and shake to distribute the sugar. Freeze for 1 to 2 hours.

2 Meanwhile, in a mixing bowl, combine the flour, salt, 3 tablespoons of the butter, the eggs and ¼ cup of the warm milk, whisking to blend thoroughly. Gradually add the remaining milk and whisk until smooth. Stir in the Armagnac and vanilla. Cover and let the batter stand at room temperature for at least 1 hour. (This will encourage a small amount of fermentation, which allows the batter to rise to the top of the skillet during baking.)

3 Use half the remaining butter to grease a 9-inch, straight-sided ovenproof skillet, preferably well-seasoned cast-iron. Dust the pan with 1 tablespoon flour; tap out remove any excess.

4 Preheat the oven to 425°F. Arrange the cherries in the pan in a single layer. Whisk the batter to a good froth and spoon over the cherries. Set the skillet in the top third of the oven and bake for 20 minutes; the surface will be barely set.

5 Sprinkle the remaining 1 tablespoon sugar over the clafoutis and dot with the remaining 1 tablespoon butter divided into small bits. Continue to bake for 20 more minutes, or until well puffed, golden brown, and set. Test by inserting a skewer into the center; it is done if it comes out clean. Transfer to a rack and let cool, before serving lukewarm, at room temperature or chilled.

VARIATION: TART CHERRY CLAFOUTIS

If substituting tart cherries, omit the lemon zest and double the sugar.

SOUFFLÉ OMELET WITH FRESH FRUITS
Soufflé Poêlée aux Fruits SERVES 2 OR 3

ONE OF THE LIGHTEST and simplest skillet desserts is a soufflé omelet. One starts out as if making a standard soufflé omelet, shaking the skillet over the heat as the bottom of the omelet cooks. But when the omelet begins to rise around the sides, it is strewn with assorted fresh fruits, and then placed in the oven where it continues to rise like a soufflé. It will rise in about five minutes in a rustic, wavy manner. It is neither omelet nor soufflé, but rather an extremely light dessert, excellent when served with a scattering of fruits.

Almost any sort of fruit can be used, depending on the season: apples macerated with sugar and rum; prunes cooked in a thick black syrup laced with Armagnac; caramelized strawberries flamed with kirsch; or oranges sautéed in butter and sugar, then flambéed with Grand Marnier.

(continued)

3 tablespoons unsalted butter

4½ tablespoons sugar

1¼ cups peeled, diced, or sliced fresh fruit: oranges, pears, peaches, assorted berries, drained and juices reserved (do not use pineapple)

2 tablespoons Grand Marnier, dark rum, kirsch, Cognac, or Armagnac

3 egg yolks, at room temperature

4 egg whites, at room temperature

Pinch of salt

Confectioners' sugar

1 Half an hour before serving, preheat the oven to 425°F. In a small skillet, melt 1 tablespoon of the butter over moderate heat. Add 1 tablespoon of the sugar and stir to blend. When the butter and sugar begin to caramelize, add the fruit and toss gently to coat. Cook 30 seconds. Add 1 tablespoon of the liqueur and ignite, shaking pan gently until flames subside. Remove the skillet from the heat. Strain the fruit and set aside. Return the juices to the pan and reduce to 3 tablespoons; reserve off heat.

2 With an electric beater, beat the egg yolks with 2 tablespoons sugar until thick and lemon colored, not less than 5 minutes. Add the remaining 1 tablespoon liqueur and beat 1 minute longer.

3 In a clean bowl with clean beaters, beat the egg whites with a pinch of salt until foamy. Gradually add 1½ tablespoons sugar and continue beating until the whites are stiff but not dry.

4 Whisk 1 heaping tablespoon of beaten egg whites into the yolk mixture, then gently fold in the remaining whites. Blend gently but thoroughly. The mixture should be firm but foamy.

5 In a 9- or 10-inch ovenproof skillet, preferably copper, melt the remaining 2 tablespoons butter over moderate heat until sizzling. Scrape in the egg mixture and let it set for an instant. Gently smooth the surface with a spatula. Reduce the heat to low and cook for 2 minutes, or until the bottom turns golden brown, gently shaking the pan back and forth to prevent sticking. When the omelet begins to rise slightly in the skillet on top of the stove, scatter the fruit on top.

6 Quickly reheat the reduced fruit juices and sprinkle over the top. Place the omelet in the top third of the oven and bake for 5 minutes, or until puffed and golden brown. Dust with confectioners' sugar and serve at once.

NOTE TO THE COOK

Success with this dessert depends upon your pan. You must find one that can go into a hot oven and can also withstand stove top heat. It must be attractive enough to serve in, too. A copper skillet will do beautifully; a good heavy black iron skillet will appeal to those who like the homespun look.

Batter Cake With Fresh Pears From the Corrèze

→→ *Flaugnarde*   SERVES 4

"IT'S OUR BEST DESSERT," says Albert Parveaux, proprietor of the Château de Castel Novel. He is speaking of the *flaugnarde* of the Corrèze, a superb soufflé-like fruit cake, similar to a German apple pancake. "But," he adds, "its simplicity is misunderstood by some of our guests, who think complexity is the same thing as excellence."

He explained the true secrets of a successful *flaugnarde*: "First, never put sugar into it the way they do in the Périgord, because it won't rise on account of the extra weight. Second, be sure to use a metal dish, since metal heats up quicker and thus will give the batter a better rise. Third, only fill the pan to one third of its height—the *flaugnarde* will thus have room to rise, and it will in fact fill the pan when baked."

You must eat this dessert while hot, though it will hold its rise as long as 10 minutes. When serving, slip it out of its pan onto a serving plate; then dust heavily with superfine granulated sugar.

3 eggs	1 tablespoon dark rum
7 ounces (about 1½ cups) unbleached pastry flour	2 tasty sweet pears, such as Comice or Anjou
Pinch of salt	2½ tablespoons unsalted butter
1 cup warm milk	Superfine sugar

1 Two to 3½ hours before serving, lightly beat the eggs in a mixing bowl. Sift the flour and salt; add to the eggs, stirring. Add 2 tablespoons warm milk and mix until the batter is completely smooth. Gradually stir in the remaining milk and the rum. Strain through a fine sieve and let stand at room temperature for 1 to 2½ hours.

2 About 1 hour before serving, preheat the oven to 450°F. Peel, halve, core, and thinly slice the pear; the 3 mm slicing disk of a food processor is perfect for the job. Using half the butter, lavishly grease a 8- or 9-inch cake pan or straight-sided ovenproof skillet. Pour in the batter and delicately lay the fruit slices on top. Dot with the remaining butter.

(continued)

3 Bake in the bottom third of the oven for 15 minutes. Reduce the oven temperature to 400°F and bake for 30 to 35 minutes longer, or until well puffed and golden brown.

4 Use a spatula around the edges and under the cake to loosen. Transfer to a serving dish. Sprinkle lavishly with sugar and serve within 5 minutes.

FARMHOUSE CRÊPES

Crêpes Fermières   MAKES ABOUT 18 CRÊPES; SERVES 4 TO 6

CRÊPES IN THE SOUTHWEST are flavored with any one of the various fragrances popular in the region: orange-flower water, anisette, rum, lemon, Armagnac, prune eau-de-vie, cherry laurel leaves, Cognac, vanilla, and almond.

For light crêpes, allow the batter to rest for a few hours before cooking. Perfect crêpes are thin, light, and dry, yet supple enough to roll. The secret of these Farmhouse Crêpes is to strain the batter so that it is perfectly smooth.

A country method for greasing the crêpe pan is to skewer half a potato or apple flat side out, dip it into melted fat, and use it as an applicator.

4½ ounces (about 1 cup) unbleached all-purpose flour, sifted

3 eggs

¾ cup milk

2 tablespoons unsalted butter, at room temperature

2 tablespoons Pernod

2½ teaspoons orange-flower water

½ teaspoon almond extract

Finely grated zest of ½ lemon, organic if available

1½ tablespoons superfine sugar

⅛ teaspoon fine salt

1 tablespoon clarified butter or rendered goose fat

Granulated sugar and lemon wedges, fruit preserves, or crushed walnuts blended with enough sweetened whipped cream to make a sauce

1 About 3½ hours before serving, with an electric beater or with a hand whisk, blend the flour and eggs.

2 Meanwhile, gently heat the milk with the butter until the butter is melted. Add the Pernod, orange-flower water, almond extract, lemon zest, superfine sugar, and salt to the warmed milk. Slowly whisk the flavored milk into the egg-flour mixture; strain so that it is absolutely smooth. Let the batter rest for at least 3 hours in a cool place.

3 Heat a 5- or 6-inch iron crêpe pan or a nonstick omelet pan and grease with butter or fat. Wipe out with a paper towel, leaving only a film of shiny grease. Stir up the batter to recombine. Ladle about 2½ tablespoons of the batter to the hot pan. Lift and tilt the pan so the batter covers the bottom completely. Pour any excess batter back into the bowl. Cook over moderate heat until the bottom is lightly browned, 20 to 30 seconds. (Be careful, because crêpes made with sugar can burn.) Flip or turn the crêpe over and cook until spotted brown on the second side, 10 to 15 seconds. As the crêpes cook, stack and keep warm on a plate set over simmering water. Cover with foil and keep hot until ready to serve. *(To make ahead, stack in piles of 6 with sheets of waxed paper in between. Keeps 1 to 2 days wrapped in foil in the refrigerator. Reheat, wrapped in foil, in a 300°F oven 10 to 15 minutes.)*

4 To serve, sprinkle each crêpe with granulated sugar and serve with lemon wedges, or spread with preserves and roll up and sprinkle with sugar, or serve stacked with layers of crushed walnuts mixed with sweetened whipped cream. Serve this last version cold, cut into wedges.

APPLES BAKED ON CABBAGE LEAVES

-»- *Grimolles*   SERVES 6

IN THIS UNUSUAL, earthy yet sophisticated dessert, cabbage leaves are used in place of a pie crust, which keeps the apples moist and tender. A skillet is first lined with the leaves, then filled with a mixture of apples and thick batter flavored with lemon rind, Cognac, and cinnamon. After baking, the slightly burnt cabbage, which can be eaten or not as you wish, imparts a marvelous smoky flavor to the fruit. Serve very warm with vanilla ice cream, unsweetened crème fraîche, or whipped cream.

¾ cup (3½ ounces) all-purpose flour

2 whole eggs

½ cup milk, at room temperature

¼ cup heavy cream, at room temperature

Pinch of salt

2 dashes of ground cinnamon

2 teaspoons grated lemon zest, organic if available

1 tablespoon Cognac

3 to 4 tablespoons granulated sugar

4 tablespoons unsalted butter, melted

1 pound flavorful cooking apples, such as Granny Smith

6 or 7 large cabbage leaves

1 tablespoon light brown sugar

Confectioners' sugar

1 At least 2 hours before serving, place the flour in a medium bowl. With a wooden spoon, make a well in the center, and add the eggs, one by one, stirring until well combined. Then slowly add the milk and cream; mix until absolutely smooth. If the mixture is not smooth, strain it. Flavor with salt, cinnamon, lemon zest, and Cognac. Sweeten with sugar to taste. Stir in half the melted butter.

2 Peel, quarter, and core the apples. Cut them into ⅛-inch-thick slices and fold them into the batter. Cover and let stand at room temperature for about 1 hour.

3 About 1 hour before serving, preheat the oven to 425°F. In a hot nonstick skillet, soften the cabbage leaves one at a time. Place a leaf on the skillet and let it wilt for a second, use tongs to turn the leaf, and let it wilt on the second side. Spread the cabbage leaves out, rib side down, in a 12-inch well-seasoned cast-iron skillet, or on a black pizza pan or round griddle. Flatten them out so they cover the pan without overlapping more than is necessary. Spread the apple batter over the cabbage in a thin, even layer. Sprinkle the brown sugar and remaining melted butter on top.

4 Bake on the middle of the oven until golden brown, about 40 minutes. (The center should still be slightly supple.) Remove the cake from the oven; dust with confectioners' sugar and serve hot from the skillet, or slide onto a large serving plate before cutting.

Pies, Cakes, and Croustades

The pastry-covered pie, called *croustade* in the Languedoc and Guyenne, *pastis* in the Quercy and the Périgord (*postis* in dialect), and *tourtière* in the Tarn and the Landes, is basically the same dish: paper-thin sheets of strudel-like pastry brushed lightly with clarified butter or goose fat and wrapped about a sweetened fruit filling, shaped according to the custom of the region, then baked. The different shapes are interesting.

In the Quercy, the *pastis* is rolled up like strudel, then shaped into a serpentine coil. In the Languedoc, the same cake shaped in this fashion is called *en cabessal*, referring to the strip of cloth wound into a spiral and placed flat on a woman's head to enable her to carry pitchers of water or baskets of grapes. In the Landes, a *tourtière* is a flattened disk; in this region, a *pastis* refers to a kugelhupf-style cake. And in Gascony, the *croustade* (or pastis in patois) is shaped like "a giant overblown tea rose," a description coined by the food writer Anne Penton in her book *Customs and Cookery in the Périgord and the Quercy*.

The name can mean very different things in different regions: Pastis in Gascony and the Quercy may be apples baked in a strudel-type dough, but in the Landes, it is a brioche-type cake flavored with anise and rum. While in the Landes, an apple cake in a strudel-type dough is called a *tourtière*, in the Quercy, it refers to a chicken and salsify pie in a pâte brisée made with pork fat taken from around the kidneys.

Whatever it is called, the pastry is considered so intricate and awesome that few regional bakers, including professionals, ever bother to make it. Local women guard the secret carefully, selling their homemade version to bakeshops, charcuteries, and personal clients. In fact, the pastry is exactly the same as strudel dough. Greek phyllo dough—available frozen or, better yet, fresh nearly everywhere in the United States—makes a fine substitute.

How did these fragile pastry leaves come to be made in France? French gastronomic historians insist they are related to the pastry in the Moroccan *bisteeya* or *pastilla*, the magnificent pie of pigeon meat, almonds, lemons, eggs, cinnamon, and myriad other spices introduced to Spain during the time of the Moorish conquest and brought into France as far as the gates of Poitiers. There are many other evidences of Moorish culinary influences in Southwest France: the preserving of meat as confit (the Moroccans preserve red-fleshed meat in exactly the same way and call it *khlea*); anise-flavored bread; orange-flower water flavoring for cakes; the use of cinnamon and nutmeg in chicken dishes; saffron-flavored tripe and poultry dishes; small almond-flavored cookies; prunes and quince in rich meat stews; fish with spices, onions, and raisins; and meat, fish, and poultry dishes smothered in onion marmalade.

CROUSTADE WITH APPLES AND PRUNES IN ARMAGNAC

➤➤ *Croustade de Pommes et de Pruneaux
à la Gasconne (Pastis Gascon)*   SERVES 6 OR 7

THE BEST GASCON CROUSTADE *(pastis)* I ever tasted was made by a woman from the Gascon town of Eauze. She mixed cooked apples with prunes that had been marinated in Armagnac for six months. This created the following recipe filling. If the decoration of roses atop the croustade seems too complicated, simply wrap the fruit in the dough, bake it, and call it a *tourtière landaise*. Serve it lukewarm. In Gascony, long, thin scissors are used to cut this cake into wedges.

For an intense apple flavor, the apples are cooked in a vacuum-pack pouch (the *sous vide* method).

2½ pounds Granny Smith or Pippin apples, peeled, cored, and thickly sliced

¾ cup plus 2 tablespoons granulated sugar

2 thin strips of lemon zest, organic if available

1 vanilla bean, split

30 Prunes in Armagnac (pages 397–398), including 5 tablespoons of the prune-Armagnac syrup

⅓ cup clarified butter, melted

½ teaspoon orange-flower water

2 teaspoons Armagnac

9 or 10 large strudel or phyllo leaves, or homemade strudel dough

Confectioners' sugar

1 Slice the apples and mix with the sugar and lemon peel. With a small sharp knife, scrape the vanilla seeds from the bean and add to apples. Vacuum pack in a boilable pouch. Steam over boiling water for 10 to 15 minutes, or until soft to the touch. Remove and drop into icy slush until completely cold, about 30 minutes. Keep apples in the pouch in the refrigerator until ready to use. (The apples will keep for up to 1 week.) Drain off liquid before using. Alternatively, combine apples with sugar, vanilla, and lemon zest in a heavy saucepan. Cover and cook over very low heat until the apples are soft, about 20 minutes. Let cool; drain just before using.

2 Pit the Armagnac-soaked prunes. Cut into ½-inch pieces and return to ¼ cup of the prune-Armagnac syrup until ready to use.

3 Mix 2 tablespoons of the melted clarified butter with the orange-flower water, 1 tablespoon sugar, the remaining 1 tablespoon prune-Armagnac syrup, and the Armagnac.

4 Two to 3 hours before serving, place a baking stone or heavy baking sheet on lowest oven rack. Preheat the oven to 400°F. Lightly brush a 15-inch round pan, such as a pizza pan (preferably with a black finish) with 1 tablespoon of the remaining clarified butter.

5 Unroll the strudel or phyllo leaves in front of you and cover with a damp towel. Working quickly (this pastry dries out fast when exposed to air), brush the top leaf lightly with melted clarified butter. Fold in half lengthwise and brush each side lightly with butter. Place one end of the folded leaf in the center of the pan, letting the sheet hang over the side of the pan (Figure 1). Repeat with the remaining leaves, arranging them spoke fashion so that the inner ends are stacked in a hub and the outer ends barely touch (Figures 2 and 3).

6 Very lightly sprinkle some of the reserved scented butter-liquid over the dough that extends over the edge of the pan. Place drained pitted prunes in a 10-inch circle in the center of the pastry. Top with drained cold apples.

7 To enclose the filling, start with the last leaf placed on the pan. Lift up the outer end and bring it toward the center, twisting the piece once so that the underside faces you. Roll up the end of the strip loosely to form a cup-shaped "rose" and set it flat on the filling, pressing lightly so it adheres (Figure 4). Repeat with the remaining leaves, placing the flowers close together to cover the top of the cake. (Do not worry if a little filling shows through.) Sprinkle the top very lightly with the remaining scented butter-liquid, drizzle with the remaining clarified butter, and dust with 3 tablespoons granulated sugar (Figure 5).

8 Place the pan in the oven on hot baking stone or baking sheet and bake for 12 minutes. Reduce the oven temperature to 350°F. Bake for 20 to 25 minutes longer, or until the croustade is golden and crisp. Slide onto a wire rack. Sprinkle 2 more tablespoons granulated sugar over the top and let cool to lukewarm. Just before serving, dust with confectioners' sugar.

(continued)

→ Strudel leaves are stronger and fewer to the pound than phyllo leaves. They do a better job of keeping the "roses" rigid after shaping, but if you can buy only the thinner phyllo leaves, that won't lessen the rustic charm of this wonderful, easy cake.

→ If you prepare the cake early in the day and wish to prevent the bottom layer of pastry from becoming too wet, use stale sponge cake or stale white bread crumbs mixed with a little sugar between the bottom leaves of the pastry. This makes an excellent foil for absorbing the moisture of the fruit fillings.

CROUSTADE WITH QUINCE AND PRUNES

➜➤ *Croustade de Languedoc* SERVES 6 TO 8

THIS CROUSTADE, an enclosed pie with a rich, intensely flavored filling of quince and prunes, originates in the Languedoc, where it is subtitled *en cabessal*. The pastry, made of strudel-type dough, is brushed lavishly with melted butter and oil so that when it is curved into a coil it will not crack or break.

This croustade is beloved in the Languedoc for its special aroma and taste. Quince preserve (rather than jelly) is full of flavor and texture. The taste of quince is tangy and balances the sweetness of the prunes. In my version I have substituted a light, flaky pastry for the strudel dough and have shaped the croustade into a simple round.

¾ pound pitted prunes

2 cups warm brewed tea, preferably linden or orange pekoe (optional)

¾ cup granulated sugar

1 teaspoon vanilla extract

1 tablespoon fresh lemon juice

½ teaspoon grated lemon zest

1½ tablespoons prune eau-de-vie, Slivovitz, or Armagnac

Pâte Brisée (page 92)

1 cup quince preserves

Egg glaze: 1 egg yolk beaten with 1 tablespoon milk

Confectioners' sugar

Crème fraîche or unsweetened whipped cream

1 If the prunes are hard, soak them in the tea until soft, 10 to 15 minutes. Drain, discarding the tea.

2 Place the sugar and 1½ cups water in a medium saucepan. Bring to a boil, stirring until sugar dissolves; boil for 5 minutes. Add the prunes to the syrup. Reduce the heat and simmer for 20 minutes. Remove from the heat and let the prunes cool in the syrup. Add the vanilla, lemon juice, and lemon zest. Cover and refrigerate for 1 hour.

3 Meanwhile, bring the pastry dough to room temperature.

4 Drain the prunes, reserving the syrup. Coarsely chop the prunes. Put in a bowl and stir in the eau-de-vie.

(continued)

5 Gently heat the quince preserves in a small saucepan until just melted. Stir in one fourth of the reserved prune syrup and let cool completely.

6 Preheat the oven to 425°F. Divide the dough into two equal parts. Roll out 1 piece of dough between two sheets of lightly floured waxed paper into an 11-inch circle. Fit the pastry into a 9- or 10-inch tart pan with a removable bottom, leaving an extra inch of overhang. Prick the bottom with the tines of a fork. Roll out the second piece of pastry.

7 Spread the quince preserves over the bottom of the pastry-lined pan. Top with the prunes in an even layer. Brush the exposed margin of pastry with egg glaze. Cover with the second round of dough, pressing the edges together to seal. Trim to ½ inch and crimp the edges to seal.

8 Brush the top of the pie with the egg glaze. Score the top of the tart pastry with crisscross lines and make a few holes on top with the point of a sharp knife so that steam can escape during baking.

9 Bake in the oven for 15 minutes. Reduce the oven temperature to 350°F and bake for 35 minutes longer. Dust the top with confectioners' sugar and bake until the top is shiny and glazed, about 10 minutes. Transfer to a wire rack and let cool. Serve lukewarm or cold with crème fraîche or unsweetened whipped cream.

Basque Cake With Pastry Cream Filling

→ *Gâteau Basque*   SERVES 6 TO 8

THERE ARE AS MANY VERSIONS of *gâteau basque* as there are people who bake it, and the Basques like nothing better than to sit around and discuss the relative merits of one baker's recipe versus another's. It's like listening to Toulousains talk about cassoulet, Provençals arguing about bouillabaisse, or Alsatians quarreling over choucroute. A combination cake and pie, *gâteau basque* is stuffed with pastry cream flavored with almonds, anise, rum, orange-flower water, and Armagnac.

The town of Itxassou along the Nive River is famous for its black cherries, which make for a most delicious variation. I have used top-quality black cherry preserves with good results and that's what I suggest in the variation that follows.

The dough is a little tricky to make because at first you think you are making a cake, then all of a sudden you discover you have made a pie. Actually, if you know how to cream butter with sugar until it is very pale in color and fluffy and how to roll out a piece of delicate dough, you should have no trouble at all.

Begin 1 day in advance.

Pastry Cream (page 377), flavored with 2 tablespoons Basque Aromatic Mixture (page 361), chilled

6 ounces (about 1¼ cups) unbleached all-purpose flour

3 ounces (⅔ cup) cake flour

1 teaspoon double-acting baking powder

⅛ teaspoon salt

9 tablespoons unsalted butter, at room temperature

½ cup plus 1 tablespoon sugar, preferably superfine

2 eggs, lightly beaten

1½ tablespoons Basque Aromatic Mixture

1 teaspoon heavy cream

1 Early in the day, prepare the Pastry Cream. Cover and refrigerate.

2 Make the dough: Sift the all-purpose flour, cake flour, baking powder, and salt into a bowl; set aside. In another bowl with a wooden spoon or an electric mixer, beat the butter until fluffy. Gradually add the sugar, creaming with the butter until very light and fluffy. The mixture must not feel granular.

(continued)

2 Set aside 2 tablespoons beaten egg for glazing the top. Add the remaining eggs to the butter and sugar by spoonfuls, beating well between additions to blend completely. If using an electric mixer, add the eggs at low speed. Add the Basque Aromatic Mixture and one fourth of the sifted flour. Fold in the remaining flour and gather into a ball. Do not overmix or knead the dough. It will be very sticky and soft. Dust lightly with flour and invert into a wide soup bowl. Wrap in waxed paper. Let rest overnight in the refrigerator at least 5 hours, or overnight.

3 Divide the dough into 2 unequal parts, one slightly larger than the other. Roll out the larger portion into a 10-inch round between sheets of lightly floured waxed paper. (Loosen the paper from time to time to facilitate rolling.) Remove the top sheet of paper and invert the dough into an 8-inch cake pan; line the bottom and sides. Peel off the paper; if the pastry tears, use edges to repair or pinch the torn pastry together. Trim the edges and fill with pastry cream. Roll out the smaller ball of dough into an 8-inch round. Remove the paper and invert onto filling; crimp edges. Chill completely.

4 Preheat oven to 425°F. Place a baking sheet or tile on lowest oven rack.

5 Brush the pastry with reserved beaten egg diluted with 1 teaspoon cream. Score the top decoratively with the back of the tines of a fork. Make 3 slashes for escaping steam. Place on the heated baking sheet or hot tile. Immediately reduce the oven temperature to 375°F. Bake for 45 to 50 minutes, or until the cake is light golden brown.

6 Remove to a rack and let cool 10 minutes. Invert out of pan and invert again onto a rack to cool completely. The cake will harden as it cools. Serve at room temperature, cut in wedges.

VARIATION I: ITXASSOU CAKE WITH BLACK CHERRY FILLING

Make the cake as directed above, but substitute 12 ounces black cherry preserves for the Pastry Cream.

VARIATION II: BAYONNE CAKE WITH PASTRY CREAM AND BLACK CHERRY PRESERVES

Place 1⅓ cups Basque Aromatic Mixture–flavored Pastry Cream on pastry; cover with about ½ cup black cherry preserves, warmed gently until spreadable.

Inspired by a recipe of Rosalie Muruamendiaraz of the restaurant Euskalduna in Bayonne.

PASTRY CREAM

Crème Pâtissière

1 cup milk

1 vanilla bean, 3 inches long, split, or ½ teaspoon vanilla extract

1½ tablespoons superfine sugar

Pinch of salt

4 teaspoons cornstarch

3 egg yolks

1 tablespoon unsalted butter

2 tablespoons heavy cream

1 tablespoon flavoring (use Basque Aromatic Mixture for Gâteau Basque, page 361)

1 Bring the milk to a boil with the vanilla bean, if using, in a small saucepan. Cover and set aside.

2. Place the sugar, salt, cornstarch, and egg yolks in a mixing bowl; beat until pale yellow and thick. Beat in the vanilla extract, if using.

3. Remove the vanilla bean from the hot milk. Gradually beat the hot milk into the egg yolk mixture. Pour into a clean saucepan and cook over moderate heat, stirring constantly, until boiling. Reduce the heat to low and whisk vigorously until the custard is smooth, 1 to 2 minutes. Remove from the heat and continue to beat vigorously for 30 seconds longer. Strain into a bowl.

4. Add the butter and stir until melted. Stir in the cream and flavoring. Let stand until cool, stirring, from time to time. Place a sheet of buttered waxed paper directly on the cream to inhibit the formation of a skin, cover, and refrigerate until chilled.

Marie-Claude's Chocolate Cake with Fleur de Sel

→ *Gâteau Chocolat, Fleur de Sel* SERVES 6

I'VE MENTIONED MY FRIEND Marie-Claude Gracia in introductions to several other recipes. As you can see I am a huge fan and couldn't resist adding one more. This cake may remind you of a particularly good brownie, but the addition of fleur de sel turns it into something quite unusual and wonderful.

The first time I tasted coarse flakes of sea salt sprinkled over a chocolate cake, I was astounded how good it was. The mild sea salt flavor played against the sweetness and brought out the chocolate flavor.

A friend who tasted the cake said all it needed was some crème anglaise, a few raspberries, and a glass of Ruby Port to make it perfect. Another friend, a professional baker, felt that the long creaming of the butter and sugar created not only a lighter than usual chocolate cake, but also an extremely moist one.

For best results, prepare the cake at least one day in advance. It will keep for several days at room temperature, improving as it "matures."

7 ounces (1 stick plus 6 tablespoons) unsalted butter, plus ½ tablespoon

7 ounces or 2 dark chocolate bars (3½ ounces each) containing at least 70 percent pure chocolate, preferably Valrhona, broken into small pieces

1 cup superfine sugar

5 eggs, at room temperature, separated

½ cup all-purpose flour

2 tablespoons cocoa powder, preferably Valrhona, not Dutch-processed

1 teaspoon baking powder

Pinch of fine salt

2 pinches of fleur de sel from the Ile de Ré, or Maldon sea salt

½ recipe (1¼ cups) Crème Anglaise (pages 380–381) without bay leaves

1 cup fresh raspberries

1 Preheat the oven to 350°F. Line a 9-inch round baking dish, preferably ceramic, with a round of parchment paper. Butter the paper with the ½ tablespoon butter.

2 Place the chocolate in a bowl set over simmering water; let it slowly melt without stirring. Remove from the heat and let cool slightly.

3 Meanwhile, cream the butter and sugar together until light, white, soft, and creamy, about 10 minutes. Add the egg yolks to the butter-sugar mixture one by one, then blend in the chocolate, until the mixture is entirely smooth and well blended. In a small bowl, combine the flour, cocoa, baking powder, and fine salt; sieve directly over the chocolate mixture and fold in to combine.

4 Beat the whites until glossy and stiff enough to "cut," then stir a large spoonful into the chocolate batter to lighten it. Add the remaining whites and fold gently, carefully lifting the heavy chocolate from the bottom of the bowl, to thoroughly mix in the whites, keeping everything light and fluffy. (The more air you lose the heavier the cake will be.)

5 Scrape the batter into the prepared baking dish, scatter the fleur de sel over the top, and set in the oven. Bake for 30 to 40 minutes, or until the edges are set but the center still jiggles slightly when shaken. Turn off the heat but leave the cake in the oven to cool with the door slightly ajar for about 15 minutes. Remove from the oven, let cool on a rack, then cover and let rest overnight at room temperature.

6 When the cake is completely cold, unmold, then turn right side up onto a round platter. Garnish each slice with a few spoonfuls of Crème Anglaise and some raspberries.

Cake on a Spit With Bay Leaf–Scented Crème Anglaise

➤ *Gâteau à la Broche, Crème Anglaise Parfumée au Laurier*

IMAGINE THAT YOU'RE at a festive dinner in the Auvergne. In the center of the table there's a two-foot-high, multi layered cake called affectionately the "pyramid of the Mountains." It looks a lot like a bronzed fir tree. When it's time for dessert, the host cuts the smoky-flavored cake in horizontal rounds, then serves them with a nice spoonful of bay leaf–scented crème anglaise.

This amazing cake took up to 5 hours to make. Cooked on a spit in front of the fire, it was patiently built out of thin layerings of batter made with sugar, flour, eggs, and butter. A true peasant dish popular in areas of the Quercy, the Pyrenees, and the Rouergue, it is a relic from another era.

Even this avid cook lacks the patience to make this *gâteau à la broche* (similar to the German *baumkuchen*). Even in Southwest France, it's usually provided on demand by specialist caterers who have their secret recipes. But now you, too, can command this cake directly from a master artisan in France. Go to the French website, Bienmanger.com, an amazing resource in English and French, and you'll find an excellent *gâteau à la broche* to order online. All you have to do is unwrap the package when it arrives and make the bay leaf–scented crème anglaise.

½ vanilla bean, split lengthwise, or 1½ teaspoons vanilla extract

6 tablespoons sugar

2 cups milk

2 imported bay leaves

1 strip of lemon zest, organic if available

5 egg yolks

Pinch of salt

1 *gâteau à la broche*

1 Scrape the seeds from vanilla bean into a small dish; reserve the pod. Add 1 tablespoon of the sugar to the vanilla seeds and rub with your fingers to blend well. Set the vanilla sugar aside.

2 Scald the milk with the vanilla bean pod, bay leaves, and lemon zest in a heavy medium saucepan. Remove from the heat and let stand until cooled to room temperature. Remove vanilla bean from milk. (The vanilla pod can be rinsed and dried and used to flavor sugar in a bin.) Discard the lemon zest and bay leaves.

3 Beat the egg yolks, vanilla sugar, and remaining 5 tablespoons sugar in a mixing bowl until the mixture is pale and forms a ribbon when the whisk is lifted, 2 to 3 minutes. Whisk in a pinch of salt. Scrape into a heavy enameled saucepan and warm over very low heat, stirring constantly.

4 Gradually stir in the hot milk. Cook over low heat, stirring constantly with a wooden spoon, until the mixture thickens enough to coat the back of the spoon heavily and the froth on the surface has disappeared, about 10 minutes; the custard will register about 165°F. Do not allow to boil. Immediately remove from the heat.

5 Strain the custard through a fine sieve into a chilled mixing bowl set over ice. Cool down quickly, stirring constantly. Blend in the vanilla extract at this point, if using. When cold, cover the surface with plastic wrap and refrigerate until needed.

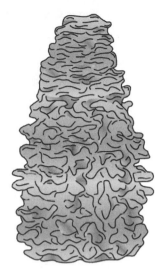

Gâteau à la Broche

6 Slice the gâteau in horizontal rounds. Serve each slice with the crème anglaise.

WALNUT TART FROM MASSEUBE

⇥ *Tarte aux Noix à la Masseube*   SERVES 10

PROVENCE, THE SAVOY, and Dauphiné all have their regional walnut cakes and tarts, as do the Périgord and the Quercy. This rich, rustic version comes from the Gascon town of Masseube. The walnuts are cooked in a toffee-like syrup and baked in a sugar crust that appears to be wavy rather than flat. Plain granulated sugar is sprinkled on top.

Fresh nuts make a huge difference in any dessert. You can shell them yourself, buy them from a reputable source, or purchase shelled walnuts in tins. Some markets now carry DOC Périgord vacuum-sealed walnut halves, which are the best.

This cake keeps about a week if well wrapped in foil and kept in a cool, dry place. It is excellent with vanilla ice cream or unsweetened crème fraîche and sliced fresh fruit or berries. This cake is extremely rich; plan on serving very thin slices. The filling can be doubled for a thicker cake.

The cake improves in flavor, so make it at least 3 days in advance.

(continued)

Sugar Crust (at right)

1 cup plus 1½ tablespoons sugar

½ pound shelled walnuts, chopped into pieces the size of small blueberries

½ cup milk or light cream, heated

7 tablespoons unsalted butter, at room temperature

Egg glaze: 1 egg yolk beaten with 1 tablespoon cream

1 Make the Sugar Crust as directed. Chill a minimum of 3 hours, or even better, overnight.

2 Roll out the larger round of pastry between 2 sheets of lightly floured waxed paper. Fit the round into a 9- or 9½-inch tart pan with a removable bottom. The pastry will be thin; if it tears, simply pinch to seal any holes. Set the tart shell in the freezer. Meanwhile, roll out the remaining pastry and trim if necessary to make a perfect round, 11 to 12 inches in diameter. Place on a cookie sheet and refrigerate until ready to use.

3 Preheat the oven to 450°F. In a heavy, deep 4-quart pot, preferably stainless steel or a copper preserving pan, bring 1 cup of the sugar and ⅓ cup water to a boil over moderate heat, stirring until the sugar dissolves. Raise heat to moderately high, cover, and cook for 2 minutes; then reduce the heat to low, uncover, and cook without stirring until the syrup is light caramel, about 10 minutes. Gently swirl the pan from time to time to even out the color as it develops. As soon as the caramel colors, immediately remove it from the heat.

4 Meanwhile, warm the chopped walnuts in a dry skillet over low heat or in the oven for 2 to 3 minutes. Do not let darken.

5 As soon as the syrup stops boiling, gradually stir in the hot milk; be very careful because the mixture bubbles up considerably. Stir in the butter and the warm walnuts. Return to moderate heat and cook, stirring, at a slow boil for 4 to 5 minutes. The temperature of the mixture should remain at 240°F on a candy thermometer.

6 Meanwhile, line a baking sheet with foil, shiny side down, and set on the rack of the oven. Remove the tart shell from the freezer and carefully pour the hot walnut mixture into the shell. Immediately, brush the rim of the pastry with egg glaze and place the refrigerated round of pastry on top. Press all around to seal; then crimp the edge decoratively. The top will be bubbly and become wavy. Brush it lightly with egg glaze; pierce once or twice in the center and set on the hot foil-lined baking sheet in the oven.

7 Immediately reduce the oven temperature to 400°F and bake for 15 minutes. Quickly brush the top crust a second time with egg glaze and sprinkle very lightly with the remaining sugar. Reduce the oven temperature to 300°F and bake for 20 minutes longer.

8 Transfer the tart to a rack and let cool for at least 4 hours. Wrap well in foil and store in an airtight container for at least 3 or up to 5 days before serving.

NOTE TO THE COOK

This dessert was given to me by the pastry chef at André Daguin's restaurant. When she first described it, I was a little apprehensive about pouring a hot caramel onto raw pastry dough. Seeing my disbelief, she very kindly decided to teach me the three important tricks for success. Once you know them, it's a cinch to make:

⇥ The milk must be hot when you add it to the caramel;

⇥ The filling must cook to the soft-ball stage on a candy thermometer (234°F to 240°F); and

⇥ The pastry dough must be ice-cold (frozen) when the hot walnut filling is added to it.

SUGAR CRUST

Pâte Sucrée   MAKES ENOUGH PASTRY FOR A THIN 9 OR 10-INCH DOUBLE CRUST TART

8½ ounces (2 cups) unbleached all-purpose flour or a mixture of pastry flour and all-purpose flour

⅓ cup sugar

Pinch of salt

9 tablespoons unsalted butter, chilled and cut into tiny dice

1 egg

3½ tablespoons heavy cream

½ teaspoon pure vanilla extract

1 Combine the flour, sugar, and salt in a food processor. "Sift" by pulsing the machine once. Scatter the butter bits on top of the flour and pulse 5 or 6 times, until the butter is the size of small peas.

2 In a small bowl, lightly beat the egg. Blend in the cream and vanilla. Add to the dough and process for 5 seconds; dump onto a sheet of waxed paper. Break off nuggets and flatten forward with the heel of your hand or a dough scraper to distribute fat and flour evenly. Gather the dough into a ball and divide in two, with one half a bit larger than the other for the bottom crust. Wrap both in waxed paper and refrigerate for at least 3 hours or overnight.

Madeleines From Dax

→ *Madeleines de Dax* MAKES ABOUT 18 3-INCH CAKES OR 24 2-INCH CAKES

THESE SOFT, SPONGY, buttery madeleines are not the same as the *madeleines de commercy*, which one finds elsewhere, or the génoise type that appear in so many cookbooks, or, for that matter, the dunking type described so vividly and nostalgically by Marcel Proust. These lovely Southwest-style madeleines are more like little cakes, in the traditional shape (like a shell on one side, with an adorable hump on the other), flavored with lemon zest or orange-flower water. These are exquisite served with sorbets, homemade jams, and fruit compotes, or simply eaten without any accompaniment at all.

The patron saint of the Landais town of Mont-de-Marsan is Sainte-Madeleine, and in the neighboring town of Dax, madeleines have been famous for many years. Both towns hold madeleine bake-offs, and recipes vary widely. At Michel Guérard's Eugénie-les-Bains establishment, the madeleines served for breakfast are actually closer to slices of orange-flavored chiffon cake.

I learned this recipe from a young male baker who gave me the recipe in "egg weights"—the old way of setting culinary proportions. "Egg weights" are determined by weighing an egg, then weighing out the flour, sugar, and butter using the weight of the egg as a constant. If you visualize an old-fashioned fulcrum-type balance scale, the method makes more sense.

Begin 1 day in advance.

2 large eggs

Pinch of salt

5 tablespoons superfine sugar

1 teaspoon vanilla extract

5½ tablespoons unbleached all-purpose flour

5½ tablespoons cake flour

1 teaspoon baking powder

5 tablespoons clarified butter or Plugra, melted and cooled

2 tablespoons heavy cream

1½ teaspoons orange-flower water

1 tablespoon softened unsalted butter

1 A day in advance, combine the eggs, salt, and sugar in a mixing bowl. Whisk until thick and light in color, about 2 minutes.

2 Mix together the all-purpose and cake flours with the baking powder. Sift them twice. Gradually stir the dry ingredients into the egg mixture. Do not overbeat. Add the clarified butter, the cream, the orange-flower water, and the vanilla; stir gently until smooth. Cover with plastic wrap and refrigerate the batter overnight.

3 The following day, preheat the oven to 425°F. Using a pastry brush, coat the ridged hollows of a madeleine pan with the softened butter. (It is not necessary to dust with flour.) Use a teaspoon and a small spatula to barely fill each hollow about two-thirds full with batter. Tap the mold on the table to allow the batter to settle.

4 Bake for 5 minutes. Reduced the oven temperature to 325°F and bake for 7 to 10 minutes longer, until the madeleines are pale golden and just turning brown around the edges.

5 Use the tip of a knife at the base of each madeleine to turn them out onto wire racks to cool slightly. Serve warm and freshly baked with fruit compotes, sorbets, and custards. Leftover madeleines may be stored in an airtight tin and reheated gently before serving.

NOTES TO THE COOK

→→ The batter must be made a day in advance so that the proteins in the flour can relax, and the madeleines will be very tender when baked.

→→ You can bake a batch of fresh madeleines each day (storing the unused batter in the refrigerator); or cook them in batches if you have only one mold with 6, 8, or 12 shapes.

→→ Madeleine pans should never be scrubbed with harsh abrasives. Scratched pans cause madeleines to bake up very pale on the ridged sides.

Fruit Desserts

Roast Figs in the Style of the Pyrenees

➤ *Figues Rôties*   SERVES 6

DURING SEPTEMBER AND OCTOBER, when small purple figs are available, you can transform them into these cool, sweet, peppery delights—crunchy on the outside, softly melting on the inside.

1 tablespoon unsalted butter

18 small purple (black Mission) figs, slightly overripe

¼ cup plus 1 teaspoon sugar

½ cup shelled walnuts pieces

1 tablespoon chestnut or acacia honey

Juice of 1 lemon

2 or 3 turns of the pepper mill

Crème fraîche, as accompaniment

1 Preheat the oven to 400°F. Butter a shallow, flameproof baking dish. Place the figs in it side by side, stems up. Sprinkle with ¼ cup of the sugar and 1 tablespoon water.

2 Bake the figs for 20 minutes, basting from time to time with the syrupy juices in the dish.

3 Scatter the walnuts over the figs; sprinkle the remaining 1 teaspoon sugar on top. Reduce the oven temperature to 300°F and bake for 10 minutes longer.

4 Transfer the figs and walnuts to a serving dish. Add the honey to the cooking juices in the baking dish. Set over low heat and cook, stirring, to blend. Spoon the syrup over figs. Sprinkle with lemon juice and pepper. Cover and refrigerate until chilled. Serve cold, with a bowl of crème fraîche on the side.

FRESH STRAWBERRIES WITH PEPPERCORNS AND RED WINE

→ *Fraises au Poivre et au Vin Rouge*   SERVES 4 TO 6

I FOUND THIS DESSERT described in a little Landais cookbook. The recipe called for a touch of cinnamon. I have substituted freshly ground black pepper—not a modern conceit, since the combination of fruit with peppercorns is traditional in the Southwest.

2 pints fresh strawberries	Squeeze of fresh lemon juice
2 to 3 tablespoons sugar	4 to 6 turns of the pepper mill
¼ cup dry red wine	

1 Wipe the strawberries if they are sandy. Hull the berries and sprinkle with 2 tablespoons of the sugar. Let stand for 2 hours in a serving dish at room temperature to draw out their juices.

2 Sprinkle with the red wine and the remaining sugar, if needed for sweetness. Let stand for 20 to 30 minutes longer.

3 Just before serving, add a squeeze of lemon juice and a grinding of fresh pepper.

PRUNES IN SAUTERNE

→→ *Pruneaux au Sauterne*   SERVES 4

THE LUSCIOUS, NECTARLIKE fruitiness and enormous fullness of Sauterne, combined with the flavor of prunes, make this an exceptional dessert. For a spectacular yet understated ending to a meal, serve with Madeleines from Dax.

The flavor improves enormously if this dessert is prepared two to three days in advance. The great French Sauternes is not needed to make this special dessert.

12 ounces pitted prunes

2 cups Sauterne or other sweet white wine

½ vanilla bean, split lengthwise

2 tablespoons sugar

2-inch piece of lemon zest, organic if available

1 cinnamon stick

1 Soak the prunes in the wine for 4 to 6 hours.

2 Scrape the seeds from the vanilla bean into a small bowl; reserve the pod. Add the sugar and rub the seeds with the sugar to blend well.

3 In an enameled or stainless steel saucepan, simmer the prunes in the wine with the vanilla sugar, vanilla bean pod, lemon zest, and cinnamon stick for 10 minutes. Let cool completely, then cover and refrigerate until well chilled, at least 6 hours and up to 3 days. Serve cool.

POACHED FIGS IN RASPBERRY AND RED WINE SAUCE

➤➤ *Figues Pochées au Vin Rouge
et au Coulis de Framboise*

SERVES 6

A COOK I KNOW once told me there is a wine for every fruit to bring out its flavor: Riesling for nectarines; Sauternes for prunes; and red wine for red berries, pears, and black fresh figs.

1 pint fresh raspberries, or 1 package frozen unsweetened raspberries, thawed and drained

2½ tablespoons fresh lemon juice

¾ cup superfine sugar

1 bottle (750 ml) dry red wine, preferably Bordeaux

12 to 18 firm small fresh purple (black Mission) figs

Zest of 1 orange, organic if available

1 In a food processor, puree the raspberries with the lemon juice and ⅓ cup of the sugar for 2 minutes. Strain through a sieve to remove the seeds.

2 Place the raspberry puree in a large nonreactive saucepan. Add the red wine and remaining sugar. Bring to a boil, reduce the heat to low, and cook, stirring constantly, until sugar is completely dissolved.

3 Add the figs to the raspberry-wine syrup and poach over low heat, uncovered, for 4 minutes, turning them every minute or so as they cook. Remove the figs with a slotted spoon and arrange them in a shallow bowl, stem side up. Boil the poaching liquid until reduced to about 1¼ cups. Spoon over the figs and refrigerate until chilled.

4 Make a garnish with the orange zest: Cut the zest into thin julienne strips. Boil in a small saucepan of water for 3 minutes; drain and rinse under cold running water. Drain well and pat dry. Decorate the top of each fig with a few strands of orange zest before serving.

NOTE TO THE COOK

The months of September and October are the time that you will find fresh, violet-hued figs at fine greengrocers. It is certainly worth trying this very easy and elegant dish during that time.

VARIATION: PEACHES IN RASPBERRY AND RED WINE SAUCE

Make the recipe as directed above, substituting 12 peeled small whole peaches for the figs. Omit the orange zest and garnish with a few whole fresh raspberries.

MELON-ANISETTE ICE

→► *Sorbet au Melon et à l'Anisette*

THIS COMBINATION IS INSPIRED by the Catalan dessert *melon con anis*. This dessert is best served the day it is prepared.

SERVES 4 TO 6

1 cup superfine sugar

1½ to 2 pounds ripe cantaloupe

3 to 4 tablespoons fresh lemon juice

5 to 8 tablespoons anisette liqueur (see Note below)

1 Make the sugar syrup: In a medium saucepan, combine the sugar with 1½ cups water. Cook over moderate heat, stirring, until the syrup is clear and the sugar is dissolved. Remove from the heat and cool completely.

2 Peel and seed the melon; cut into large cubes. Puree in a food processor, then strain through a sieve into a bowl. Stir in the sugar syrup. Add enough lemon juice to bring up flavor and offset sweetness. Cover and refrigerate until cold.

3 Pour into an ice cream maker and freeze according to the manufacturer's directions. Toward the end, add the anisette to taste and finish freezing.

4 Pack into a covered container and freeze for up to 8 hours before serving. Spoon a teaspoon or two of the remaining anisette over each serving.

NOTE TO THE COOK

Different brands of anisette liqueur are of different strengths; I use ¼ cup if using Marie Brizard.

Green Izarra Sorbet

Sorbet à la Vieille Liqueur du Pays Basque: Izarra

IT IS NOT ALWAYS EASY to find Izarra, the old herbal liqueur of the Basque country. Izarra means star. There are two types: yellow and green. The yellow is lighter in flavor, while the green is lustier and drier in taste. Izarra is prepared from an ancient secret formula, using exotic plants from the Pyrenees, herbs, honey, Armagnac, and spices, including saffron. The yellow type is made from as many as thirty-two plants; the green from forty-eight. When I visited the Izarra distillery in Bayonne I saw such things as mint, coriander, anise, cardamom, star anise, caraway, angelica, vanilla, nutmeg, bitter almonds, dried celery, all laid out in boxes as they are sometimes in health food stores.

Tradition has it that in the Pyrenees Izarra was sprinkled on snow, then eaten—a forerunner, perhaps, to this sorbet. If Izarra is unobtainable, try the variation made with Chartreuse at the end of this recipe; it's not authentically Southwest, but it's good.

This ice is best if made a day ahead and allowed to ripen.

2 cups minus 2 tablespoons superfine sugar

¼ cup green Izarra plus more for pouring over each serving

⅓ cup fresh orange juice

¼ cup fresh lemon juice

Green food coloring (optional)

½ cup heavy cream

1 A day in advance, dissolve the sugar in 4 cups water over moderate heat, stirring. If sugar crystals appear on the inner sides of the pan, brush down with a brush dipped in cold water. Boil undisturbed for 5 minutes. Remove from the heat. Let cool slightly, then add the Izarra. Let the syrup cool completely.

2 Stir the orange juice and lemon juice into the Izarra syrup. If desired, add a few drops of food coloring to obtain a mint-green hue.

3 Pour into an ice cream maker and freeze according to the manufactuer's instructions, adding the cream just before it freezes solid. Pack into a covered container and freeze for at least 4 hours, or overnight. Pour about 1 tablespoon Izarra over each serving.

VARIATION: GREEN CHARTREUSE SORBET

Make the sorbet as described above, but substitute ½ cup green Chartreuse for the Izarra, and use ⅔ cup orange juice and ¼ cup lemon juice.

Inspired by a recipe from Bernard Cousseau.

Red Wine Sorbet

→ *Sorbet au Vin Rouge*

IN A BORDELAISE COOKBOOK, I read a description of a fruit soup made with cherries and a St.-Emilion wine, spiced with cinnamon and cloves. I thought it would be fun to adapt the recipe to make a true sorbet—not a slushy granita—with red wine and fresh fruit.

When fresh fruit is out of season, I have found better-quality frozen raspberries than cherries. (If you do use frozen cherries, add a little kirsch to bring up their flavor.) I add a little eau de framboise to frozen raspberries, a colorless eau-de-vie or *alcool blanc* produced from many pounds of fresh fruit—expensive but worth it. (Avoid fruit-flavored brandies, which will only give this sherbet a cheap taste.)

Begin 1 to 2 days in advance.

¾ cup superfine sugar

1½ cups fruity red wine, such as Zinfandel or Chiroubles

1 pint fresh raspberries, or 1 package (10 ounces) frozen unsweetened raspberries, thawed

1 cinnamon stick

1 whole clove

¾ teaspoon vanilla extract

⅔ cup fresh orange juice

¼ cup fresh lemon juice

1½ tablespoons raspberry (framboise) eau-de-vie

1 A day or 2 in advance, combine the sugar and 1⅔ cups water in a medium saucepan. Cook, stirring, over moderate heat until the syrup is clear and the sugar is dissolved. Boil undisturbed for 5 minutes. Remove from the heat and let cool completely.

2 Meanwhile, in a nonreactive saucepan, simmer the wine with the raspberries, cinnamon stick, and clove for 15 minutes. Remove from the heat and let cool completely.

3 Combine sugar syrup, spiced wine, vanilla, orange juice, and lemon juice in a glass or stainless steel bowl. Cover and refrigerate for 1 to 2 days to ripen.

4 Early the day of serving, strain the liquid; discard spices and raspberry seeds. You should have about 1 quart liquid. Pour into an ice-cream maker and freeze according to the manufacturer's instructions, adding the eau-de-vie just before the sorbet hardens completely.

5 Pack into a covered container and freeze until ready to serve. This is best if served the same day.

NOTE TO THE COOK

If the sorbet crystallizes, dump it into the work bowl of a food processor and process 5 seconds. The sorbet will only be better and lighter for this last-minute *truc*.

Prune and Armagnac Ice Cream

➤➤ *Glace aux Pruneaux à l'Armagnac*   MAKES 2 QUARTS; SERVES 10 TO 12

THIS IS A VARIATION of a marvelous creation by André Daguin. It is perhaps the most elegant ice cream I know. It should be made with prunes that have been soaked in Armagnac for at least 2 weeks. To give an illusion of extra richness but not too many extra calories, I add a little heavy cream when the ice cream has nearly solidified. This way, the butterfat in the cream will "glide" into the chilled ice cream, endowing it with a satiny texture.

Prepare 1 day in advance.

1 quart milk, heated

1 small piece of vanilla bean, split down one side, or 1½ teaspoons vanilla extract

10 egg yolks

1 cup plus 1 tablespoon superfine sugar

Pinch of salt

30 Prunes in Armagnac (pages 397–398), pitted, plus ¼ cup of the syrup, plus extra prunes for garnish, if you have them

½ cup heavy cream

1 A day before serving, in a heavy enameled saucepan, scald the milk with the vanilla bean; set aside, covered, to keep warm.

2 In a mixing bowl, beat the egg yolks and sugar together until thick and pale, and a ribbon forms when the whisk is lifted. Whisk in a pinch of salt.

3 In a heavy enameled or stainless steel saucepan, warm the beaten eggs and sugar over very low heat, stirring constantly. Gradually stir in the hot milk. Cook, over low heat, stirring constantly with a wooden spoon, until the custard thickens enough to coat the back of the spoon, the froth on the surface has disappeared, and the custard registers about 165°F on a candy thermometer. Do not let boil. Immediately remove from the heat.

(continued)

4 Strain the custard into a chilled mixing bowl set over ice. Cool down quickly, stirring constantly. If using vanilla extract, stir it in at this point. Pour into an ice cream maker and freeze according to the manufacturer's directions.

5 Meanwhile, coarsely chop the prunes with a large sharp knife or by pulsing in a food processor. When the ice cream is half frozen, add the prunes and the Armagnac syrup.

6 When almost frozen, add the cream. When the ice cream is done, pack into a 2-quart ice cream mold and set in the freezer overnight.

7 About 20 minutes before serving, transfer the ice cream to the refrigerator to soften slightly, 5 to 10 minutes. Invert onto a serving plate. To help loosen the ice cream, soak a kitchen towel in hot water, wring it out, and wrap around the mold. If necessary, tap the mold lightly with your fingers and shake it to loosen. If the surface needs a little patching up, smooth it with a spatula dipped in hot water. Return the unmolded ice cream to the freezer for 5 to 10 minutes to firm up. Place a whole, soaked prune on top of each portion and drizzle with a teaspoon or so of the syrup.

LEMON MERINGUE BOMBE WITH A BITTERS MOUSSE AND BLACK CURRANT SAUCE

➢➤ *La Mousse Glace au Parfum de Racine de Gentian*   SERVES 10 TO 12

I LEARNED THE FOLLOWING dessert when I spent time in the kitchen with Michel Bras. He worked virtually like an alchemist. Beneath the underlying sweetness of the mousse there is strong and rewarding interaction among the bitters, the acid of the lemon, and the tart black currants. When they are combined, the sensation is dazzling—all the tastes explode together in the mouth.

Begin 3 to 4 days in advance to make the parfait and the sauce.

½ cup superfine sugar

3 large egg whites, at room temperature

Pinch of salt

2 pinches of cream of tartar

1 cup heavy cream, well chilled

1 teaspoon high-quality pure lemon extract

Bitters Mousse (page 396)

2 tablespoons dry red wine

1¼ teaspoons grated lemon zest, organic if available

1 jar (12 ounces) black currant jam

1 Line an 8½ x 4 x 3–inch (5-cup) loaf pan with enough plastic wrap to overhang the edges by several inches. If you do not have a pan this size, a disposable foil loaf pan will work.

2 In a small, heavy saucepan, preferably unlined copper, combine ½ cup water with 6 tablespoons of the sugar and a pinch of cream of tartar. Cook over low heat, stirring, until the sugar dissolves. With a small wet brush, wash down the inside of the pan to the syrup. Boil, without stirring, until the syrup reaches the soft-ball stage, 234°F on a candy thermometer. Immediately remove the pan from the heat and place in icy water to stop the cooking.

3 Beat the egg whites with an electric mixer until frothy. Add a pinch each of salt and cream of tartar and 1 teaspoon of the sugar. Continue beating until soft peaks forms, then gradually add the remaining sugar. Beat until the whites are shiny and stiff.

4 Gently reheat the sugar syrup until hot. Gradually beat the hot syrup into the egg whites in a slow, steady stream. When all the syrup has been incorporated, continue to beat for 5 to 7 minutes longer, slowly reducing the speed as the meringue becomes cold and thick. Set it aside covered with a damp cloth until completely cold.

5 In a chilled bowl, using cold beaters, whip the heavy cream until soft mounds form. Add the lemon extract and continue to beat until the cream forms soft peaks. Gradually fold the whipped cream into the cold meringue. Scoop the mixture into the prepared loaf pan. Cover with the extra plastic wrap, then cover with foil and freeze for 3 hours. *(Can be prepared up to 1 week ahead.)*

6 Make the Bitters Mousse when the Lemon Meringue has chilled at least 3 hours.

7 Make the black currant sauce: Combine the wine, lemon zest, and the preserves in a small saucepan and cook, stirring, for 3 to 4 minutes. Let cool, press through a sieve, and refrigerate. Bring to room temperature before serving.

8 To assemble the bombe: Line a 9 x 5 x 3–inch loaf pan with enough plastic wrap to allow generous overhanging edges. Pour half of the bitters mousse into the prepared mold and tap lightly on the counter to settle the mousse. Unwrap the frozen lemon meringue parfait and place it in the center. Cover with the remaining bitters mousse. Enclose in plastic wrap and freeze for at least 6 hours or overnight.

9 About half an hour before serving, transfer the mold to the refrigerator and let soften for 25 to 30 minutes. To serve, invert the dessert to unmold. Cut the loaf into ¾-inch-thick slices. Set the slices on dessert plates. Thin the black currant sauce with water if necessary and spoon into a

(continued)

squeeze bottle or a heavy plastic bag with a corner snipped off. Drizzle the sauce over and around each portion and serve at once.

BITTERS MOUSSE

4 tablespoons unsalted butter

1 teaspoon unflavored gelatin

2 tablespoons Angostura bitters

5 whole eggs, separated, at room temperature

7½ tablespoons sugar

1 Melt the butter in a heavy, small saucepan over low heat. Let cool it to room temperature (the butter should be liquid) and set aside. In another saucepan combine the gelatin and bitters. Set in a pan of simmering water and stir to dissolve. Remove it from the heat and cool it slightly. Using an electric mixer, beat the yolks until pale yellow and a slowly dissolving ribbon foams when the beaters are lifted. Stir the syrupy gelatin mixture into the beaten eggs; set aside, stirring occasionally, until mixture mounds when dropped from a spoon.

2 Using clean dry beaters and a dry bowl slowly beat the egg whites until they begin to froth. Raise the speed to medium and "tighten" the whites by adding 2 tablespoons of the sugar. Continue beating for 1 minute. Then add the remaining sugar in a steady stream, beating continuously on medium speed until the whites are stiff, thick, and glossy, about 2 minutes. (The whites should feel smooth and silky.) Use a large wire whisk to fold in one fourth of whites into the egg-yolk mixture to lighten. Gently fold in remaining whites. Very delicately fold in the cool but liquid butter (the mixture will slightly deflate at this point).

Preserves

My book on Southwest French food wouldn't be complete without including some of the famous regional recipes for preserving fruits. Most of these recipes involve preserving in alcohol; remember that the fruits must always be completely covered by the liquid. Check your shelf of preserves from time to time to see if any of the fruits inside have swollen up above the liquid line. If they have, add some eau-de-vie or brandy until the fruits are again submerged. (This isn't necessary with peaches, pears, or prunes preserved in red wine and Armagnac; once these processed jars are opened they must be refrigerated and their contents used.)

PRUNES IN ARMAGNAC

⇥ *Pruneaux à l'Armagnac*   MAKES 1½ QUARTS

THIS IS AN ESSENTIAL RECIPE, since the prunes and their Armagnac syrup are used in Prune and Armagnac Ice Cream (pages 397–398), the Pastry Cake Filled With Apples and Prunes in Armagnac (pages 370–372), and in various fruit flans and omelets. They are excellent, too, eaten alone, after which one should drink off the thick, dark, aromatic syrup as slowly as possible, the longer to savor it.

In the Southwest there are the world-famous prunes of Agen. Our California prunes, which have been cultivated in America since the early nineteenth century, are the same variety and are just as luscious.

2 pounds extra-large prunes, unpitted	1 cup superfine sugar
3 cups warm brewed tea, preferably linden or orange pekoe	About 3 cups Armagnac

1 Soak the prunes in the tea overnight so that they swell up.

2 The following day, drain the prunes, discarding the tea. Roll each prune in paper towels to dry well. Place the prunes in a sterilized 1½-quart wide-mouth glass canning jar.

(continued)

3 Make a syrup with the sugar and ½ cup water; bring to a boil, stirring. Boil undisturbed 2 minutes. Remove from heat and allow to cool. Pour over the prunes. Completely cover the prunes with Armagnac; stir. If prunes rise above the line of liquid, add more Armagnac. Let soak a minimum of 2 weeks in a cool, dark place or in the refrigerator. Use clean wooden tongs or wooden spoon to remove prunes as needed. Keeps up to one year.

NOTES TO THE COOK

→ In the Southwest they soak prunes in chamomile tea to bring out the full flavor of the fruit.

→ If prunes become uncovered, add more Armagnac to cover.

SWEET AND SOUR CHERRIES

→ *Cerise à l'Aigre-Doux*   MAKES 1 QUART

PICKLED CHERRIES AND the pickled prunes that follow make an ideal accompaniment to pâtés, confits, foie gras, or any rich daube in this book. This recipe has been adapted to use the cherries available in the market when they are not too sweet.

Prepare at least 3 months in advance.

1½ pounds (about 1 quart) firm, not too sweet cherries

1 cup sugar

3 cups white wine tarragon vinegar

2 whole cloves

1 piece mace or ¼ teaspoon ground mace

90-proof vodka or plain eau-de-vie

1 Carefully inspect, wash, and dry each cherry. Discard any that are bruised. Prick each once or twice with a needle. Trim each stem, leaving about ½ inch attached.

2 In a nonreactive saucepan, combine the sugar and vinegar. Cook, stirring, until sugar is dissolved. Add the cloves and mace; boil 1 minute. Remove from the heat and allow to cool. Add the cherries, cover, and let stand 1 day.

3 The following day, sterilize two 1-pint canning jars and their rubber rings: Cover with warm water in a pan, bring to a boil, and boil covered 10 minutes. Drain upside down on kitchen towels.

4 Meanwhile, drain the cherries (reserve liquid) and place in the clean jars. Bring the liquid to a boil and boil 7 to 8 minutes. Cool completely, then pour over the cold cherries. Add vodka or eau-de-vie to cover. Seal and let stand in a cool, dry, dark place for 3 months before serving.

NOTE TO THE COOK

The cherries will lose their bright color; according to some old cookbooks, this is the sign that the cherries are ready to be eaten.

SWEET AND SOUR PRUNES

→ *Pruneaux à l'Aigre-Doux*   MAKES 2 CUPS

THESE ARE ABSOLUTELY luscious with terrines, pâtés, and Confit of Pig's Tongue (see variation on page 282, Confit of Calf's Tongue).

Prepare at least 6 weeks in advance.

12 ounces large prunes with pits	2 cups tarragon white wine vinegar
1 cup brewed tea, preferably chamomile or orange pekoe	1 cinnamon stick
	2 whole cloves
1⅓ cups granulated sugar	About 1 cup vodka

1 Simmer the prunes in the tea or in water for 10 minutes. Let stand for 2 to 3 hours. Meanwhile, in a nonreactive saucepan, slowly cook the sugar and vinegar, stirring until dissolved. Add the cinnamon and cloves: simmer 10 minutes. Remove from heat and let stand until cold.

2 Drain the prunes. Roll in paper towels to dry. Prick each 2 or 3 times with a pin. Place in a bowl, and strain the vinegar-sugar solution over them. Let the prunes rest 24 hours.

3 The following day, strain the vinegar solution into a nonreactive pan and slowly boil 6 to 8 minutes. Cool completely.

4 Place the prunes in a very clean 1-pint glass preserving jar. Cover with the cold vinegar solution. Add enough vodka to cover the prunes. Seal and place in a dry dark place for at least 6 weeks. Refrigerate after opening.

Preserved Spiced Pears in Red Wine With Armagnac

⇥ *Poires au Poivre et à l'Armagnac*   SERVES 8

INVENTED BY ANDRÉ DAGUIN, this preserve is based on the Gascon tradition of using pepper to heighten the flavor of fruits. The recipe can be doubled or even tripled easily. Keep in mind the pears need to marinate for 3 months before eating. They are fabulous with grilled duck breasts, roast goose, or Toulouse sausages.

4 perfect, but not completely ripe, pears, preferably Anjou

Juice of ½ lemon

3½ cups full-bodied red wine such as Madiran, California Petite Sirah, or Spanish Rioja, plus ¼ cup before serving

1½ cups sugar

1 scant tablespoon black peppercorns, rinsed and patted dry

½ cup Armagnac

1 For 4 pears, wash and drain two 3½ cup glass preserving jars with lids and new rubber rings. Place in a pan of water and slowly heat to boiling. Drain upside down on a clean kitchen towel.

2 Peel and drop the pears into a bowl of water acidulated with the juice of ½ lemon to prevent discoloration.

3 In an enameled or stainless steel saucepan, bring the wine and sugar to a boil, stirring until the sugar dissolves; boil for 1 minute. Drain the pears and add to the wine syrup. Simmer for 3 minutes.

4 Pack 2 pears in each clean, hot jar. Bring the wine syrup to a boil and boil 4 to 5 minutes to intensify flavor. Add the peppercorns and Armagnac, return to a boil, and pour boiling syrup over the pears, filling to within ½ inch of the top of the jar, or until the indicated level. Do not overpack jars. (If there is any leftover juice, freeze for a tiny granita—see Note at right.)

5 Use a clean wooden spoon to stir the fruit gently to let any air bubbles escape. With a paper towel, wipe the mouths of the jars clean of any syrup. Set the new rubber rings in place and seal the jars at once. Gently lower onto a rack set in a deep pot or water canner filled with enough lukewarm water to cover the jars by at least 1 inch. Bring to a boil. Cover the pot and boil vigorously 1 hour. Don't be tempted to reduce the cooking time—the wine must be fully cooked. Let the jars cool in the water before removing. Using tongs, transfer the jars to a rack to rest overnight.

6 The following day, test for a full seal by loosening the clamps and holding the jars from the top. If they don't open, the seals have been completed. (Be sure to have your other hand underneath to catch a jar, if necessary.) If there is a bad seal, do not plan to store the fruits. Instead, refrigerate and use within the week. Label fully sealed jar or jars and store in a cool place for 3 months before opening.

7 The day before you plan to serve the pears, open the jars and stir ¼ cup uncooked red wine into each. Chill overnight. Serve ½ pear per serving, with a little of the syrup. Serve with an extra grinding of fresh black pepper. If too sweet, add a dash of lemon juice.

NOTE TO THE COOK

Leftover juices make a delicious granita. Add orange and lemon juice to taste (about 3 tablespoons orange juice and 1 tablespoon lemon juice for each cup leftover red wine syrup.) Simply freeze until slushy. Break up mixture in food processor, return to freezer, and freeze until hard.

GREEN FIG AND WALNUT JAM
Confiture de Figues Vertes aux Noix

MAKES 1 QUART, 2 PINTS,
OR FOUR 8-OUNCE JARS

ALAIN DUTOURNIER TOLD ME the combination of figs and walnuts brought back memories of his childhood. As he described it to me, his eyes filled with tears. This delectable jam is wonderful with fresh cheese.

2 pounds firm (slightly underripe) fresh green figs

2 large organic lemons

1½ pounds sugar

¾ cup shelled fresh walnuts

1 Wash the figs and remove the stem tips if they are hard. Halve the figs.

2 Rinse the lemons; remove the zest and cut into fine julienne strips. Cut away all the white pith from the lemon and thinly slice the fruit. Remove any seeds and put them into a small cheesecloth bag.

3 In a large heavy saucepan, combine the sugar with 1¼ cups water. Bring to a boil, stirring until the sugar dissolves. Cook the syrup undisturbed until it reaches a temperature of 220°F.

(continued)

Immediately add the figs, lemon zest, lemon slices, and seed bag. Return to the boil, then reduce the heat to low. Cook slowly until setting point is reached, about 2 hours. The setting point is determined by dipping a spoon into the liquid and letting a few drops fall onto a saucer; if they set quickly, it is done. Remove and discard the bag of seeds. Use a spoon to remove any scum on the surface. Add the walnuts and cook for 5 minutes longer.

4 Sterilize jars, rings, and lids: Cover with hot water, bring to a boil, and boil 10 minutes. Drain upside down on a kitchen towel. Fill hot, dry jars, leaving a ½-inch headspace. Cool and seal. Keep the jam in the refrigerator after opening.

ORANGE RATAFIA

→→ *Ratafia d'Orange*   MAKES ABOUT 1½ QUARTS

RATAFIAS ARE LIQUEURS produced by steeping fruits and peels in Armagnac. Oranges are especially enhanced with the perfume of France's oldest brandy.

This wonderful recipe comes from l'Estanquet in the town of Gastes in the Landes. Pepette Arbulo, the young woman chef there, makes many different fruit and brandy concoctions. She claims this one is especially good for digestion as well as for enlivening the appetite.

6 large juice oranges, preferably organic	4 cinnamon sticks
1 cup sugar	1 liter Armagnac

1 Wash 2 of the oranges well and dry. Using a zester or a swivel-bladed vegetable peeler, remove the outer zest only and cut very thin strips.

2 Juice all of the oranges and strain; you will need 2 cups juice. Combine the orange juice and sugar in medium nonreactive saucepan and bring to a boil, stirring to dissolve the sugar. Remove from the heat and let stand until completely cool. Add the Armagnac.

3 Put the orange zest and cinnamon sticks in a glazed stoneware crock or glass pitcher. Pour in the orange juice mixture, cover and let stand for 1 month at room temperature, stirring from time to time with a clean wooden spoon. Strain through coffee filter papers into bottles. Cover tightly and let age for at least 1 month before serving.

STOCKS AND SAUCE BASES

*S*omeone once said that "England has three sauces and sixty religions while France has three religions and sixty sauces." In fact, there are far more sauces than that in the famous catalog of Austin de Croze.

Most of the sauces for the dishes in this book are included with the recipes. But I am adding a few base preparations here: an all-purpose chicken stock, an all-purpose demi-glace, a dark, rich duck stock, a duck and wine demi-glace, a fish stock, a fish fumet, and a few others.

I particularly like my all-purpose demi-glace; it keeps up to a year in the freezer, takes up hardly any room, and is available in an instant to enhance and sometimes even save a dish. You may notice that this version does not require browning the bones. The reason is that when you make most modern sauces, you are reducing to such an extent that there is the possibility of a bitter taste from well-browned meat and bones. On the other hand, I do caramelize the vegetables so that their flavor will be strong, and the sauce will have good color. Color is also the reason I suggest blackening an onion over flames or under the broiler, a process that will also offset any possible bitterness.

To avoid spending a good deal of time skimming, I often cover the bones of veal and chicken with warm water and quickly bring it to a boil. After 3 minutes of boiling, I drain the bones, rinse them, and start cooking in fresh water. This procedure removes most of the scum. It does not remove protein or taste; the nutrients and flavor of stock come from long simmering.

Chicken Stock

→ *Fond de Volaille*

USE THIS RICH STOCK for soups, pot-au-feu, and some stews. It can be stored in the refrigerator for up to 3 days or frozen in covered containers for up to 3 months.

5 pounds chicken necks, backs, and wings, plus leftover roasted carcasses, if available

2 or 3 chicken gizzards

1 veal shank or a few marrowbones (optional)

2 onions, halved

Green tops from 2 or 3 leeks

2 small celery ribs, halved

1 carrot, halved

Peel and seeds from 2 tomatoes or 1 plum tomato, quartered (see Note below)

2 garlic cloves

2 whole cloves

1 Place the chicken parts, gizzards, and veal shank and marrowbones (if you have them) in a large stockpot. Cover with warm water and quickly bring to a boil over high heat. Boil vigorously for 3 minutes. Drain; rinse the bones and return them to the pot.

2 Cover with 6 quarts cold water; slowly bring to a boil. Skim off any scum that surfaces until only a small amount of foam rises to the top. Add the onions, leek greens, celery, carrot, tomato or tomatoes, garlic, and cloves. Return to a boil. Reduce the heat to low, partially cover the pot, and simmer slowly, without disturbing, for 4 to 5 hours.

3 Ladle the stock through a colander into a deep bowl. Then ladle it again through a strainer lined with several thicknesses of damp cheesecloth. Skim the fat off the top. If you have time, chill the stock, then scrape off all the congealed fat.

4 Put the degreased stock in a large, heavy saucepan and bring to a boil. Slide the pan half off the heat and cook at a slow boil, skimming, for 25 to 30 minutes, or until the stock is reduced to 2 quarts.

NOTE TO THE COOK

Peel and seeds from fresh tomatoes will flavor the stock as well as attract scum. Use the best part of the tomato for some other purpose.

DEMI-GLACE

→ *Demi-Glace*

THIS IS AN INTENSE, all-purpose reduced meat and poultry sauce base that you'll find called for in many recipes in this book. It can be stored in the refrigerator for 6 months or frozen for up to 1 year.

8 to 10 pounds veal bones

2 to 3 pounds chicken carcasses, plus 1 heart and 1 gizzard

Several chunks of fatty veal (optional)

3 tablespoons rendered duck or goose fat or butter

2 ounces fatty cured ham, chopped (optional)

2 medium carrots, chopped

2 medium onions, chopped, plus 1 onion, halved

1 leek, split and sliced (white and green parts separated)

1 small celery rib, sliced

6 sprigs of parsley

1 head of garlic, halved horizontally

1 large tomato, halved, with skin and seeds

1 imported bay leaf

¼ teaspoon freshly grated nutmeg

1 Crack the veal bones and chicken carcasses with a cleaver into very small pieces or have the butcher do this for you. Place them in a deep stockpot, cover with warm water, and quickly bring to a boil. Boil hard for 3 minutes. Drain, rinse, and return to the pot.

2 Cover the bones with 6 quarts cold water. Add the fatty pieces of veal if you have them. Slowly bring to a boil over moderate heat, skimming off the scum as it rises to the top. Simmer, skimming, for 1 hour.

3 Meanwhile, in a large skillet, heat the fat. Add the ham, carrots, and chopped onions. Cover and cook over low heat for 10 minutes to sweat the vegetables.

4 Add the white parts of the leek and the celery. Raise the heat to moderate and cook the vegetables, stirring occasionally, until lightly browned, about 15 minutes. Caramelize the cut sides of the halved onion by placing them close to burner flames or under a hot broiler until blackened.

5 When bones have simmered for 1 hour and the liquid is clear, add the browned vegetables, caramelized onion, leek greens, celery, parsley, garlic, tomato, bay leaf, and nutmeg. Return

406 ❧ THE COOKING OF SOUTHWEST FRANCE

to a boil, reduce the heat to low, and simmer, uncovered, skimming from time to time without stirring, for at least 4 hours.

6 Strain the stock through a colander into a deep bowl, discarding the solids. Then ladle the stock through a sieve lined with several thicknesses of damp cheesecloth. Chill uncovered until the fat congeals, then scrape it all off.

7 Return the degreased stock to a clean heavy saucepan. Bring to a boil. Slide the pan half off the heat and cook at a slow boil, skimming, until reduced to 2½ cups, about 1 hour. The demi-glace should just lightly coat a spoon.

Dark, Rich Duck Stock

→← *Fond de Canard*   MAKES 1½ QUARTS

A GOOD DUCK STOCK can be the basis for a slew of stews, ragouts, sauces, and soups. If you do not have sufficient duck pieces, use a mixture of duck and chicken bones. If you have cooked duck or chicken carcasses, use them, too. This stock can be stored in the refrigerator for 6 months or frozen for up to 1 year.

Carcasses, necks, and wing tips of 4 ducks

1 large onion, halved

1½ cups cubed carrots

2 medium onions, coarsely chopped, plus 1 large onion, halved

2 leeks, trimmed, halved, and cut into 1-inch pieces (white and green parts separated)

1 cup red wine vinegar

½ cup dry red wine

1 large tomato, halved, with skin and seeds

12 whole black peppercorns, lightly cracked

1 garlic clove, crushed gently

Herb bouquet: 8 sprigs parsley, ¾ teaspoon fresh thyme leaves, and 1 imported bay leaf tied together in cheesecloth

1 Preheat the oven to 450°F. Break up or crack the carcasses, necks, and wing tips with a cleaver or mallet. Spread out pieces in a large, deep roasting pan and place in the hot oven. Brown the bones, turning them once or twice. This should take about 15 minutes.

(continued)

2 Transfer the bones to a large stockpot. Add fresh cold water to cover and slowly bring to a boil.

3 Meanwhile, pour off all but 2 tablespoons fat from the roasting pan. Scatter the carrots, chopped onions, and white parts of leeks in the pan; toss to coat lightly with fat. Return to the oven for 30 minutes to brown, turning the vegetables from time to time.

4 Transfer the browned vegetables to a side bowl. Deglaze the roasting pan with the vinegar and wine, scraping up any brown bits that cling to the bottom and sides of the pan. Boil until reduced to ¾ cup. Add to the vegetables.

5 Preheat the broiler. Place the halved onion and tomatoes, cut sides up, on a small baking sheet and broil until nicely browned, 5 to 7 minutes. Remove and set aside.

6 When the water in the stockpot with the bones reaches a boil, begin skimming until only a little foam is left on the surface. Add the vegetables and juices in the bowl, the browned onion and tomato, the peppercorns, garlic, and herb bouquet. Simmer, partially covered, for 4 hours, skimming occasionally. If at any time the bones and vegetables are not covered with liquid, add enough water to cover.

7 Strain the stock through a sieve lined with several thicknesses of damp cheesecloth, pressing on the solids to extract as much liquid as possible. Chill until the fat congeals. Carefully remove all the fat.

8 Return the degreased stock to a heavy saucepan. Bring to a boil. Slide the pan half off the heat and cook at a slow boil, skimming often, for 25 minutes, or until reduced to 1½ quarts.

Duck Demi-Glace

→ *Demi-Glace de Canard*   MAKES ABOUT 2 CUPS

WHEN DUCK STOCK is reduced, the result is a concentrated sauce base that can be used in the sauces of many dishes or to add flavor to pâtés, stews, and duck liver flans. With occasional skimming, the reducing should take a total of about 45 minutes. The demi-glace can be stored in the refrigerator for 6 months or frozen for up to 1 year.

1½ quarts Dark, Rich Duck Stock (pages 407–408)

1 Carefully degrease duck stock. In a heavy saucepan, boil steadily, uncovered, half over the heat, until reduced to about 3 cups, skimming often.

2 Strain into a small, heavy saucepan. Slowly reduce to 2 cups. Do not reduce further; stocks from deeply browned bones often make a bitter glaze.

Duck or Game, Red Wine Flavored Demi-Glace

→ *Demi-Glace de Canard au Vin Rouge*   MAKES ABOUT 1½ CUPS

USE THIS FOR Duck Liver Flans With Caramel Vinegar Sauce (pages 95–97), for Slow-Cooked Duck Legs in Red Wine (pages 187–188), or for enriching red wine sauces for game.

Begin 2 days in advance. You can store this demi-glace in the refrigerator for 6 months or frozen for up to 1 year.

2 duck or game carcasses with all fat and skin removed

1 bottle (750 ml) full-bodied red wine, such as Petite Sirah or a Côtes-du-Rhône

Herb bouquet: 8 sprigs parsley, about ¾ teaspoon thyme leaves, and 1 imported bay leaf, tied together with a string or wrapped in cheesecloth

1 carrot, sliced

1 onion, sliced

1 leek (white and green parts), sliced

1 quart Chicken Stock (page 405) or Dark, Rich Duck Stock (pages 407–408), degreased

(continued)

1 Two days in advance, crush the bones of the carcasses into very small pieces. (This allows the marrow in the bones to release and enrich the sauce.) Place the pieces in a deep, nonreactive saucepan or earthenware crock. Cover with the red wine and let soak overnight.

2 The following day, add the herb bouquet and bring to a boil. Reduce the heat to very low and cook slowly until reduced to a glaze, about 3 hours. (A slow cooker set on medium is perfect here.)

3 Add the vegetables and stock. Bring to a boil, lower the heat, and reduce slowly by half, about 2 to 3 hours, skimming (see Variation below).

4 Ladle contents of pan into a strainer lined with damp cheesecloth set over a large bowl, pressing on the solids to extract all possible liquid. Let cool completely, then chill. Remove all surface fat. Spoon out only the clear jellied demi-glace, leaving behind the granular scum at the bottom of the container. Reduce the demi-glace further, if necessary, boiling sauce half over the heat, to 1½ cups, skimming often. The demi-glace can be stored in the refrigerator for 1 week or frozen for up to 3 months.

VARIATION To make a quick duck-wine sauce, slowly reduce red wine–soaked carcasses to a glaze. Add 2 cups demi-glace and simmer for 15 minutes, skimming. Strain and degrease. Use at once or keep refrigerated up to 1 week. It can also be frozen.

Inspired by a recipe from Jean-Louis Palladin.

FISH STOCK

>+> *Fond de Poisson*

IT'S STILL DIFFICULT to find fish bones for stock except in coastal areas, but fish glazes are now available in most supermarket freezers. Still, the motivated cook will manage to make up his or her own fish stock. Bottled clam juice does not make a good substitute, though mussel broth or fresh clam broth will do.

A rather desperate method but one that works is to puree a few shrimp in their shells in a food processor and cook them in chicken stock for 30 minutes, then strain it carefully; you will come up with a satisfactory stock.

Fish glazes, or concentrates, are merely fish stocks that have been greatly reduced. If you want to boil a stock down into a glaze, I suggest you do it in the oven, to contain most of the strong fish odor. Fish glazes are easier to store than stocks and can be kept up to 1 year in the freezer. Though their odors are strong, they can be most helpful when stretched with cream and butter plus other flavorings; they can give body and deep background flavor to a sauce.

I like to use red snapper frames and heads for my stock, but you can just as easily use the frames of sole, sea bass, halibut, whiting, or a mixture of these. The heads and bones are important, for they give a stock good body. Frozen fillets of sole and flounder don't give sufficient body. Twenty-five minutes of slow simmering is ideal; longer simmering won't release any more gelatin and taste from the bones and has the negative effect of making the stock somewhat bitter and "fishy tasting."

This recipe can easily be halved or quartered and can also be increased.

6 pounds fish bones, heads, and tails, with gills removed

1 leek, halved and cut into 1-inch pieces

1 medium carrot, sliced

1 small onion, sliced

1 celery rib, cut into 1-inch pieces

3 garlic cloves, halved

5 sprigs of parsley

½ imported bay leaf

Pinch of crumbled fresh thyme leaves

1½ teaspoons lightly crushed black peppercorns

1½ cups dry white wine

(continued)

1 With a knife, cut the fish trimmings to remove any traces of blood, liver, intestines, and eggs. Rinse the trimmings under cold running water until water runs clear. Place them in a stockpot or deep kettle, preferably enameled or stainless-steel (aluminum tends to discolor fish stock but doesn't affect it otherwise). Add 6 quarts of cold water and bring to a boil, skimming well for 2 to 3 minutes.

2 Add all the remaining ingredients, reduce the heat to low, and simmer, uncovered, for 25 minutes, skimming as needed.

3 Strain the stock. Boil, if necessary, to reduce to 3 quarts. Let cool, then cover and refrigerate. As it cools, fat will rise to the top and can be easily removed. The stock can be refrigerated or frozen.

FISH GLAZE Boil 3 quarts of strained and degreased Fish Stock until reduced to 2 cups. Store in the refrigerator for 1 month or frozen for up to 1 year.

FISH FUMET

➤➤ *Fumet de Poisson*

THIS IS A SHORT concentrated base used to flavor sauces.

1½ tablespoons unsalted butter

½ medium onion, chopped

1 celery rib, chopped

1 small carrot, chopped

1 leek (white part and half the green), well washed and thinly sliced

Herb bouquet: 5 sprigs parsley, 2 sprigs thyme, and 1 small imported bay leaf tied together with string

2 to 3 pounds fish heads and frames from nonoily fish, washed and cut into small pieces

1½ cups dry red or white wine

1 Melt the butter in a large saucepan or deep skillet. Add the onion, celery, and carrot. Cover and cook over low heat for 5 minutes.

2 Add the leek, herb bouquet, and fish heads and bones. Cook, uncovered, for 5 minutes longer, stirring.

3 Add 2 quarts cold water and slowly bring to a boil. Boil, skimming, for 2 to 3 minutes. Reduce the heat to moderately low and simmer, uncovered, for 25 minutes, skimming as necessary.

4 Strain the liquid, cool, and skim off fat. Return to a clean saucepan, add the wine, and boil over moderate heat until reduced to 1 cup, about 20 minutes.

NOTE TO THE COOK

To avoid excessive fish odors in your kitchen, bring liquid to a boil, set in a 375°F oven, and reduce to 1 cup.

Stocks and Sauce Bases 413

Mail Order Sources

Beans

Tarbais: www.chefshop.com,
www.frenchselections.com

Lentilles de Puy:
www.frenchselections.com

Lingots: www.frenchfoodexports.com

Frozen fresh favas, peeled (preferably
Montana or Mideast Brands):
www.intlgourmet.com

Butter

From Charente: www.gourmetfood.com

Caviar of Aquitaine

www.dartagnan.com

Dried Cèpes

www.frenchselections.com

Cheeses

Roquefort Le Vieux Berger:
www.murrayscheese.com

French cheeses by Jean d'Alos, Bordeaux,
France: www.cowgirlcreamery.com

Assorted: www.artisanalcheese.com

Chestnuts

Roasted, packed in jars or *cryovac*:
www.frenchselection.com

Duck

Fat: www.dartagnan.com,
www.frenchselections.com,
www.preferredmeats.com

Legs, *magrets*, and foie gras; prepared
confit, gizzards, glazes, Moulard, and
Muscovy: www.dartagnan.com,
www.frenchselections.com,
www.preferredmeats.com

Superior Pekin: www.libertyducks.com,
www.mapleleaffarms.com

Artisan foie gras:
www.frenchselections.com,
www.preferredmeats.com

Eel

Pibales (real baby eel) or Angulas:
www.tienda.com

Surimi eel: www.thespanishtable.com

Essences and Extracts

www.thespicehouse.com

Gâteau à la Broche

www.bienmanger.com

Goose, Fresh

www.dartagnan.com

Grapewood

(Ask for Napa Valley "Sam's Vine Chips"—chips from grapevines): www.napageneralstore.com

Green Peppercorns

www.salttraders.com

Ham

Jambon de Bayonne: www.dartagnan.com

Hare, Wild (in Season)

www.dartagnan.com

Liqueurs

Armagnac, Chestnut liqueur *(petit liqueur de chataigne)*, Izarra: www.wine-searcher.com

Mulberry Syrup (Mymouni Brand)

www.kalustyans.com

Mushrooms

Fresh chanterelles: www.earthy.com, www.primagourmet.com

Fresh cèpes: www.primagourmet.com

Moutarde Violette

www.zingermans.com, www.frenchfoodexports.com, www.primagourmet.com

Piment d'Espelette

www.chefshop.com, www.piperade.com

Pineau de Charentes

www.wine-searcher.com

Quince Preserves

www.kalustyans.com, www.artisanpreserves.com

Pork

Rind, pork fat, pork belly, pancetta, and other pork products: www.nimanranch.com

Pork Toulouse sausages: www.frenchselections.com

Blood sausages: www.frenchselections.com, www.tienda.com, www.spanishtable.com

Ventrèche: www.dartagnan.com

Ramps, fresh, or leeks, wild

www.earthy.com

Salsify

Canned from France:
www.frenchselections.com

Sea Salt

Finishing salts (fleur de sel; Esprit du Sel;
sea salt from Necton, Portugal):
www.salttraders.com,
www.realgoodfood.com

Snails

www.frenchselections.com,
www.frenchfoodexports.com

Squid "in Its Own Ink" (Calamares en Su Tinta)

www.netgrocer.com

Truffles and French Black Truffle Oil

www.plantin.com

Truffle shavings from China packed in
France: www.frenchselections.com

Veal Demi-Glace

www.chefshop.com

Verjus

www.earthy.com,
www.fusion.com,
www.frenchfoodexports.com

Vinegar, Banyuls

www.formaggiokitchen.com,
www.frenchfoodexports.com,
www.chefshop.com

Wines of the French Southwest

www.kermitlynch.com,
www.wine-searcher.com

Yellow Stoneware Cassoulet Bowl

www.claycoyote.com

Index to Recipes by Region and Course

Notes on Equipment

WHEN I SAT DOWN TO WRITE THIS BOOK, I assumed it would not be the only French cookbook my readers would own. Thus I decided to eliminate that old warhorse list of equipment that has been published and republished so many times: *la batterie de cuisine*.

You'll need nothing special to prepare the recipes here beyond what you already own, assuming you're serious and reasonably well-equipped home cook. The only possible exception is an electric slow cooker, such as a Crock-pot. Such a cooker is not necessary, but it can be economical and convenient, since many of my recipes call for long, slow cooking with a simple reheating just before they're served.

You can do this well in any large pot, preferably one of earthenware or enameled cast iron with a tight-fitting lid. But if you have a large oven as I do, you'll use up a lot of gas or electricity. I've made good use of an electric cooker with a removable glazed earthenware inset when preparing confits, stews, cassoulets, and for making stocks, knowing that I can leave it on all day even when I leave the house and that the newer models have a temperature control that is precise. Another advantage of such a cooker is that one can remove the insert, cool it, and place it in the refrigerator, allowing the fat to rise, congeal, and then be easily removed.

For preserving confit, I like to use large mason jars or stoneware jugs that are glazed only on the interior. And in case you don't have various sizes of terra-cotta or porcelain deep dishes, a lasagna pan will work well for many of the dishes in this book. A large earthen mixing bowl or the insert from a large Crock-pot can be used for cassoulet.

Sous Vide at Home

It was in the Southwest of France that I first learned to cook in vacuum-sealed plastic bags—in effect, cooking food in its own juices. Chef Francis Garcia in Bordeaux showed me how to prepare fish using a enormously expensive Swiss-made professional vacuum sealer to retain flavor, juiciness, and nutrition.

I adapted his ideas to American products (parchment, plastic wrap, and boilable plastic pouches), wrapping food (chicken breasts, mussels, shrimps, salmon, and fruit) airtight before poaching. See the recipe for Steamed Salmon With Cooked Egg Sauce (pages 116–117) for an example. Suzanne Hamlin, a New York–based food journalist at the time of the writing of the first edition, called these experiments with water-immersion cooking "the gastronomic equivalent of stereophonic sound."

The concept of cooking food in its own moisture is very similar to another greater Southwest gastronomic triumph, the mussel dish *éclade*, from Charente, in which mussels are packed together so tightly they can barely open during cooking, forcing them to absorb their own juices (see page 102). You can produce the same effect by vacuum-packing the mussels and cooking them in simmering water for about 3 minutes.

In the last few years, a machine has arrived on the market that does the job better than hand wrapping: the Tilia FoodSaver Vacuum Sealer. It's available in housewares stores as well as most department stores. To avoid bacterial buildup, completely chill down cooked food in the bags and then refrigerate.

Bibliography

Books Consulted in Preparation of This Book:

Alexander, Stephanie. *Cooking & Travelling in South-West France*. Victoria, Australia: Penquin Books, 2002.

Barberousse, Michel. *Cuisine Basque et Béarnaise*. Paris: Barberousse.

Brown, Michael and Sybil. *Food and Wine of South-West France*. London: Batsford, 1980.

Bontou, Alcide. *Traité de Cuisine Bourgeoise Bordelaise*. 7th ed. Bordeaux: Feret et Fils, 1977.

Boulestin, Marcel. *What Shall We Have Today?* London: William Heinemann, 1931.

Carreras, Marie-Thérèse. *Les Bonnes Recettes du Pays Catalan*. Paris: Presses de la Renaissance, 1979.

Couffignal, Huguette. *La Cuisine des Pays d'Oc*. Paris: Solar, 1976.

Coulon, Christian. *Le Cuisinier Medoquin*. Bordeaux: Éditions Confluences, 2000.

Coulon, Christian. *Ce Que Mange 'Sud-Ouest' Veut Dire*. Bordeaux: Éditions Confluences, 2003.

Courtine, Robert. *Grand Livre de la France à Table*. Paris: Bordas, 1979.

de Croze, Austin. *Les Plats Régionnaux de France*. Paris: Montaigne, 1928.

Daguin, André. *Le Nouveau Cuisinier Gascon*. Paris: Stock, 1981.

Daguin, Ariane, George Faison, and Joanna Pruess. *D'Artagnan's Glorious Game Cookbook*. New York: Little, Brown and Company, 1999.

David, Elizabeth. *French Provincial Cooking*. London: Penguin, 1972.

Dubarry, Gabriel. *Cuisine et Poésie, Vieilles Recettes Gasconnes*. Gimont: Published privately, 1975.

Dumonteil, Fulbert. *La France Gourmande*. Paris: Librairie Universelle, 1906.

Dupouy, L. En Chalosse, *Recettes d'Hier et d'Aujourd'Hui*. Aire sur l'Adour: Published privately, 1977.

de Echeverria, Juan. *Gastronomia Vasconum*. Bilbao: Izquierdo, 1979.

Escurignan, Maïté. *Manuel de Cuisine Basque*. Bayonne: Harriet, 1982.

Galan, Alain. *Au Marché de Brive-la-Gaillarde*. Brive: René Dessagne.

Guillot, André. *La Vraie Cuisine Légère*. Paris: Flammarion, 1981.

———. *La Grande Cuisine Bourgeoise*. Paris: Flammarion, 1976.

Guinaudeau-Franc, Zette. *Les Secrets des Fermes en Périgord Noir*. Paris: Serg, 1978.

Hamlin, Suzanne. "Bagging Nutrition and Flavor." *New York Daily News*: January 5, 1983.

Hirigoyen, Gerald. *The Basque Kitchen*. New York: HarperCollins, 1998.

Kimball, Christopher. *The Kitchen Detective*. Brookline: Boston Common Press, 2003.

Malaurie. Jean-Paul. *Ma Cuisine des Quatre Saisons*. Perigueux: Éditions Fanlac, 1998.

La Mazille. *La Bonne Cuisine du Périgord*. Paris: Flammarion, 1929.

Molinier, Fernand. *Promenade Culinaire en Occitanie*. Albi: Privately printed (about 1930). Reprinted 1978.

Oyler, Philip. *The Generous Earth*. London: Hodder & Stoughton, 1950.

Palay, Simin. *La Cuisine du Pays*, 8th ed. Pau: Marrimpouey Jeune, 1978.

Palladin, Jean-Louis. *Cooking With the Seasons*. Charlottesville: Thomasson-Grant, 1989.

Para, Christian. *Mon Cochon de la Tête aux Pieds*. Paris: Payot & Rivages, 1998.

Penton, Anne. *Customs and Cookery in the Périgord and Quercy*. Newton Abbot, Devon (England): David & Charles, 1973.

de Pesquidoux, Joseph. *Chez Nous en Gascogne*. Paris: Plon, 1921. Reprint 1981.

Philippon, Henri. *La Cuisine du Quercy et du Périgord*. Paris: Denoël, 1979.

Progneaux, J.-E. *Recettes et Spécialités Gastronomiques Bordelaises et Girondines*. La Rochelle: Quartier Latin, 1969.

Rieux, Louis. *Au Pays de Cocagne, le Livre de Cuisine Albigeoise*. Albi: Privately published, 1913.

de Rivoyre, Éliane and Jacquette. *La Cuisine Landaise*. Paris: Noël, 1980.

St.-Martin, Paul. *Mes Secrets de Cuisine*. Mont-de-Marsan: Jean-Lacoste, 1964.

Toussaint, Jean-Luc. *The Walnut Cookbook*. Berkeley, CA: Ten Speed Press, 1998.

Vanel, Lucien. *Saveurs et Humeurs*. Dremil-Lafage: Éditions Daniel Briand, 1993.

Wolfert, Paula. *Paula Wolfert's World of Food*. New York: Harper & Row, 1988.

———. *The Slow Mediterranean Kitchen*. New York: John Wiley & Sons, 2003.

Acknowledgments
for the New Edition

MANY PEOPLE HAVE HELPED ME prepare this revised edition.

I want to particularly thank Susan Wyler for her friendship, vision, and wonderful and creative editing. It was her idea to put out a revised edition of this book, and she worked with me on every recipe, wanting nothing less than perfection.

I also want to thank the great team at John Wiley & Sons: my supportive publisher, Natalie Chapman, and equally supportive in-house editor, Linda Ingroia. Thanks to Michele Sewell; the great food photographer, Christopher Hirsheimer; the food stylist, Julie Lee; the copy editor, Suzanne Fass; the production editor, Ava Wilder; the cover art director, Jeff Faust; and the book designers, Joel Avirom and Jason Snyder.

I want to thank Janet Fletcher for her precise counsel on cheese; Steven Kolpan, professor of Wine Studies at The Culinary Institute of America, for his advice on Southwest French wines; and the following chefs and cooks for sharing recipes: Michel Bras, Pascal Condomine, Philip Dedlow, Mary Dumont, Martin Etchémaïtć, Michel Trama, and, of course, the three chefs, Gerald Hirigoyen, Laurent Manrique and Jean-Pierre Moullé, whose contributions are spelled out in the introduction.

For guidance and thoughtful advice, I also wish to thank: Barbara and Jon Beckmann, Ginette Bras, Ariane Daguin, Dr. Adam Drewnowski, Suzanne Hamlin, Dr. Nathan Myhrvold, professor emeritus Robert Wolke, Dr. André Parcé, Russ Parsons, Professor Serge Renaud, Bill Staggs, and my husband, best friend, and rigorously positive live-in food-taster, Bill Bayer.

Finally, I want to thank those members at the not-for-profit public service organization, the eGullet Society for Culinary Arts & Letters, who volunteered to act as testers for this book. These "eGulleteers," a thriving community of enthusiastic home cooks, have become a great resource for me. Their warm encouragement and friendly testing notes have been invaluable: Richard Alexander, Adam Balic, Judith Benton, Monica Bhide, Christopher Brown, John Cook, Cassy Fannin, Suzanne Fass, Seth Gross, Wayne Jackson, Michelle Kemp, Reese Kolsky, Flory Loonin, Elissa Meyers, Elie Nassar, Dana Noffsinger, Maureen O'Reilly, Charlie Osborn, Susan Fahning, Jorge Saavedra, Helena Sarin, Craig Schweickert, Nancy Smith, Carolyn Tillie, Jenna B. Umansky, Lucy Vanel, Tommy Weir, Joseph Willey, and Kit Williams.

Finally, I want to thank the Sonoma-based Ramekins Cooking School volunteers for their help: Kay Austin, Royann Francini, Mary Karlin, Lisa Lavagetto, and Elizabeth Skylan.

Acknowledgments for the 1983 Edition

MANY WONDERFUL, GENEROUS PEOPLE helped me with this book, and I hope every one of them will find his or her name in the various lists below, arranged alphabetically within each region. There were three people who particularly influenced and helped me in special and major ways. If this book is unique, different from others published in its field, then their collective assistance must be the reason.

The first is André Daguin. This extraordinary Gascon chef opened the doors of Aquitaine for me and delivered the entire Southwest. He sent me everywhere, to all the corners of the region, to meet, talk, eat, and learn. And then, too, he and his wife, Jo, gave me my own little room under the roof of their home in Auch, overlooking the top of

Cathédrale Sainte-Marie and the plains that spread from the Gers River. Here I sorted out papers, studied my notes, and read books loaned to me from the library downstairs, and if I had a question, André was always there to answer it. He is an exceptional chef—original, controversial, always experimenting, applying new concepts and techniques to traditional Gascon food. He was the first to show me how to update classic regional cuisine. Daring, intelligent, generous-spirited, he is a Gascon's Gascon.

Lucien Vanel of Toulouse opened the kitchen of his restaurant and all the "secrets" of his mother's famous *cuisine quercynoise*. It has been said of this kind and unpretentious man that he has done for country cooking what the brothers Troisgros have done for *cuisine bourgeoise* and the restaurant Taillevent has done for *haute cuisine*; he has updated it without losing the strengths, subtleties, and depths of what had gone before. He takes simple country food and gives it extraordinary lightness and flavor. He and his two sous-chefs, Jean Tillot and Luc Zwolinski, left nothing of the Périgord, Toulouse, Bordeaux, and the Quercy unturned. They wanted me to learn it all, and if I missed anything, that's my fault and not theirs.

The third is André Guillot, who is not from the Southwest. The foremost cooking teacher in France, Guillot truly and viscerally loves the culinary arts, to which he brings a keen and probing intelligence. I think he is the only teacher I have ever met who seems to exist within his subject and, simultaneously, outside it. To listen to him is to bask in culinary wisdom and to catch his own passion for the subject. Among the most important things I learned from Guillot is that there need be no incompatibility between great food and good health, that I have a responsibility toward my readers to think of their health as well as their delight, and that one can lower the quantity of fat in a dish without sacrificing any of its flavor. A recipe is an outline. The cook need not act as slave to the recipe; we have each of us our own interpretation, and it is the quality of our individual spirits that is the essence of finesse.

I am sincerely grateful to Alain Dutournier for allowing me to work in his kitchen and for giving generously of his time and knowledge.

With thanks to Pepette Arbulo, Noël and Michel Baris, Jean-Pierre Capelle, Maurice Coscuella, Bernard Cousseau, Jo Daguin, Louis Darmanté, Roger Duffour, Robert Garrapit, Christine and Michel Guérard, Robert and Fabienne Labeyrie, Claude Laffitte, Gustav Ledun, Huguette Melier, Jean-Louis Palladin, Jacques Pastour, Maïté Sandrini, Marie-Claude Soubiran-Gracia, Marylyse and Dominique Toulousy, and Monique Veilletet for recipes and notes on Gascony and the Landes.

With thanks to Firmin Arrambide, André Canal, Robert Casau, André Darraidoü, Pierre LaPorte, Geneviève and Rosalie Muruamendiaraz, and the Urguty family for recipes and notes on the Basque country and the Béarn.

With thanks to Jean-Marie Amat, Christian Clément, Jean-David Dickson, Isabelle Dussauge, Francis Garcia, Jean Ramet, Pierre Veilletet, and Jean-Pierre Xiradakis for recipes and notes on Bordeaux.

With thanks to Max Ambert, Madame Ambert-Molinier, Monique Darras, Vivienne Gautier, Pierrette Lejanou, and Jacques Rieux for recipes and notes on the Languedoc. With thanks to Pierre Escorbiac, Georgie Géry, Madame "Marthou," Madame Danièle Mazet-Delpeuch, Robert Meyzen, René Mommejac, Albert Parveaux, Jacques Pébeyre, Jean-Pierre Pébeyre, Charlou Reynal, the Rougié family, Paul Turon, and Lucienne Vanel for recipes and notes on the Lot, the Corrèze, and the Dordogne.

With thanks to all those who worked with me here in America: William Bayer, Patricia Brown, Ariane Daguin, Hallie Donnelly, Suzanne Hamlin, Barbara Kafka, Annick Klein, Susan and Robert Lescher, Frances McCullough, Anne Mendelsohn, Leslie Newman, Anne Otterson, Carol Robertson, Carl Sontheimer, Ronnellie van der Merwe, James Villas, and Roger Yaseen.

A special thank-you to Bill Otterson for his wonderful word processor, Lexor, which helped me put the whole thing together with a lot less labor and a lot more joy than I thought possible. I owe a particular debt to Ariane and Michael Batterberry for sending me to the Southwest of France in the first place. Particular thanks to Gloria Adelson and Jerry Joyner, who made the original edition of this book look so appealing.

Index

Ramps (Wild Leeks) and Mushroom Torte, 90–91

Raspberry(ies)

in Armagnac, 4–5

Kir Royale, Southwest Style, 4

and Red Wine Sauce, Poached Figs in, 389

Ratafia, Orange, 402

Red Beans With Pork and Carrots, 286–287

Red Cabbage, Duck Confit, Salad of, With Chestnuts, Watercress and, 206–207

Red Onion Sauce, Chicken With, 140–141

Red Pepper. *See* Piment d'Espelette

Red Peppers, Tomatoes, and Zucchini, Sauté of, 352

Red Wine

Beans, –Flavored, Confit of Toulouse Sausage and Duck Cooked With, 320–321

Duck Demi-Glace, -Flavored, 409–410

Onions, -Cooked, 348

Pears, Preserved Spiced, in, With Armagnac, 400–401

Sorbet, 392–393

Strawberries, Fresh, With Peppercorns and, 387

Red Wine Sauce

Artichoke Hearts in, 328–329

Baby Chickens in, 136–137

and Cocoa, Fish Fillets in, 127–128

Duck Legs in, Slow-Cooked, 187–188

and Raspberry, Poached Figs in, 389

Steak Bordelaise With Marrow and Shallot Garnish, 252–253

Steak With Shallots in, in the Style of Albi, 255–256

See also Daube

Relish, Onion and Raisin, Sweet and Sour, 290–291

Renaud, Serge, 229

Reynal, Charlou, 300

Rieux, Jacques, 255

Rieux, Louis, 255

Rillettes of Duck, Shredded, 249–250

Rillettes, Salmon, 80–81

Rimotes, 355

Root, Waverley, 310

Roquefort, 8

Sauce, Beef, Fillet of, With Mixed Nuts and, 258–260

Terrines, Cheese, 11–12

S

Salad(s)

of Bitter Greens With Truffle Vinaigrette, 245

of Duck Confit With Red Cabbage, Chestnuts, and Watercress, 206–207

of Duck Ham, Home-Cured, With Chestnuts and Walnuts, 85

Lentil, Warm, Preserved Gizzards With, 212–213

Mâche, With Moutarde Violette, 24

Melon, Mixed, Home-Cured Duck Ham With, 84

of Mixed Greens, Confit of Duck Gizzards With, 211

Mussel, Hot, With Curly Endive and Cream, 104–105

Tomato and Artichoke, With Roasted Herb Bread, Anchovy-Olive Dip, and Salmon Rillettes, 77–81

Saldas, 58

Salmon

    With Crackling Wafers, 114–116

    Rillettes, 80–81

    Slices With Fresh Oysters, 113–114

    Steamed, With Cooked Egg Sauce, 116–117

Salsify, With Chicken in Pastry, 161–163

Salt

    about, 25

    Brine for Muscovy Duck Breast, 172

    Chocolate Cake With Fleur de Sel, Marie-Claude's, 378–379

    for confit, 27

    Duck Breasts Baked in, 183–185

    Foie Gras Cured in, 246

    Pork Belly, -Cured, With Fresh Fava Bean Ragout, 301–303

    Potatoes Baked in Sea Salt, 26–27

    Truffles, Baked Whole, in, 31

Salt Cod. See Cod, Salt

Samalens, Georges, 4

Sarlat Potatoes, 342

Sardine and Potato Cake, La Tupina's, 124–125

Sauce(s)

    Asparagus, Asparagus With, 74–76

    base. See Demi-Glace

    Basquaise With Eggs and Ham (Pipérade), 353–354

    Black Currant, Lemon Meringue Bombe With a Bitters Mousse and, 394–396

    Caramel Vinegar, 96

    Cèpe-Prune, Braised Short Ribs in, 261–263

    double degreasing, 266

    Egg, Cooked, Steamed Salmon With, 116–117

    Green, 145

    Lemon-Garlic, Baby Chicken With, 134–135

    Mulberry Cream, Duck Breasts With, 179

    Red Onion, Chicken With, 140–141

    Roquefort, Fillet of Beef With Mixed Nuts and, 258–260

    stratification (reduction), 97

    Tangerine, Scallops in, 111–112

    Tarragon, Lamb Chops With, 305–306

    Tomato and Caper, Fresh, 49

    Tomato Fondue, 54–55

    Walnut, Garlic, and Oil Liaison, Languedoc, 36–37

    See also Red Wine Sauce; Verjus (Sour Grape Sauce); Wine Sauce

Sausage(s)

    Blood, With Apples and Potatoes, 300–301

    and Bread Stuffing, 192

    Cabbage Cake With, 332–333

    Confit of, Toulouse, 299

    in Lamb, Shoulder of, With Garlic and White Beans, Catalan-Style, 322–324

    Pot-au-Feu in the Style of Albi, 52–54

    Toulouse, 298

    Toulouse, and Duck, Confit of, Cooked With Red Wine–Flavored Beans, 320–321

    in Veal, Stuffed Breast of, Pot-au-feu With, 47–49

Sauternes, Chicken With Garlic Pearls in, 138–140

Sauterne, Prunes in, 388

Scallops, Roasted Sea, on a Bed of Chestnuts and Mushrooms, 109–111

Scallops in Tangerine Sauce, 111–112

Scrambled Eggs, Asparagus With, 76